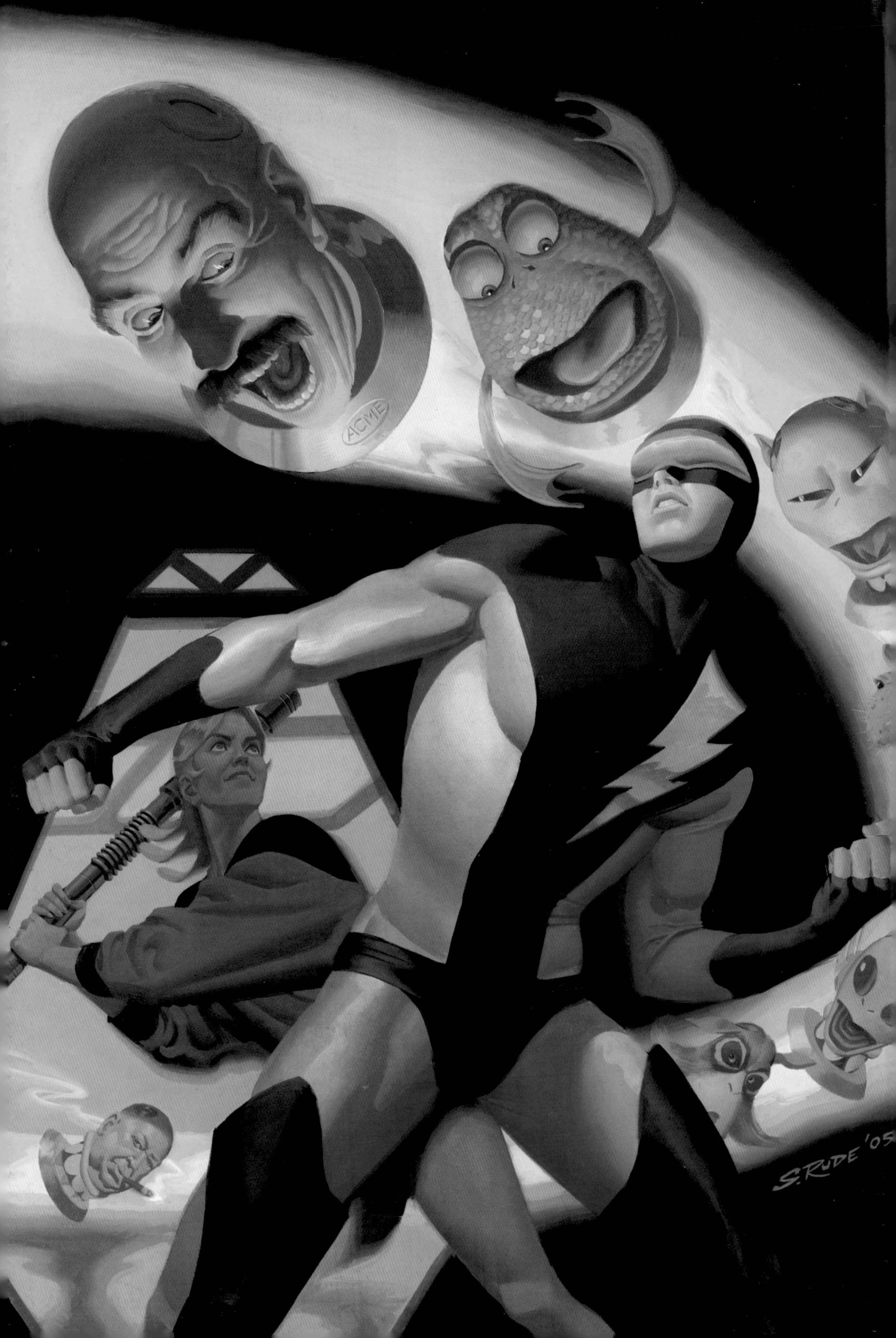
ACME
S.RUDE '05

Mike Baron • Steve Rude

NEXUS™

Volume Two

NEXUS CREATED BY
Mike Baron
and **Steve Rude**

FOREWORD BY
Joe Casey

DARK HORSE BOOKS™

PUBLISHER
Mike Richardson

COLLECTION DESIGNER
Heidi Fainza

COLLECTION EDITOR
Dave Land

ART DIRECTOR
Lia Ribacchi

Published by
Dark Horse Books
A division of Dark Horse Comics, Inc.

Dark Horse Comics, Inc.
10956 SE Main Street
Milwaukie, Oregon 97222

darkhorse.com
bloodyredbaron.com
steverude.com

To find a comic shop in your area, call the
Comic Shop Locator Service: (888) 266-4226

First Edition: March 2006
ISBN: 1-59307-455-7

1 3 5 7 9 10 8 6 4 2

Printed in China

NEXUS™ ARCHIVES: VOLUME TWO

This volume collects issues five and six of Nexus Volume Two originally published by Captial Comics and issues seven through eleven of Nexus Volume Two originally published by First Comics.

TABLE OF CONTENTS

WRITTEN BY MIKE BARON
ART BY STEVE RUDE

FOREWORD
by Joe Casey

Great Goulessarian, I love this comic book!

I understand what you all must be thinking. How can any rational human being actually experience feelings of genuine love towards what is essentially words and pictures working together to tell a story?

If you've ever read *Nexus*, you'd already know the answer.

Nexus #3, one of Capital's "new color" comics, as the ads proudly proclaimed at the time, was the first non-Marvel, non-DC comic book I ever bought. This, in itself, was a major turning point in my admittedly short life. The idea of "independent comics" didn't exist for me until I picked up this one amazing comic book. But, honestly, at the time I couldn't have cared less about labels, "independent" vs. "mainstream," and all those other so-called market divisions that now seem to consume us in the early twenty-first century. I just remember thinking one thing at that moment, reading that comic book:

"This is so much better than any Marvel or DC comic book I've ever seen!"

Okay, so there was a little hyperbole involved there. What can I say? It was 1983, and I barely had body hair, so of course I was prone to grandiose statements. But as it turns out, respected writers like Harlan Ellison enthusiastically—and publicly—agreed with me. So, this being a book introduction, it's time to introduce you to what you're about to read—or, for some of us, re-read . . .

Nexus is a man, Horatio Hellpop. He dreams of mass murderers. When he awakens he is compelled to execute them using his fusion-casting powers derived from the stars. He lives on the moon of Ylum. He wears an ultra-cool costume (probably the coolest superhero costume design since the Silver Age Flash). He's got a hot girlfriend named Sundra Peale. He's got a best friend, a wise old Thune named Dave. Dave's son is Judah Maccabee, the independent adjudicator also known as the Hammer. Any one of those characters could carry their own series. But all of this is just the tip of the iceberg. There's a lot more to be found within these pages. And, y'know, not one of these things would exist without the blood, sweat, and tears of two men: Baron and Rude. You have no idea how significant that statement is for me. So, in that spirit, let the unabashed gushing begin...

First off, there's Mike Baron. Gimme some room here. When I was a teenager, Baron was the writer I always wanted to be. The guy seemed as cool as his comics were. As it turns out, I ended up becoming my own kind of writer (for better or worse), but I always go back to Baron for the deepest kind of inspiration: the inspiration to be *original*. In other words, the kind of inspiration that really can't be measured. Then there're the man's pure skills. His wit, his use of language, his turns of phrase, his economy of words . . . I'm still in awe. Simply put, the man has one of the most unique voices in comic books (which, being such a visual, art-driven medium, is quite a feat indeed). Who else on earth would've dreamed up a rhyming battle that ends with the famous line, "Won't you have—an ORANGE?" Only Baron.

And then there's Steve Rude. He *is* "the Dude." Now, when it comes to the Dude, I need to admit something right off the bat . . . I love the guy. I love his Loomis-meets-Toth-meets-Kirby art. I love his spirit. I love his complete and total commitment to his craft. I love his uncompromising stance on what comic books should be. I love the way he built the visual world that you, lucky reader, are about to experience in this collection. If you don't want to live in the Dude's depiction of Ylum (or the greater Web), then you might just be style deficient . . . because who wouldn't want to live in the worlds the Dude creates? On a personal note, it's not often a writer gets to work with one of his heroes, but with the Dude, I got that chance. And, for me, my admiration for everything he's ever done in comic books all goes back to his work on *Nexus*, because everything I just described was obviously there from the beginning.

Of course, we now come to the ultimate product of these two minds colliding. The meat of the matter. The reason we're all here. The stories you're about to read (and re-read) . . .

Take it from me: when it comes to comic books, it just doesn't get any better than this. Beginning with "Drinking Man's Tour of the Galaxy," and followed by "The Ultimate Bizarre Object," "The Bowl-Shaped World," "Up and Out" (collectively comprising the aptly named "Trialogue Trilogy"), "Teen Angel," "Talking Heads," and, last but certainly not least, "Get Clausius!" these stories have it all. Imagination, sex, violence, humor, unique characterization, evil villains, exotic locales, and plenty of twists and turns. The treachery of Ursula. The political savvy of Tyrone. The hilarity of Clonezone. The nobility of the Heads. The evil of Clausius. The sexiness of Jil. And, of course, the insanity of the Badger (arguably the ultimate guest star). These stories draw you in so completely . . . well, to me they just feel like home. They feel like great comics *should* feel. And Baron and Rude gave these gifts to us at a mere $1.75 a pop. For

me, personally, I feel like they've generously given me something that I can never repay them for. Publicly waxing their car in this introduction is just a drop in the bucket.

"Light-years ahead." That was the tag line in those early *Nexus* ads.

Even twenty-eight years later, this comic book is *still* light-years ahead. Of practically everything else on the stands.

Joe Casey
Los Angeles, CA
September 1, 2005

Joe Casey is a writer who's been so inspired by Nexus *to the point where he's co-created original comic book series like* Automatic Kafka, Gødland, The Intimates, The Milkman Murders, Codeflesh, The Harvest King, *and the upcoming* Secret I.D. *He's also worked on mainstream superhero franchises. He lives and writes in Los Angeles, CA.*

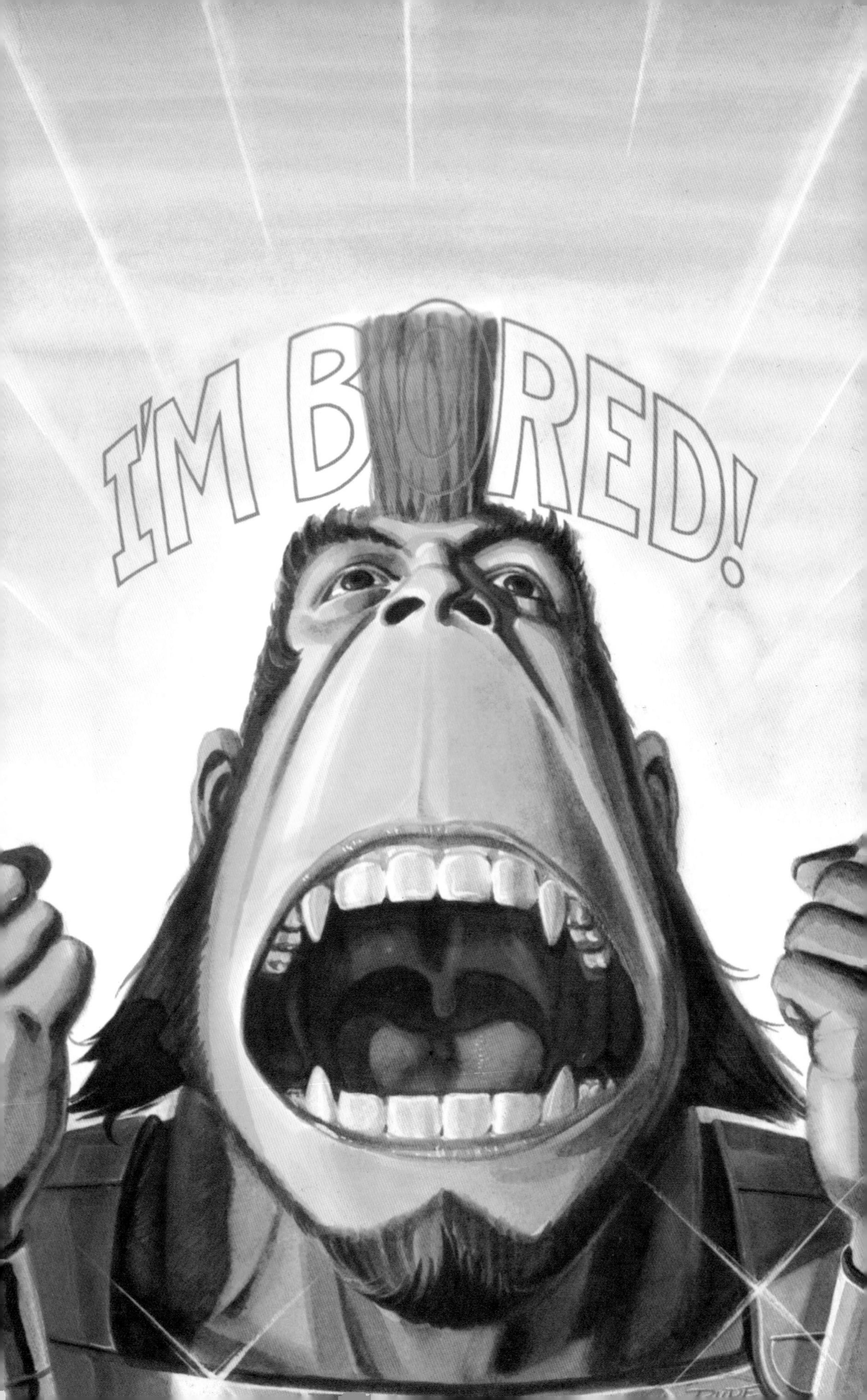
I'M BORED!

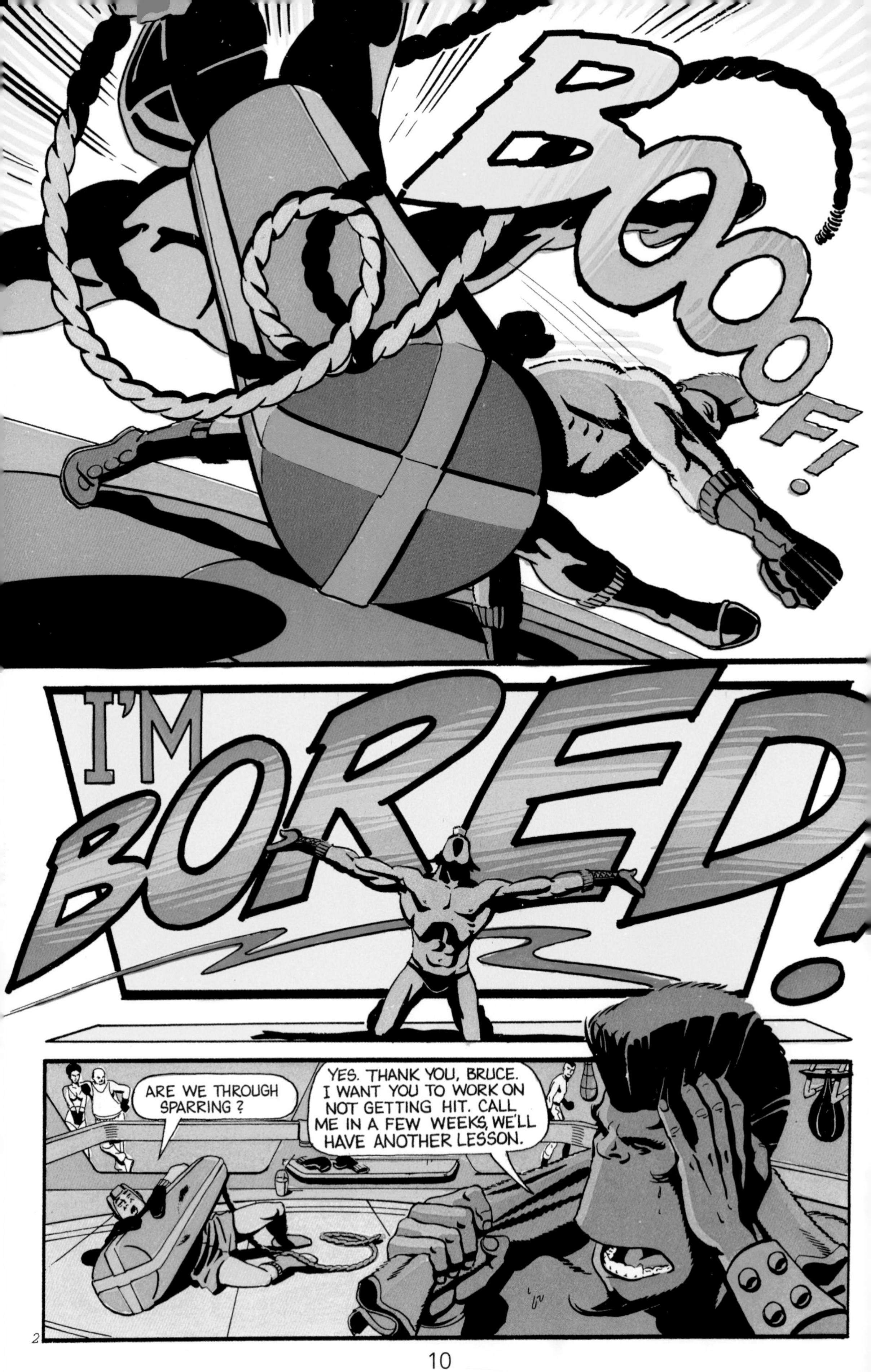
BOOOOF!
I'M BORED!
ARE WE THROUGH SPARRING ?
YES. THANK YOU, BRUCE. I WANT YOU TO WORK ON NOT GETTING HIT. CALL ME IN A FEW WEEKS, WE'LL HAVE ANOTHER LESSON.

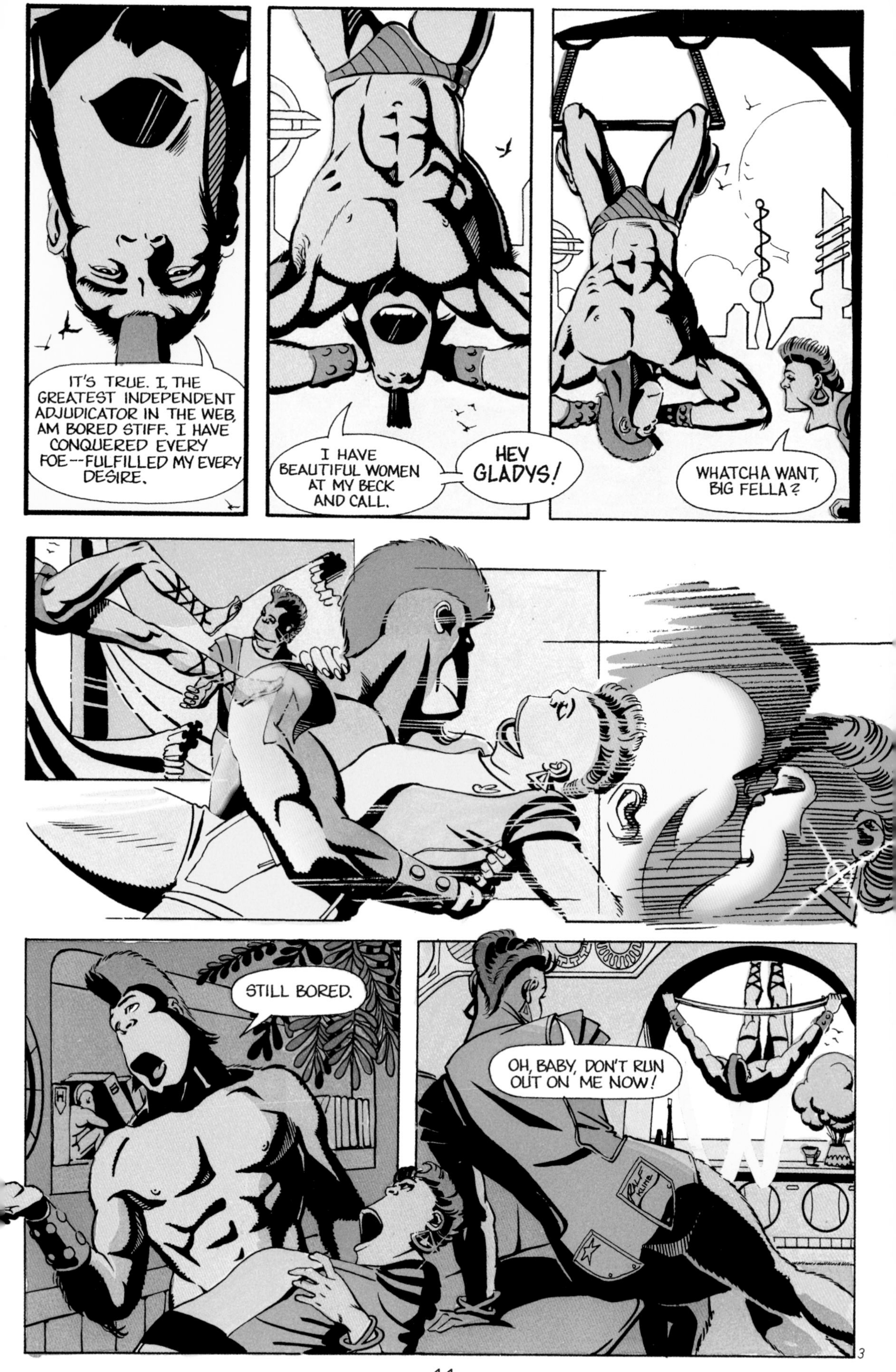
IT'S TRUE. I, THE GREATEST INDEPENDENT ADJUDICATOR IN THE WEB, AM BORED STIFF. I HAVE CONQUERED EVERY FOE--FULFILLED MY EVERY DESIRE.
I HAVE BEAUTIFUL WOMEN AT MY BECK AND CALL.
HEY GLADYS!
WHATCHA WANT, BIG FELLA?
STILL BORED.
OH, BABY, DON'T RUN OUT ON ME NOW!
3

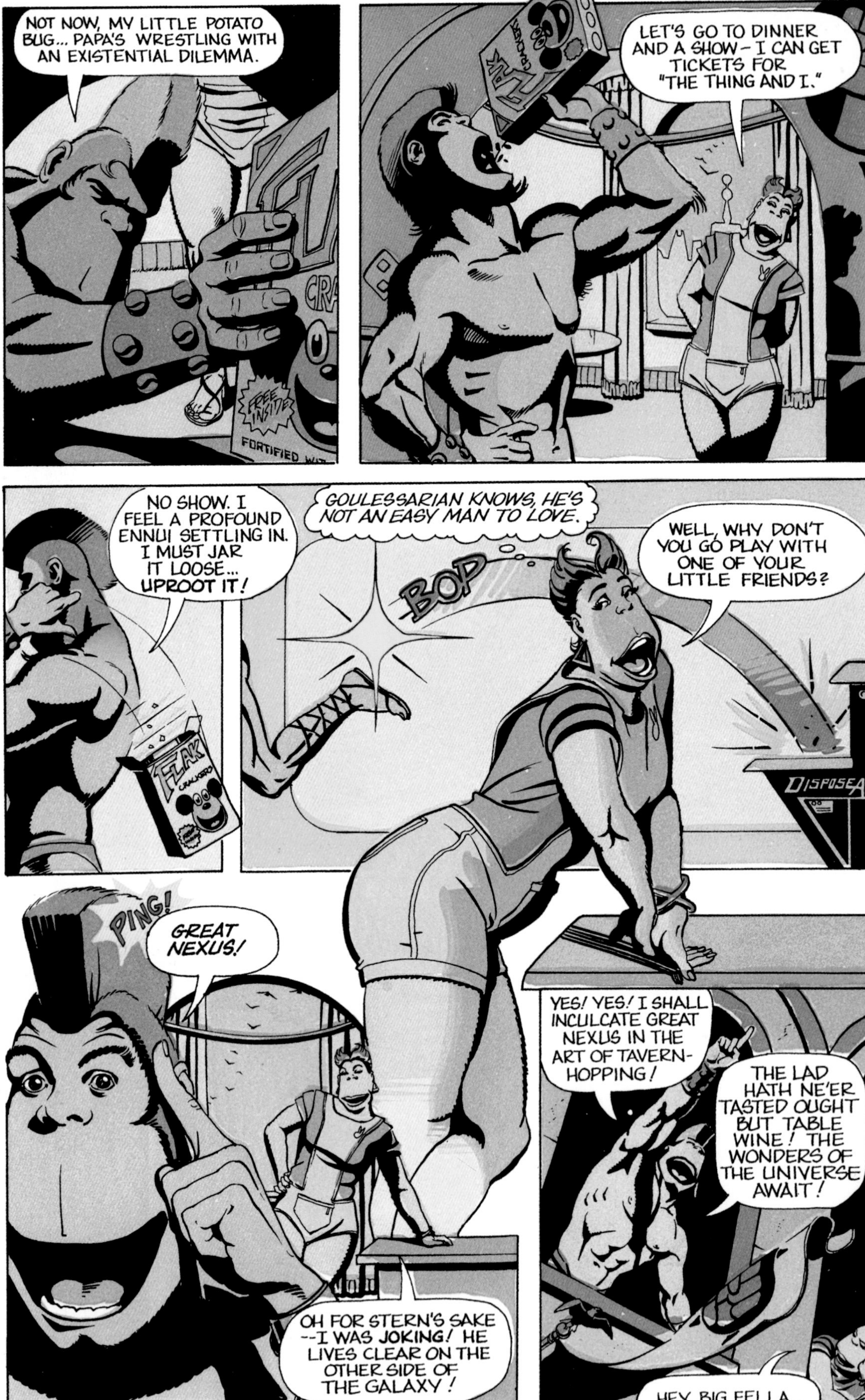
NOT NOW, MY LITTLE POTATO BUG... PAPA'S WRESTLING WITH AN EXISTENTIAL DILEMMA.
FREE INSIDE
FORTIFIED WI
LET'S GO TO DINNER AND A SHOW – I CAN GET TICKETS FOR "THE THING AND I."
NO SHOW. I FEEL A PROFOUND ENNUI SETTLING IN. I MUST JAR IT LOOSE... UPROOT IT!
GOULESSARIAN KNOWS, HE'S NOT AN EASY MAN TO LOVE.
BOP
WELL, WHY DON'T YOU GO PLAY WITH ONE OF YOUR LITTLE FRIENDS?
FLAK CRACKERS
DISPOSEALL
PING!
GREAT NEXUS!
OH FOR STERN'S SAKE --I WAS JOKING! HE LIVES CLEAR ON THE OTHER SIDE OF THE GALAXY!
YES! YES! I SHALL INCULCATE GREAT NEXUS IN THE ART OF TAVERN-HOPPING!
THE LAD HATH NE'ER TASTED OUGHT BUT TABLE WINE! THE WONDERS OF THE UNIVERSE AWAIT!
HEY, BIG FELLA...
4

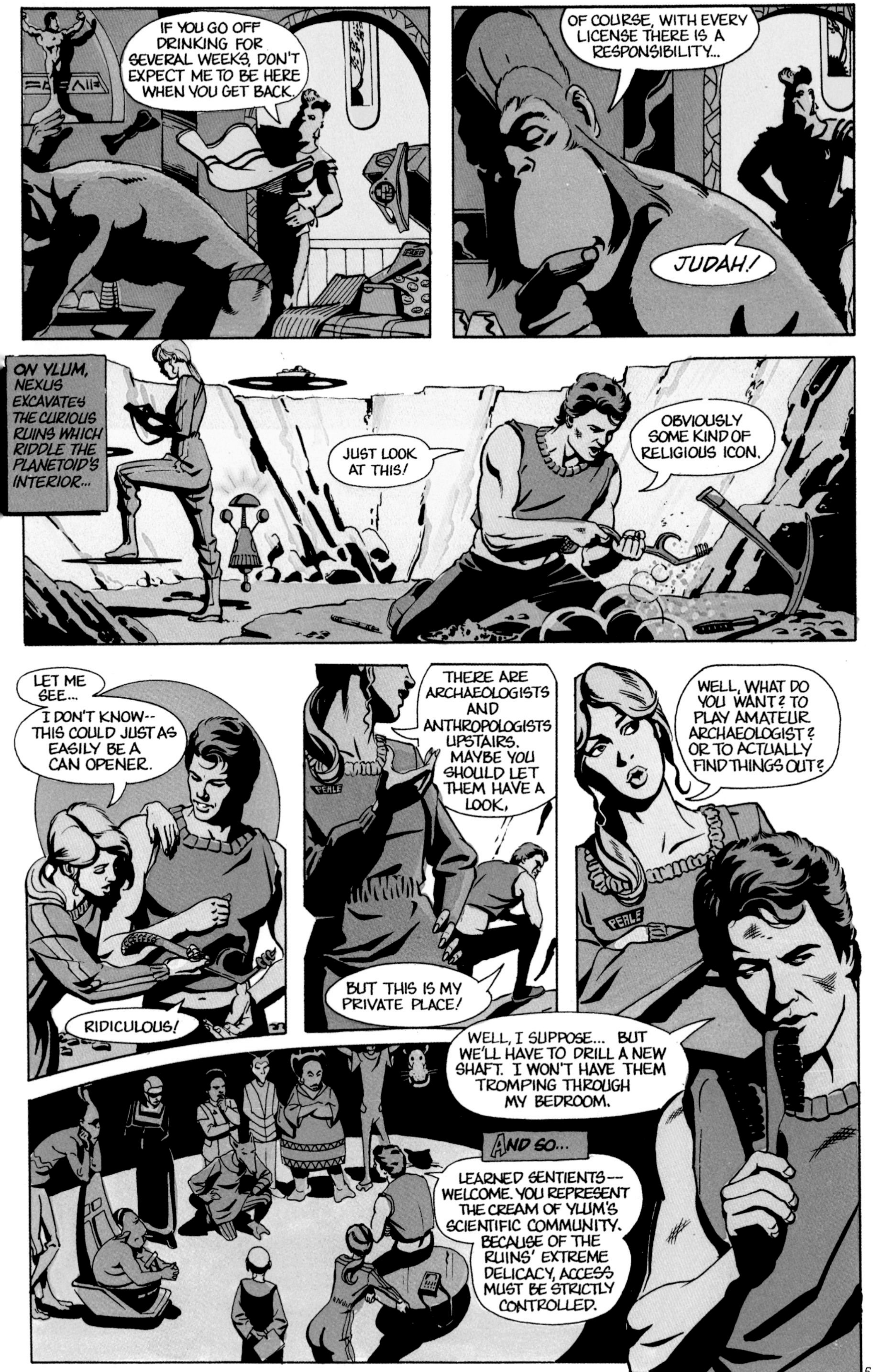
IF YOU GO OFF DRINKING FOR SEVERAL WEEKS, DON'T EXPECT ME TO BE HERE WHEN YOU GET BACK.
OF COURSE, WITH EVERY LICENSE THERE IS A RESPONSIBILITY...
JUDAH!
ON YLUM, NEXUS EXCAVATES THE CURIOUS RUINS WHICH RIDDLE THE PLANETOID'S INTERIOR...
JUST LOOK AT THIS!
OBVIOUSLY SOME KIND OF RELIGIOUS ICON.
LET ME SEE...
I DON'T KNOW-- THIS COULD JUST AS EASILY BE A CAN OPENER.
RIDICULOUS!
THERE ARE ARCHAEOLOGISTS AND ANTHROPOLOGISTS UPSTAIRS. MAYBE YOU SHOULD LET THEM HAVE A LOOK.
BUT THIS IS MY PRIVATE PLACE!
WELL, WHAT DO YOU WANT? TO PLAY AMATEUR ARCHAEOLOGIST? OR TO ACTUALLY FIND THINGS OUT?
WELL, I SUPPOSE... BUT WE'LL HAVE TO DRILL A NEW SHAFT. I WON'T HAVE THEM TROMPING THROUGH MY BEDROOM.
AND SO...
LEARNED SENTIENTS-- WELCOME. YOU REPRESENT THE CREAM OF YLUM'S SCIENTIFIC COMMUNITY. BECAUSE OF THE RUINS' EXTREME DELICACY, ACCESS MUST BE STRICTLY CONTROLLED.
5

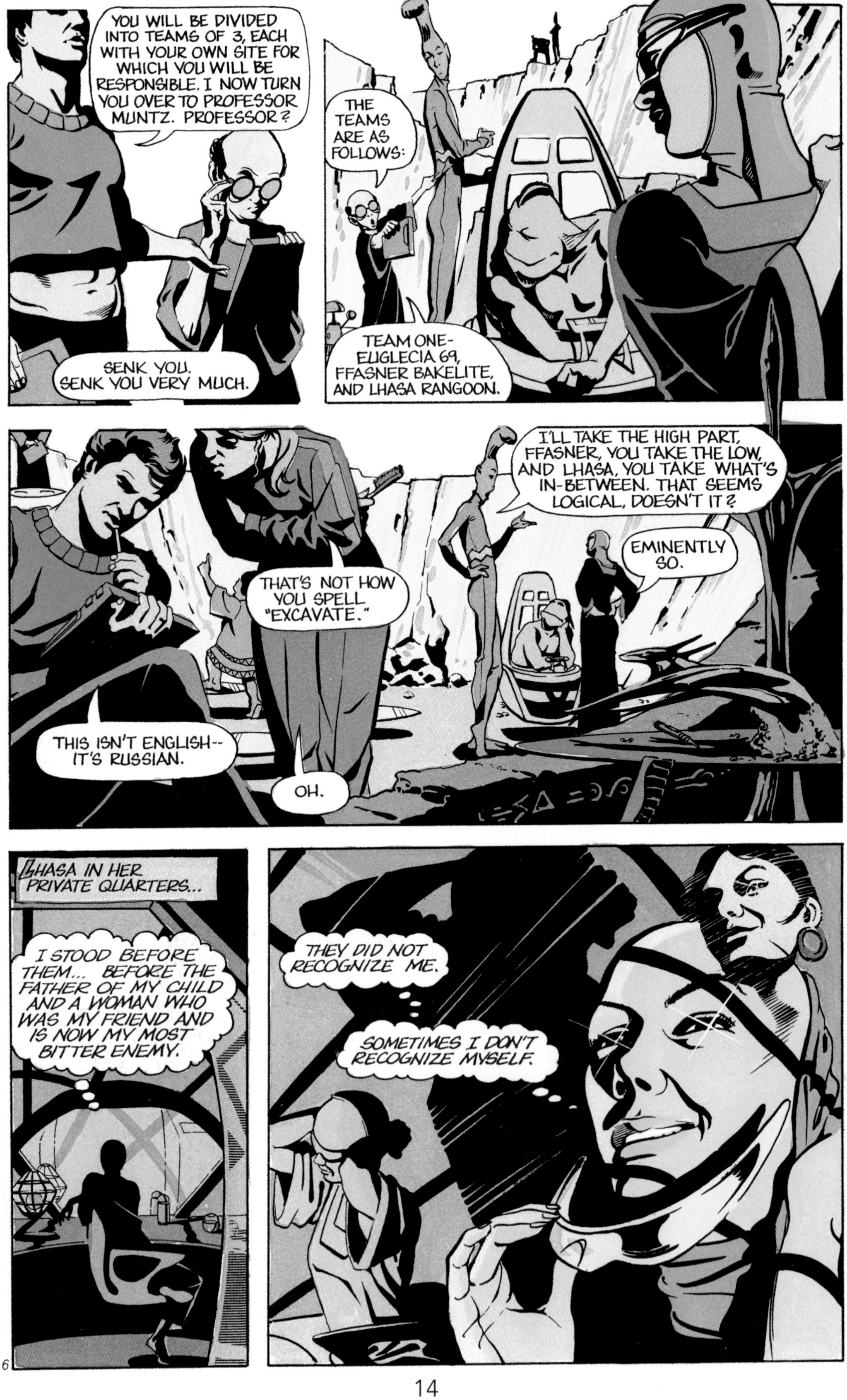
YOU WILL BE DIVIDED INTO TEAMS OF 3, EACH WITH YOUR OWN SITE FOR WHICH YOU WILL BE RESPONSIBLE. I NOW TURN YOU OVER TO PROFESSOR MUNTZ. PROFESSOR?
SENK YOU. SENK YOU VERY MUCH.
THE TEAMS ARE AS FOLLOWS:
TEAM ONE- EUGLECIA 69, FFASNER BAKELITE, AND LHASA RANGOON.
I'LL TAKE THE HIGH PART, FFASNER, YOU TAKE THE LOW, AND LHASA, YOU TAKE WHAT'S IN-BETWEEN. THAT SEEMS LOGICAL, DOESN'T IT?
EMINENTLY SO.
THAT'S NOT HOW YOU SPELL "EXCAVATE."
THIS ISN'T ENGLISH-- IT'S RUSSIAN.
OH.
LHASA IN HER PRIVATE QUARTERS...
I STOOD BEFORE THEM... BEFORE THE FATHER OF MY CHILD AND A WOMAN WHO WAS MY FRIEND AND IS NOW MY MOST BITTER ENEMY.
THEY DID NOT RECOGNIZE ME.
SOMETIMES I DON'T RECOGNIZE MYSELF.
6

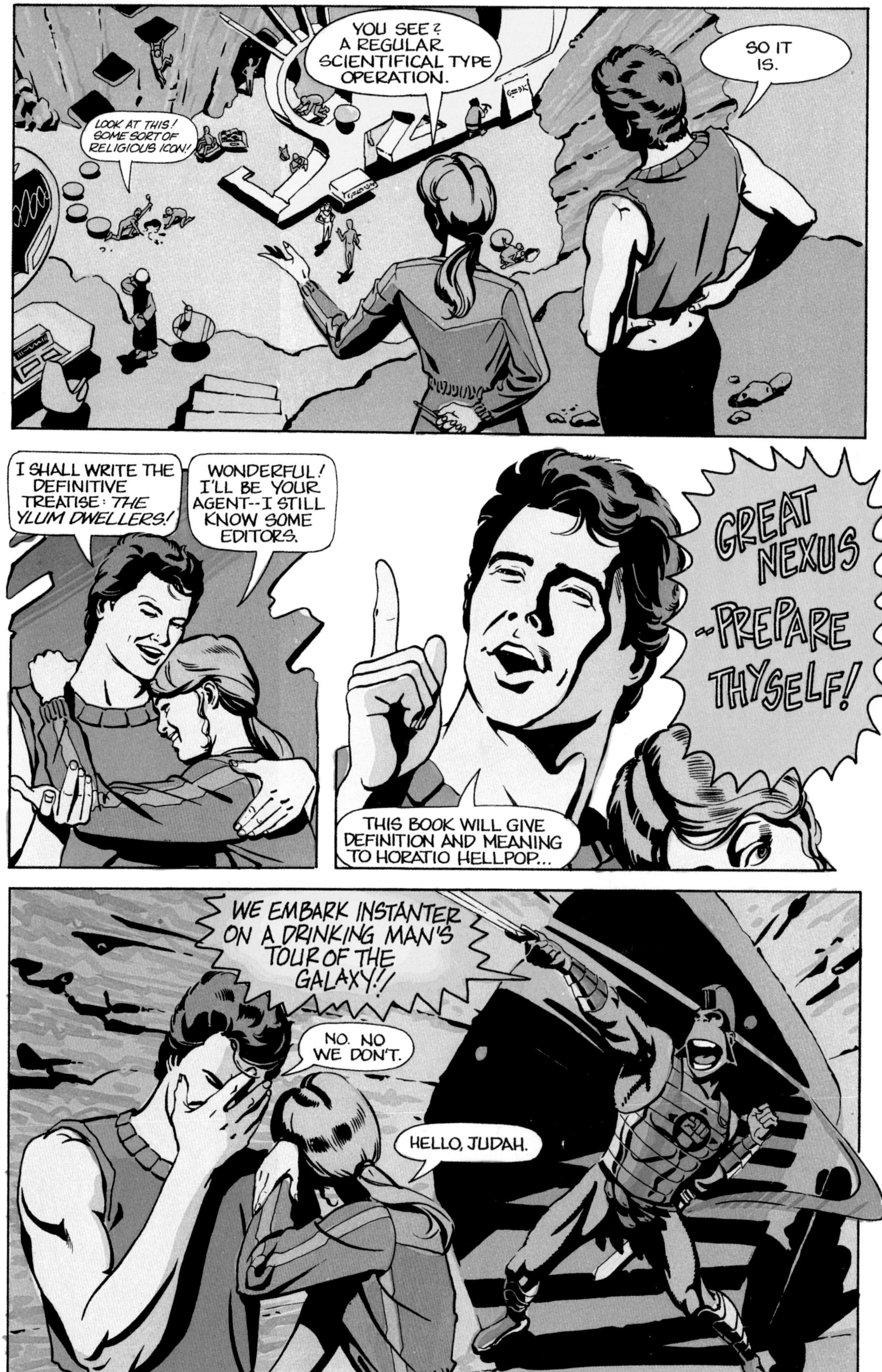
LOOK AT THIS! SOME SORT OF RELIGIOUS ICON!
YOU SEE? A REGULAR SCIENTIFICAL TYPE OPERATION.
SO IT IS.
I SHALL WRITE THE DEFINITIVE TREATISE: THE YLUM DWELLERS!
WONDERFUL! I'LL BE YOUR AGENT--I STILL KNOW SOME EDITORS.
GREAT NEXUS --PREPARE THYSELF!
THIS BOOK WILL GIVE DEFINITION AND MEANING TO HORATIO HELLPOP...
WE EMBARK INSTANTER ON A DRINKING MAN'S TOUR OF THE GALAXY!!
NO. NO WE DON'T.
HELLO, JUDAH.
7

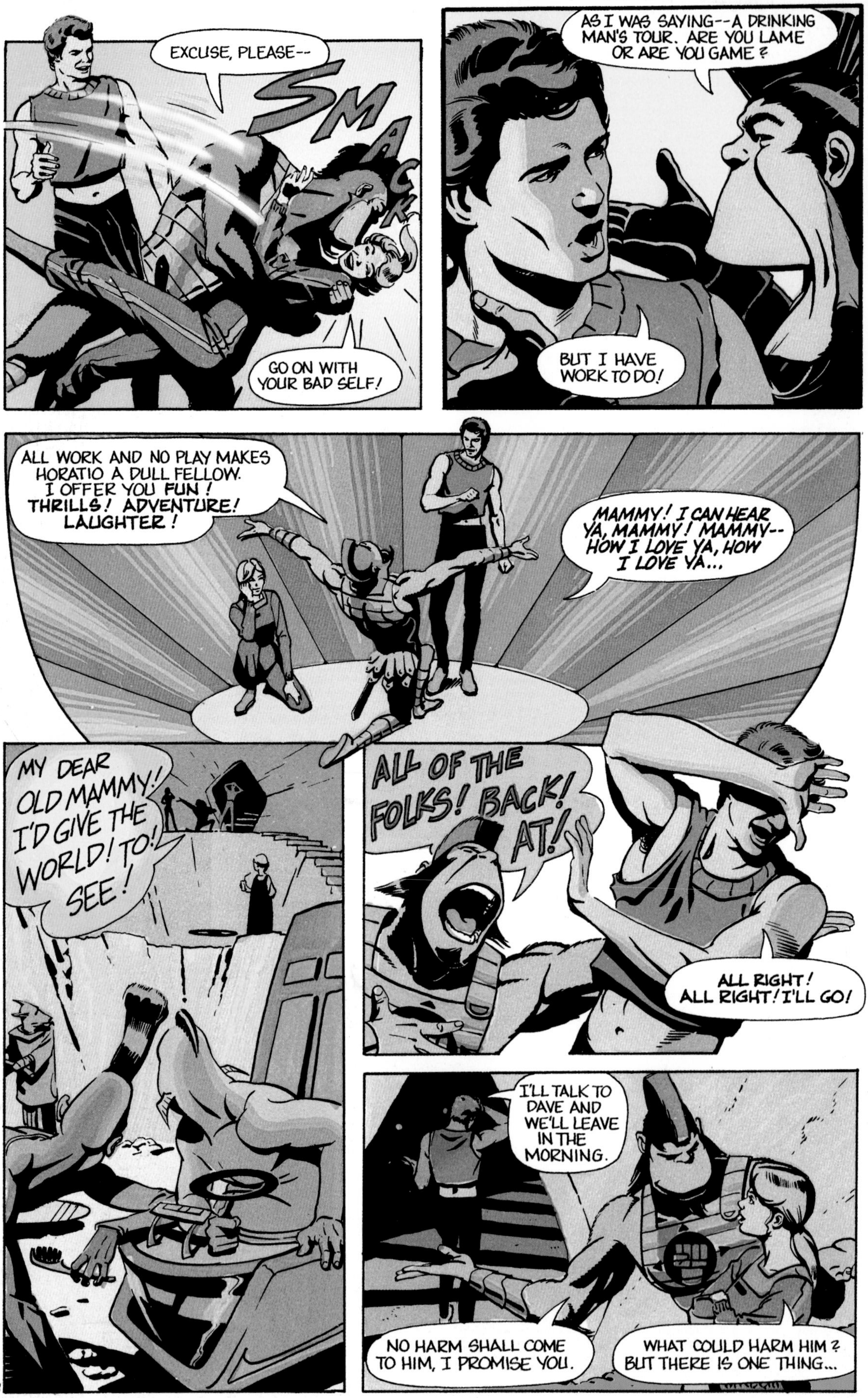
EXCUSE, PLEASE--
SMACK
GO ON WITH YOUR BAD SELF!
AS I WAS SAYING--A DRINKING MAN'S TOUR. ARE YOU LAME OR ARE YOU GAME?
BUT I HAVE WORK TO DO!
ALL WORK AND NO PLAY MAKES HORATIO A DULL FELLOW. I OFFER YOU FUN! THRILLS! ADVENTURE! LAUGHTER!
MAMMY! I CAN HEAR YA, MAMMY! MAMMY-- HOW I LOVE YA, HOW I LOVE YA...
MY DEAR OLD MAMMY! I'D GIVE THE WORLD! TO! SEE!
ALL OF THE FOLKS! BACK! AT!
ALL RIGHT! ALL RIGHT! I'LL GO!
I'LL TALK TO DAVE AND WE'LL LEAVE IN THE MORNING.
NO HARM SHALL COME TO HIM, I PROMISE YOU.
WHAT COULD HARM HIM? BUT THERE IS ONE THING...

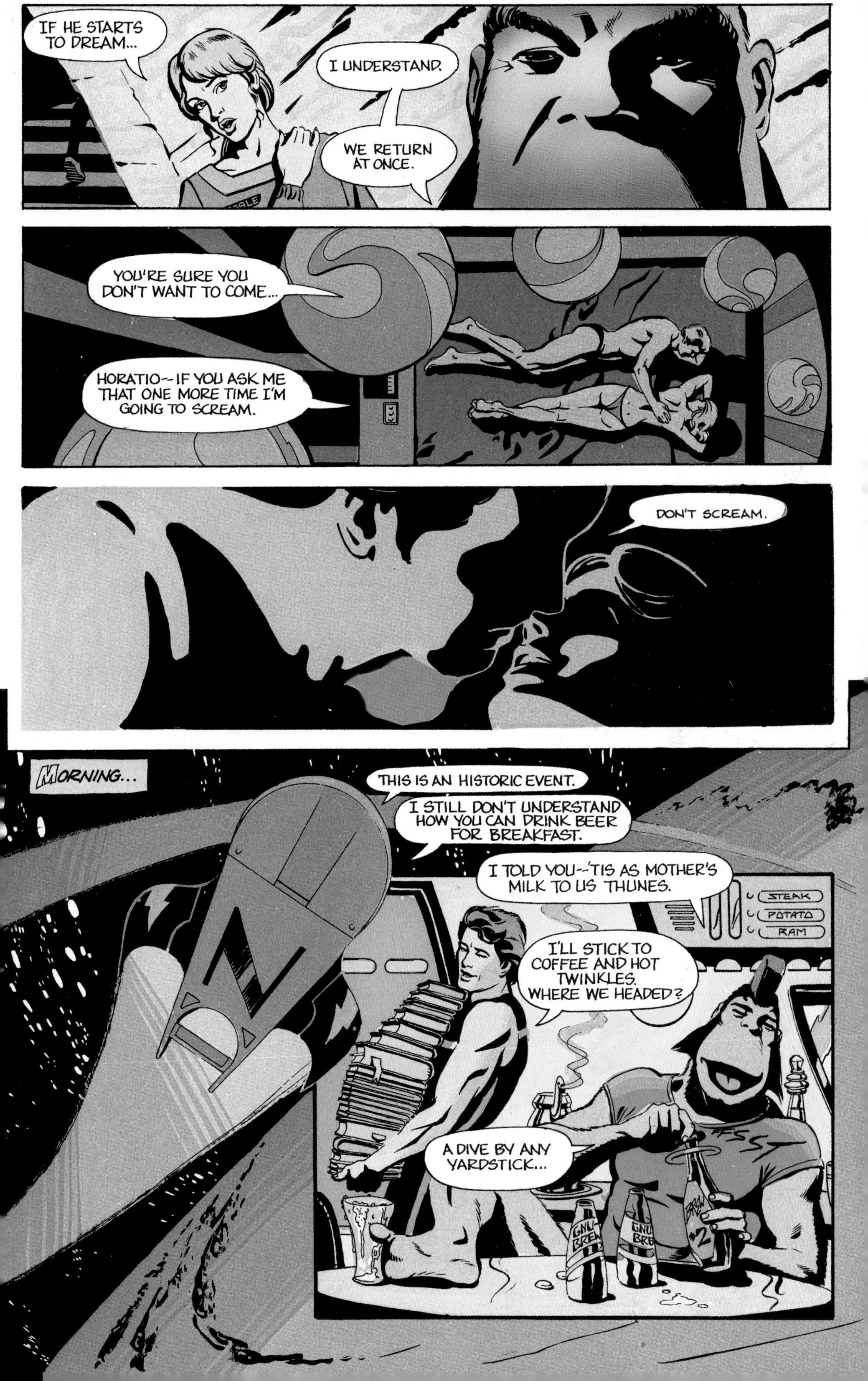
IF HE STARTS TO DREAM...
I UNDERSTAND.
WE RETURN AT ONCE.
YOU'RE SURE YOU DON'T WANT TO COME...
HORATIO-- IF YOU ASK ME THAT ONE MORE TIME I'M GOING TO SCREAM.
DON'T SCREAM.
MORNING...
THIS IS AN HISTORIC EVENT.
I STILL DON'T UNDERSTAND HOW YOU CAN DRINK BEER FOR BREAKFAST.
I TOLD YOU--'TIS AS MOTHER'S MILK TO US THUNES.
STEAK
POTATO
RAM
I'LL STICK TO COFFEE AND HOT TWINKLES. WHERE WE HEADED?
A DIVE BY ANY YARDSTICK...
FSST

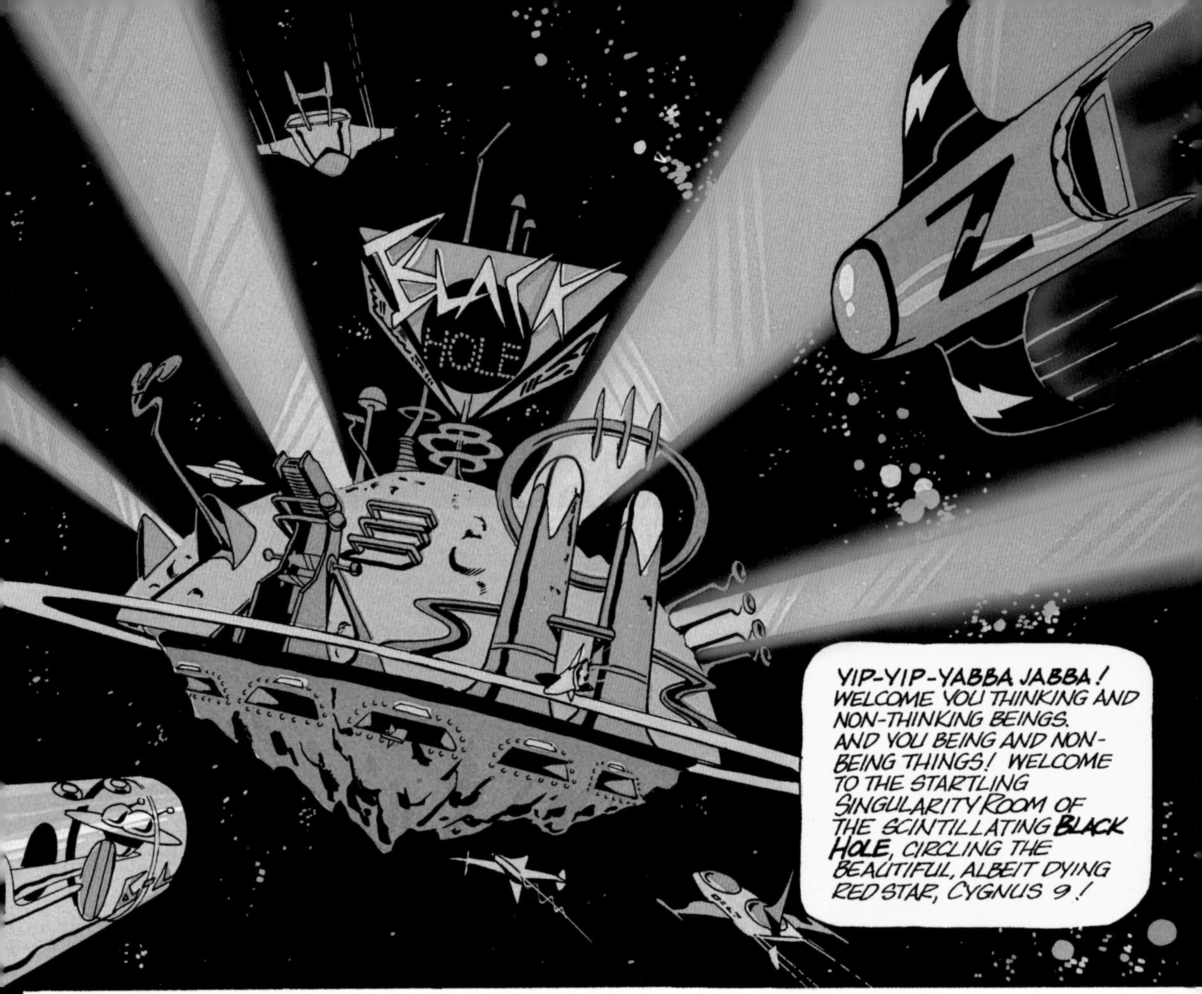
BLACK HOLE
YIP-YIP-YABBA JABBA! WELCOME YOU THINKING AND NON-THINKING BEINGS. AND YOU BEING AND NON-BEING THINGS! WELCOME TO THE STARTLING SINGULARITY ROOM OF THE SCINTILLATING BLACK HOLE, CIRCLING THE BEAUTIFUL, ALBEIT DYING RED STAR, CYGNUS 9!

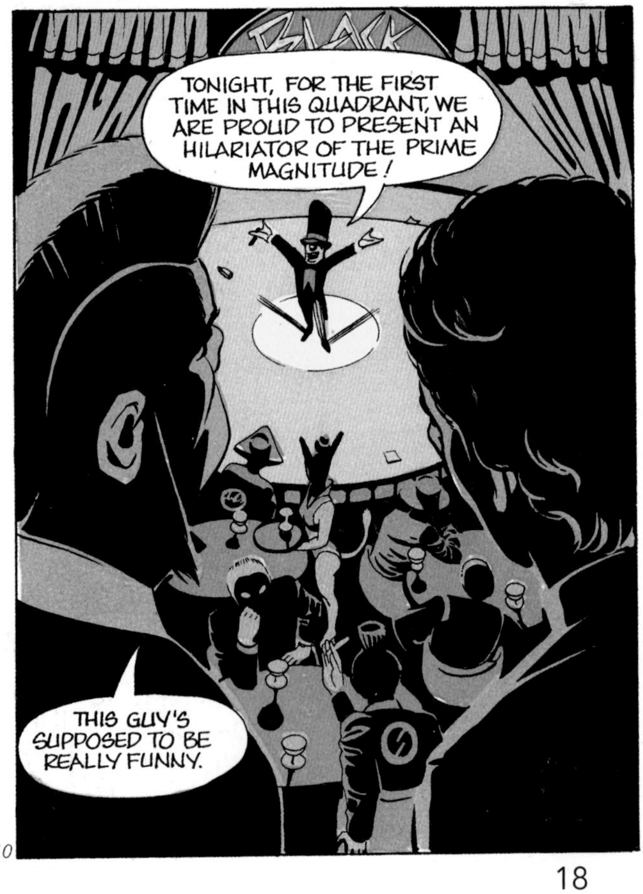
TONIGHT, FOR THE FIRST TIME IN THIS QUADRANT, WE ARE PROUD TO PRESENT AN HILARIATOR OF THE PRIME MAGNITUDE!
THIS GUY'S SUPPOSED TO BE REALLY FUNNY.

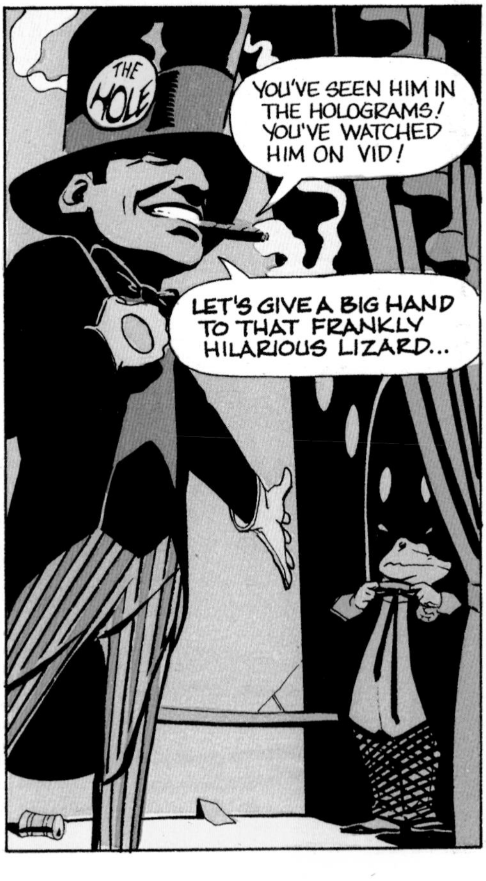
THE HOLE
YOU'VE SEEN HIM IN THE HOLOGRAMS! YOU'VE WATCHED HIM ON VID!
LET'S GIVE A BIG HAND TO THAT FRANKLY HILARIOUS LIZARD...

10

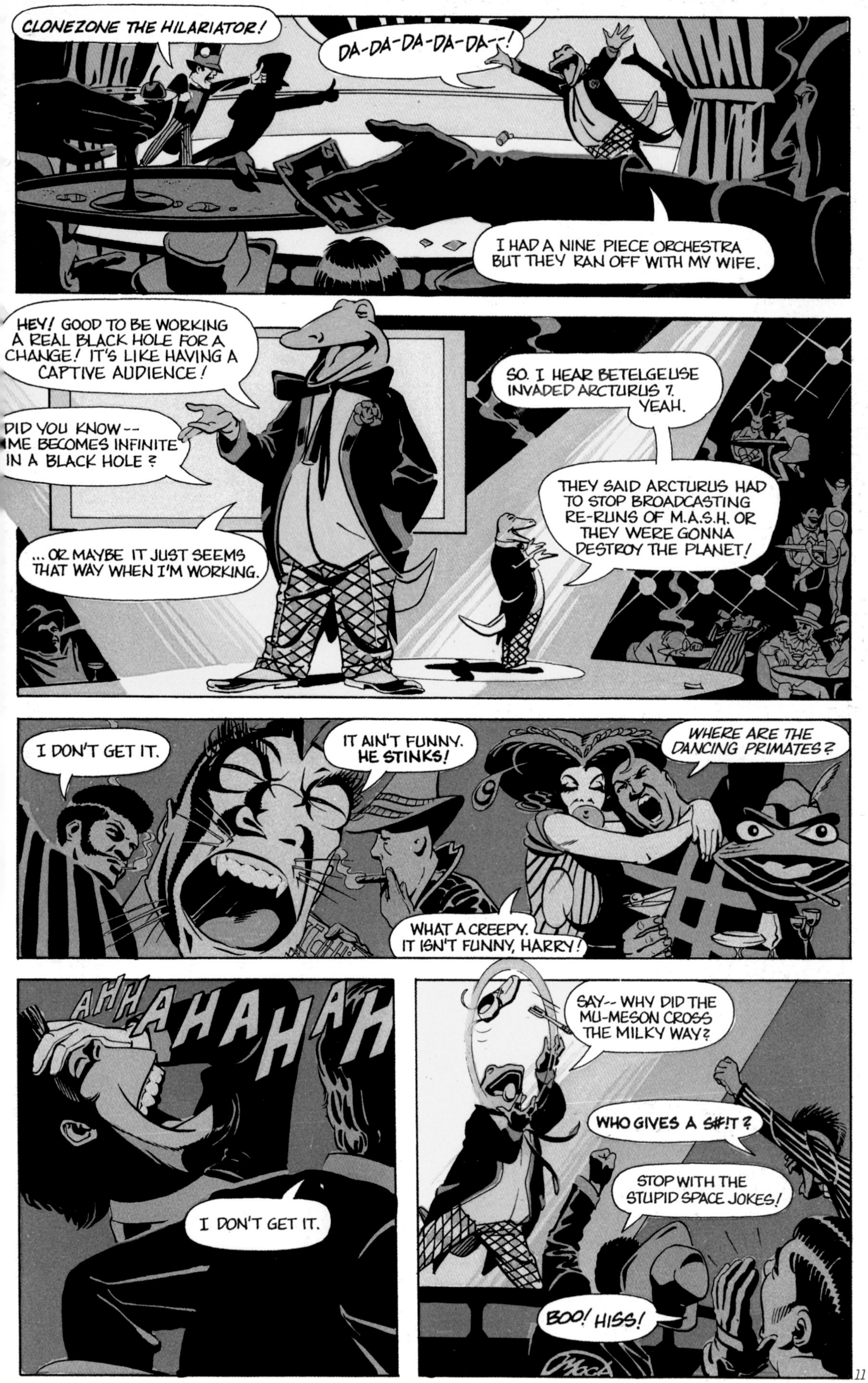
CLONEZONE THE HILARIATOR!
DA-DA-DA-DA-DA--!
I HAD A NINE PIECE ORCHESTRA BUT THEY RAN OFF WITH MY WIFE.
HEY! GOOD TO BE WORKING A REAL BLACK HOLE FOR A CHANGE! IT'S LIKE HAVING A CAPTIVE AUDIENCE!
DID YOU KNOW-- IME BECOMES INFINITE IN A BLACK HOLE?
...OR MAYBE IT JUST SEEMS THAT WAY WHEN I'M WORKING.
SO. I HEAR BETELGEUSE INVADED ARCTURUS 7.
YEAH.
THEY SAID ARCTURUS HAD TO STOP BROADCASTING RE-RUNS OF M.A.S.H. OR THEY WERE GONNA DESTROY THE PLANET!
I DON'T GET IT.
IT AIN'T FUNNY. HE STINKS!
WHERE ARE THE DANCING PRIMATES?
WHAT A CREEPY. IT ISN'T FUNNY, HARRY!
AHHAHAHAHAH
I DON'T GET IT.
SAY-- WHY DID THE MU-MESON CROSS THE MILKY WAY?
WHO GIVES A S#!T?
STOP WITH THE STUPID SPACE JOKES!
BOO! HISS!
11

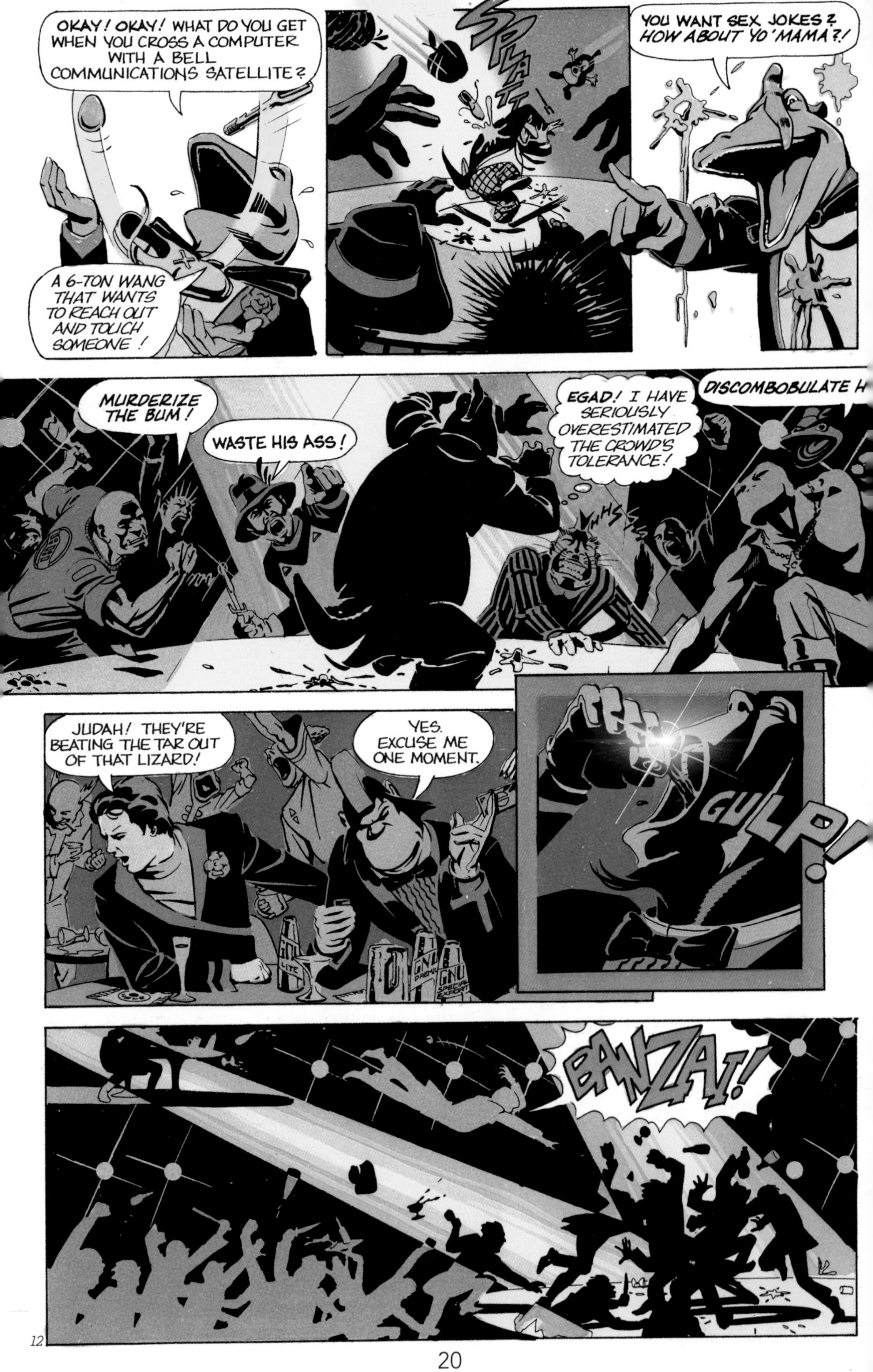
OKAY! OKAY! WHAT DO YOU GET WHEN YOU CROSS A COMPUTER WITH A BELL COMMUNICATIONS SATELLITE?
A 6-TON WANG THAT WANTS TO REACH OUT AND TOUCH SOMEONE!
SPLATT
YOU WANT SEX JOKES? HOW ABOUT YO' MAMA?!
MURDERIZE THE BUM!
WASTE HIS ASS!
EGAD! I HAVE SERIOUSLY OVERESTIMATED THE CROWD'S TOLERANCE!
DISCOMBOBULATE H
JUDAH! THEY'RE BEATING THE TAR OUT OF THAT LIZARD!
YES. EXCUSE ME ONE MOMENT.
GULP!!
BANZAI!

12

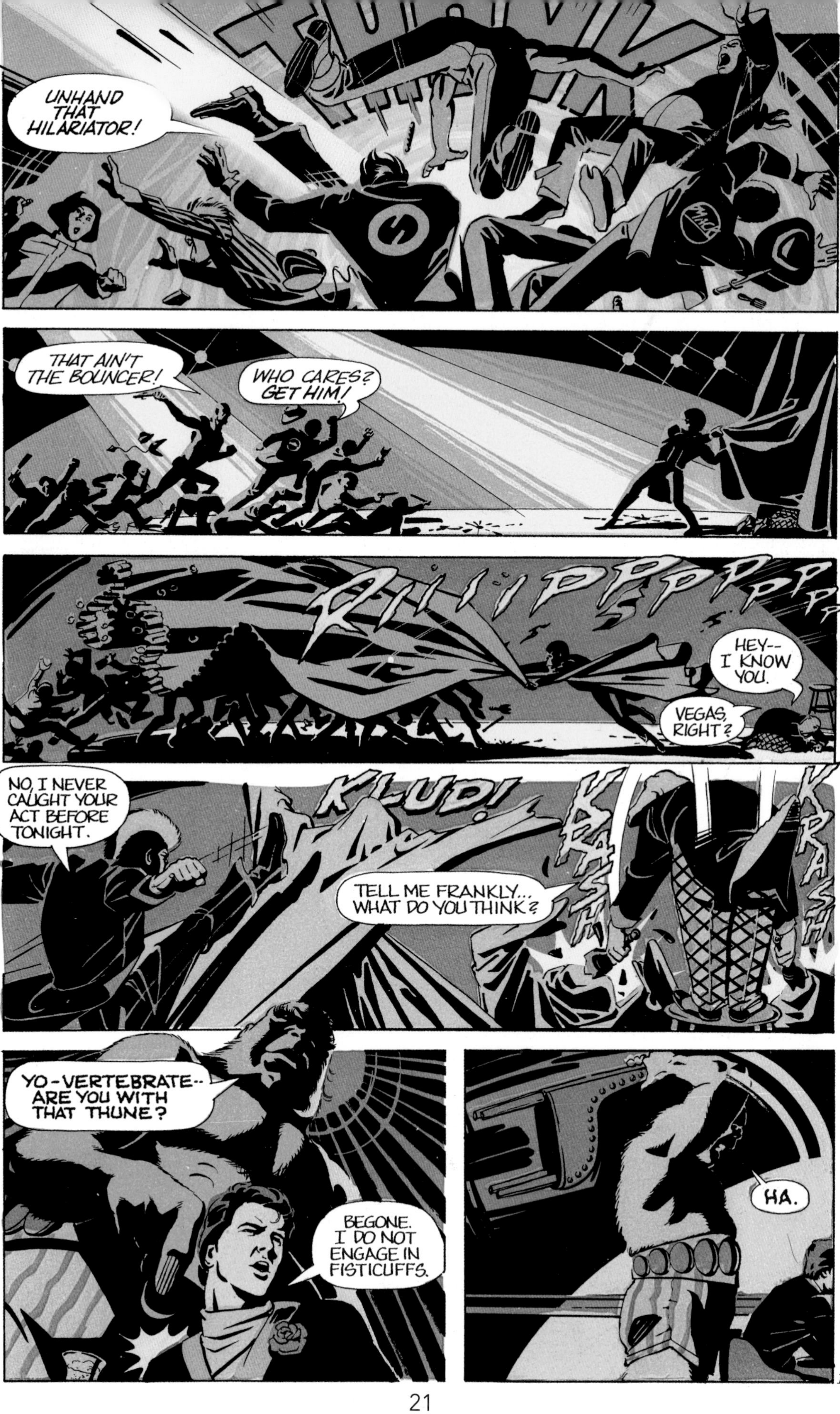
UNHAND THAT HILARIATOR!
THAT AIN'T THE BOUNCER!
WHO CARES? GET HIM!
RIIIIPPPPPPP
HEY-- I KNOW YOU.
VEGAS, RIGHT?
NO, I NEVER CAUGHT YOUR ACT BEFORE TONIGHT.
KLUD!
KRASH
KRASH
TELL ME FRANKLY... WHAT DO YOU THINK?
YO-VERTEBRATE-- ARE YOU WITH THAT THUNE?
BEGONE. I DO NOT ENGAGE IN FISTICUFFS.
HA.

13

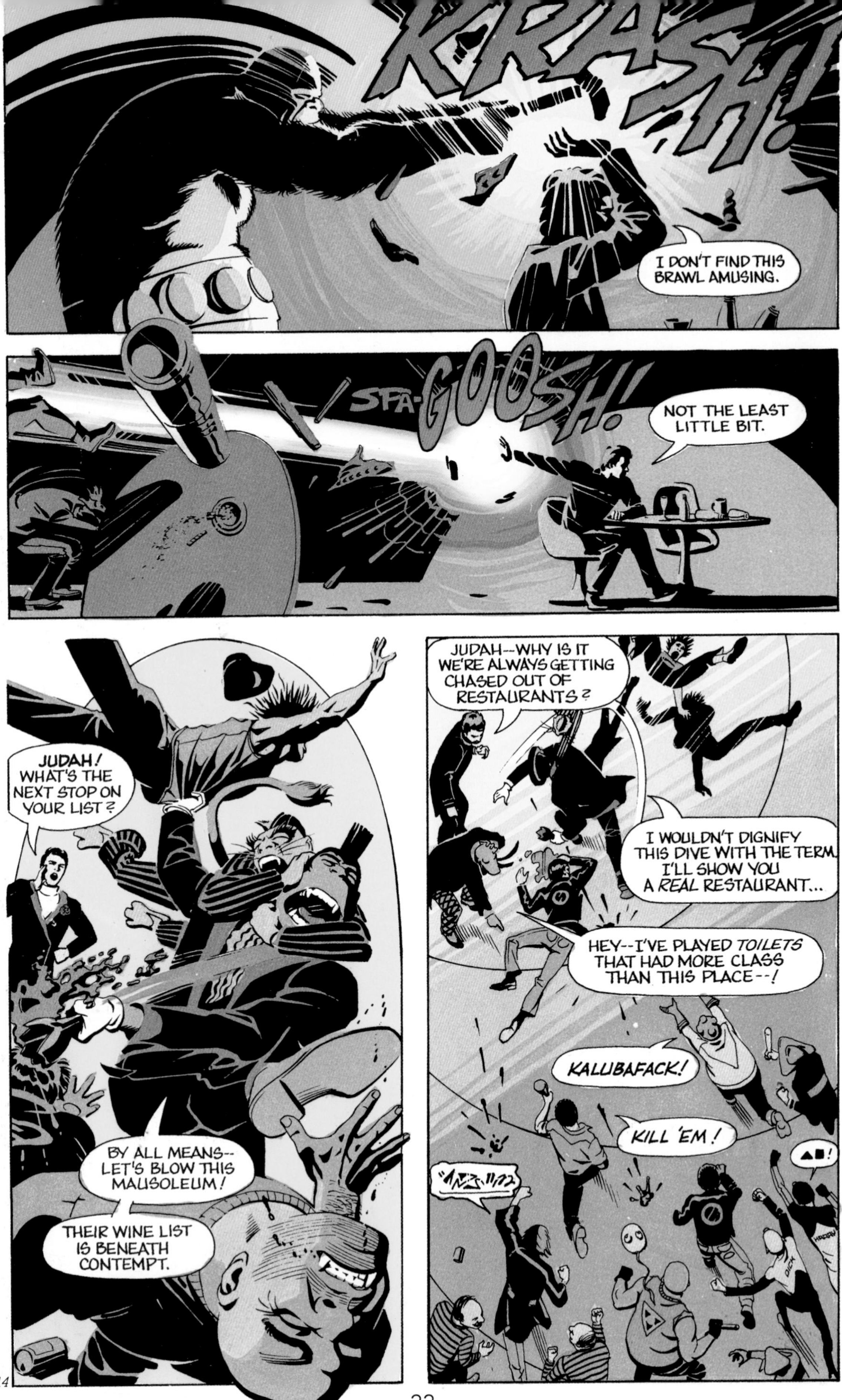
KRASH!
I DON'T FIND THIS BRAWL AMUSING.
SFA-GOOSH!
NOT THE LEAST LITTLE BIT.
JUDAH! WHAT'S THE NEXT STOP ON YOUR LIST?
BY ALL MEANS-- LET'S BLOW THIS MAUSOLEUM!
THEIR WINE LIST IS BENEATH CONTEMPT.
JUDAH--WHY IS IT WE'RE ALWAYS GETTING CHASED OUT OF RESTAURANTS?
I WOULDN'T DIGNIFY THIS DIVE WITH THE TERM. I'LL SHOW YOU A *REAL* RESTAURANT...
HEY--I'VE PLAYED *TOILETS* THAT HAD MORE CLASS THAN THIS PLACE--!
KALUBAFACK!
KILL 'EM!

KILL!

KALUBAFACK!

TICM!

DISCOMBOBULATE!

ALL RIGHT ALREADY! I'M A SENSITIVE SOUL! I CAN'T TAKE IT ANY MORE!

ENOUGH OF THIS.

BOOM

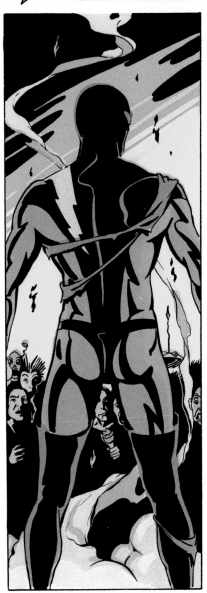

LOOK...

WHOA! I BEEN CRACKIN' WISE ABOUT THIS GUY ALL OVER THE UNIVERSE...

BASTA ES BASTA.

VERILY, THOU SAYEST BUCKETS

KA-RASH

15

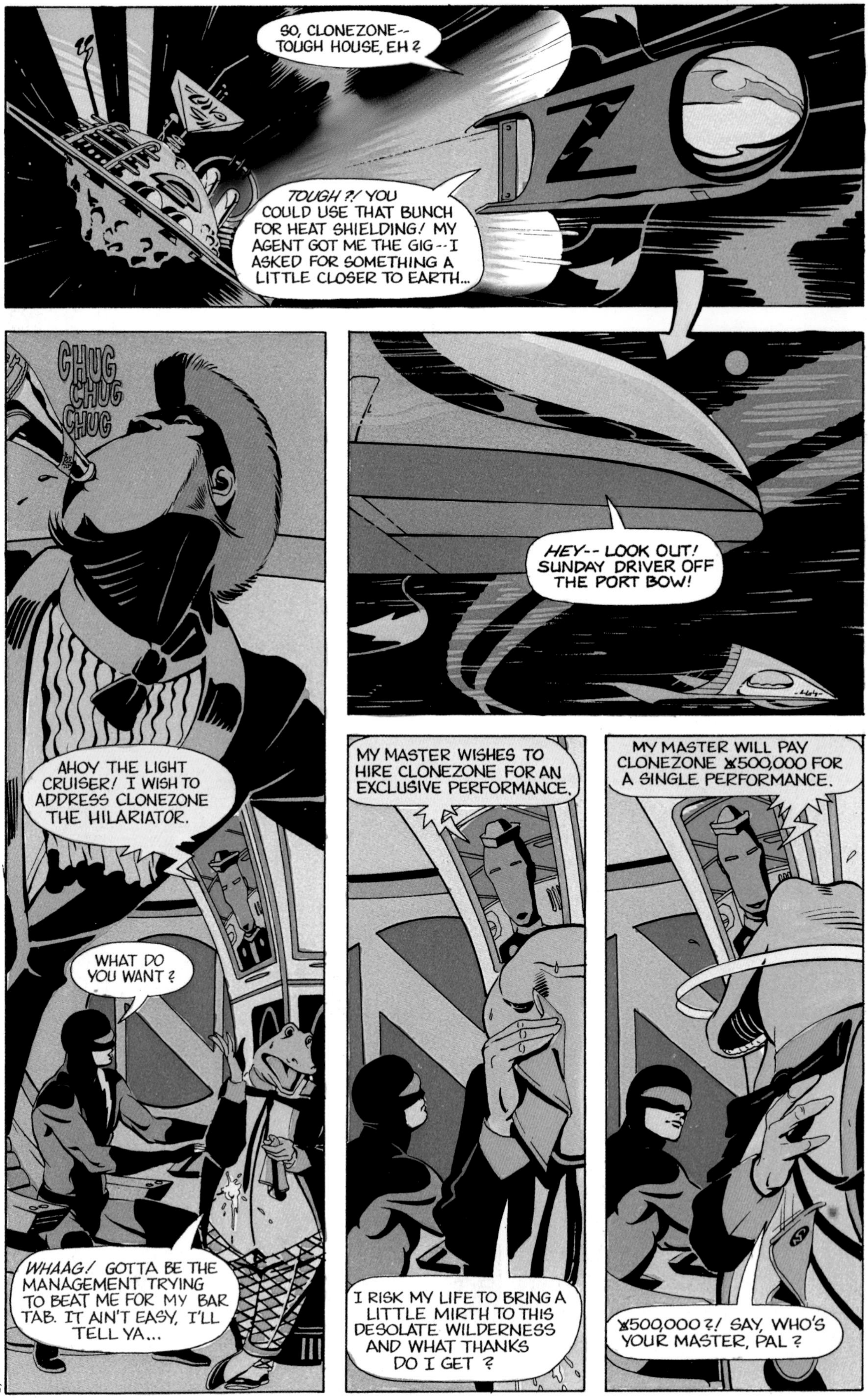
SO, CLONEZONE-- TOUGH HOUSE, EH?
TOUGH?! YOU COULD USE THAT BUNCH FOR HEAT SHIELDING! MY AGENT GOT ME THE GIG--I ASKED FOR SOMETHING A LITTLE CLOSER TO EARTH...
HEY--LOOK OUT! SUNDAY DRIVER OFF THE PORT BOW!
CHUG CHUG CHUG
AHOY THE LIGHT CRUISER! I WISH TO ADDRESS CLONEZONE THE HILARIATOR.
WHAT DO YOU WANT?
WHAAG! GOTTA BE THE MANAGEMENT TRYING TO BEAT ME FOR MY BAR TAB. IT AIN'T EASY, I'LL TELL YA...
MY MASTER WISHES TO HIRE CLONEZONE FOR AN EXCLUSIVE PERFORMANCE.
I RISK MY LIFE TO BRING A LITTLE MIRTH TO THIS DESOLATE WILDERNESS AND WHAT THANKS DO I GET?
MY MASTER WILL PAY CLONEZONE ¥500,000 FOR A SINGLE PERFORMANCE.
¥500,000?! SAY, WHO'S YOUR MASTER, PAL?

16

MY MASTER IS A FAMOUS PERSONALITY WHO WISHES TO REMAIN ANONYMOUS. HIS IDENTITY WILL BE REVEALED TO YOU IN DUE TIME. WILL YOU COME?

WILL I!? FOR ¥500,000, I'D EAT A PLATE OF CHILI PEPPERS!

GENTLEMEN, I BID YOU A CHEESE FONDUE. REMEMBER--WHENEVER CLONEZONE'S IN TOWN, THE SHOW, THE DINNER, THE DRINKS ARE ON ME.

DROP DEAD HILARIATOR!*

* TRADITIONAL GOOD LUCK WISH FOR HILARIATORS.

YAS, THIS HILARIATOR'S FORTUNES ARE DEFINITELY ON THE ASCENDANT...

TIC TIC TIC TIC

WE REGRET THAT WE MUST LEAVE CLONEZONE AT THIS TIME, BUT WE'LL BE BACK TO FOLLOW AN HILARIATOR'S PROGRESS!

WHAT THE HELL IS THIS?

WHAT'S WHAT?

BZZK

THIS...THIS GROTESQUE SINGULARITY. IT'S SPINNING THE WRONG WAY!

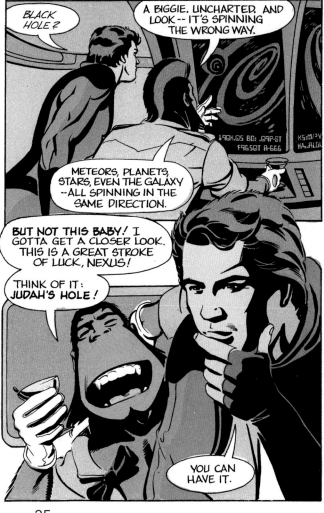

BLACK HOLE?

A BIGGIE. UNCHARTED. AND LOOK -- IT'S SPINNING THE WRONG WAY.

METEORS, PLANETS, STARS, EVEN THE GALAXY --ALL SPINNING IN THE SAME DIRECTION.

BUT NOT THIS BABY! I GOTTA GET A CLOSER LOOK. THIS IS A GREAT STROKE OF LUCK, NEXUS!

THINK OF IT: JUDAH'S HOLE!

YOU CAN HAVE IT.

17

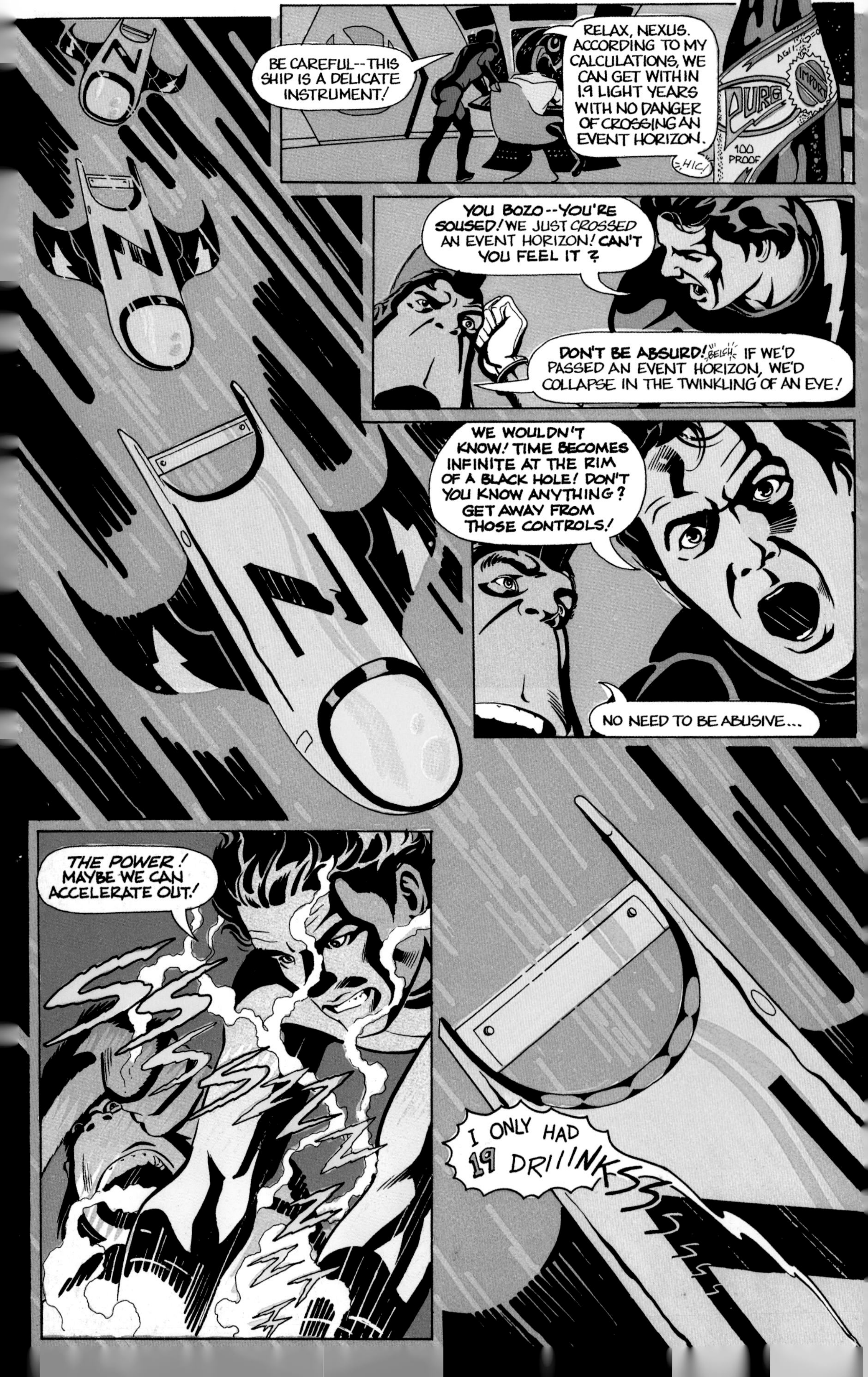
BE CAREFUL--THIS SHIP IS A DELICATE INSTRUMENT!
RELAX, NEXUS. ACCORDING TO MY CALCULATIONS, WE CAN GET WITHIN 1.9 LIGHT YEARS WITH NO DANGER OF CROSSING AN EVENT HORIZON.
HIC!
DURG
IMPORT
100 PROOF
YOU BOZO--YOU'RE SOUSED! WE JUST CROSSED AN EVENT HORIZON! CAN'T YOU FEEL IT?
DON'T BE ABSURD! BELCH IF WE'D PASSED AN EVENT HORIZON, WE'D COLLAPSE IN THE TWINKLING OF AN EYE!
WE WOULDN'T KNOW! TIME BECOMES INFINITE AT THE RIM OF A BLACK HOLE! DON'T YOU KNOW ANYTHING? GET AWAY FROM THOSE CONTROLS!
NO NEED TO BE ABUSIVE...
THE POWER! MAYBE WE CAN ACCELERATE OUT!
I ONLY HAD 19 DRIIINKSSSSSS

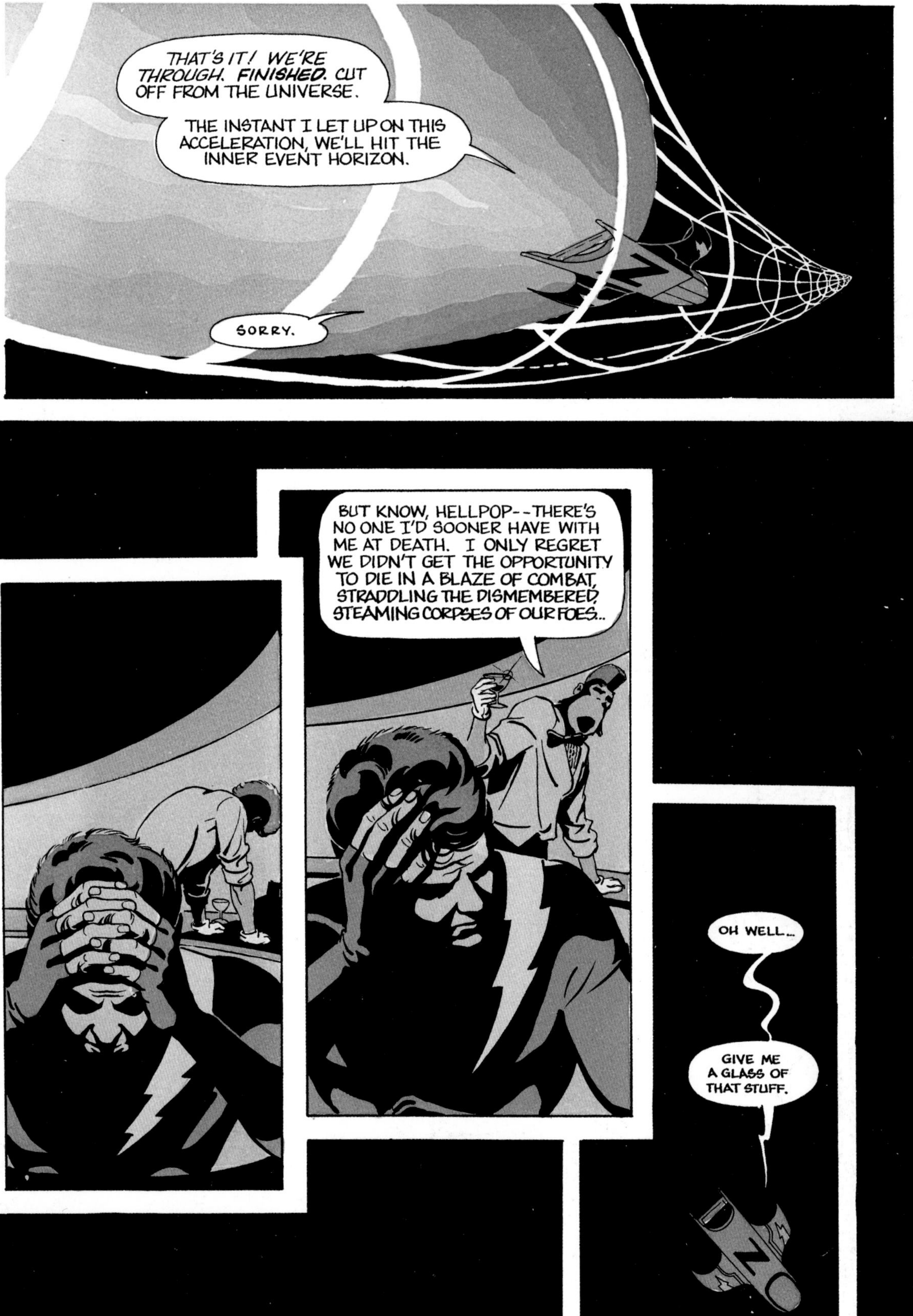
THAT'S IT! WE'RE THROUGH. FINISHED. CUT OFF FROM THE UNIVERSE.
THE INSTANT I LET UP ON THIS ACCELERATION, WE'LL HIT THE INNER EVENT HORIZON.
SORRY.
BUT KNOW, HELLPOP--THERE'S NO ONE I'D SOONER HAVE WITH ME AT DEATH. I ONLY REGRET WE DIDN'T GET THE OPPORTUNITY TO DIE IN A BLAZE OF COMBAT, STRADDLING THE DISMEMBERED, STEAMING CORPSES OF OUR FOES..
OH WELL...
GIVE ME A GLASS OF THAT STUFF.

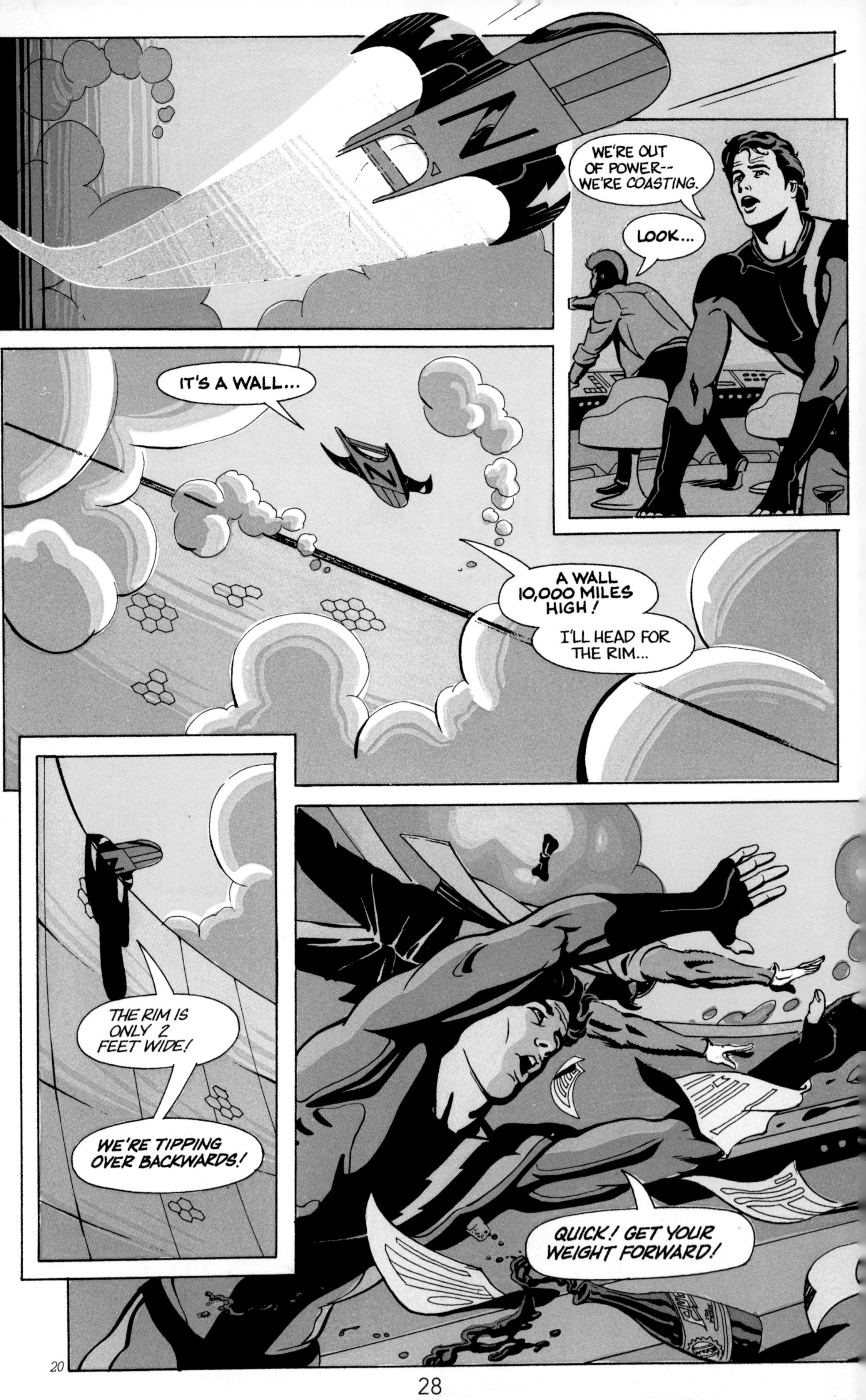
WE'RE OUT OF POWER-- WE'RE COASTING.
LOOK...
IT'S A WALL...
A WALL 10,000 MILES HIGH!
I'LL HEAD FOR THE RIM...
THE RIM IS ONLY 2 FEET WIDE!
WE'RE TIPPING OVER BACKWARDS!
QUICK! GET YOUR WEIGHT FORWARD!

20

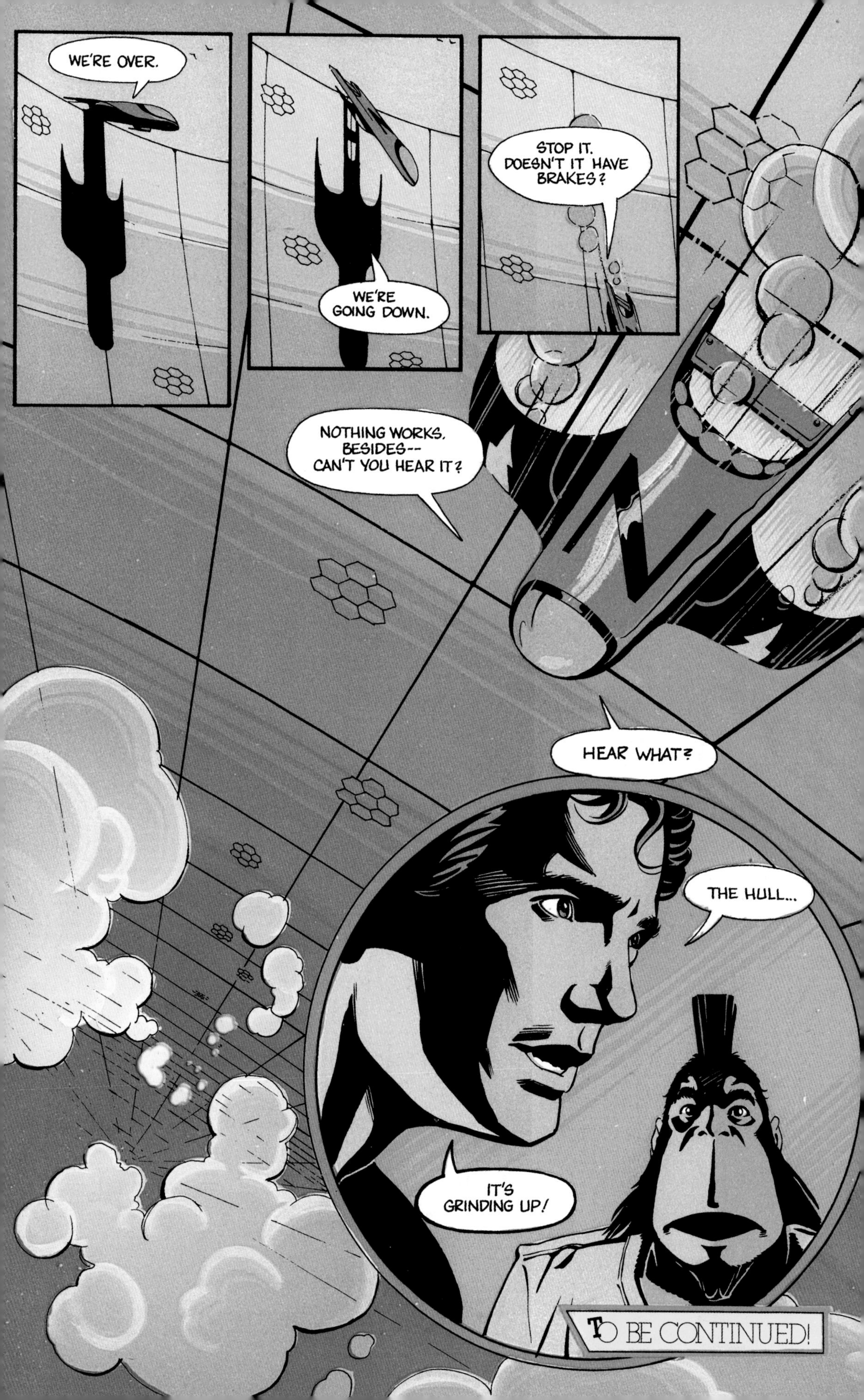
WE'RE OVER.
WE'RE GOING DOWN.
STOP IT. DOESN'T IT HAVE BRAKES?
NOTHING WORKS. BESIDES-- CAN'T YOU HEAR IT?
HEAR WHAT?
THE HULL...
IT'S GRINDING UP!
TO BE CONTINUED!

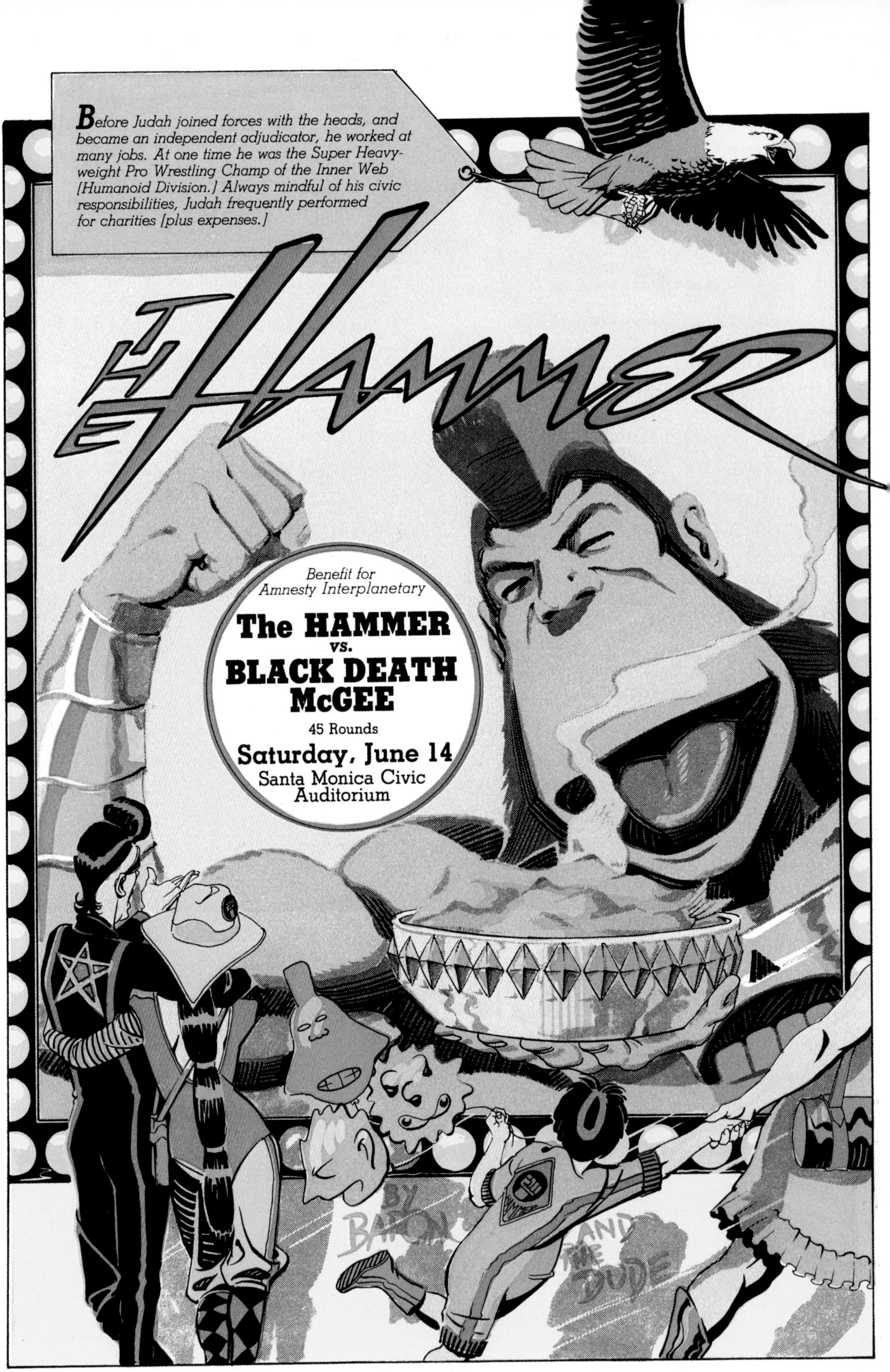
Before Judah joined forces with the heads, and became an independent adjudicator, he worked at many jobs. At one time he was the Super Heavyweight Pro Wrestling Champ of the Inner Web [Humanoid Division.] Always mindful of his civic responsibilities, Judah frequently performed for charities [plus expenses.]
THE HAMMER
Benefit for Amnesty Interplanetary
The HAMMER
vs.
BLACK DEATH McGEE
45 Rounds
Saturday, June 14
Santa Monica Civic Auditorium

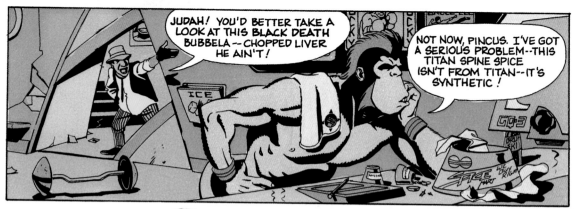

JUDAH! YOU'D BETTER TAKE A LOOK AT THIS BLACK DEATH BUBBELA--CHOPPED LIVER HE AIN'T!
NOT NOW, PINCUS. I'VE GOT A SERIOUS PROBLEM--THIS TITAN SPINE SPICE ISN'T FROM TITAN--IT'S SYNTHETIC!
ICE
SPICE MART WE BUY RIGHT
DO YOU HAVE ANY IDEA WHAT THIS SYNTHETIC CRAP WILL DO TO MY SOUFFLE? DO YOU?
JUDAH--TAKE A LOOK AT BLACK DEATH McGEE--I'M BEGGIN'.
MR. HAMMER--THEY'RE PLAYING YOUR THEME MUSIC.
MY PUBLIC CALLS.
JUST REMEMBER--THIS GIG WASN'T MY IDEA.
AND IN THE BLACK CORNER--BLACK DEATH McGEE, WEIGHING IN AT A TRIM, SLIM 237 KG., AND UNDEFEATED IN 753 PROFESSIONAL BOUTS--!
THE SUPER HEAVYWEIGHT CHAMPEEN WILL ATTEMPT TO BAKE HIS PRIZE-WINNING SALMON SOUFFLÉ BETWEEN ROUNDS, WHILE HIS OPPONENT IS HORS DE COMBAT.
TONIGHT'S SOUFFLE WILL BE ENTERED IN THE INTERPLANETARY BAKE-OFF!
NO HAY PROBLEMA, PINCUS.
BOYCHIK, I'M ONLY YOUR MANAGER. YOU THINK YOU CAN TAKE HIM, I'M GONNA ARGUE?
23

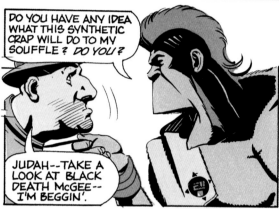

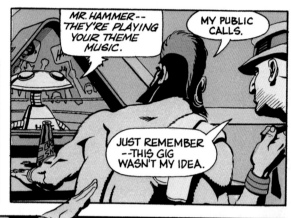

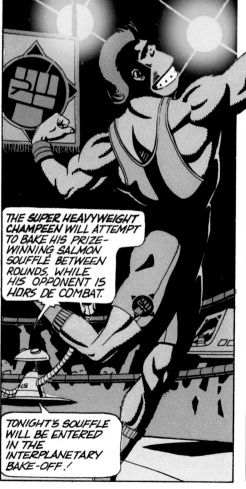

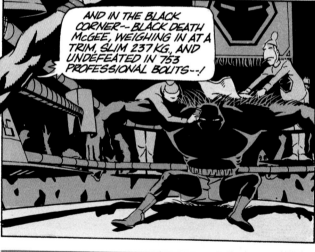

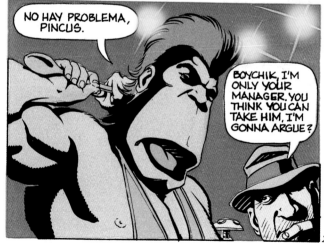

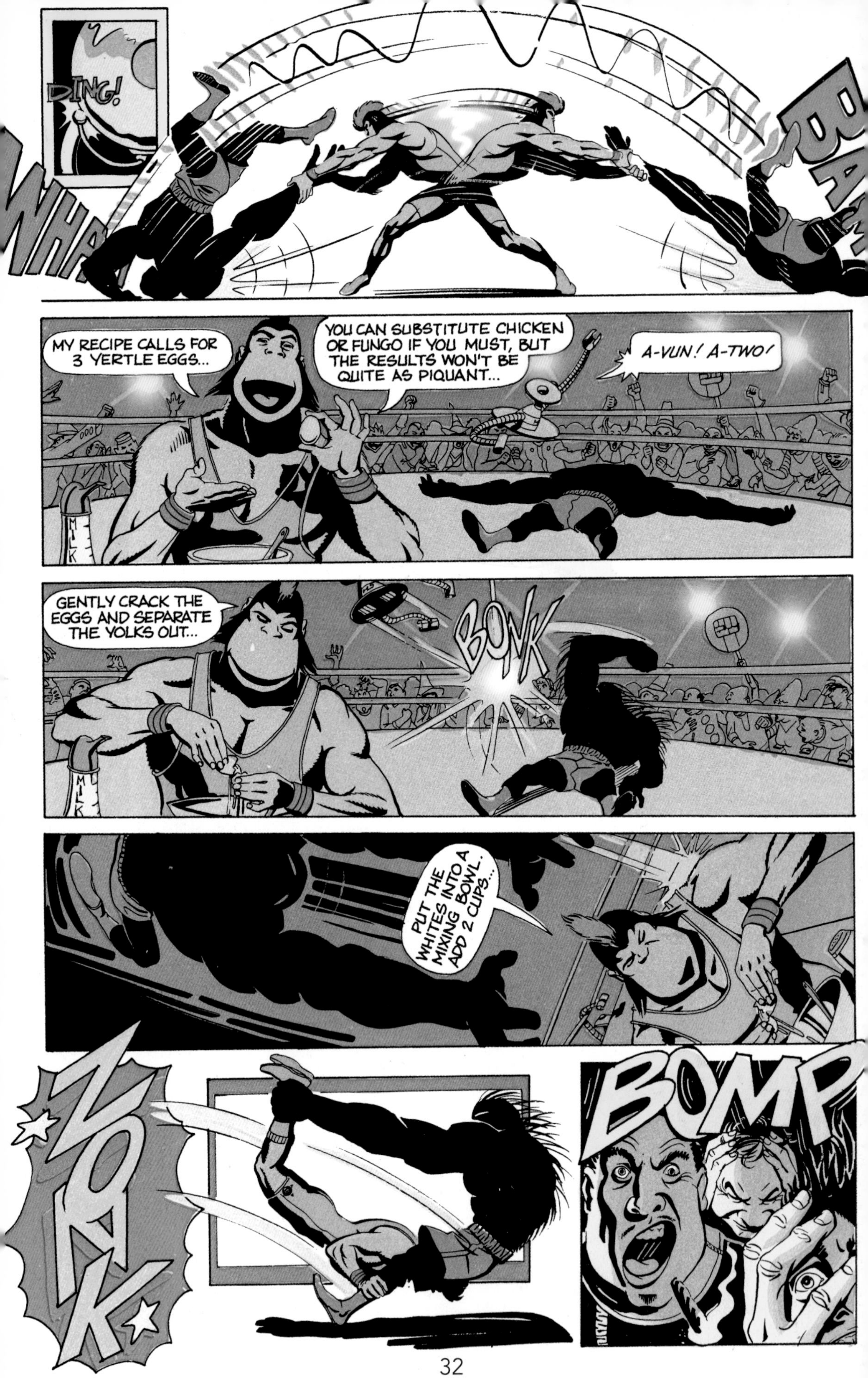
DING!
WHAP
BAM
MY RECIPE CALLS FOR 3 YERTLE EGGS...
YOU CAN SUBSTITUTE CHICKEN OR FUNGO IF YOU MUST, BUT THE RESULTS WON'T BE QUITE AS PIQUANT...
A-VUN! A-TWO!
MILK
GENTLY CRACK THE EGGS AND SEPARATE THE YOLKS OUT...
BONK
MILK
PUT THE WHITES INTO A MIXING BOWL. ADD 2 CUPS...
NOK
BOMP

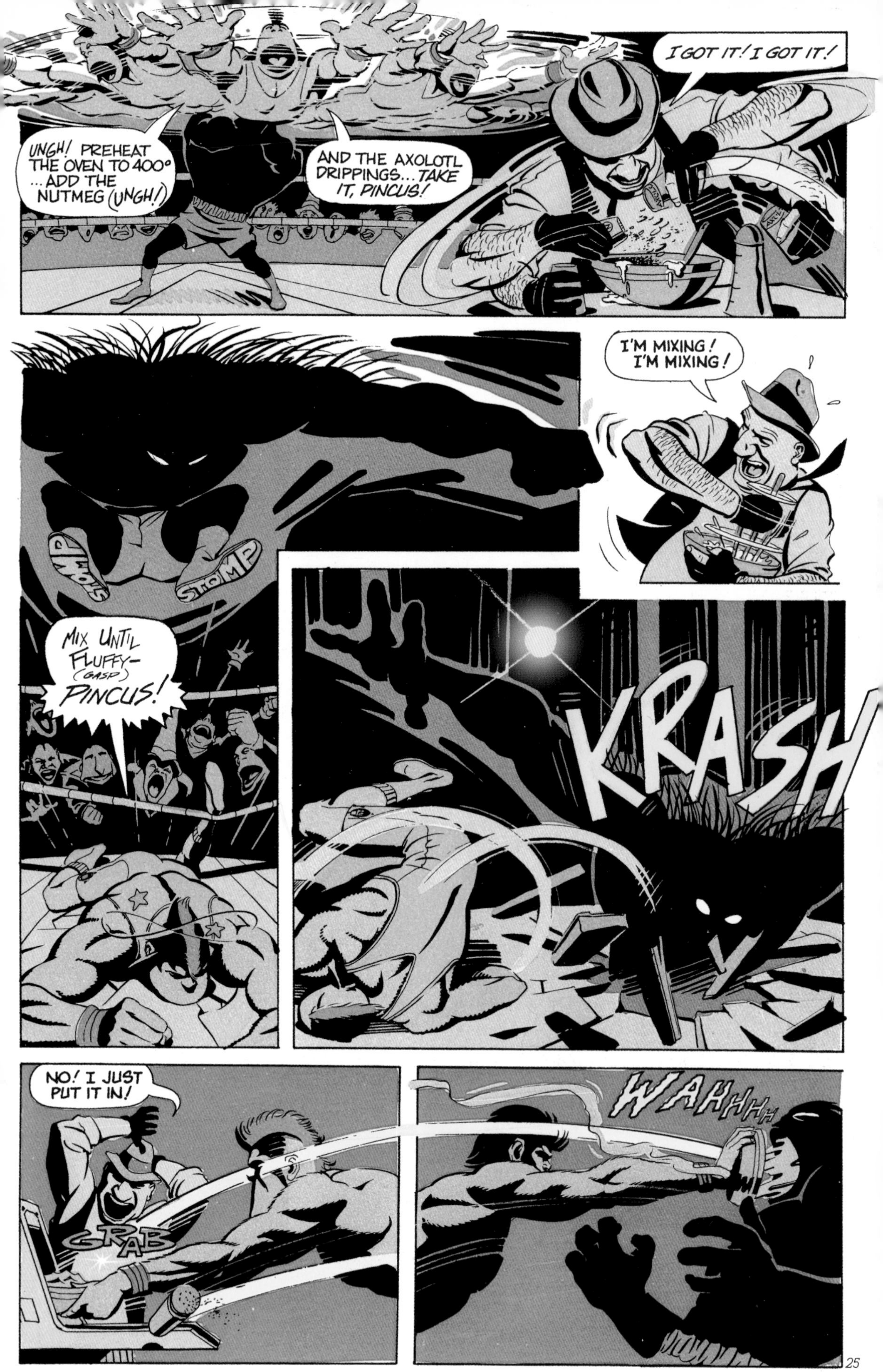
I GOT IT! I GOT IT!
UNGH! PREHEAT THE OVEN TO 400° ...ADD THE NUTMEG (UNGH!)
AND THE AXOLOTL DRIPPINGS... TAKE IT, PINCUS!
I'M MIXING! I'M MIXING!
STOMP STOMP
MIX UNTIL FLUFFY- (GASP) PINCUS!
KRASH
NO! I JUST PUT IT IN!
GRAB
WAHHHH
25

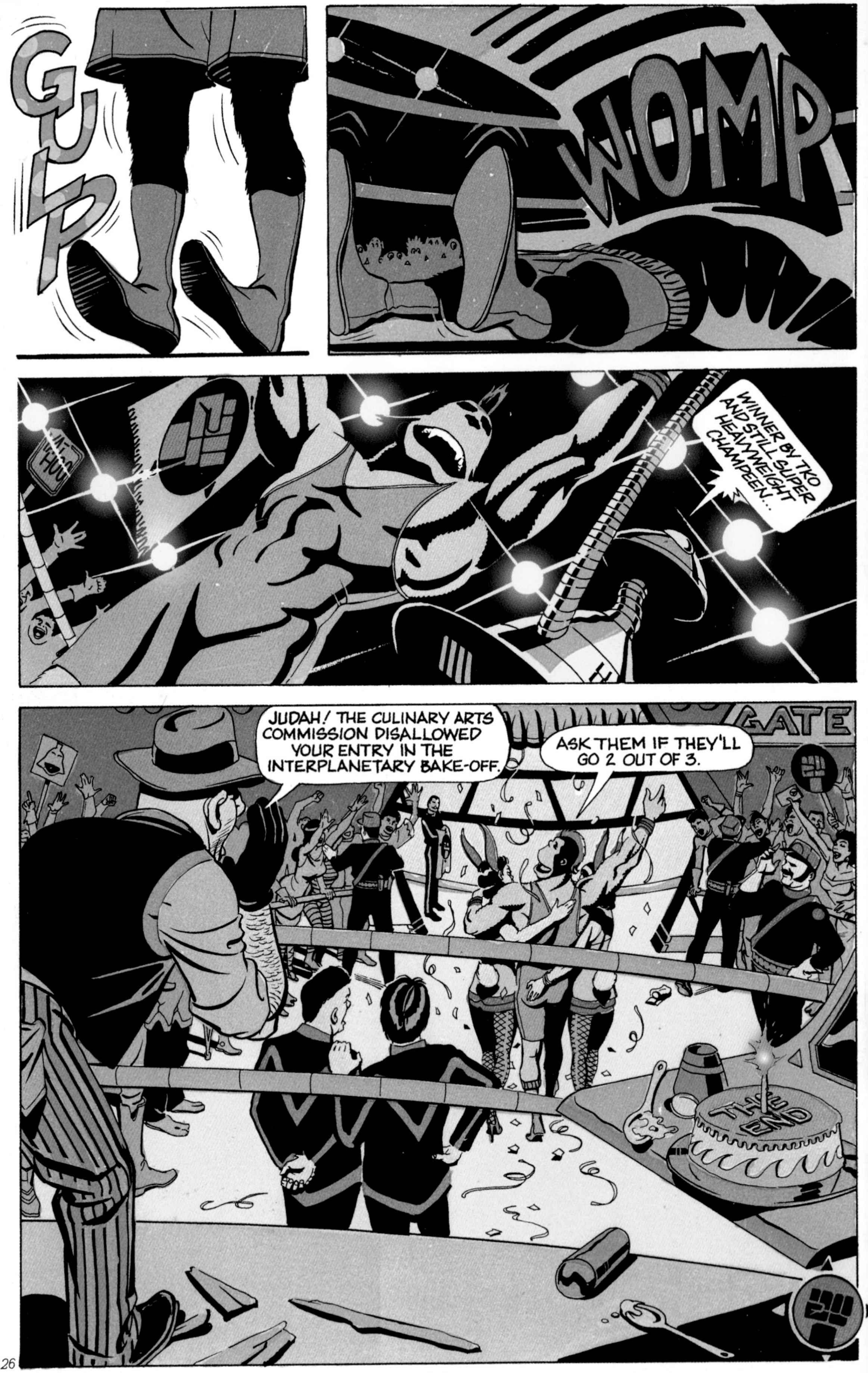
GULP
WOMP
WINNER BY TKO AND STILL SUPER HEAVYWEIGHT CHAMPEEN...
GATE
JUDAH! THE CULINARY ARTS COMMISSION DISALLOWED YOUR ENTRY IN THE INTERPLANETARY BAKE-OFF.
ASK THEM IF THEY'LL GO 2 OUT OF 3.

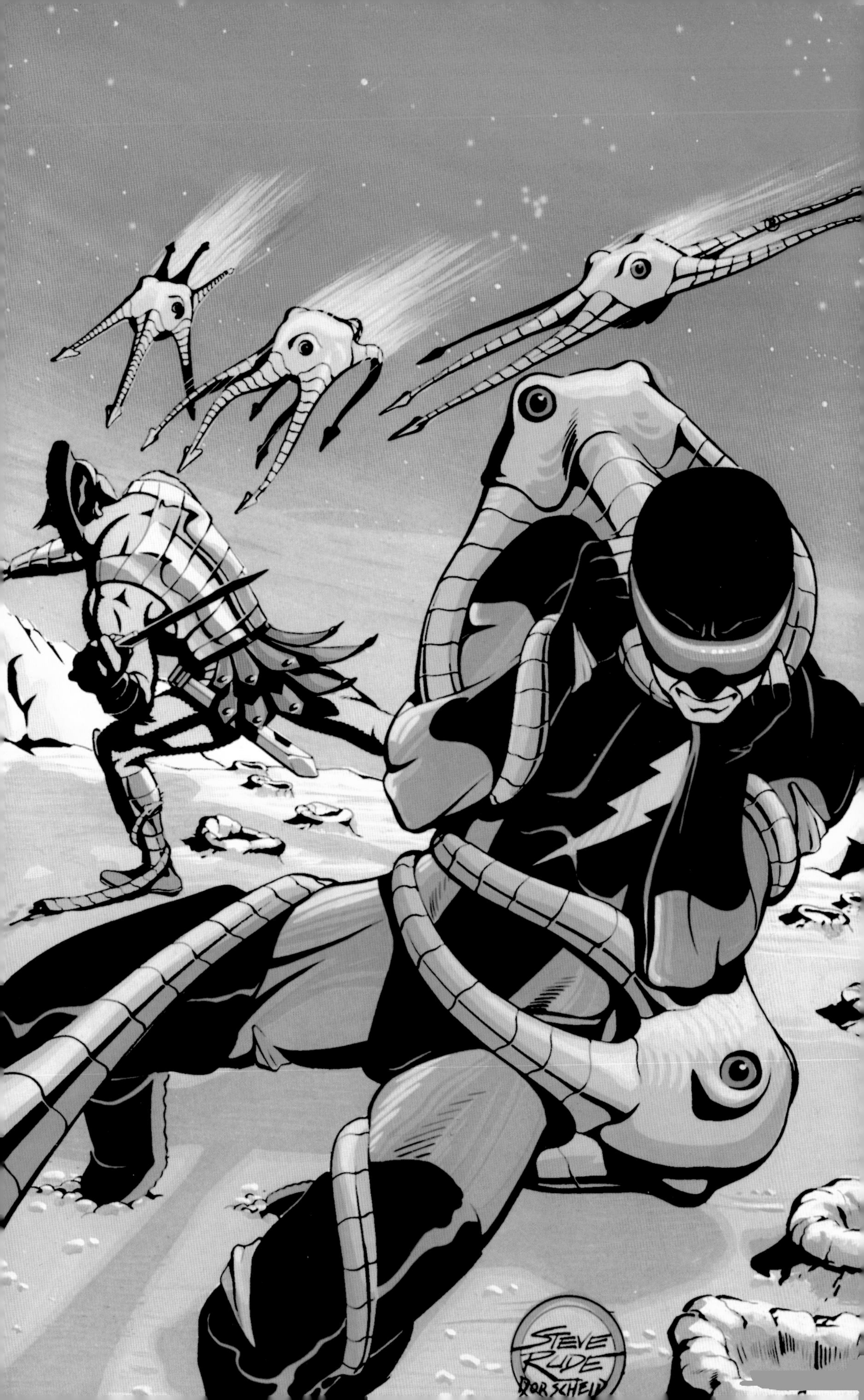
STEVE RUDE
DORSCHEID

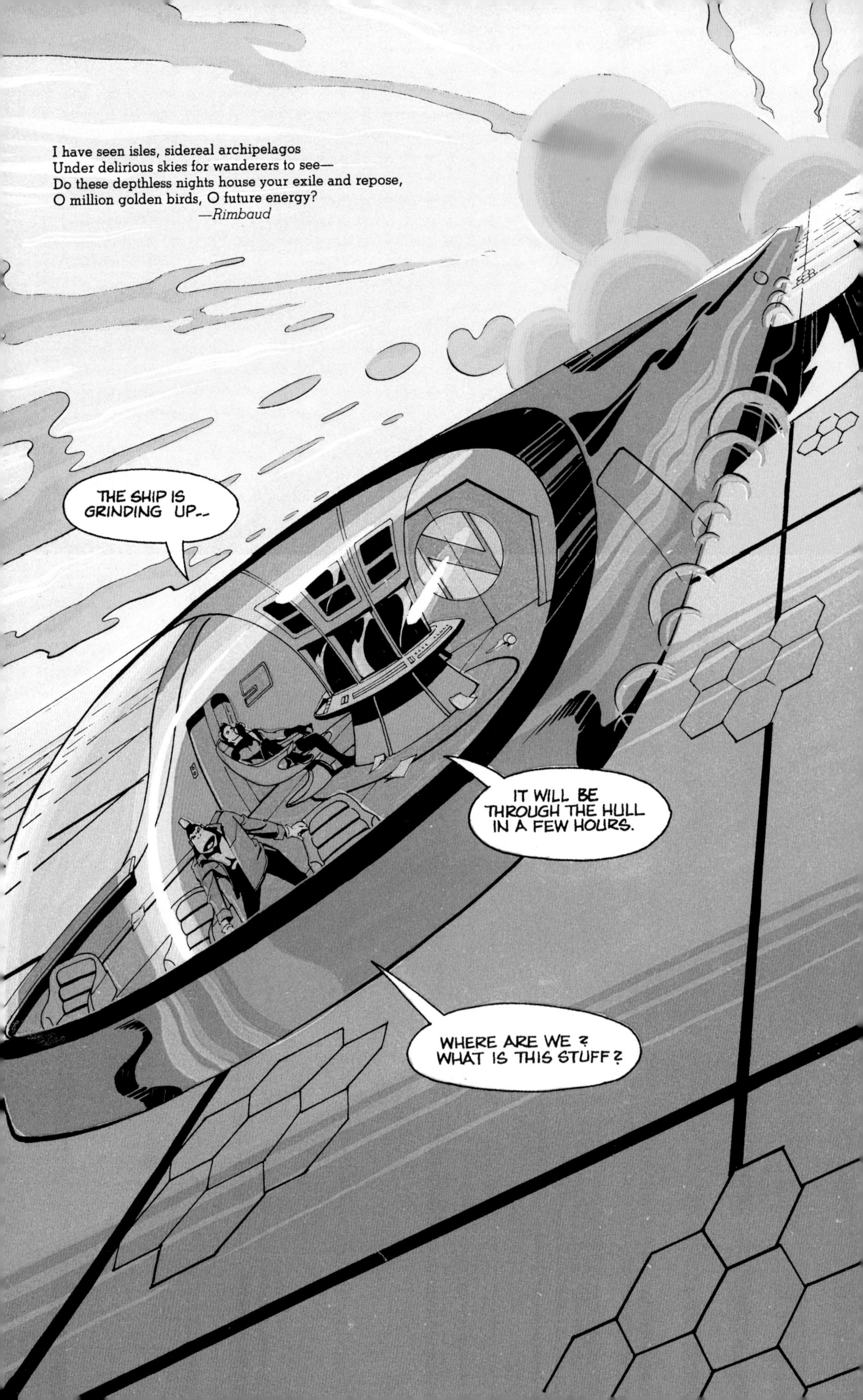
I have seen isles, sidereal archipelagos
Under delirious skies for wanderers to see—
Do these depthless nights house your exile and repose,
O million golden birds, O future energy?
—Rimbaud
THE SHIP IS GRINDING UP--
IT WILL BE THROUGH THE HULL IN A FEW HOURS.
WHERE ARE WE? WHAT IS THIS STUFF?

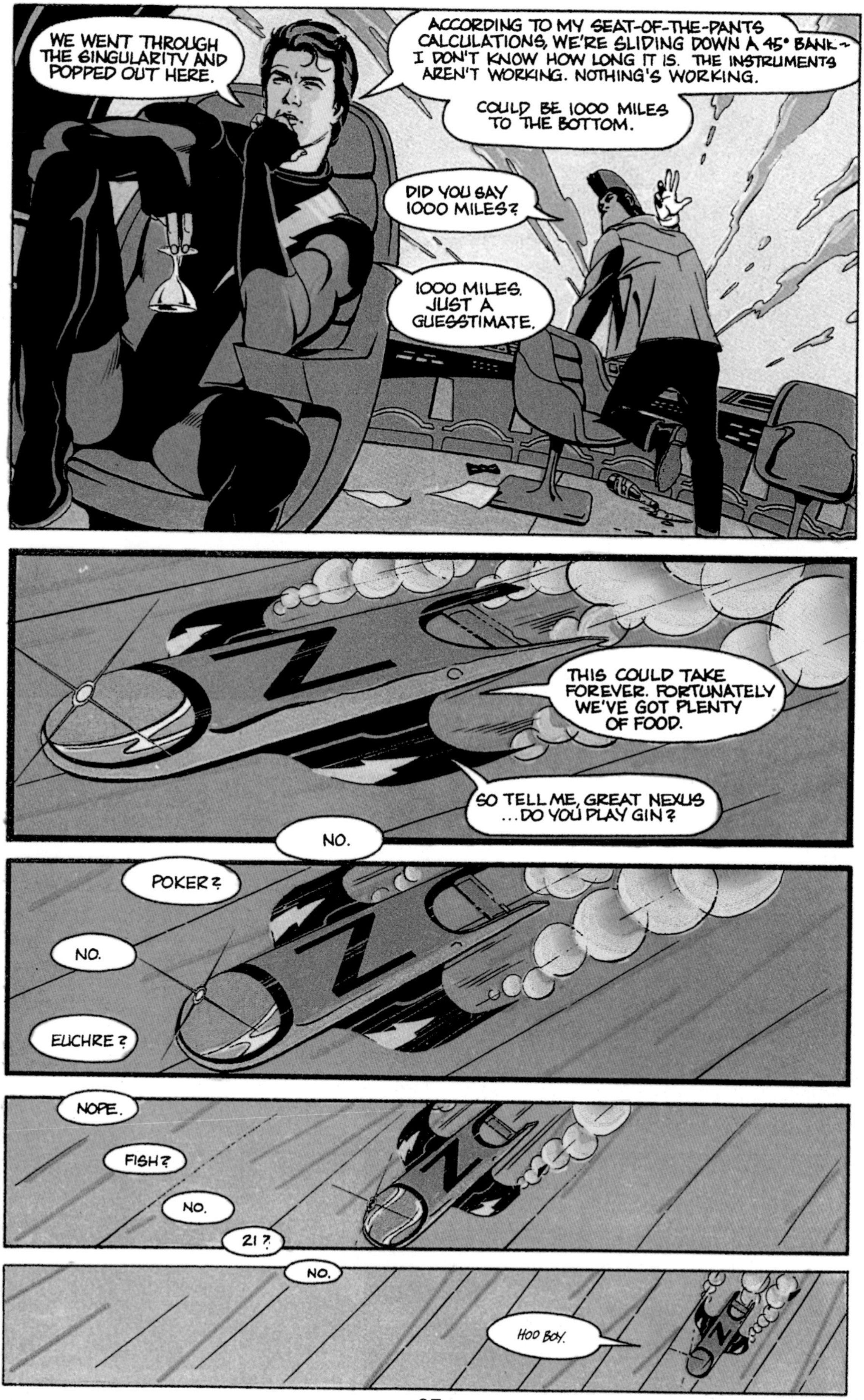
WE WENT THROUGH THE SINGULARITY AND POPPED OUT HERE.
ACCORDING TO MY SEAT-OF-THE-PANTS CALCULATIONS, WE'RE SLIDING DOWN A 45° BANK– I DON'T KNOW HOW LONG IT IS. THE INSTRUMENTS AREN'T WORKING. NOTHING'S WORKING.
COULD BE 1000 MILES TO THE BOTTOM.
DID YOU SAY 1000 MILES?
1000 MILES. JUST A GUESSTIMATE.
THIS COULD TAKE FOREVER. FORTUNATELY WE'VE GOT PLENTY OF FOOD.
SO TELL ME, GREAT NEXUS ...DO YOU PLAY GIN?
NO.
POKER?
NO.
EUCHRE?
NOPE.
FISH?
NO.
21?
NO.
HOO BOY.

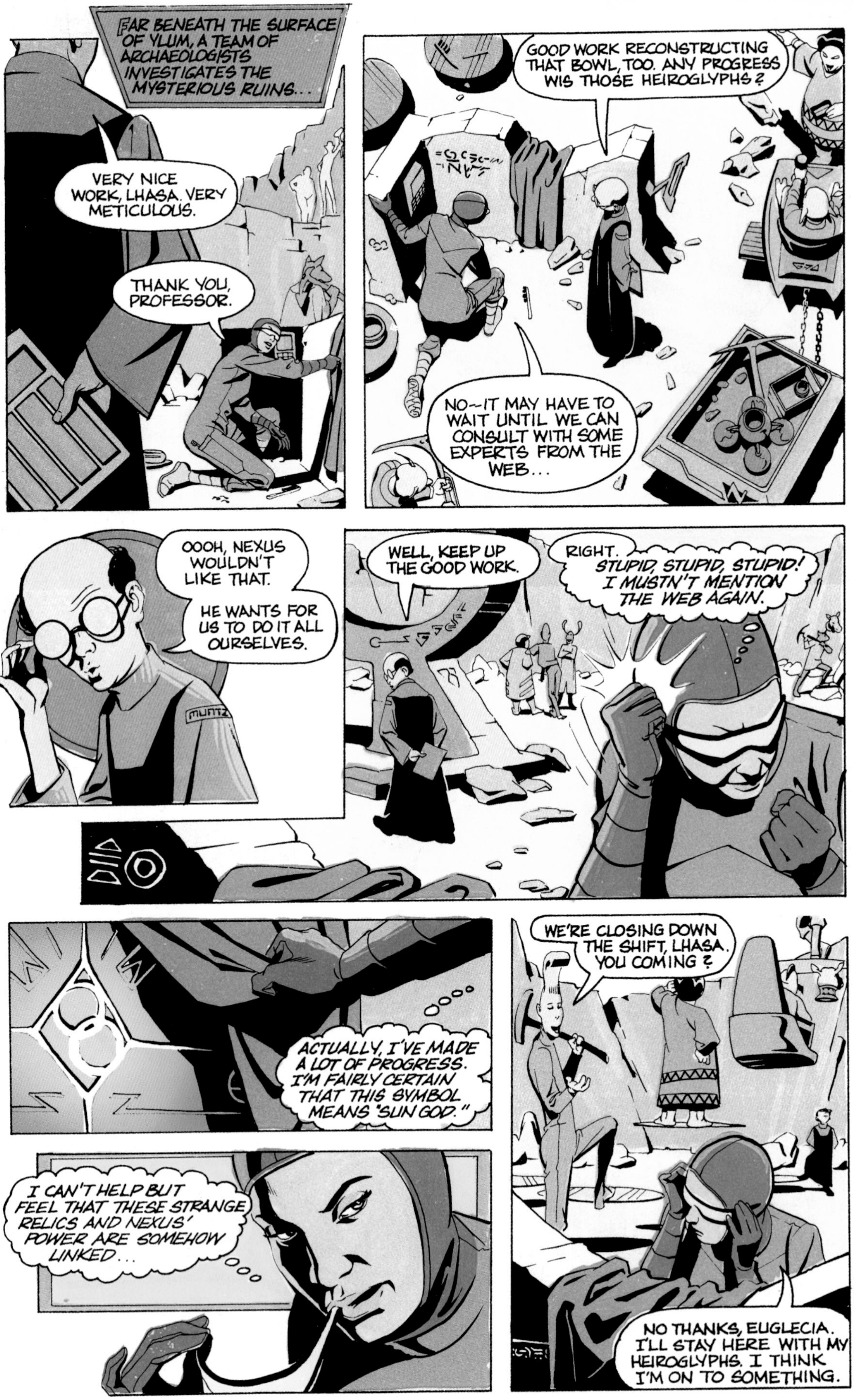

FAR BENEATH THE SURFACE OF YLUM, A TEAM OF ARCHAEOLOGISTS INVESTIGATES THE MYSTERIOUS RUINS...
VERY NICE WORK, LHASA. VERY METICULOUS.
THANK YOU, PROFESSOR.
GOOD WORK RECONSTRUCTING THAT BOWL, TOO. ANY PROGRESS WIS THOSE HEIROGLYPHS?
NO--IT MAY HAVE TO WAIT UNTIL WE CAN CONSULT WITH SOME EXPERTS FROM THE WEB...
OOOH, NEXUS WOULDN'T LIKE THAT.
HE WANTS FOR US TO DO IT ALL OURSELVES.
MUNTZ
WELL, KEEP UP THE GOOD WORK.
RIGHT. STUPID, STUPID, STUPID! I MUSTN'T MENTION THE WEB AGAIN.
ACTUALLY, I'VE MADE A LOT OF PROGRESS. I'M FAIRLY CERTAIN THAT THIS SYMBOL MEANS "SUN GOD."
I CAN'T HELP BUT FEEL THAT THESE STRANGE RELICS AND NEXUS' POWER ARE SOMEHOW LINKED...
WE'RE CLOSING DOWN THE SHIFT, LHASA. YOU COMING?
NO THANKS, EUGLECIA. I'LL STAY HERE WITH MY HEIROGLYPHS. I THINK I'M ON TO SOMETHING.

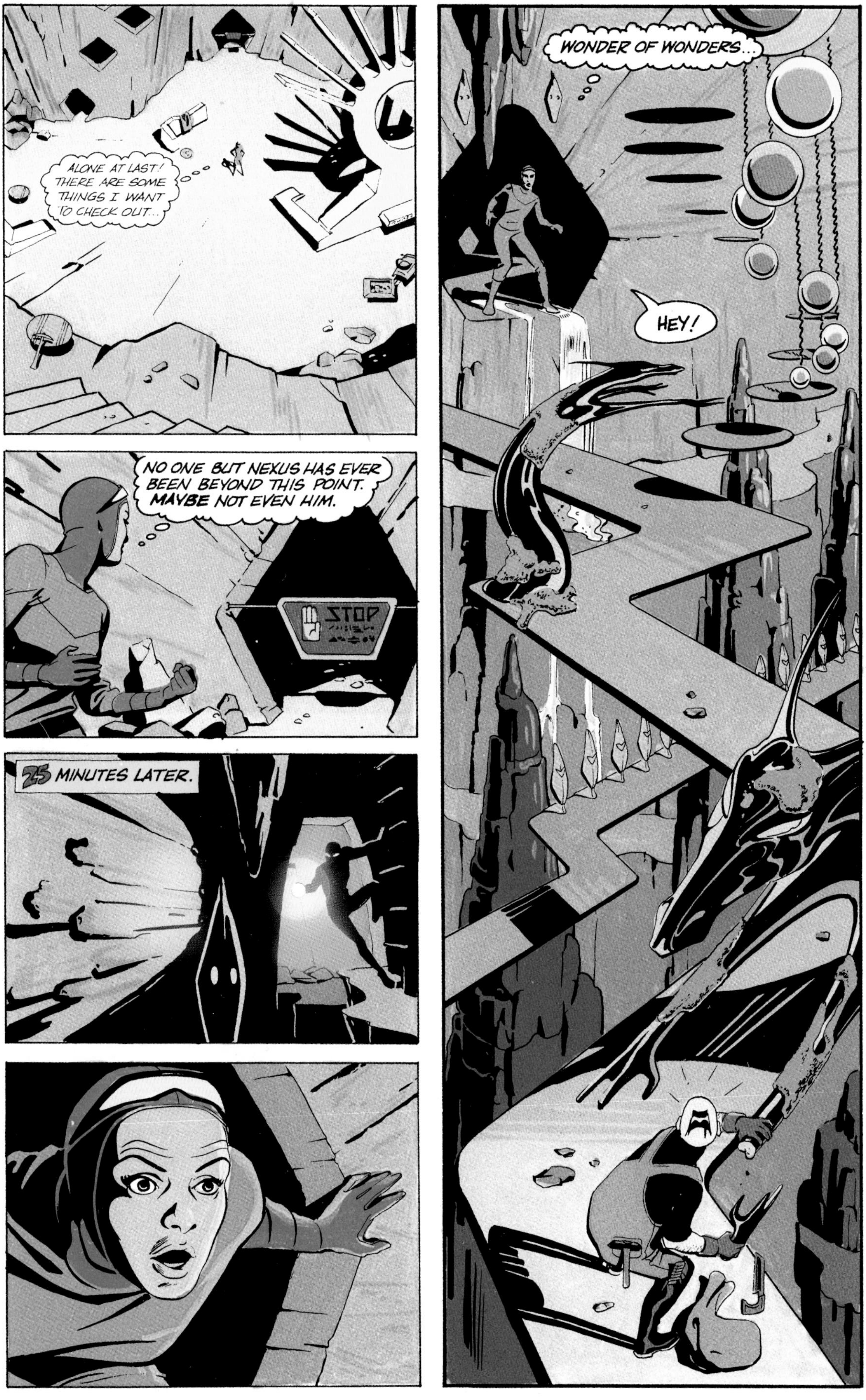
ALONE AT LAST! THERE ARE SOME THINGS I WANT TO CHECK OUT...
NO ONE BUT NEXUS HAS EVER BEEN BEYOND THIS POINT. MAYBE NOT EVEN HIM.
STOP
25 MINUTES LATER.
WONDER OF WONDERS...
HEY!

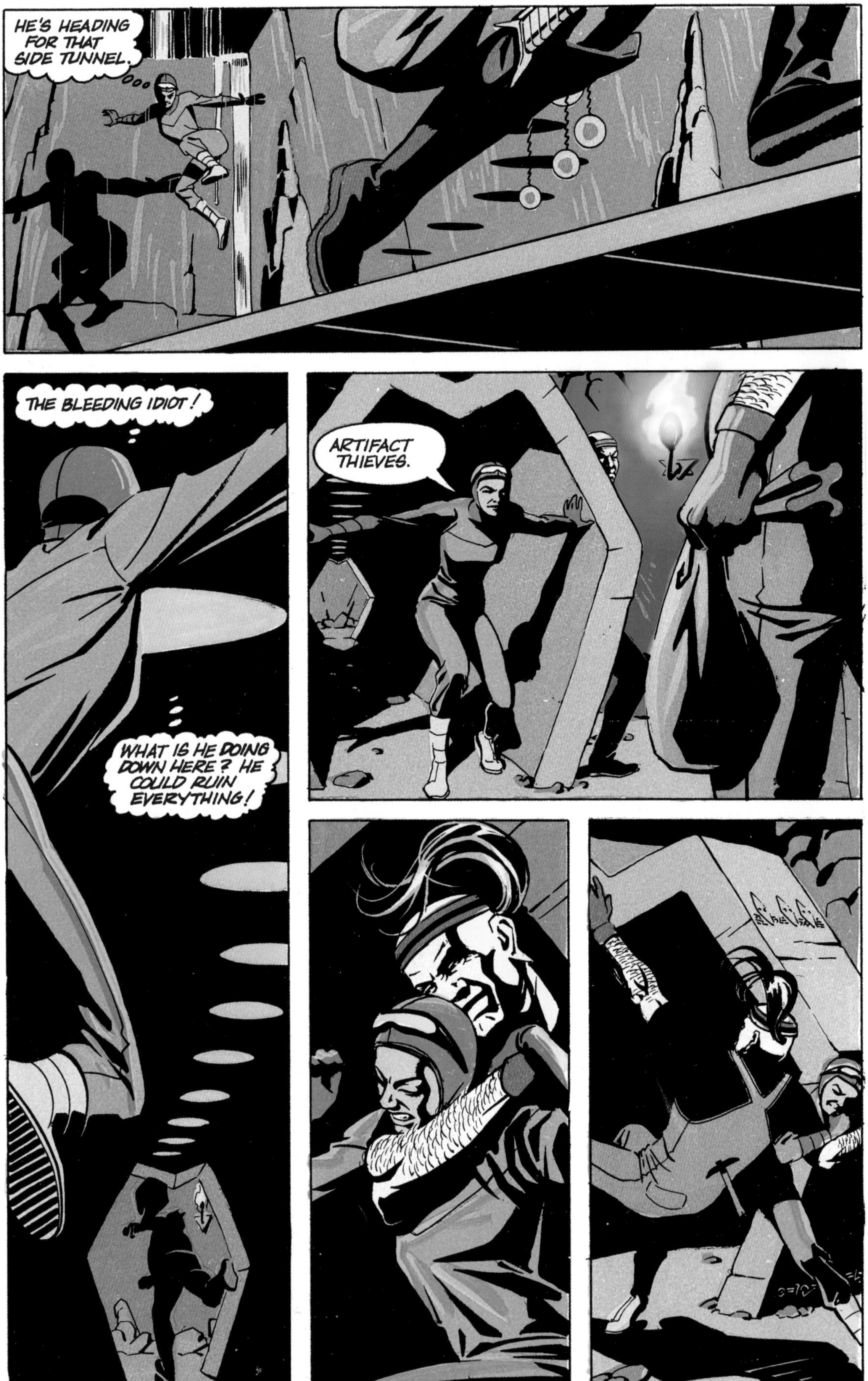
HE'S HEADING FOR THAT SIDE TUNNEL.
THE BLEEDING IDIOT!
WHAT IS HE DOING DOWN HERE? HE COULD RUIN EVERYTHING!
ARTIFACT THIEVES.

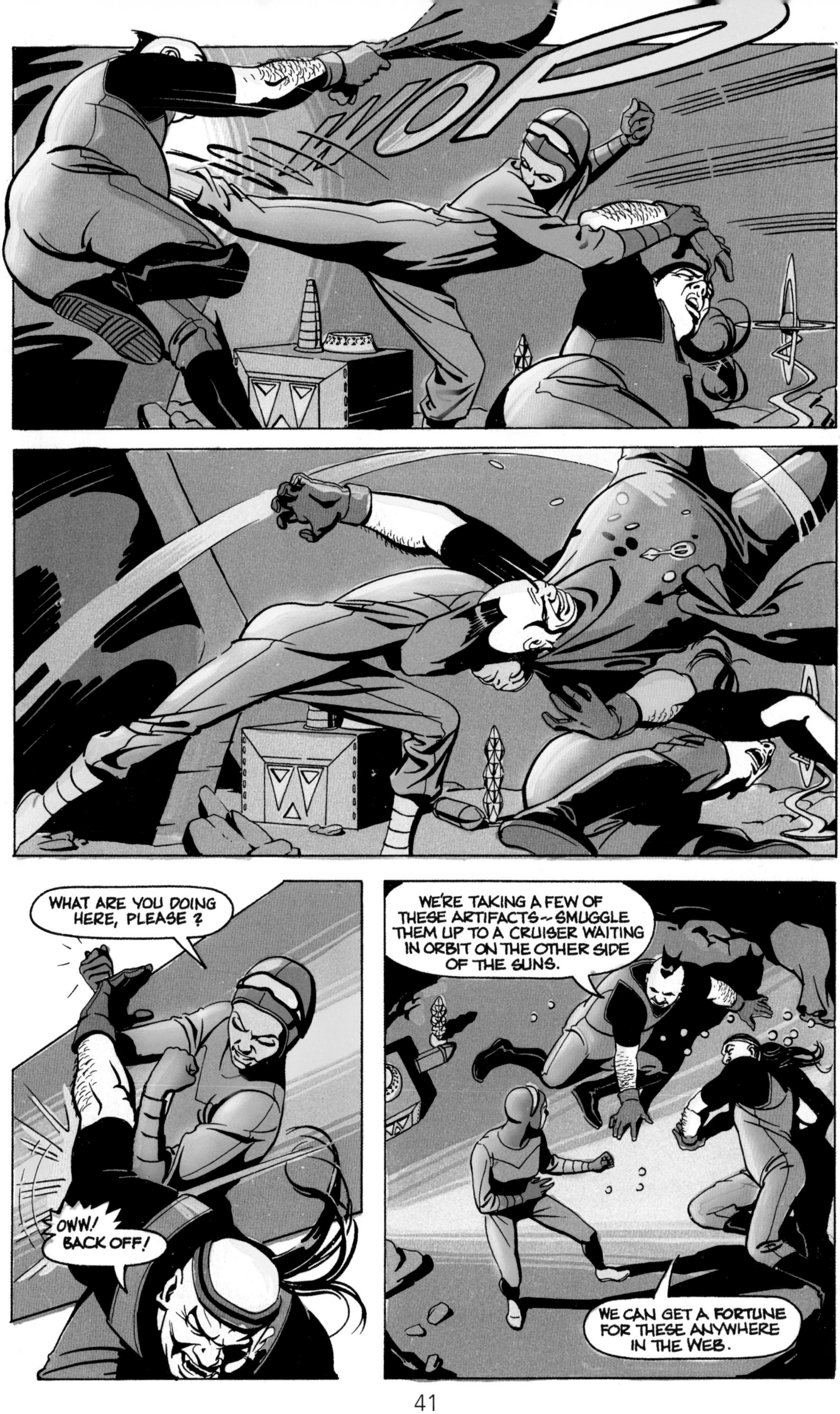
WHAT ARE YOU DOING HERE, PLEASE ?
OWW! BACK OFF!
WE'RE TAKING A FEW OF THESE ARTIFACTS-- SMUGGLE THEM UP TO A CRUISER WAITING IN ORBIT ON THE OTHER SIDE OF THE SUNS.
WE CAN GET A FORTUNE FOR THESE ANYWHERE IN THE WEB.

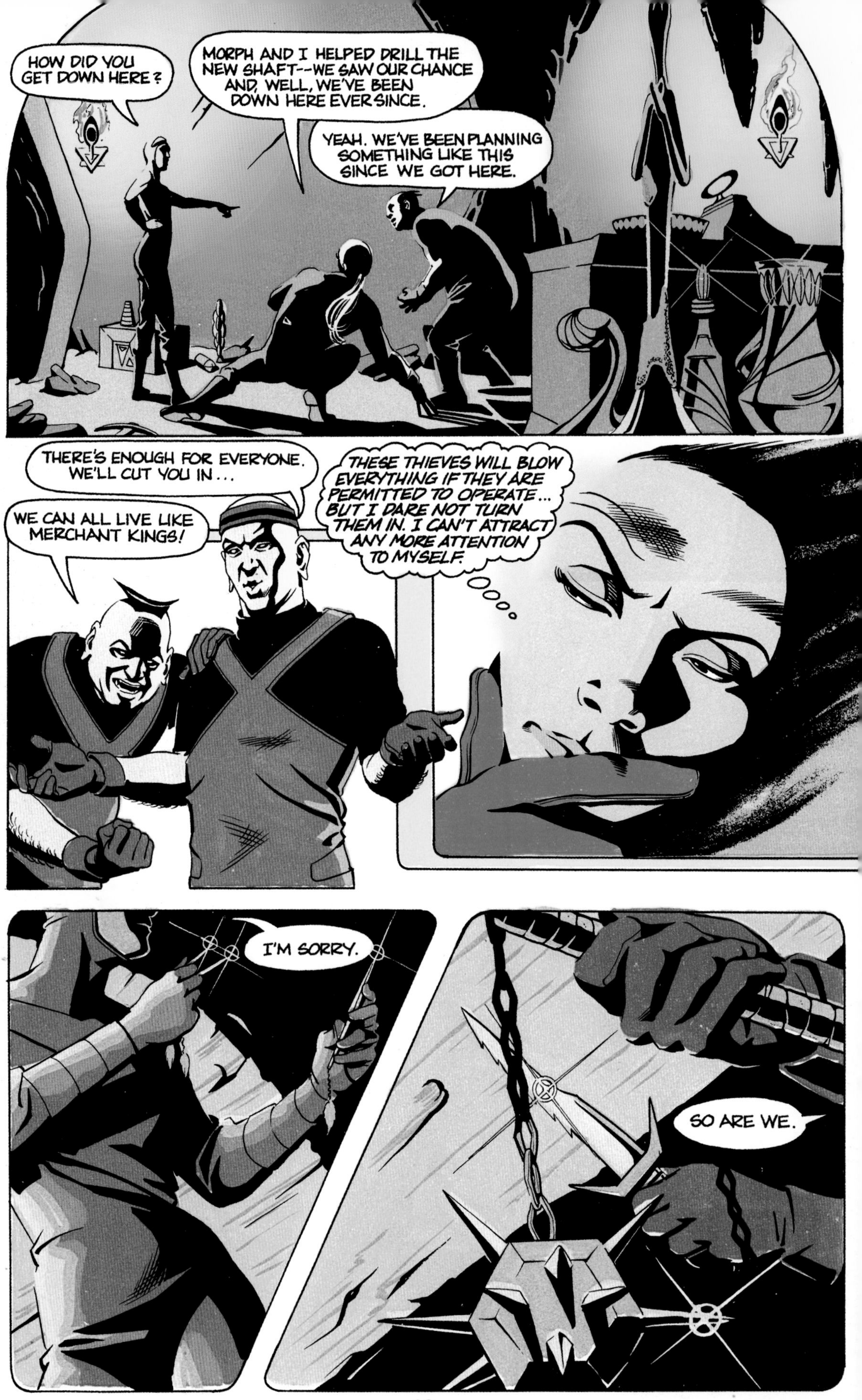
HOW DID YOU GET DOWN HERE?
MORPH AND I HELPED DRILL THE NEW SHAFT--WE SAW OUR CHANCE AND, WELL, WE'VE BEEN DOWN HERE EVER SINCE.
YEAH. WE'VE BEEN PLANNING SOMETHING LIKE THIS SINCE WE GOT HERE.
THERE'S ENOUGH FOR EVERYONE. WE'LL CUT YOU IN...
WE CAN ALL LIVE LIKE MERCHANT KINGS!
THESE THIEVES WILL BLOW EVERYTHING IF THEY ARE PERMITTED TO OPERATE... BUT I DARE NOT TURN THEM IN. I CAN'T ATTRACT ANY MORE ATTENTION TO MYSELF.
I'M SORRY.
SO ARE WE.

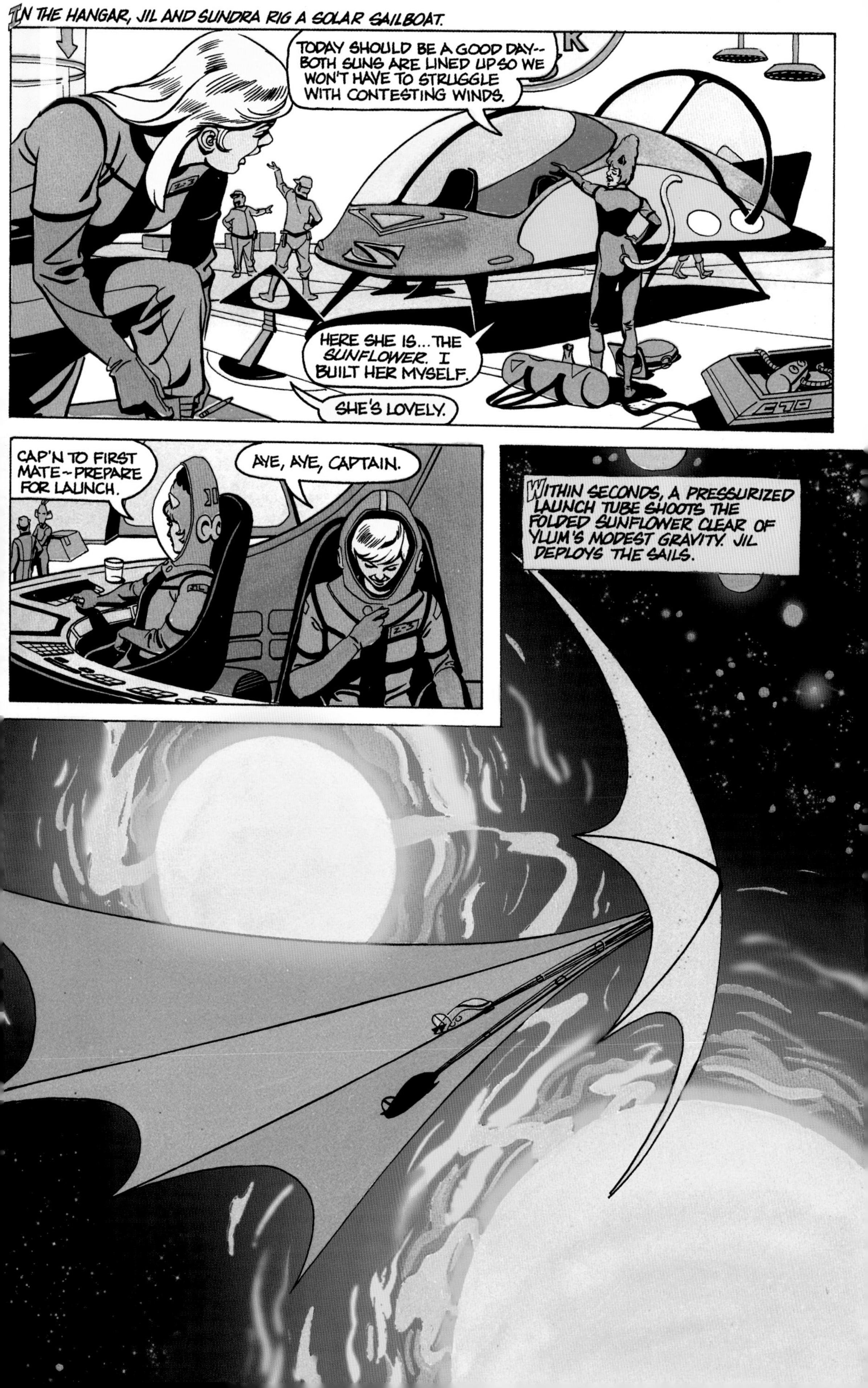
IN THE HANGAR, JIL AND SUNDRA RIG A SOLAR SAILBOAT.
TODAY SHOULD BE A GOOD DAY-- BOTH SUNS ARE LINED UP SO WE WON'T HAVE TO STRUGGLE WITH CONTESTING WINDS.
HERE SHE IS... THE SUNFLOWER. I BUILT HER MYSELF.
SHE'S LOVELY.
CAP'N TO FIRST MATE-- PREPARE FOR LAUNCH.
AYE, AYE, CAPTAIN.
WITHIN SECONDS, A PRESSURIZED LAUNCH TUBE SHOOTS THE FOLDED SUNFLOWER CLEAR OF YLUM'S MODEST GRAVITY. JIL DEPLOYS THE SAILS.

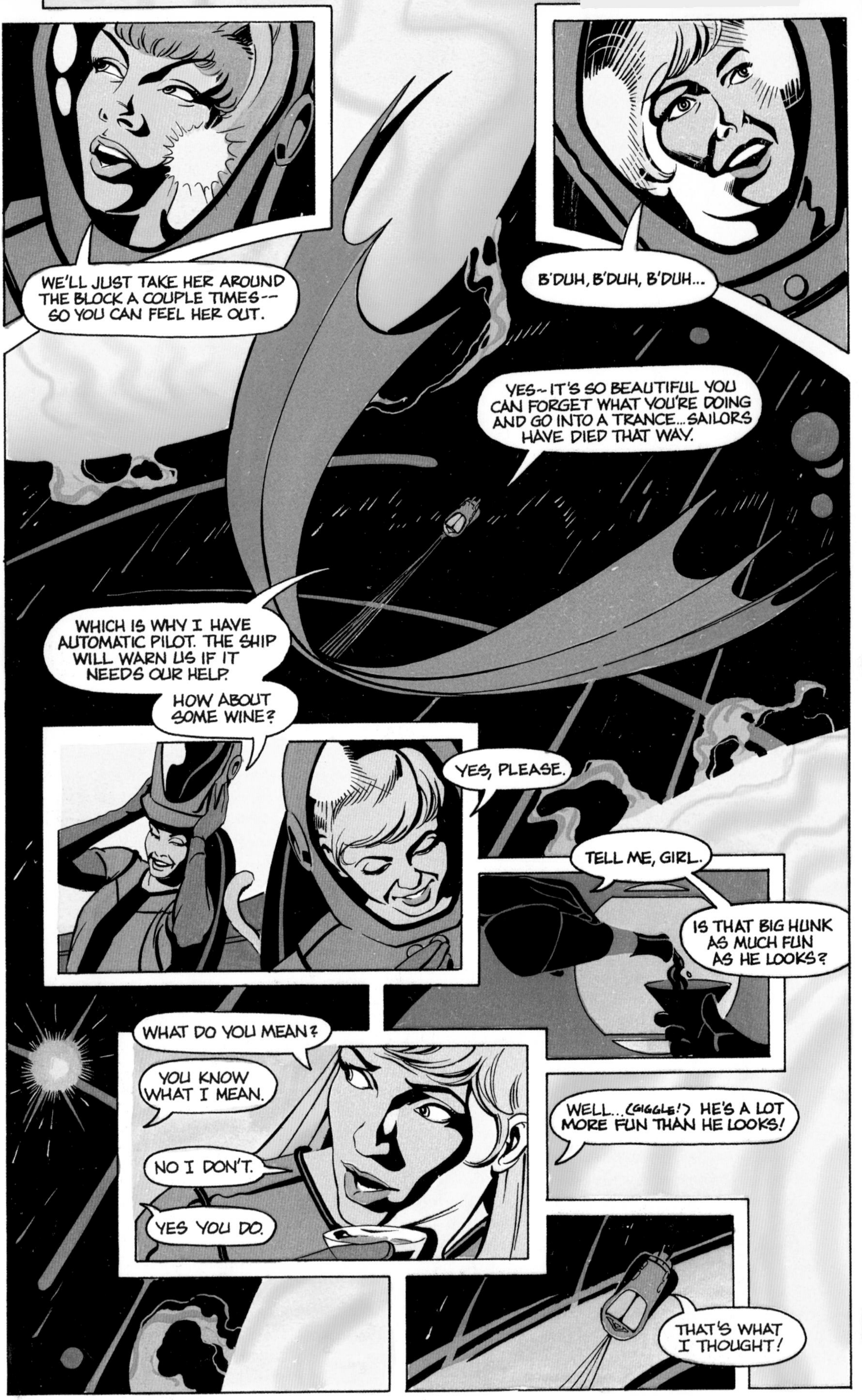

WE'LL JUST TAKE HER AROUND THE BLOCK A COUPLE TIMES-- SO YOU CAN FEEL HER OUT.
B'DUH, B'DUH, B'DUH...
YES-- IT'S SO BEAUTIFUL YOU CAN FORGET WHAT YOU'RE DOING AND GO INTO A TRANCE...SAILORS HAVE DIED THAT WAY.
WHICH IS WHY I HAVE AUTOMATIC PILOT. THE SHIP WILL WARN US IF IT NEEDS OUR HELP.
HOW ABOUT SOME WINE?
YES, PLEASE.
TELL ME, GIRL.
IS THAT BIG HUNK AS MUCH FUN AS HE LOOKS?
WHAT DO YOU MEAN?
YOU KNOW WHAT I MEAN.
NO I DON'T.
YES YOU DO.
WELL... (GIGGLE!) HE'S A LOT MORE FUN THAN HE LOOKS!
THAT'S WHAT I THOUGHT!

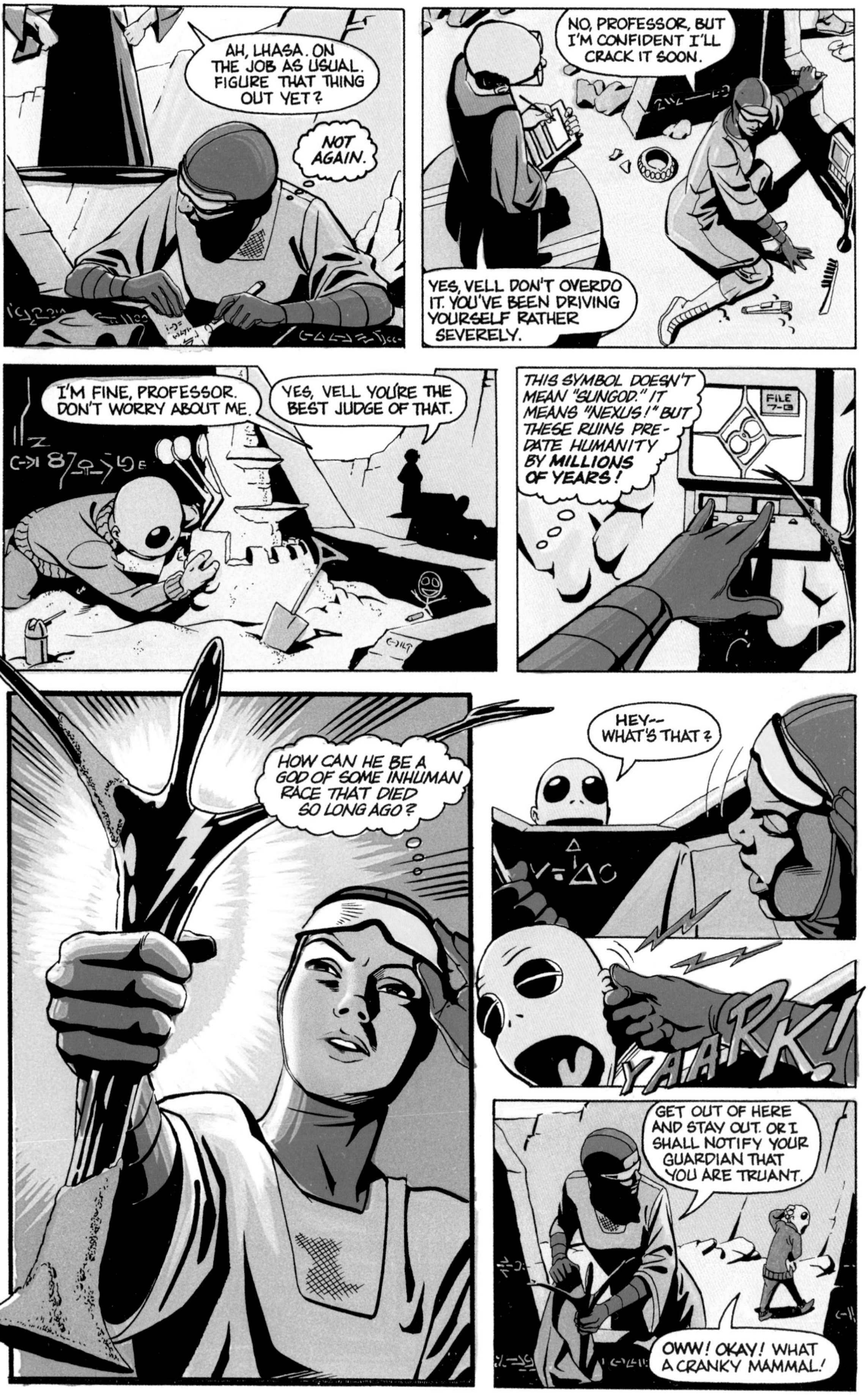
AH, LHASA. ON THE JOB AS USUAL. FIGURE THAT THING OUT YET?
NOT AGAIN.
NO, PROFESSOR, BUT I'M CONFIDENT I'LL CRACK IT SOON.
YES, VELL DON'T OVERDO IT. YOU'VE BEEN DRIVING YOURSELF RATHER SEVERELY.
I'M FINE, PROFESSOR. DON'T WORRY ABOUT ME.
YES, VELL YOU'RE THE BEST JUDGE OF THAT.
THIS SYMBOL DOESN'T MEAN "SUNGOD." IT MEANS "NEXUS!" BUT THESE RUINS PRE-DATE HUMANITY BY MILLIONS OF YEARS!
FILE 7-B
HOW CAN HE BE A GOD OF SOME INHUMAN RACE THAT DIED SO LONG AGO?
HEY-- WHAT'S THAT?
YAARK!
GET OUT OF HERE AND STAY OUT. OR I SHALL NOTIFY YOUR GUARDIAN THAT YOU ARE TRUANT.
OWW! OKAY! WHAT A CRANKY MAMMAL!

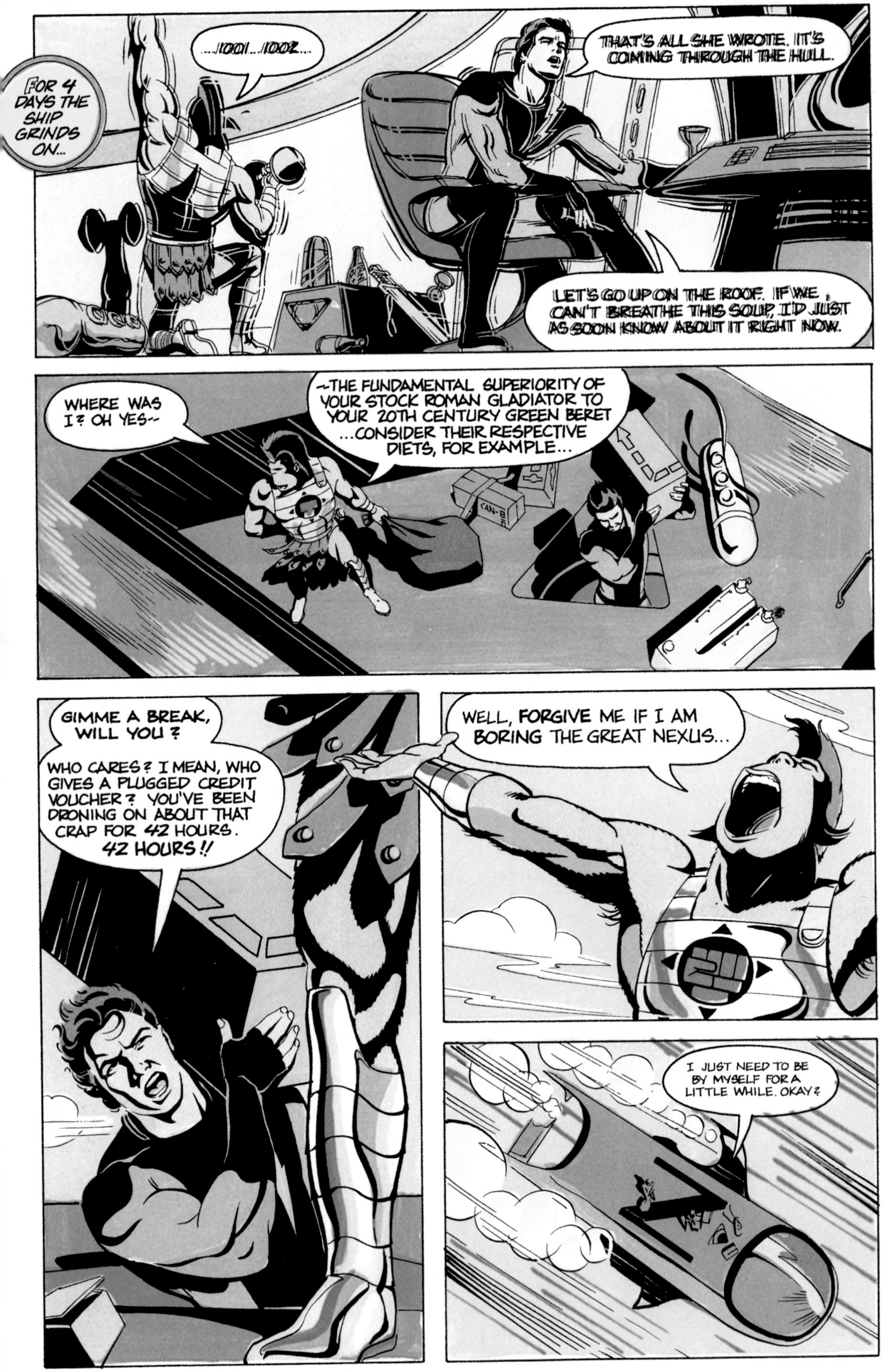
FOR 4 DAYS THE SHIP GRINDS ON...
...1001...1002...
THAT'S ALL SHE WROTE. IT'S COMING THROUGH THE HULL.
LET'S GO UP ON THE ROOF. IF WE CAN'T BREATHE THIS SOUP, I'D JUST AS SOON KNOW ABOUT IT RIGHT NOW.
WHERE WAS I? OH YES--
--THE FUNDAMENTAL SUPERIORITY OF YOUR STOCK ROMAN GLADIATOR TO YOUR 20TH CENTURY GREEN BERET ...CONSIDER THEIR RESPECTIVE DIETS, FOR EXAMPLE...
GIMME A BREAK, WILL YOU?
WHO CARES? I MEAN, WHO GIVES A PLUGGED CREDIT VOUCHER? YOU'VE BEEN DRONING ON ABOUT THAT CRAP FOR 42 HOURS. 42 HOURS!!
WELL, FORGIVE ME IF I AM BORING THE GREAT NEXUS...
I JUST NEED TO BE BY MYSELF FOR A LITTLE WHILE. OKAY?

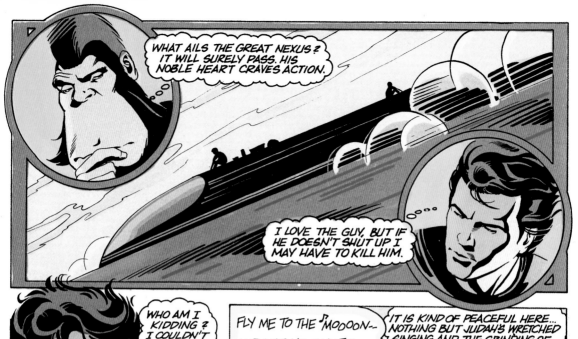

WHAT AILS THE GREAT NEXUS? IT WILL SURELY PASS. HIS NOBLE HEART CRAVES ACTION.

I LOVE THE GUY, BUT IF HE DOESN'T SHUT UP I MAY HAVE TO KILL HIM.

WHO AM I KIDDING? I COULDN'T KILL A MICROBE.

MY POWER'S GONE-- THE BEST I CAN DO IS MAKE MY FINGER SPARKLE. JUST ENOUGH TO SHAVE.

FLY ME TO THE ♪MOOOON-- AND LET ME GAAAZE ♪UPON THE STAAAARS♪

IT IS KIND OF PEACEFUL HERE... NOTHING BUT JUDAH'S WRETCHED SINGING AND THE GRINDING OF THE HULL...

NO STRIDENT POLITICAL TYPES DEMANDING THINGS...

...NO RESPONSIBILITIES...

...NO DREAMS...

47

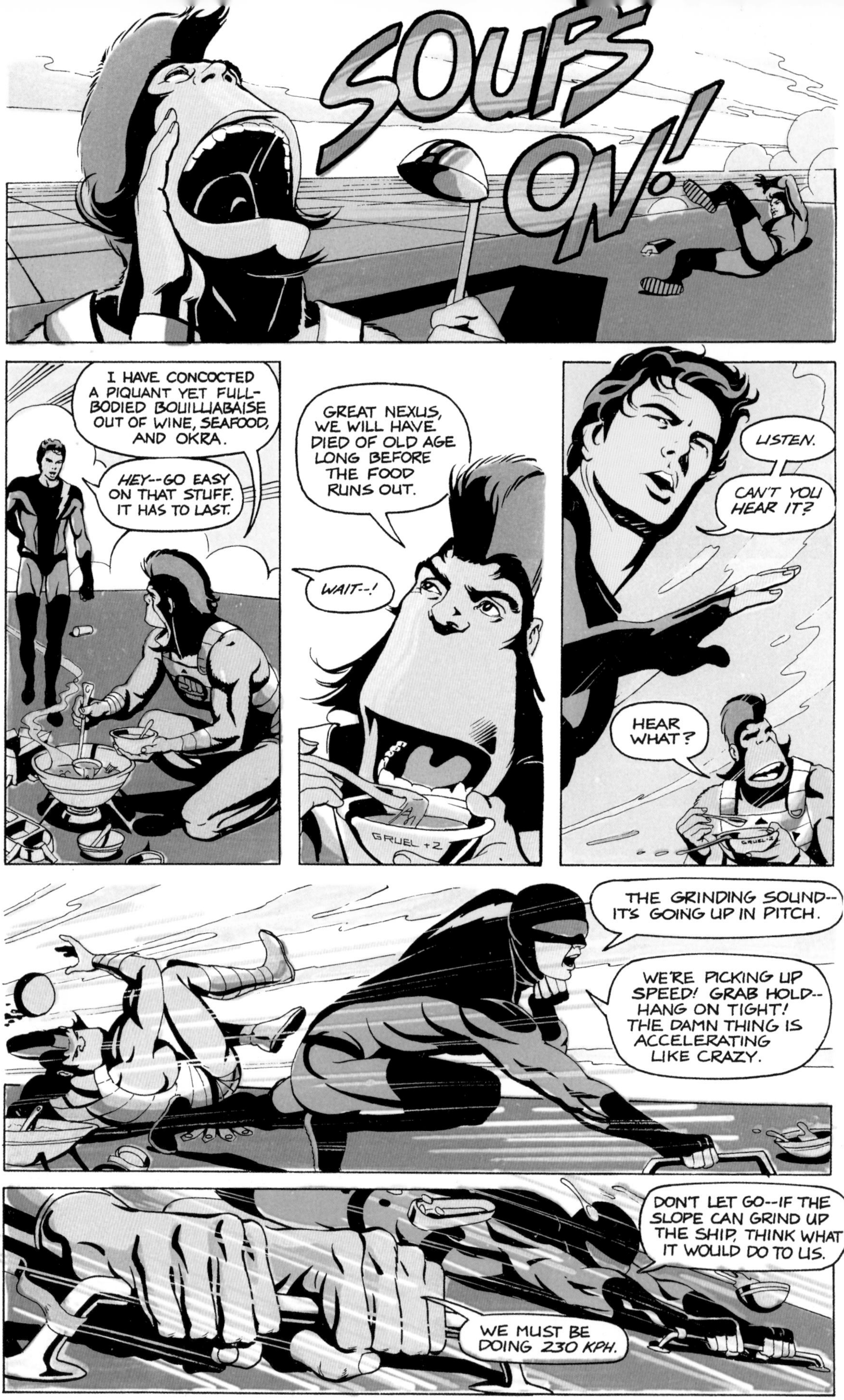
SOUP'S ON!
I HAVE CONCOCTED A PIQUANT YET FULL-BODIED BOUILLIABAISE OUT OF WINE, SEAFOOD, AND OKRA.
HEY--GO EASY ON THAT STUFF. IT HAS TO LAST.
GREAT NEXUS, WE WILL HAVE DIED OF OLD AGE LONG BEFORE THE FOOD RUNS OUT.
WAIT--!
GRUEL +2
LISTEN.
CAN'T YOU HEAR IT?
HEAR WHAT?
GRUEL-2
THE GRINDING SOUND-- IT'S GOING UP IN PITCH.
WE'RE PICKING UP SPEED! GRAB HOLD-- HANG ON TIGHT! THE DAMN THING IS ACCELERATING LIKE CRAZY.
DON'T LET GO--IF THE SLOPE CAN GRIND UP THE SHIP, THINK WHAT IT WOULD DO TO US.
WE MUST BE DOING 230 KPH.

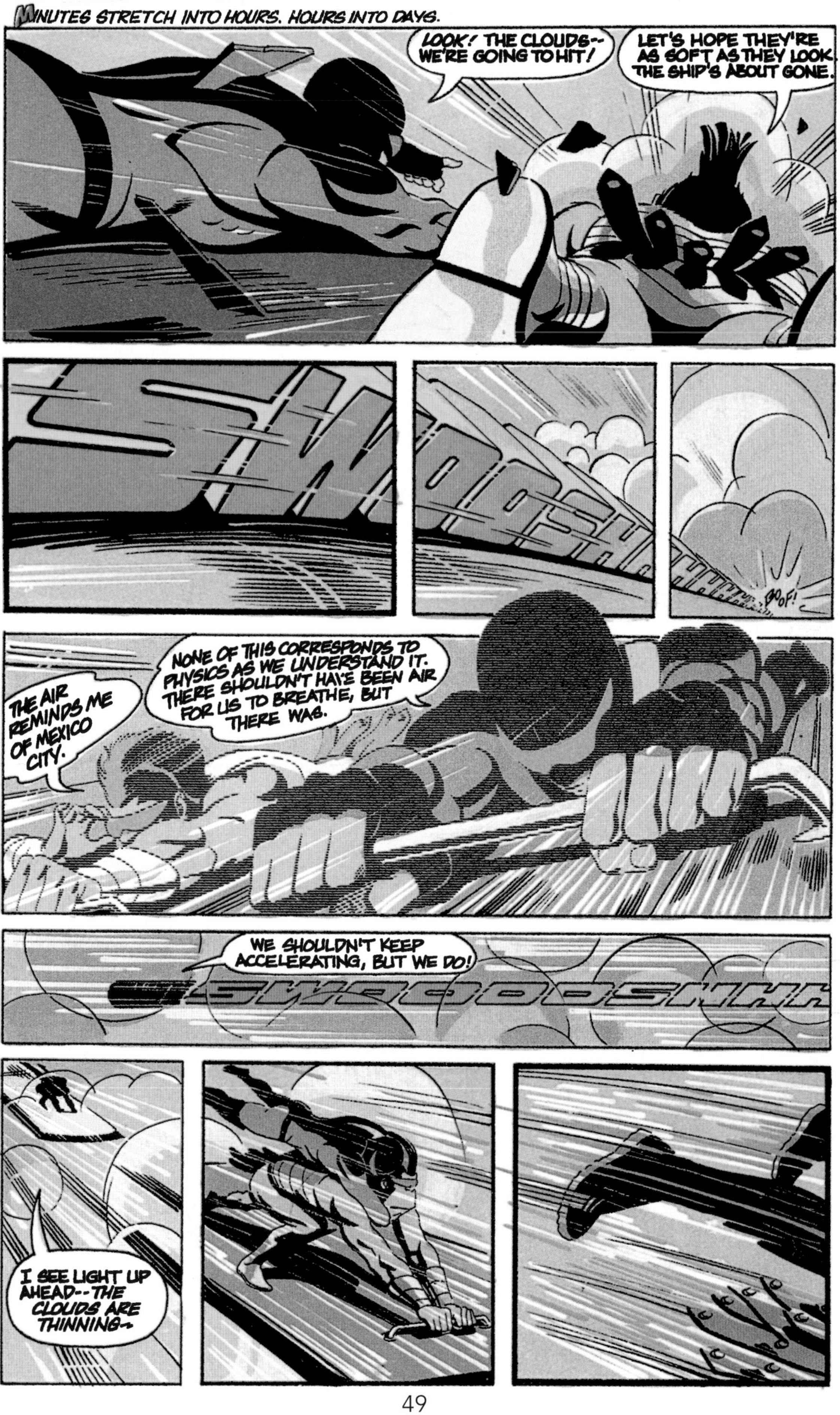
MINUTES STRETCH INTO HOURS. HOURS INTO DAYS.
LOOK! THE CLOUDS--WE'RE GOING TO HIT!
LET'S HOPE THEY'RE AS SOFT AS THEY LOOK. THE SHIP'S ABOUT GONE.
SWOOSHHHH
POOF!
THE AIR REMINDS ME OF MEXICO CITY.
NONE OF THIS CORRESPONDS TO PHYSICS AS WE UNDERSTAND IT. THERE SHOULDN'T HAVE BEEN AIR FOR US TO BREATHE, BUT THERE WAS.
WE SHOULDN'T KEEP ACCELERATING, BUT WE DO!
SWOOOOSHHH
I SEE LIGHT UP AHEAD--THE CLOUDS ARE THINNING--

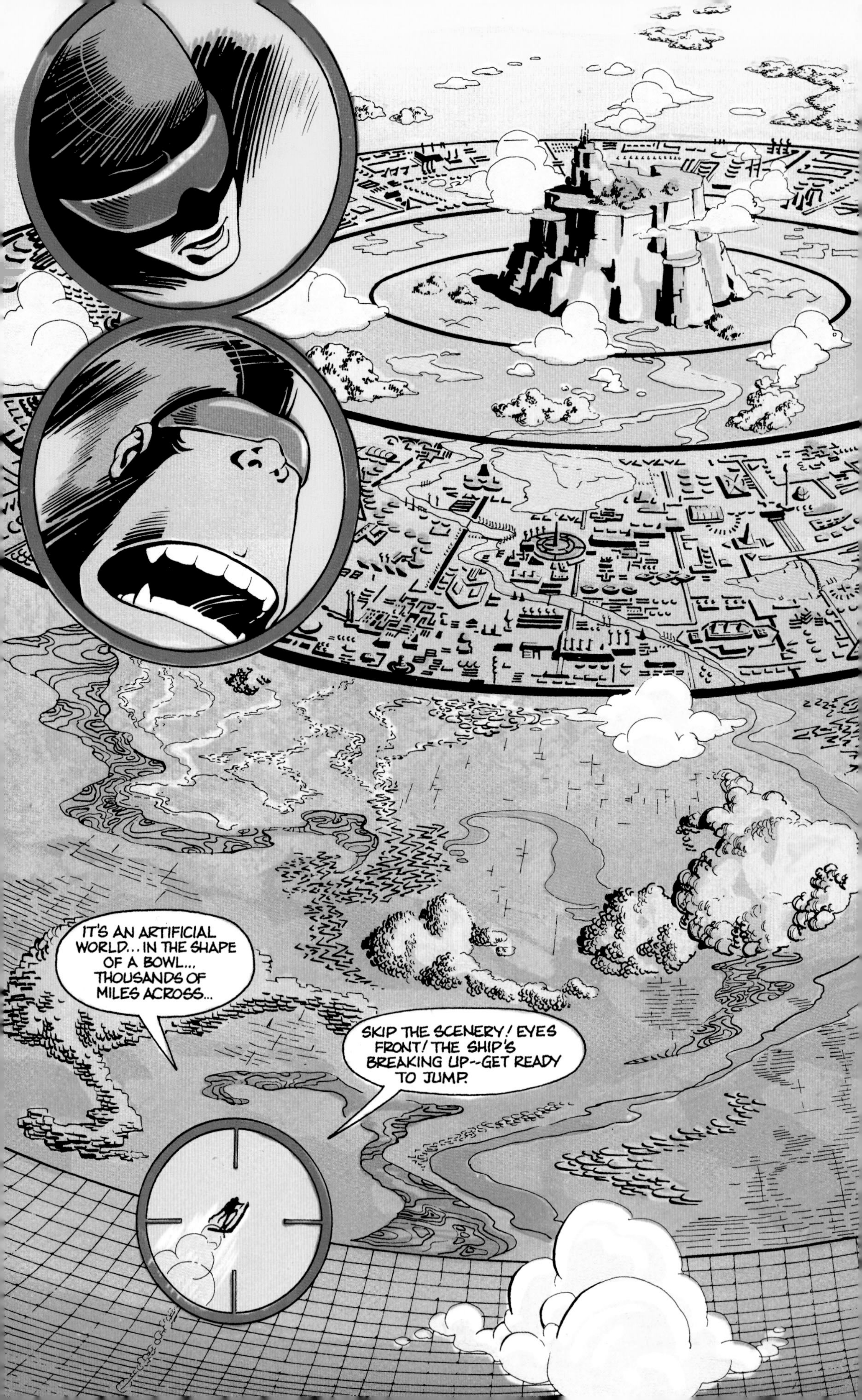
IT'S AN ARTIFICIAL WORLD... IN THE SHAPE OF A BOWL... THOUSANDS OF MILES ACROSS...
SKIP THE SCENERY! EYES FRONT! THE SHIP'S BREAKING UP--GET READY TO JUMP.

TUCK YOUR HEAD AND ROLL!
(GROAN-) MY BACK. MY HEAD. WHAT DO WE DO NOW?
FROM WHAT WE SAW ON THE WAY DOWN, THE SIDES ARE AS SMOOTH AS A BABY'S BEHIND. WE HEAD FOR THE CENTER.
WHAT!? ON FOOT?
CERTAINLY, GREAT NEXUS. WITH JUDAH MACCABEE AT YOUR SIDE, YOU HAVE NOTHING TO FEAR.
EXCEPT POSSIBLY WILD BEASTS...
STARVATION...
DISEASE...
HOSTILE NATIVES...
INCLEMENT WEATHER...

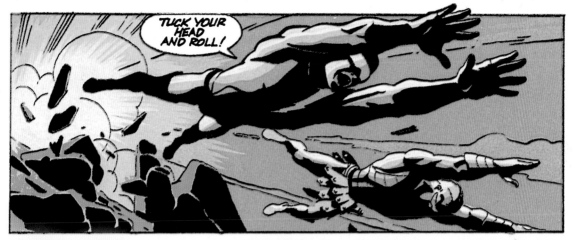

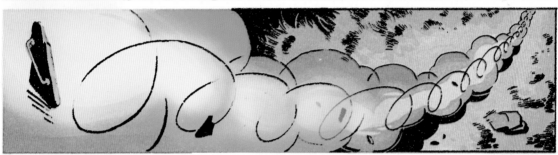

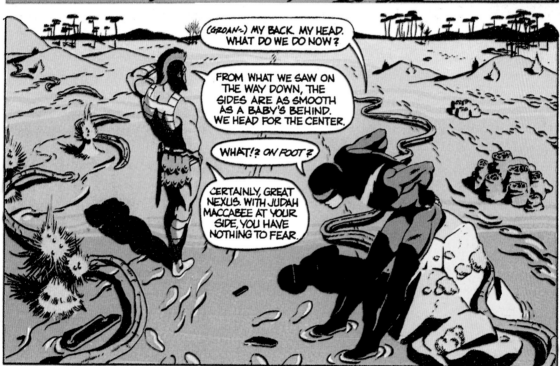

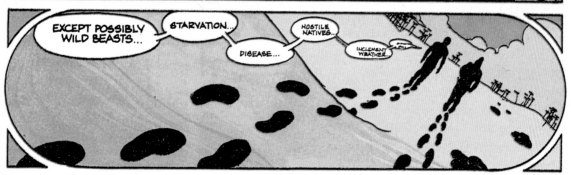

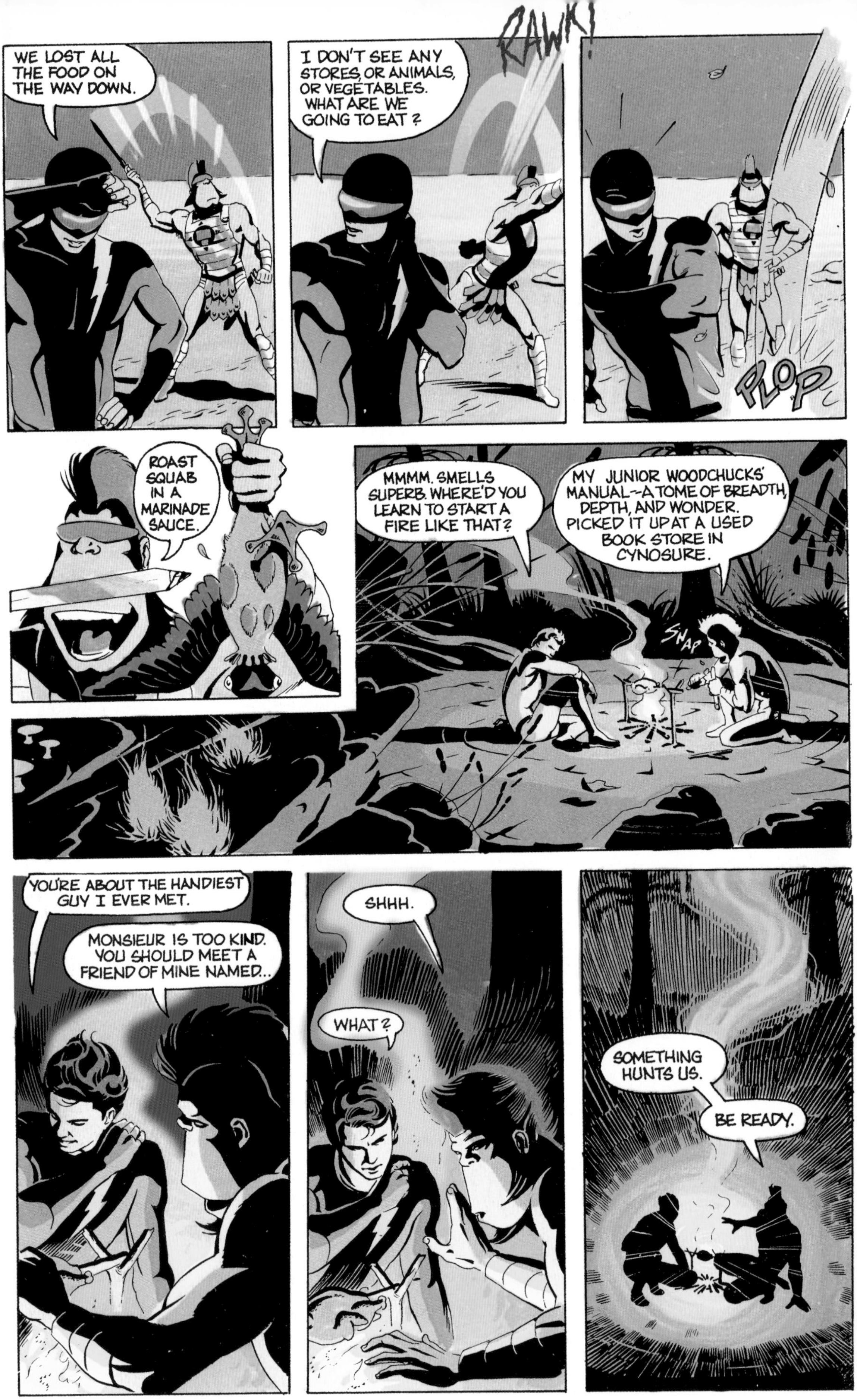
WE LOST ALL THE FOOD ON THE WAY DOWN.
I DON'T SEE ANY STORES, OR ANIMALS, OR VEGETABLES. WHAT ARE WE GOING TO EAT ?
RAWK!
PLOP
ROAST SQUAB IN A MARINADE SAUCE.
MMMM. SMELLS SUPERB. WHERE'D YOU LEARN TO START A FIRE LIKE THAT?
MY JUNIOR WOODCHUCKS' MANUAL--A TOME OF BREADTH, DEPTH, AND WONDER. PICKED IT UP AT A USED BOOK STORE IN CYNOSURE.
SNAP
YOU'RE ABOUT THE HANDIEST GUY I EVER MET.
MONSIEUR IS TOO KIND. YOU SHOULD MEET A FRIEND OF MINE NAMED...
SHHH.
WHAT ?
SOMETHING HUNTS US.
BE READY.

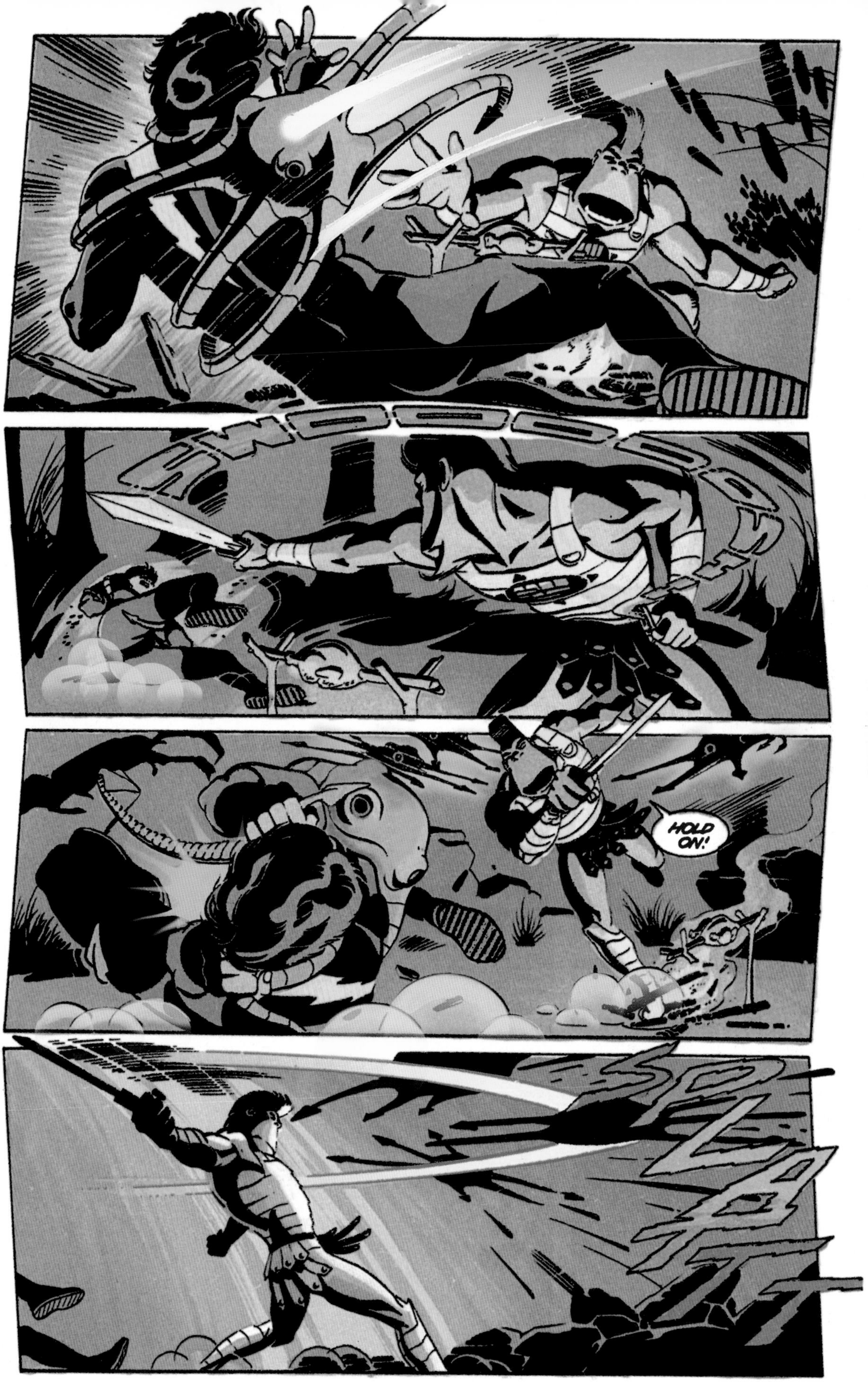
HOLD ON!

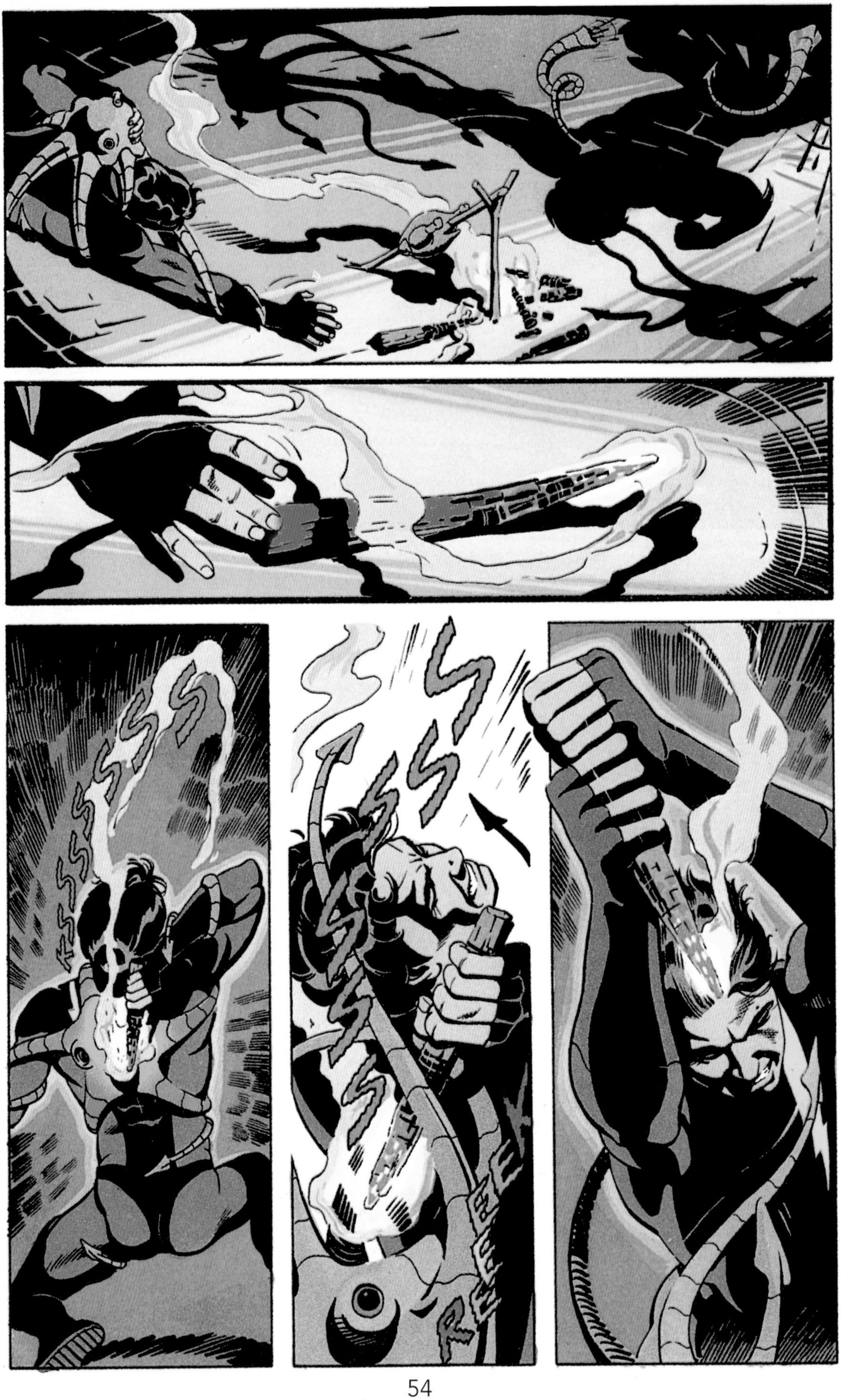
KSSSSSS
SSSSSSS
REEEK

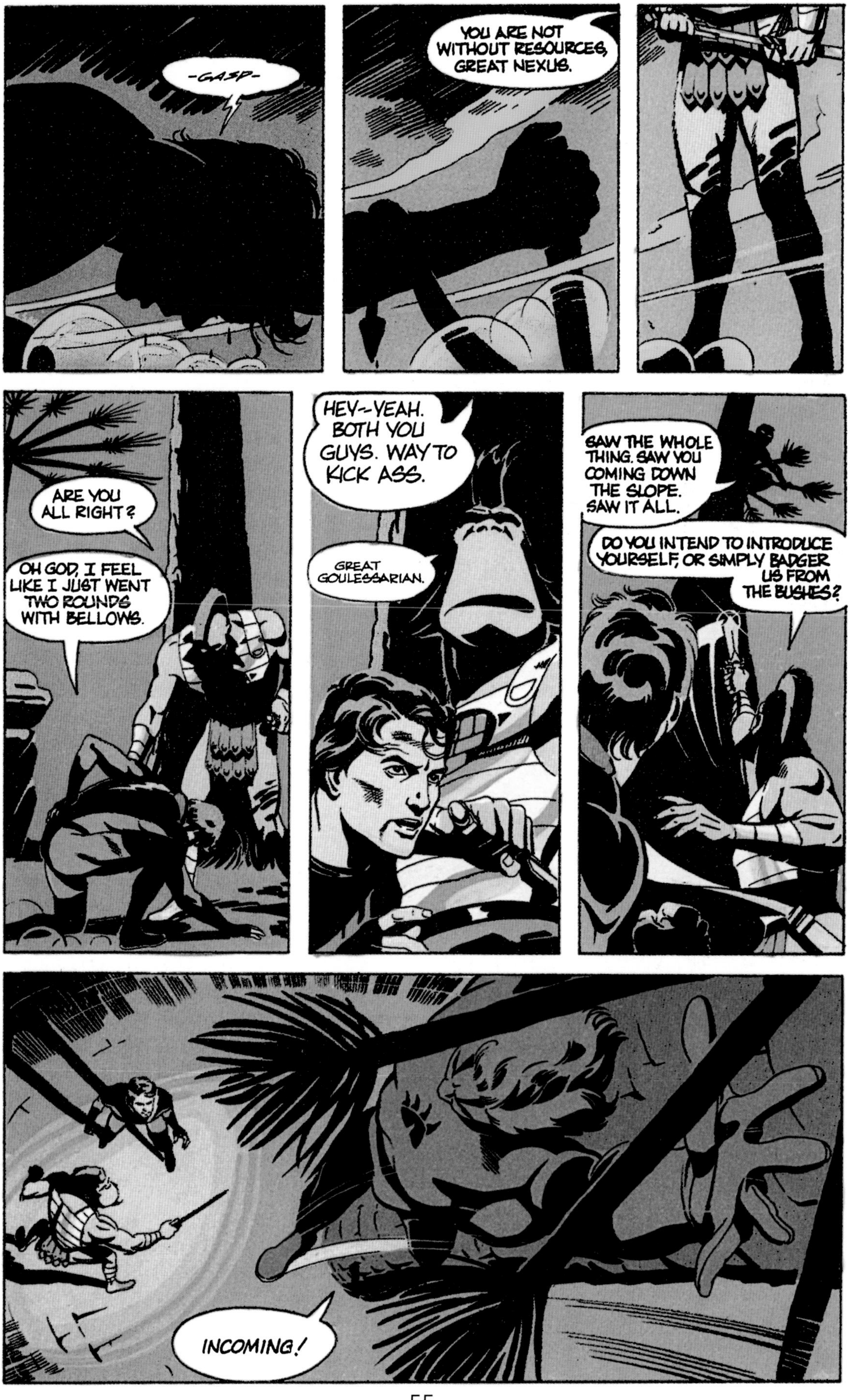
-GASP-
YOU ARE NOT WITHOUT RESOURCES, GREAT NEXUS.
ARE YOU ALL RIGHT?
OH GOD, I FEEL LIKE I JUST WENT TWO ROUNDS WITH BELLOWS.
HEY--YEAH. BOTH YOU GUYS. WAY TO KICK ASS.
GREAT GOULESSARIAN.
SAW THE WHOLE THING. SAW YOU COMING DOWN THE SLOPE. SAW IT ALL.
DO YOU INTEND TO INTRODUCE YOURSELF, OR SIMPLY BADGER US FROM THE BUSHES?
INCOMING!

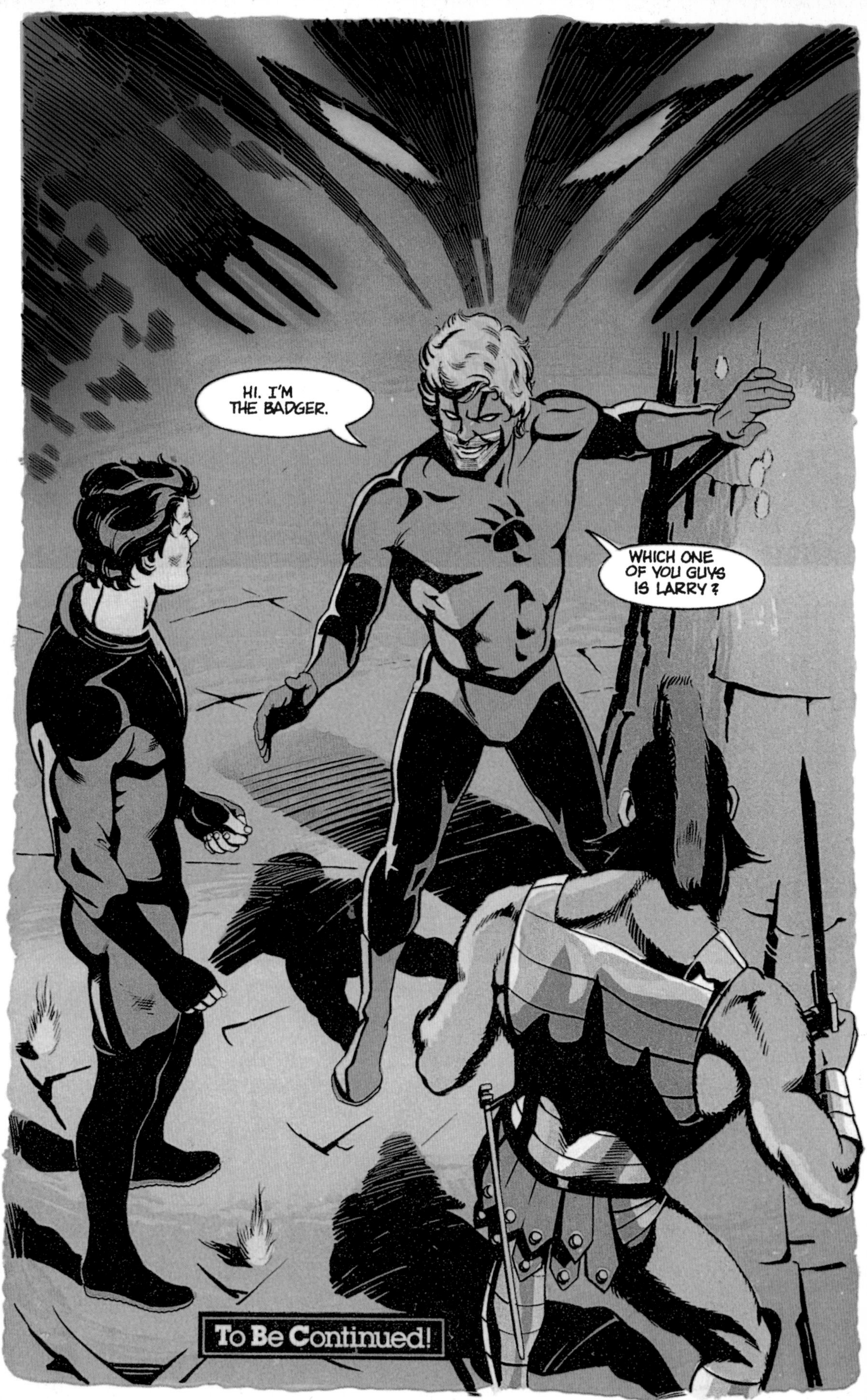
HI. I'M THE BADGER.
WHICH ONE OF YOU GUYS IS LARRY?
To Be Continued!

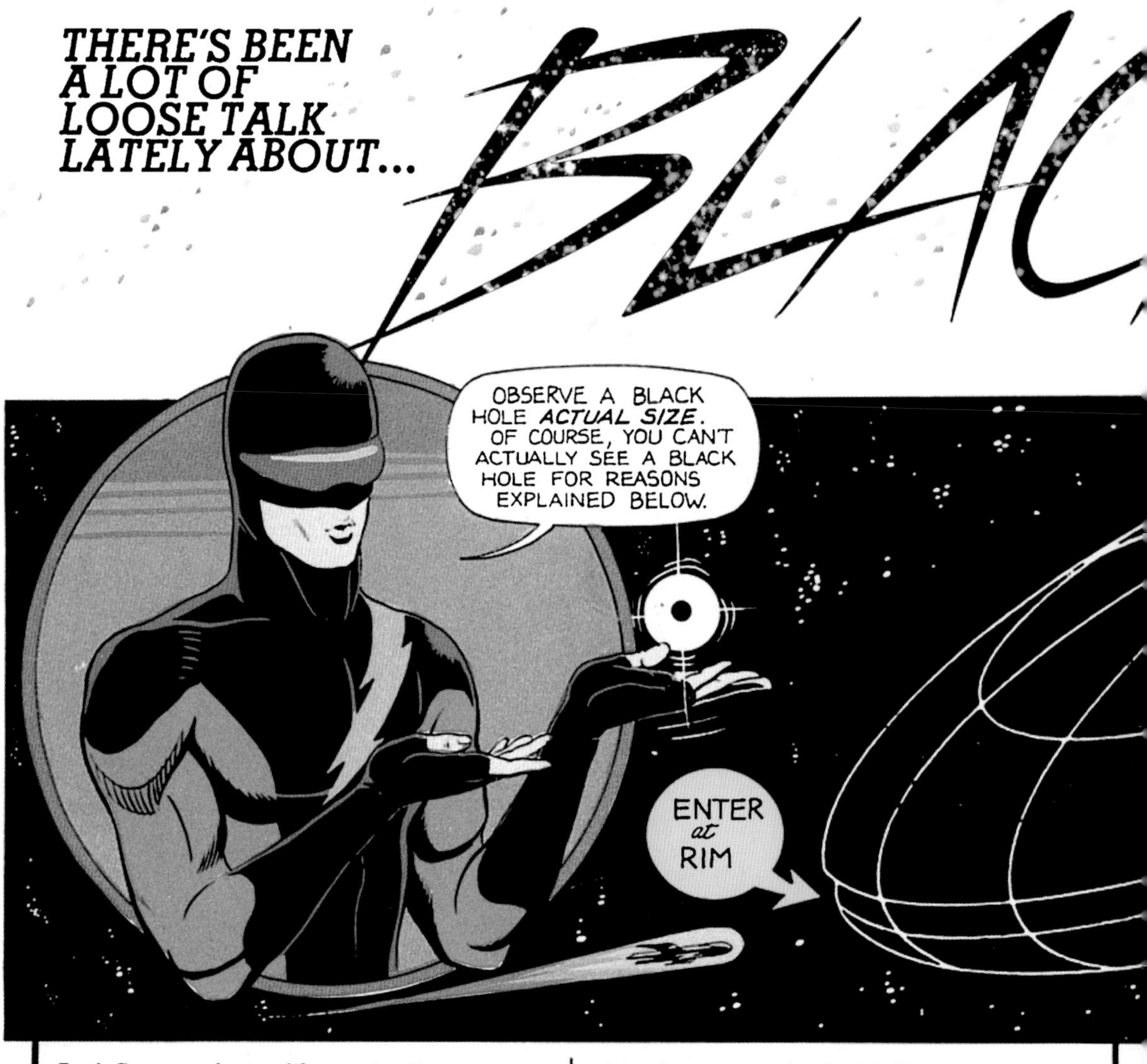
THERE'S BEEN A LOT OF LOOSE TALK LATELY ABOUT...
BLAC
OBSERVE A BLACK HOLE *ACTUAL SIZE*. OF COURSE, YOU CAN'T ACTUALLY SEE A BLACK HOLE FOR REASONS EXPLAINED BELOW.
ENTER at RIM

Earth Correspondents: *We occasionally get inquiries on how it is possible for our ships to travel from sun to sun when the distances between stars is so vast that light, travelling at the stupendous velocity of 670 million m.p.h., takes 4.33 years to travel from Sol (your sun, Earthlings) to its nearest neighbor. The answer is relatively simple. We use black holes. Of course you cannot see a real black hole, for it is a collapsed star of such immense mass not even light can escape its gravity. Hence, the name.*

As far back as 1935 the physicists Albert Einstein and Nathan Rosen proposed the existence of Einstein-Rosen Bridges, passages directly connecting one part of the Universe with another. We know today that black holes are the gateways to these passages. In our galaxy alone, there are millions of them.

All heavenly bodies, including stars, spin. When a star collapses (an event which occurs over a long period of time in discernible stages) it spins at a faster and faster rate. Imagine an ice skater spinning with her arms extended. What happens when she suddenly draws her arms into her body? She spins much faster. Assuming a black hole ten times the mass of Sol (our preferred size), the black hole throws out a frisbee-shaped gravitational field spinning at one thousand revolutions per second. Each part of this gravitational disc moves at a speed of 116,000 miles per second or just over 400 million m.p.h. (six/tenths the speed of light).

Our craft must match this speed exactly if we hope to make constructive use of the forces involved. Approaching the very rim of this magical gravitational field at the appropriate speed, we "see" a rectangular aperture along the edge, precisely 640 yards in height. This aperture is a gateway to another region of space. If our ship enters this region at the correct speed, we will pass inexorably, harmlessly through the black hole's event horizons (the point beyond which there can be no escape), avoid the crushing densities of the singularity, and pop out of a white hole, some light years distant. That's right: for every black hole sucking in matter, there must be a white hole from which the matter escapes-- the other end of the Einstein-Rosen Bridge.

I have found some ancient texts useful in the preparation of this explanation, notably:
The Iron Sun, Adrian Berry, Warner Books (1977) and
Cosmology Plus 1 (Readings from **Scientific American**), W.H. Freeman & Co. (1977)

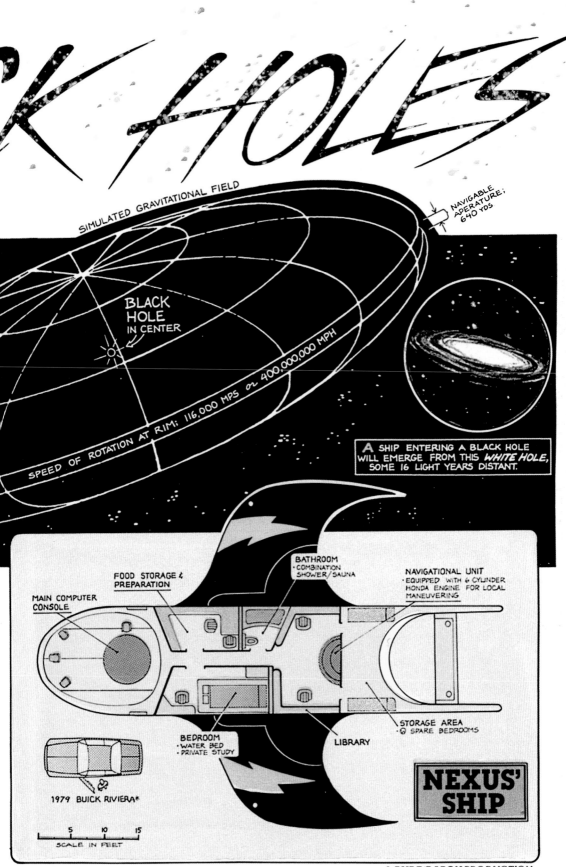

CK HOLES

SIMULATED GRAVITATIONAL FIELD

NAVIGABLE APERATURE; 640 YDS.

BLACK HOLE IN CENTER

SPEED OF ROTATION AT RIM; 116,000 MPS or 400,000,000 MPH

A SHIP ENTERING A BLACK HOLE WILL EMERGE FROM THIS *WHITE HOLE,* SOME 16 LIGHT YEARS DISTANT.

MAIN COMPUTER CONSOLE

FOOD STORAGE & PREPARATION

BATHROOM
· COMBINATION SHOWER/SAUNA

NAVIGATIONAL UNIT
· EQUIPPED WITH 6 CYLINDER HONDA ENGINE FOR LOCAL MANEUVERING

STORAGE AREA
· 2 SPARE BEDROOMS

BEDROOM
· WATER BED
· PRIVATE STUDY

LIBRARY

NEXUS' SHIP

1979 BUICK RIVIERA*

5 10 15
SCALE IN FEET

* 20TH CENTURY LAND VEHICLE
COURTESY BULLIS AUTOMOTIVE MUSEUM, NEW MINNEAPOLIS, PLUTO.

A *RUDE/BARON* PRODUCTION

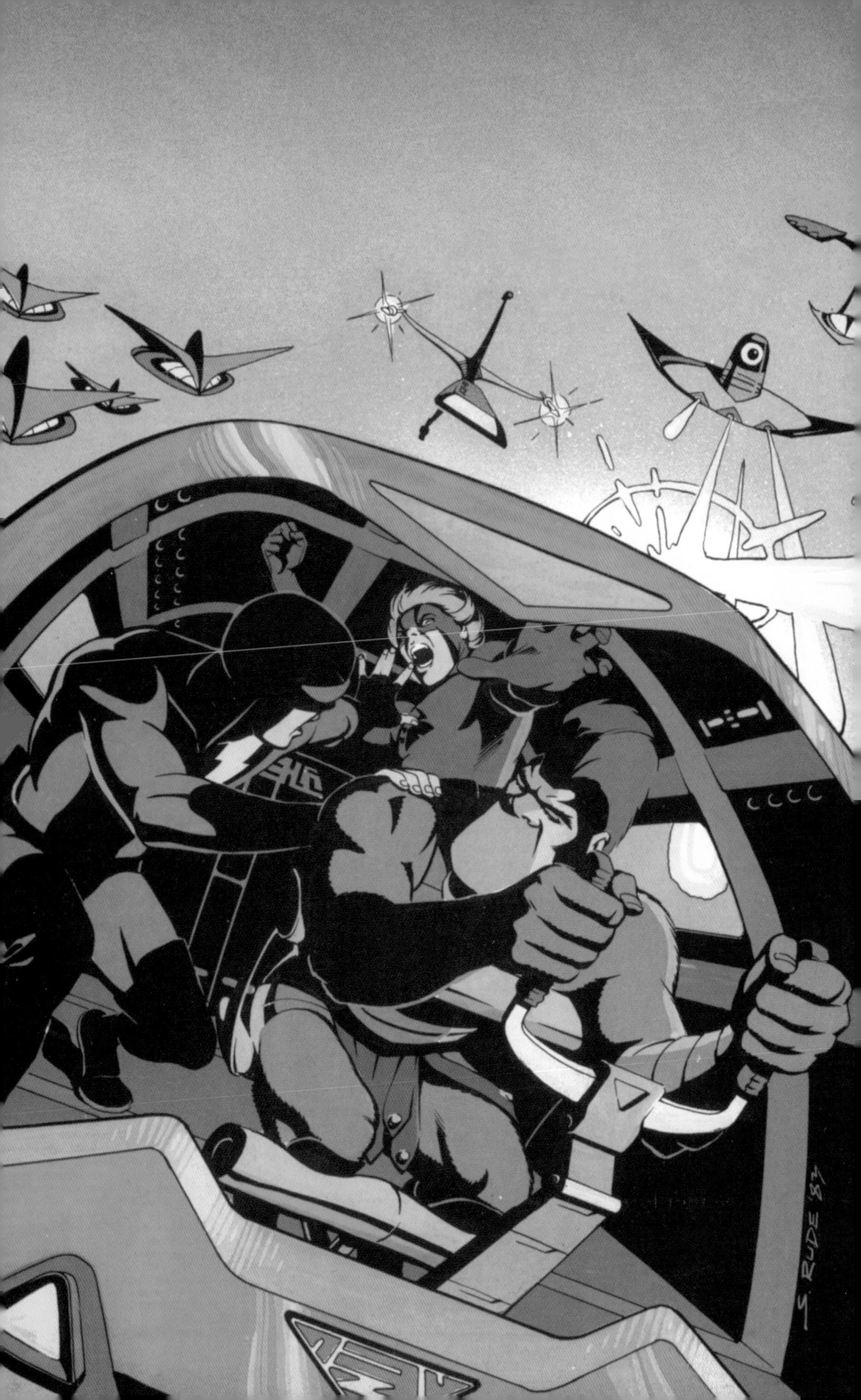
S. RUDE '83

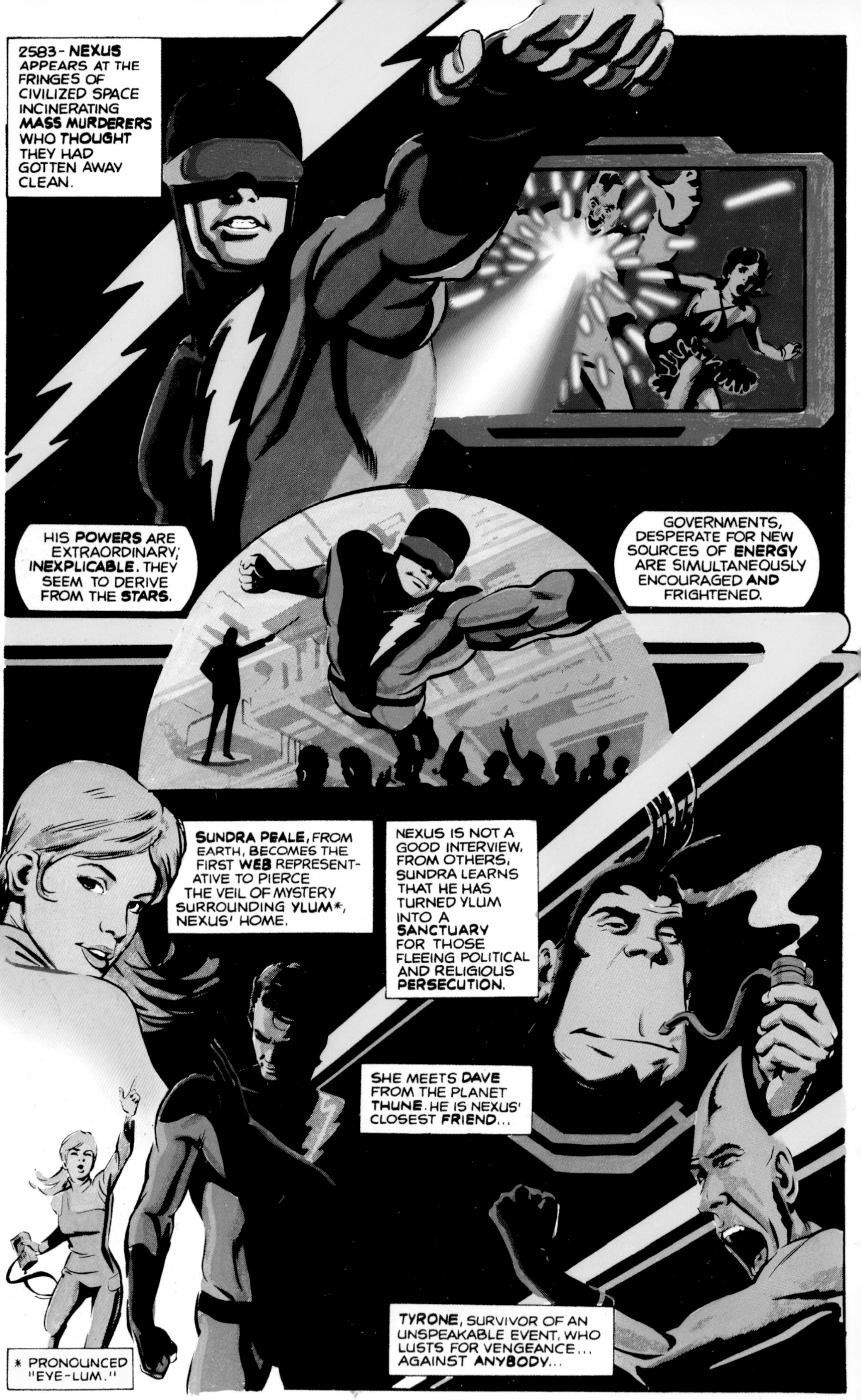
2583 - NEXUS APPEARS AT THE FRINGES OF CIVILIZED SPACE INCINERATING MASS MURDERERS WHO THOUGHT THEY HAD GOTTEN AWAY CLEAN.
HIS POWERS ARE EXTRAORDINARY; INEXPLICABLE. THEY SEEM TO DERIVE FROM THE STARS.
GOVERNMENTS, DESPERATE FOR NEW SOURCES OF ENERGY ARE SIMULTANEOUSLY ENCOURAGED AND FRIGHTENED.
SUNDRA PEALE, FROM EARTH, BECOMES THE FIRST WEB REPRESENT-ATIVE TO PIERCE THE VEIL OF MYSTERY SURROUNDING YLUM*, NEXUS' HOME.
NEXUS IS NOT A GOOD INTERVIEW. FROM OTHERS, SUNDRA LEARNS THAT HE HAS TURNED YLUM INTO A SANCTUARY FOR THOSE FLEEING POLITICAL AND RELIGIOUS PERSECUTION.
SHE MEETS DAVE FROM THE PLANET THUNE. HE IS NEXUS' CLOSEST FRIEND...
TYRONE, SURVIVOR OF AN UNSPEAKABLE EVENT, WHO LUSTS FOR VENGEANCE... AGAINST ANYBODY...
* PRONOUNCED "EYE-LUM."

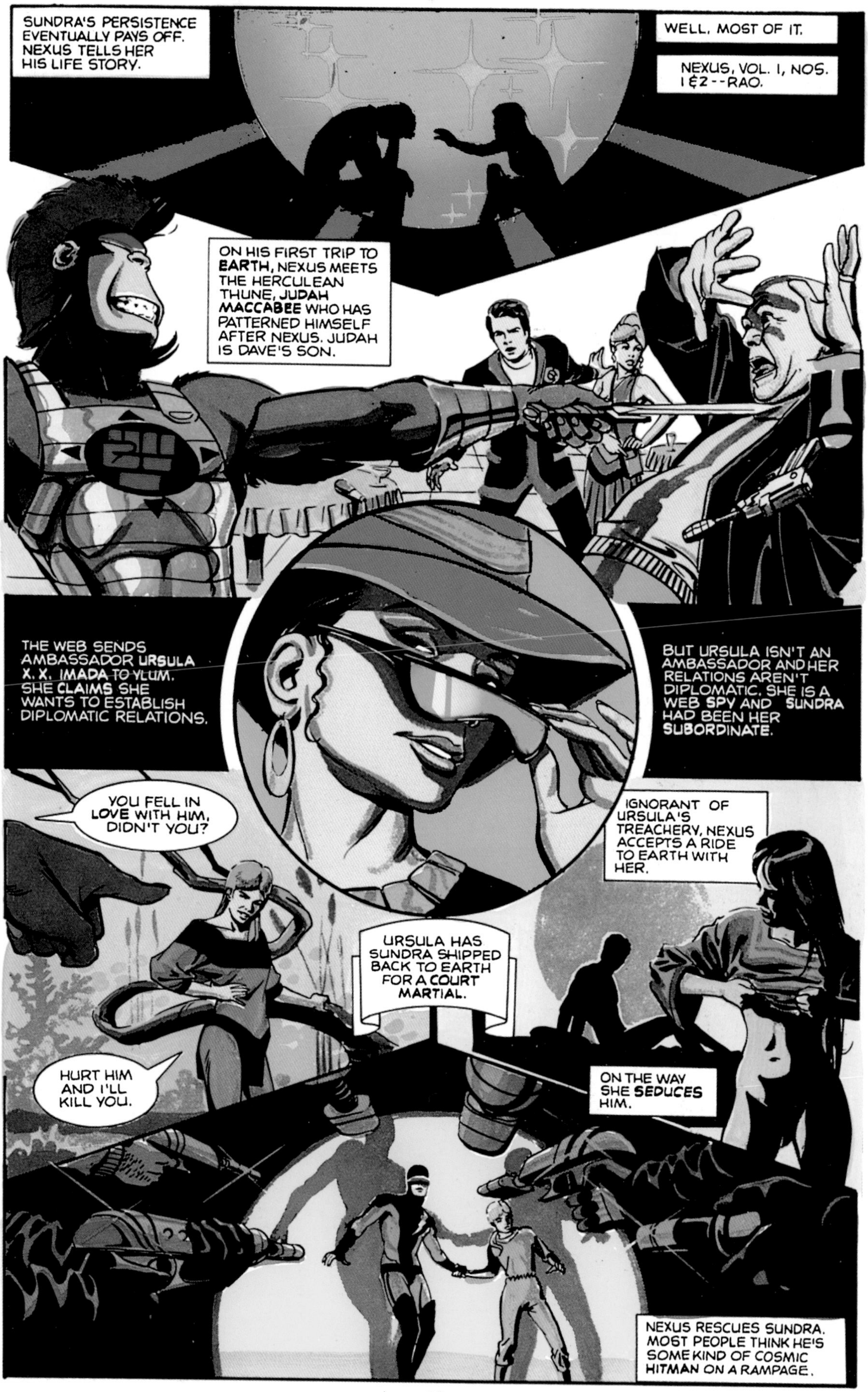
SUNDRA'S PERSISTENCE EVENTUALLY PAYS OFF. NEXUS TELLS HER HIS LIFE STORY.
WELL, MOST OF IT.
NEXUS, VOL. 1, NOS. 1 & 2 --RAO.
ON HIS FIRST TRIP TO EARTH, NEXUS MEETS THE HERCULEAN THUNE, JUDAH MACCABEE WHO HAS PATTERNED HIMSELF AFTER NEXUS. JUDAH IS DAVE'S SON.
THE WEB SENDS AMBASSADOR URSULA X. X. IMADA TO YLUM. SHE CLAIMS SHE WANTS TO ESTABLISH DIPLOMATIC RELATIONS.
BUT URSULA ISN'T AN AMBASSADOR AND HER RELATIONS AREN'T DIPLOMATIC. SHE IS A WEB SPY AND SUNDRA HAD BEEN HER SUBORDINATE.
YOU FELL IN LOVE WITH HIM, DIDN'T YOU?
IGNORANT OF URSULA'S TREACHERY, NEXUS ACCEPTS A RIDE TO EARTH WITH HER.
URSULA HAS SUNDRA SHIPPED BACK TO EARTH FOR A COURT MARTIAL.
HURT HIM AND I'LL KILL YOU.
ON THE WAY SHE SEDUCES HIM.
NEXUS RESCUES SUNDRA. MOST PEOPLE THINK HE'S SOME KIND OF COSMIC HITMAN ON A RAMPAGE.

NEXUS AND SUNDRA RETURN TO YLUM CERTAIN THAT THEY HAVE SEEN THE LAST OF URSULA. HA!

SHE IS BACK IN A MATTER OF WEEKS, WITH HORDES OF *REFUGEES* STREAMING IN DAILY, IT IS *IMPOSSIBLE* TO KEEP TRACK OF EVERYONE.

THE WEB NEEDS *ENERGY.* URSULA BELIEVES THAT THE *KEY* TO NEXUS' *POWER* LIES HIDDEN DEEP IN THE *RUINS* THAT RIDDLE THE YLUM'S INTERIOR.

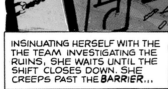

INSINUATING HERSELF WITH THE THE TEAM INVESTIGATING THE RUINS, SHE WAITS UNTIL THE SHIFT CLOSES DOWN. SHE CREEPS PAST THE *BARRIER...*

DEEPER INTO THE RUINS THAN ANYONE HAD EVER GONE... OR SO SHE *THINKS*

SHE ENCOUNTERS TWO ARTIFACT *THEIVES...*

WHERE IS *NEXUS* WHILE THIS IS OCCURRING?

A DRINKING MAN'S TOUR! ARE YOU LAME OR ARE YOU GAME?

THEY GO TO A PLACE CALLED...

OKAY!

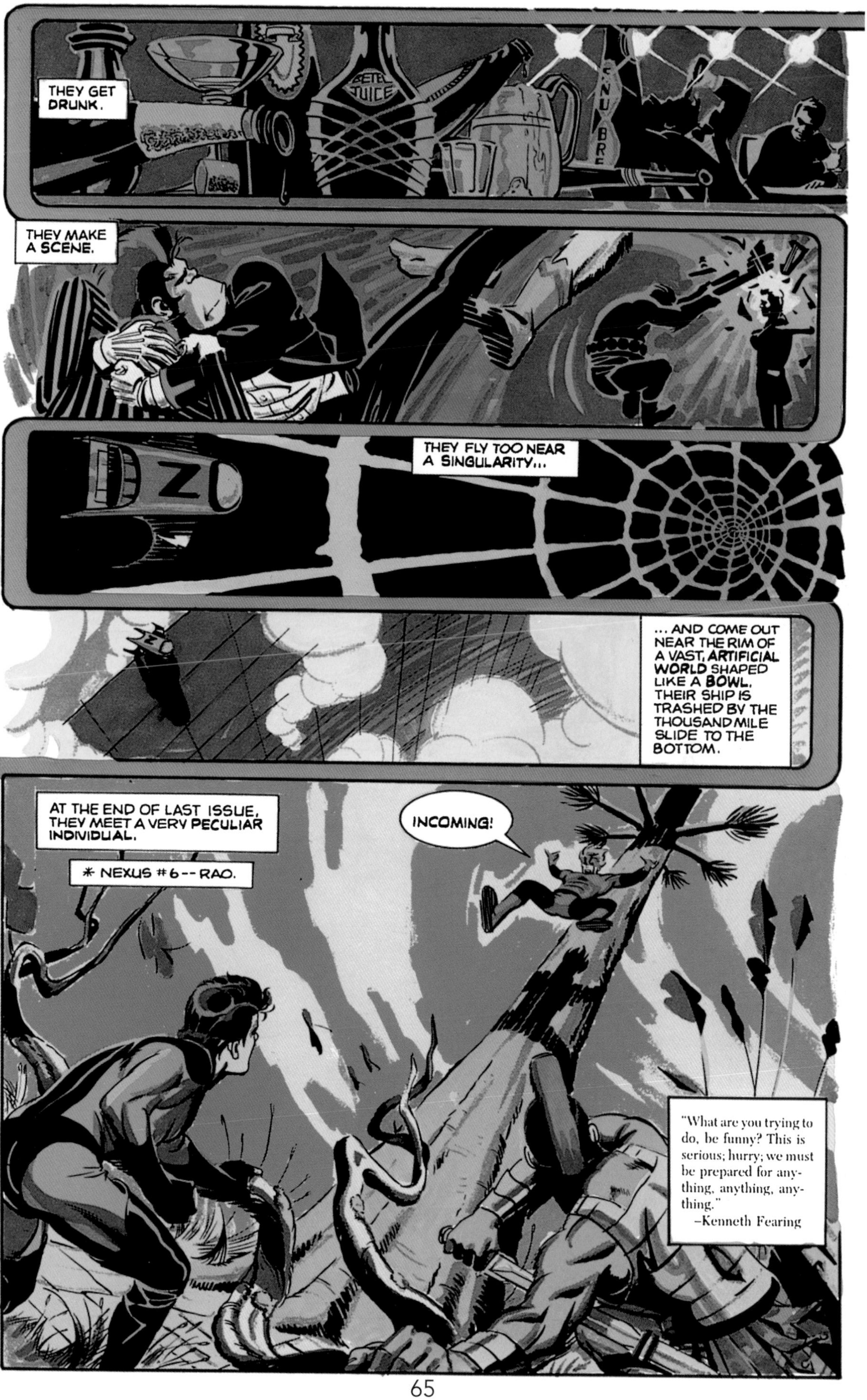
THEY GET DRUNK.
BETEL JUICE
THEY MAKE A SCENE.
THEY FLY TOO NEAR A SINGULARITY...
... AND COME OUT NEAR THE RIM OF A VAST, ARTIFICIAL WORLD SHAPED LIKE A BOWL. THEIR SHIP IS TRASHED BY THE THOUSAND MILE SLIDE TO THE BOTTOM.
AT THE END OF LAST ISSUE, THEY MEET A VERY PECULIAR INDIVIDUAL.
* NEXUS #6 -- RAO.
INCOMING!
"What are you trying to do, be funny? This is serious; hurry; we must be prepared for anything, anything, anything."
–Kenneth Fearing

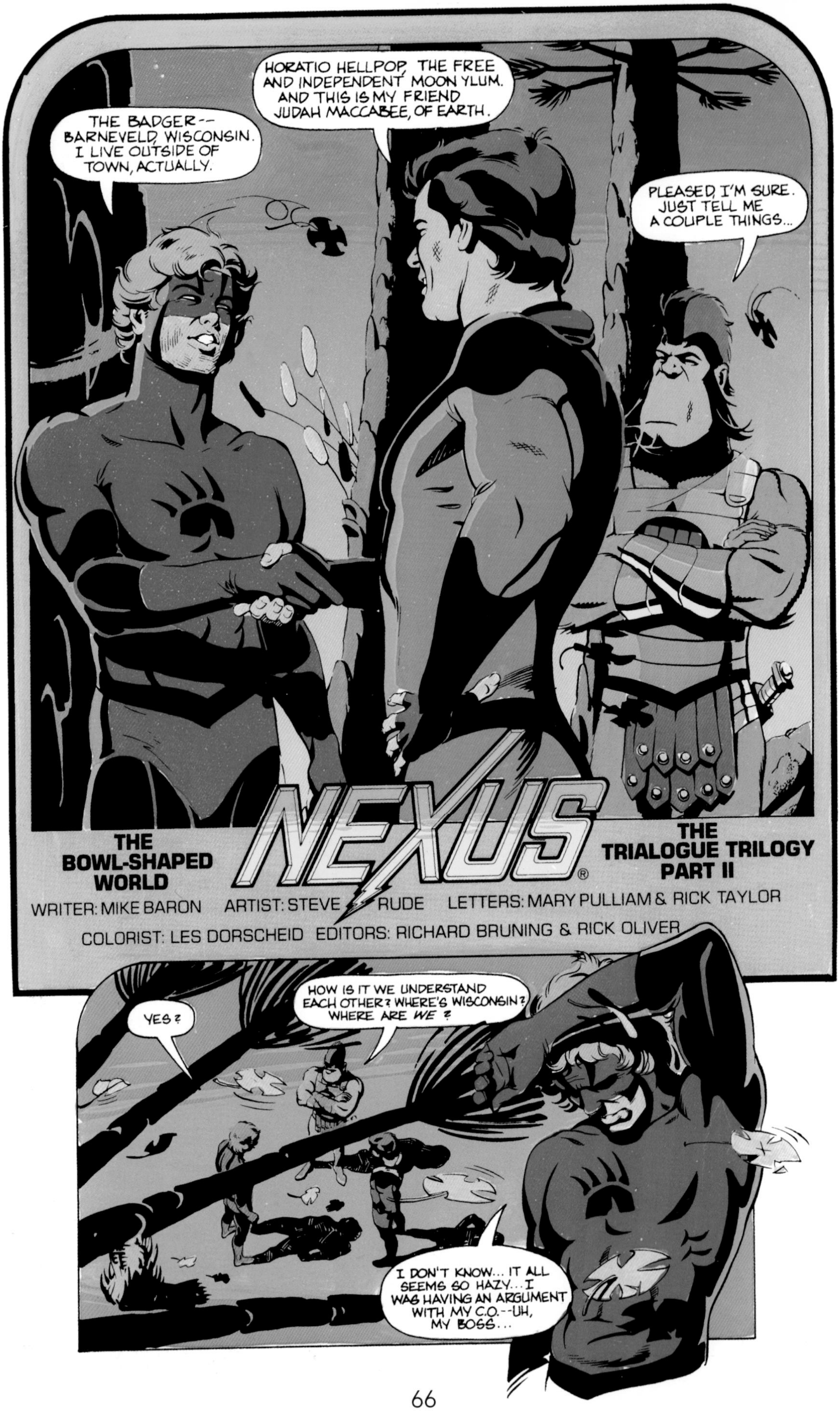
THE BADGER-- BARNEVELD, WISCONSIN. I LIVE OUTSIDE OF TOWN, ACTUALLY.
HORATIO HELLPOP, THE FREE AND INDEPENDENT MOON YLUM. AND THIS IS MY FRIEND JUDAH MACCABEE, OF EARTH.
PLEASED, I'M SURE. JUST TELL ME A COUPLE THINGS...
THE BOWL-SHAPED WORLD
NEXUS®
THE TRIALOGUE TRILOGY PART II
WRITER: MIKE BARON ARTIST: STEVE RUDE LETTERS: MARY PULLIAM & RICK TAYLOR
COLORIST: LES DORSCHEID EDITORS: RICHARD BRUNING & RICK OLIVER
YES?
HOW IS IT WE UNDERSTAND EACH OTHER? WHERE'S WISCONSIN? WHERE ARE *WE*?
I DON'T KNOW... IT ALL SEEMS SO HAZY... I WAS HAVING AN ARGUMENT WITH MY C.O.--UH, MY BOSS...

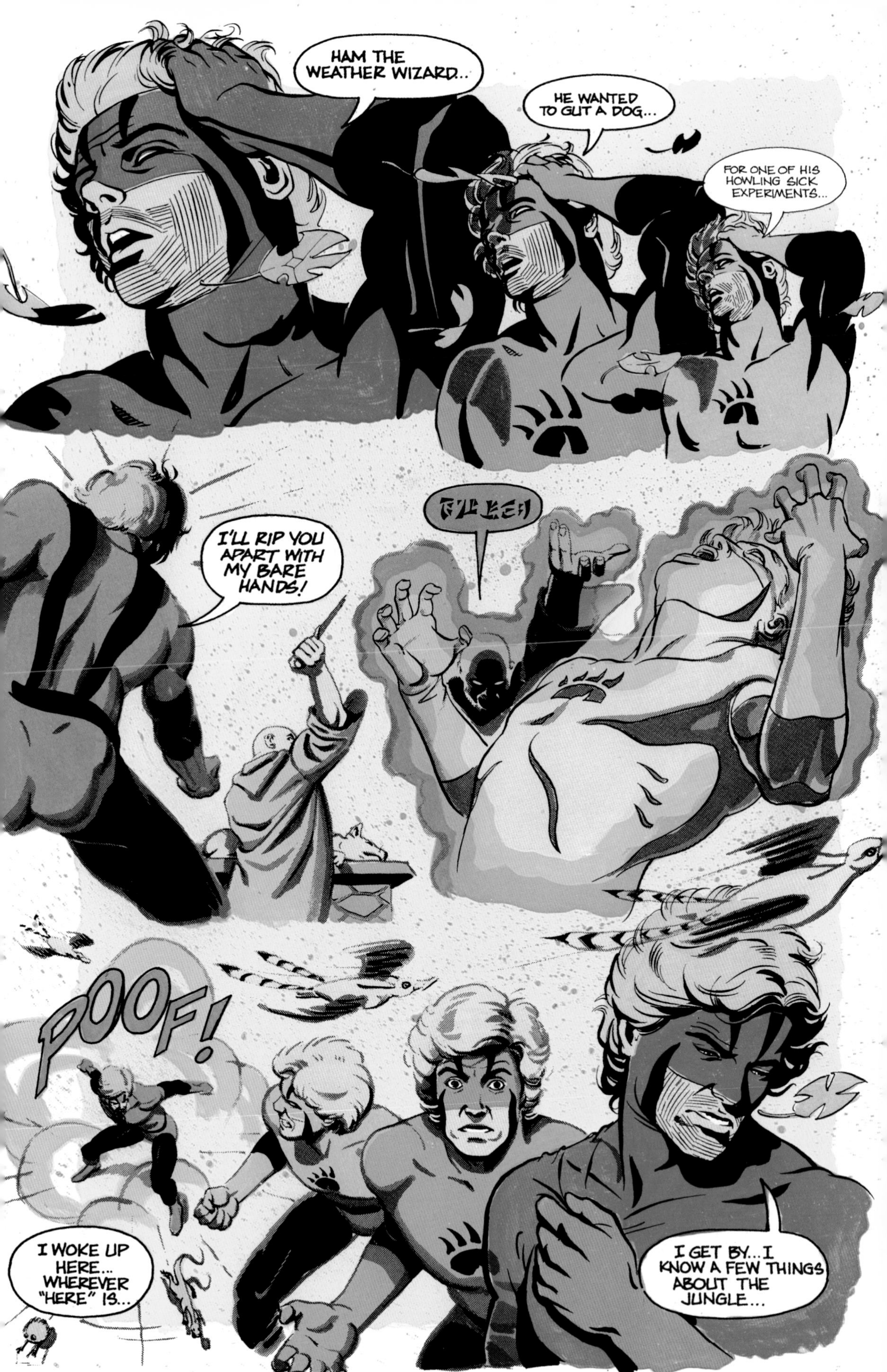
HAM THE WEATHER WIZARD...
HE WANTED TO GUT A DOG...
FOR ONE OF HIS HOWLING SICK EXPERIMENTS...
I'LL RIP YOU APART WITH MY BARE HANDS!
POOF!
I WOKE UP HERE... WHEREVER "HERE" IS...
I GET BY... I KNOW A FEW THINGS ABOUT THE JUNGLE...

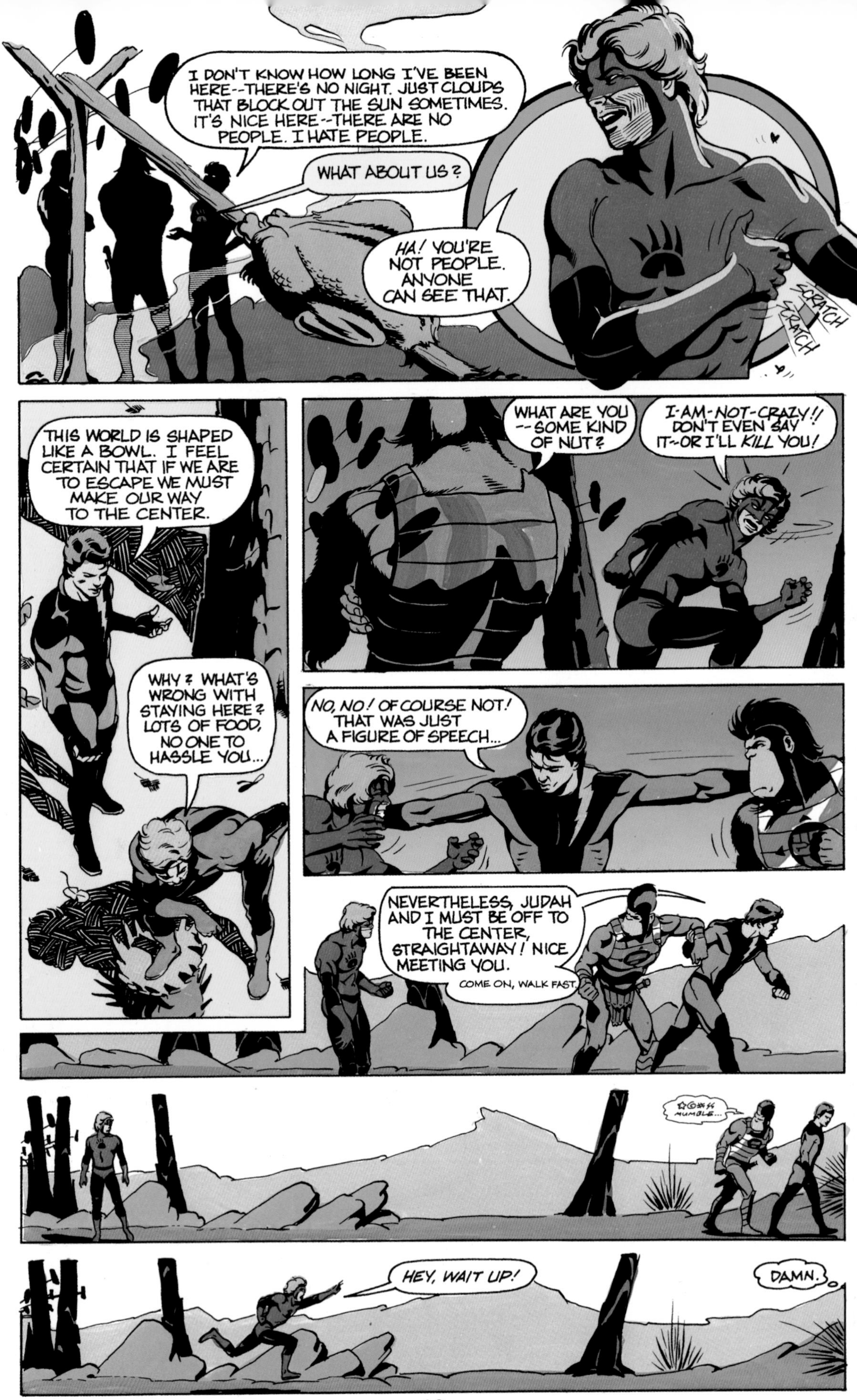

I DON'T KNOW HOW LONG I'VE BEEN HERE--THERE'S NO NIGHT. JUST CLOUDS THAT BLOCK OUT THE SUN SOMETIMES. IT'S NICE HERE--THERE ARE NO PEOPLE. I HATE PEOPLE.
WHAT ABOUT US?
HA! YOU'RE NOT PEOPLE. ANYONE CAN SEE THAT.
SCRATCH
SCRATCH
SCRATCH
THIS WORLD IS SHAPED LIKE A BOWL. I FEEL CERTAIN THAT IF WE ARE TO ESCAPE WE MUST MAKE OUR WAY TO THE CENTER.
WHY? WHAT'S WRONG WITH STAYING HERE? LOTS OF FOOD, NO ONE TO HASSLE YOU...
WHAT ARE YOU --SOME KIND OF NUT?
I-AM-NOT-CRAZY!! DON'T EVEN SAY IT--OR I'LL KILL YOU!
NO, NO! OF COURSE NOT! THAT WAS JUST A FIGURE OF SPEECH...
NEVERTHELESS, JUDAH AND I MUST BE OFF TO THE CENTER, STRAIGHTAWAY! NICE MEETING YOU.
COME ON, WALK FAST.
MUMBLE...
HEY, WAIT UP!
DAMN.

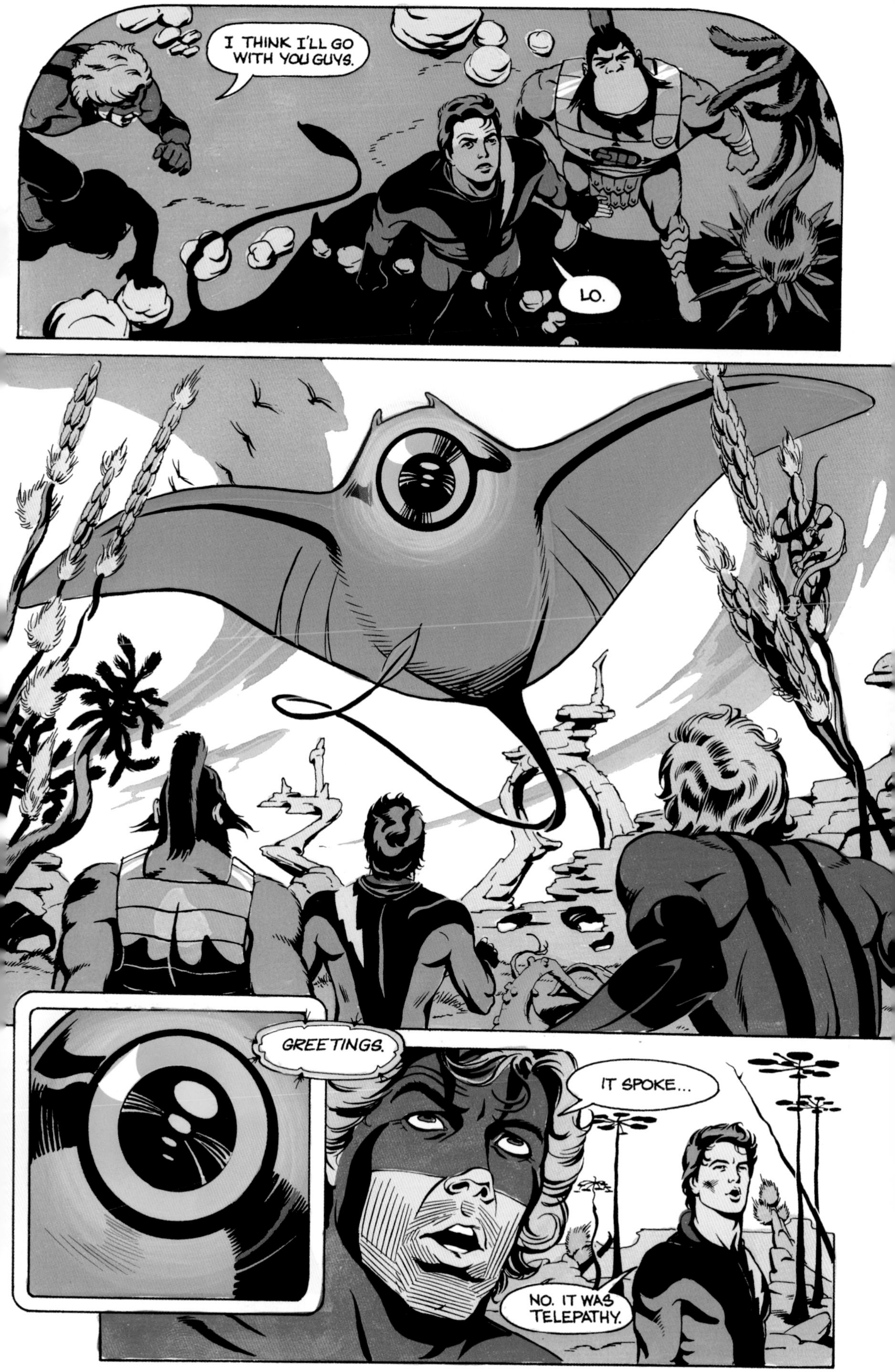
I THINK I'LL GO WITH YOU GUYS.
LO.
GREETINGS.
IT SPOKE...
NO. IT WAS TELEPATHY.

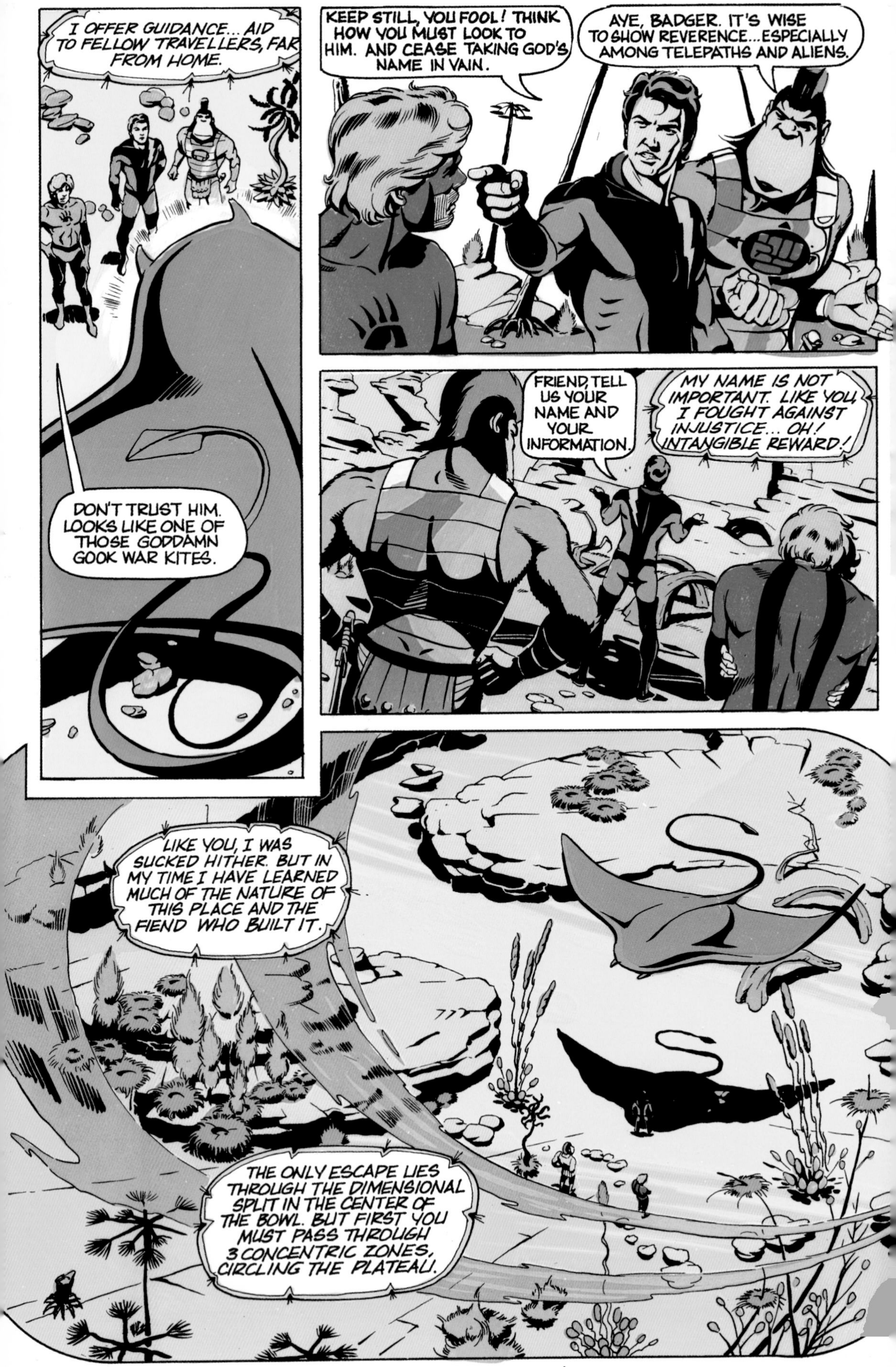
I OFFER GUIDANCE... AID TO FELLOW TRAVELLERS, FAR FROM HOME.
KEEP STILL, YOU FOOL! THINK HOW YOU MUST LOOK TO HIM. AND CEASE TAKING GOD'S NAME IN VAIN.
AYE, BADGER. IT'S WISE TO SHOW REVERENCE...ESPECIALLY AMONG TELEPATHS AND ALIENS.
DON'T TRUST HIM. LOOKS LIKE ONE OF THOSE GODDAMN GOOK WAR KITES.
FRIEND, TELL US YOUR NAME AND YOUR INFORMATION.
MY NAME IS NOT IMPORTANT. LIKE YOU, I FOUGHT AGAINST INJUSTICE... OH! INTANGIBLE REWARD!
LIKE YOU, I WAS SUCKED HITHER. BUT IN MY TIME I HAVE LEARNED MUCH OF THE NATURE OF THIS PLACE AND THE FIEND WHO BUILT IT.
THE ONLY ESCAPE LIES THROUGH THE DIMENSIONAL SPLIT IN THE CENTER OF THE BOWL. BUT FIRST YOU MUST PASS THROUGH 3 CONCENTRIC ZONES, CIRCLING THE PLATEAU.

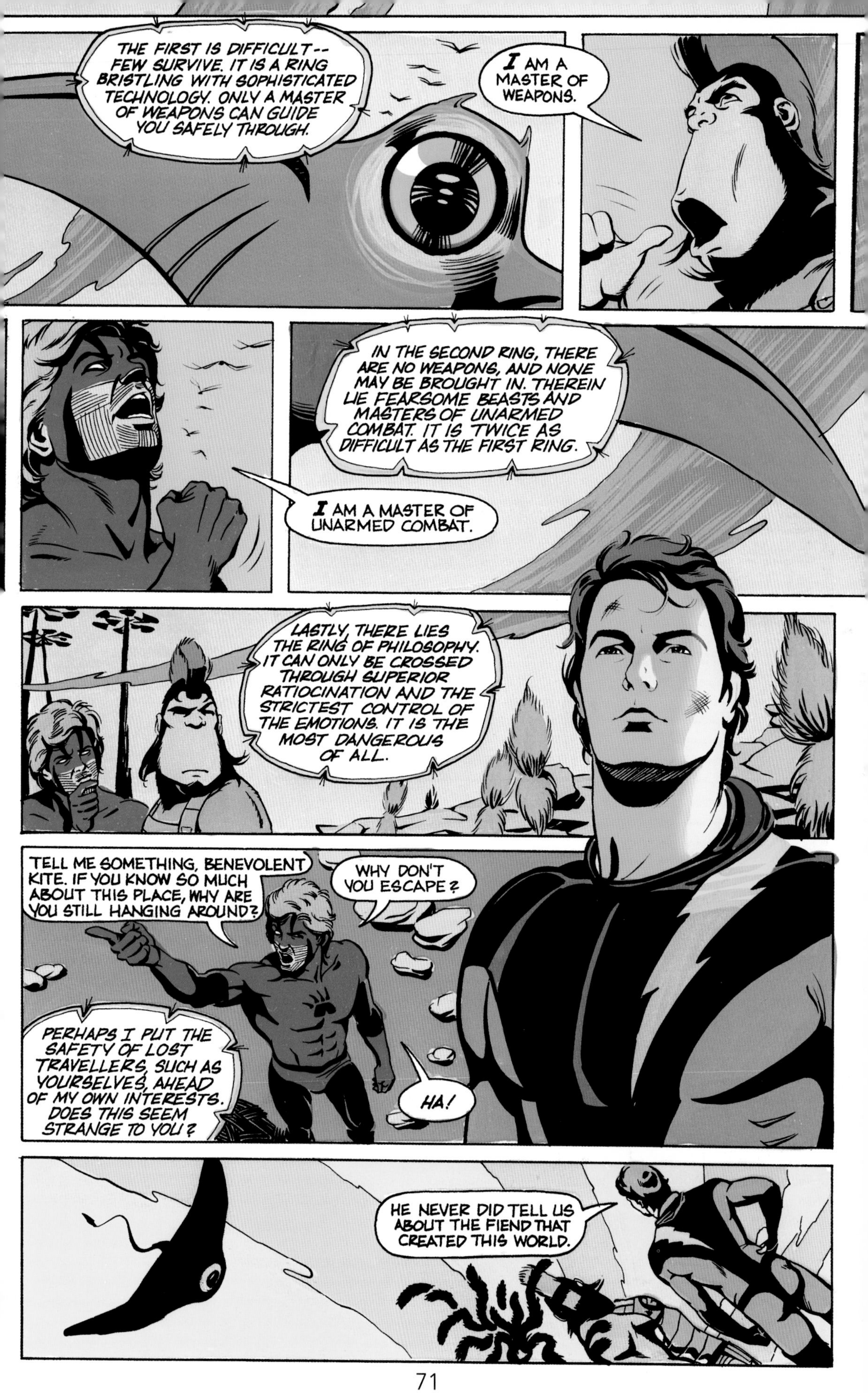
THE FIRST IS DIFFICULT-- FEW SURVIVE. IT IS A RING BRISTLING WITH SOPHISTICATED TECHNOLOGY. ONLY A MASTER OF WEAPONS CAN GUIDE YOU SAFELY THROUGH.
I AM A MASTER OF WEAPONS.
IN THE SECOND RING, THERE ARE NO WEAPONS, AND NONE MAY BE BROUGHT IN. THEREIN LIE FEARSOME BEASTS AND MASTERS OF UNARMED COMBAT. IT IS TWICE AS DIFFICULT AS THE FIRST RING.
I AM A MASTER OF UNARMED COMBAT.
LASTLY, THERE LIES THE RING OF PHILOSOPHY. IT CAN ONLY BE CROSSED THROUGH SUPERIOR RATIOCINATION AND THE STRICTEST CONTROL OF THE EMOTIONS. IT IS THE MOST DANGEROUS OF ALL.
TELL ME SOMETHING, BENEVOLENT KITE. IF YOU KNOW SO MUCH ABOUT THIS PLACE, WHY ARE YOU STILL HANGING AROUND?
WHY DON'T YOU ESCAPE?
PERHAPS I PUT THE SAFETY OF LOST TRAVELLERS, SUCH AS YOURSELVES, AHEAD OF MY OWN INTERESTS. DOES THIS SEEM STRANGE TO YOU?
HA!
HE NEVER DID TELL US ABOUT THE FIEND THAT CREATED THIS WORLD.

FAR BENEATH YLUM'S LIFELESS SURFACE, "LHASA" GASPS IN AMAZEMENT...
SKREEEK
SCREEEEEEEE
UP ABOVE.
DOWN BELOW.
I KNOW WHAT IT SAYS!
"CURSE BEYOND DEATH (IT) WHO GOES BEYOND THIS SACRED SEAL--SPACE CLAIMED BY THE SUN GOD, NEXUS."
UP ABOVE.
DOWN BELOW.
HOW INSIGNIFICANT OUR PETTY SQUABBLES SEEM AGAINST SUCH REVELATIONS...
HEY, GANG-- EVERYBODY REMEMBER SUTTA LE BERQ'S GOON, YALTA, FROM BLACK AND WHITE NEXUS #27. HE'S BEEN IN A COMA FOR TWO YEARS! --M.B.

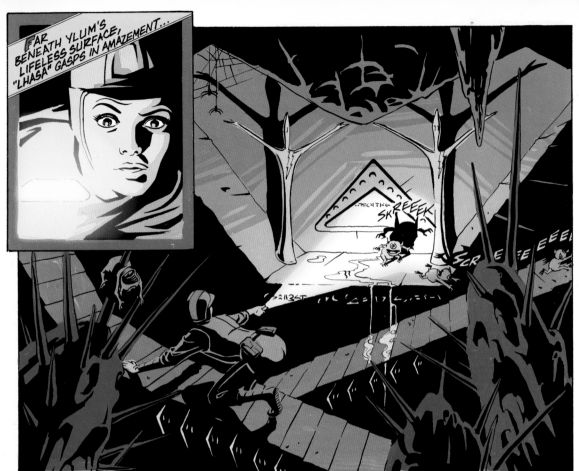

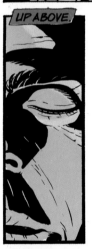

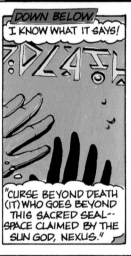

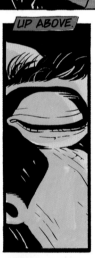

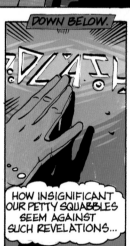

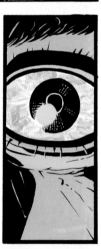

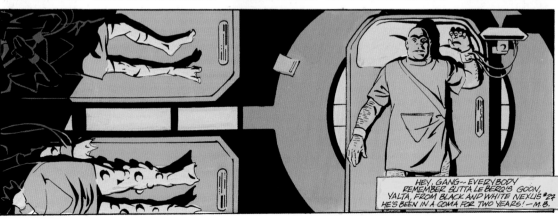

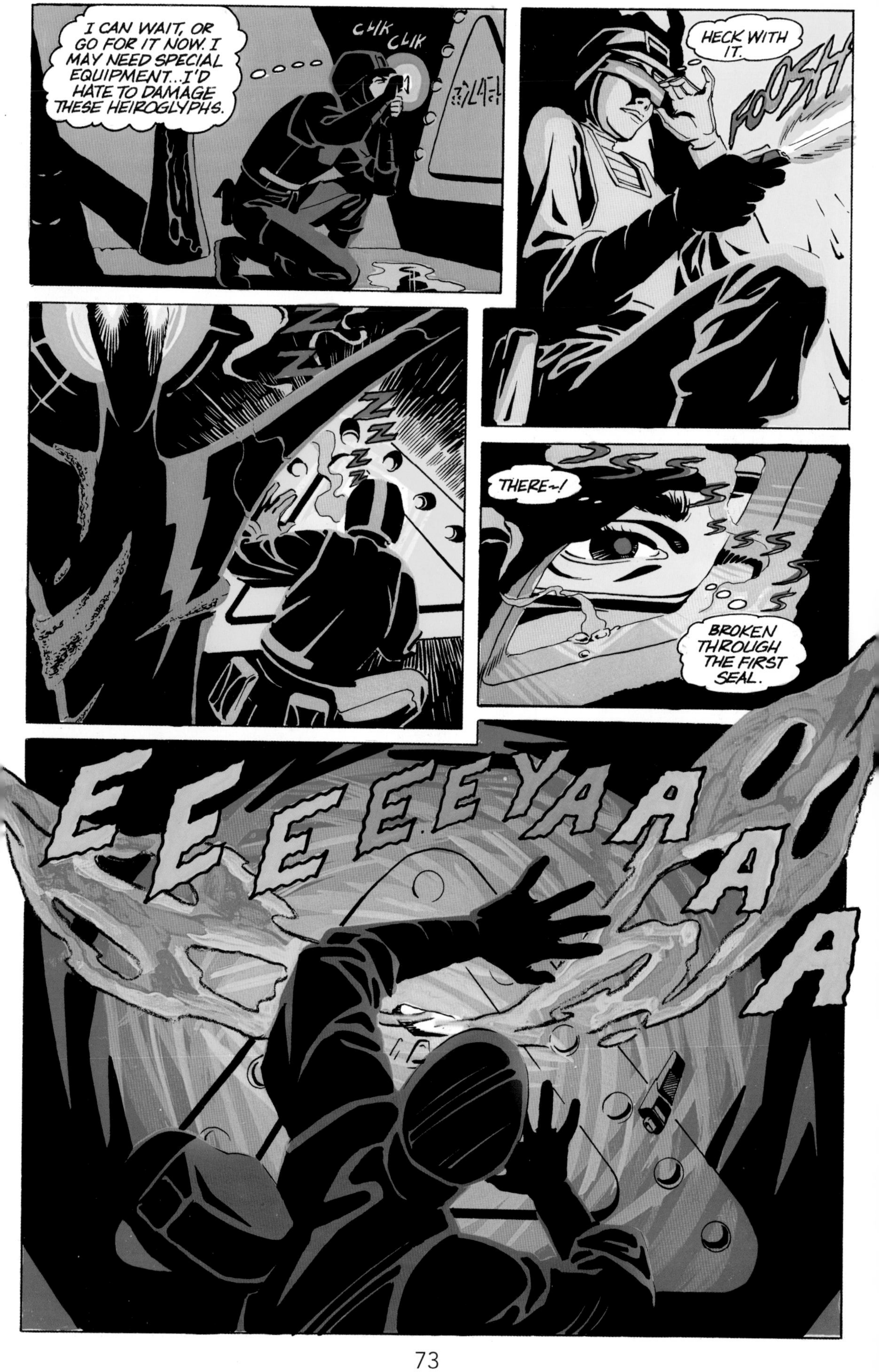
I CAN WAIT, OR GO FOR IT NOW. I MAY NEED SPECIAL EQUIPMENT...I'D HATE TO DAMAGE THESE HEIROGLYPHS.
CLIK CLIK
HECK WITH IT.
FOOSH
THERE--!
BROKEN THROUGH THE FIRST SEAL.
EEEEEYAAAAA

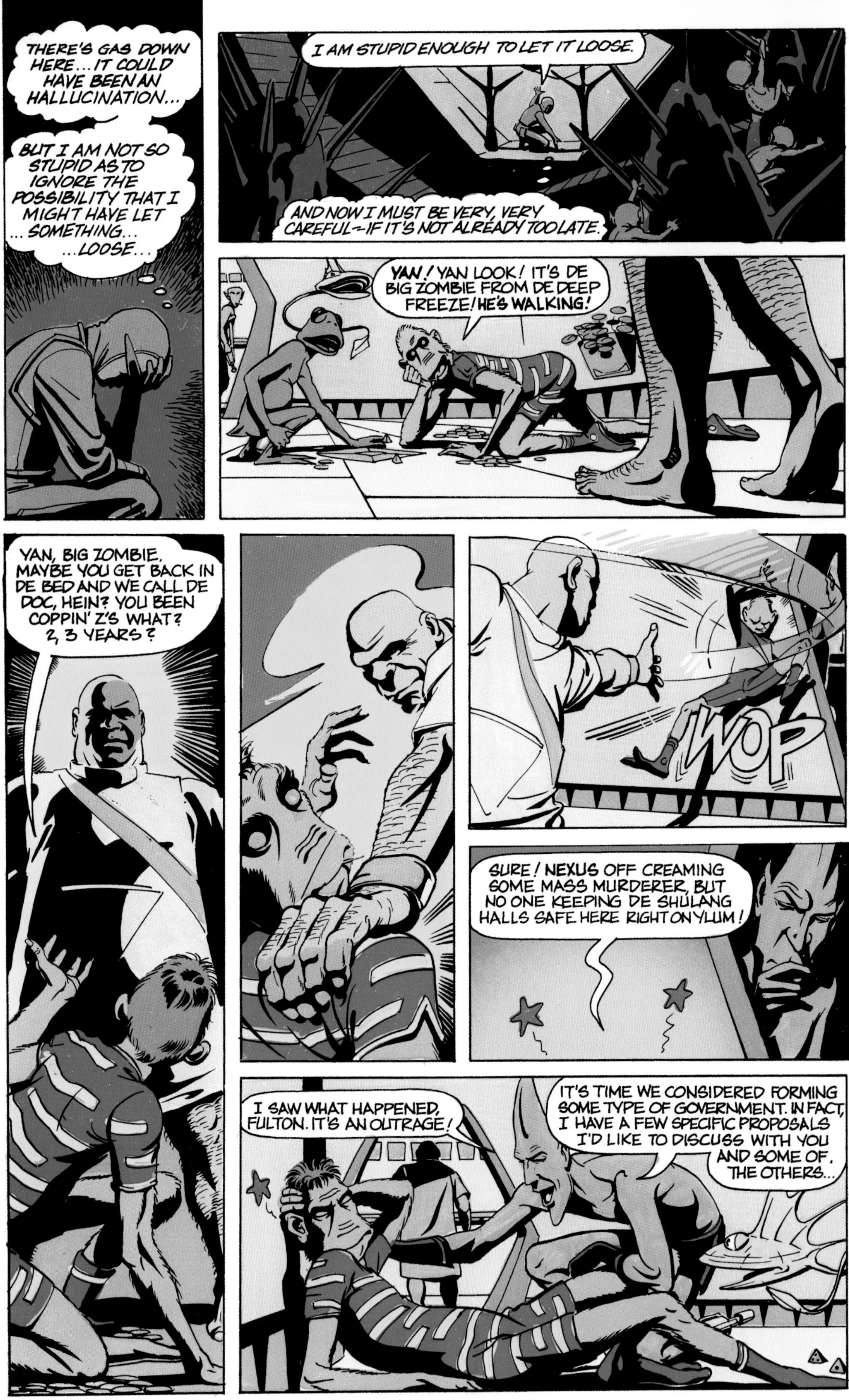
THERE'S GAS DOWN HERE... IT COULD HAVE BEEN AN HALLUCINATION...
BUT I AM NOT SO STUPID AS TO IGNORE THE POSSIBILITY THAT I MIGHT HAVE LET ...SOMETHING... ...LOOSE...
I AM STUPID ENOUGH TO LET IT LOOSE.
AND NOW I MUST BE VERY, VERY CAREFUL--IF IT'S NOT ALREADY TOO LATE.
YAN! YAN LOOK! IT'S DE BIG ZOMBIE FROM DE DEEP FREEZE! HE'S WALKING!
YAN, BIG ZOMBIE, MAYBE YOU GET BACK IN DE BED AND WE CALL DE DOC, HEIN? YOU BEEN COPPIN' Z'S WHAT? 2, 3 YEARS?
WOP
SURE! NEXUS OFF CREAMING SOME MASS MURDERER, BUT NO ONE KEEPING DE SHULANG HALLS SAFE HERE RIGHT ON YLUM!
I SAW WHAT HAPPENED, FULTON. IT'S AN OUTRAGE!
IT'S TIME WE CONSIDERED FORMING SOME TYPE OF GOVERNMENT. IN FACT, I HAVE A FEW SPECIFIC PROPOSALS I'D LIKE TO DISCUSS WITH YOU AND SOME OF THE OTHERS...

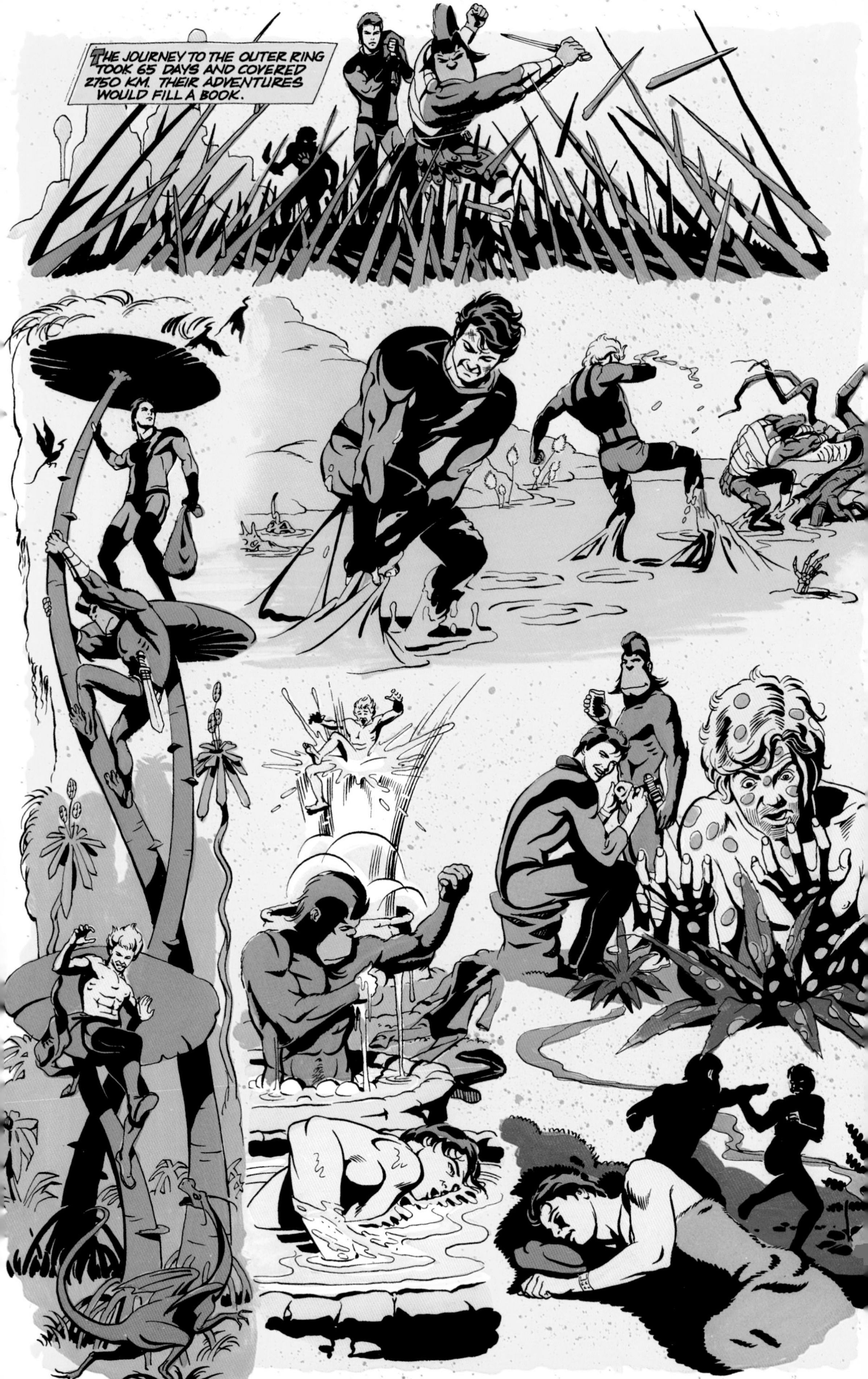
THE JOURNEY TO THE OUTER RING TOOK 65 DAYS AND COVERED 2750 KM. THEIR ADVENTURES WOULD FILL A BOOK.

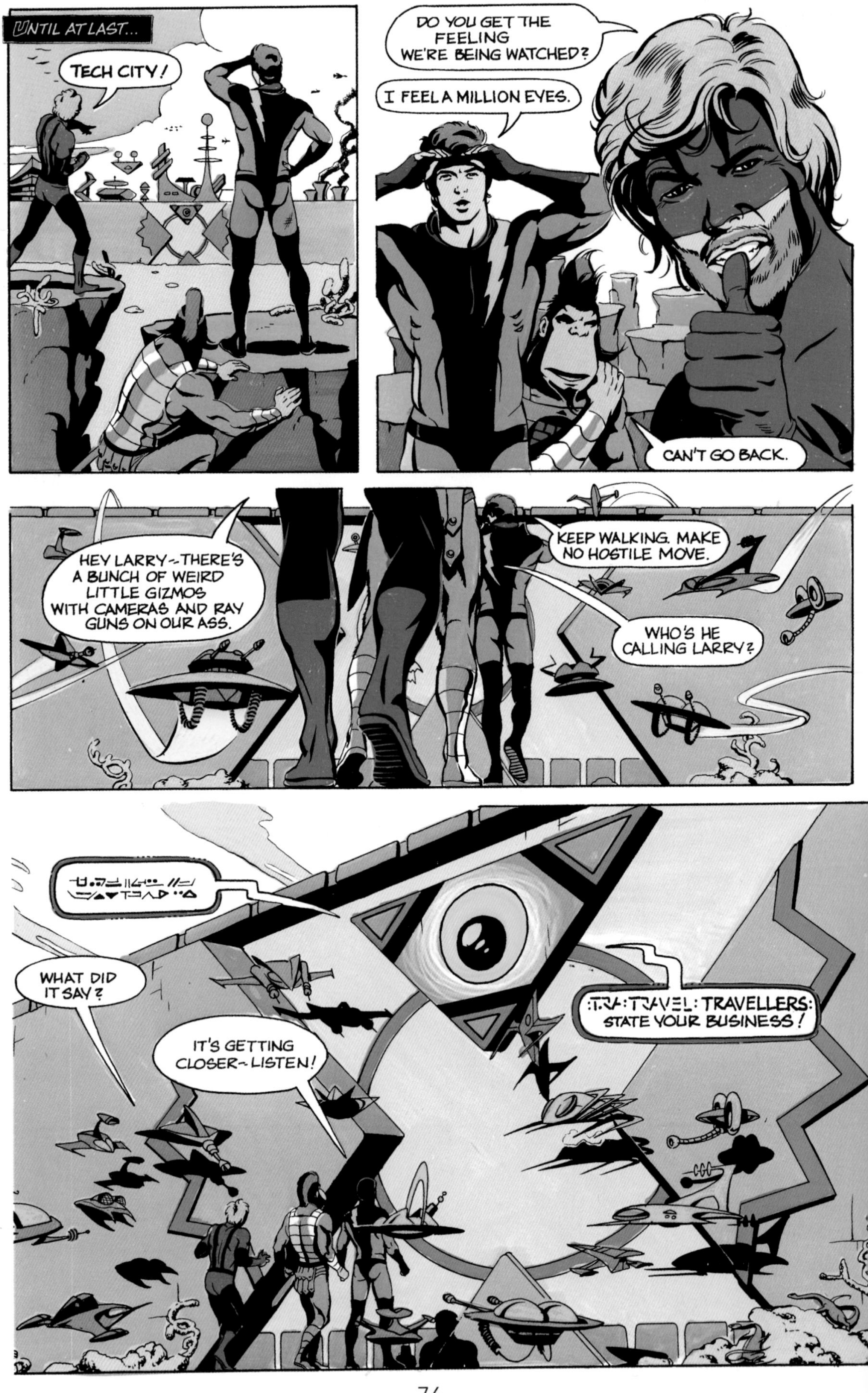
UNTIL AT LAST...
TECH CITY!
DO YOU GET THE FEELING WE'RE BEING WATCHED?
I FEEL A MILLION EYES.
CAN'T GO BACK.
HEY LARRY-- THERE'S A BUNCH OF WEIRD LITTLE GIZMOS WITH CAMERAS AND RAY GUNS ON OUR ASS.
KEEP WALKING. MAKE NO HOSTILE MOVE.
WHO'S HE CALLING LARRY?
WHAT DID IT SAY?
IT'S GETTING CLOSER-- LISTEN!
:TRA:TRAVEL: TRAVELLERS: STATE YOUR BUSINESS!

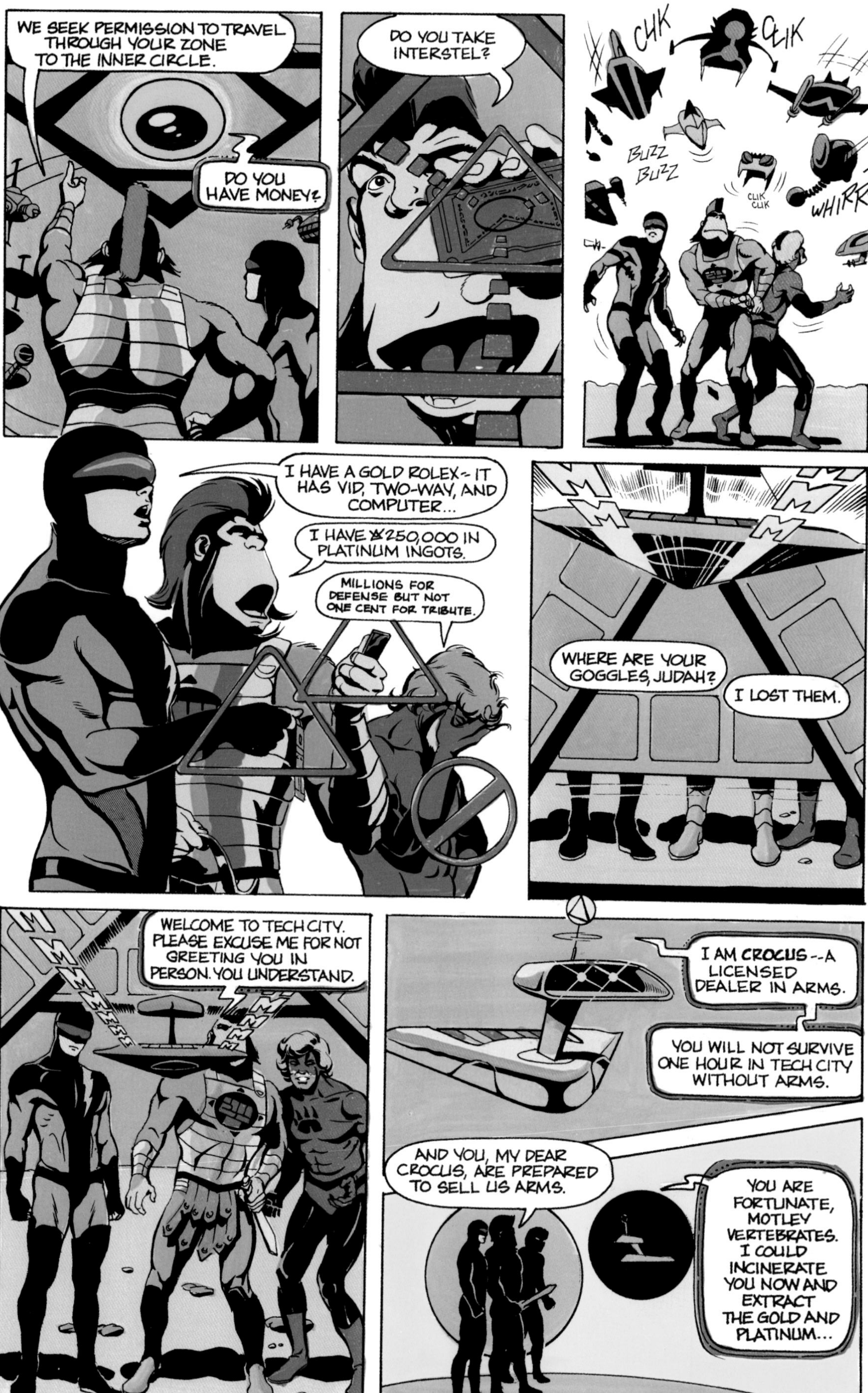
WE SEEK PERMISSION TO TRAVEL THROUGH YOUR ZONE TO THE INNER CIRCLE.
DO YOU HAVE MONEY?
DO YOU TAKE INTERSTEL?
CLIK
CLIK
BUZZ BUZZ
CLIK CLIK
WHIRRR
I HAVE A GOLD ROLEX-- IT HAS VID, TWO-WAY, AND COMPUTER...
I HAVE ¥250,000 IN PLATINUM INGOTS.
MILLIONS FOR DEFENSE BUT NOT ONE CENT FOR TRIBUTE.
WHERE ARE YOUR GOGGLES, JUDAH?
I LOST THEM.
WELCOME TO TECH CITY. PLEASE EXCUSE ME FOR NOT GREETING YOU IN PERSON. YOU UNDERSTAND.
I AM **CROCUS**--A LICENSED DEALER IN ARMS.
YOU WILL NOT SURVIVE ONE HOUR IN TECH CITY WITHOUT ARMS.
AND YOU, MY DEAR CROCUS, ARE PREPARED TO SELL US ARMS.
YOU ARE FORTUNATE, MOTLEY VERTEBRATES. I COULD INCINERATE YOU NOW AND EXTRACT THE GOLD AND PLATINUM...

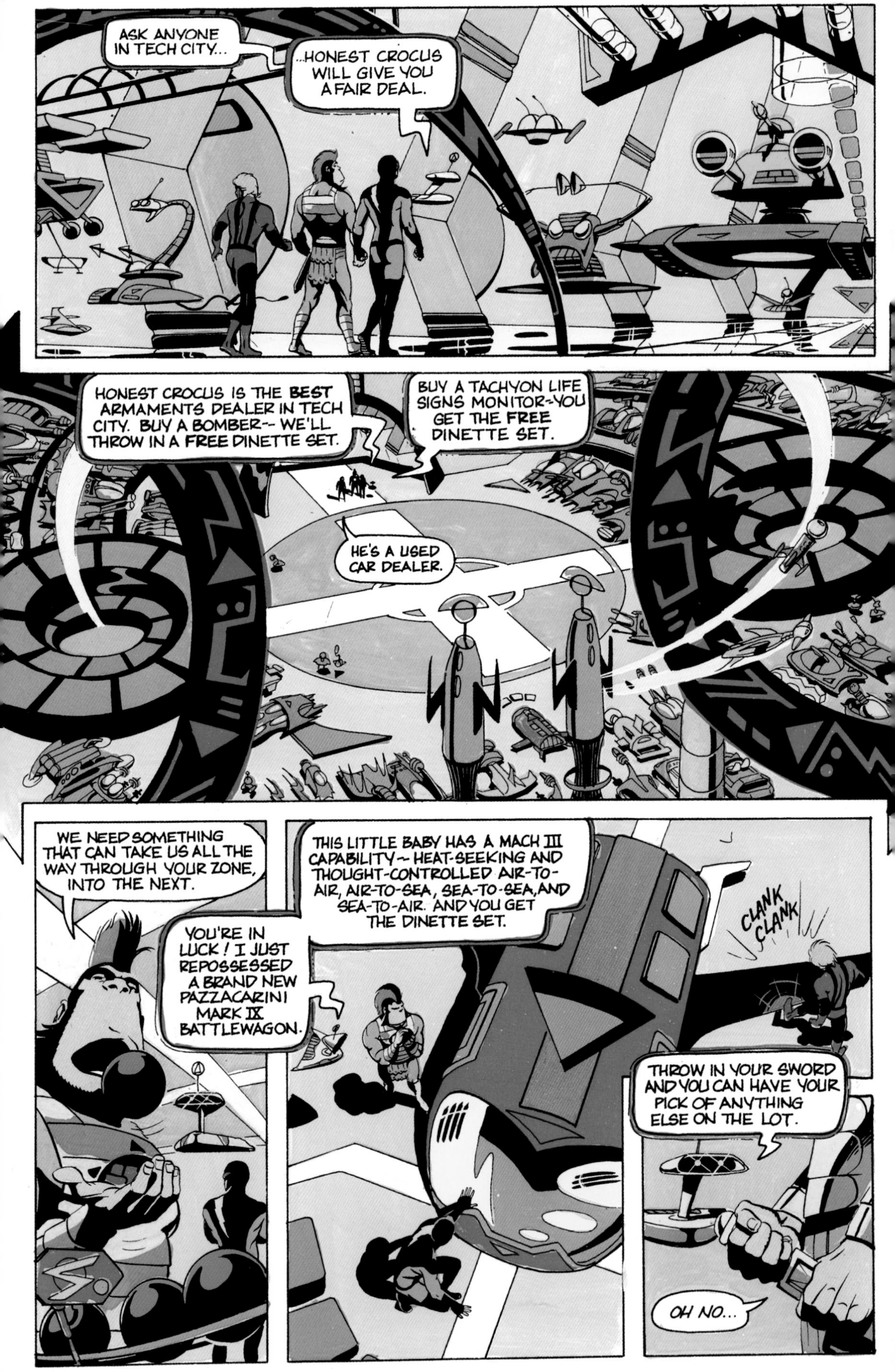
ASK ANYONE IN TECH CITY...
...HONEST CROCUS WILL GIVE YOU A FAIR DEAL.
HONEST CROCUS IS THE BEST ARMAMENTS DEALER IN TECH CITY. BUY A BOMBER-- WE'LL THROW IN A FREE DINETTE SET.
BUY A TACHYON LIFE SIGNS MONITOR--YOU GET THE FREE DINETTE SET.
HE'S A USED CAR DEALER.
WE NEED SOMETHING THAT CAN TAKE US ALL THE WAY THROUGH YOUR ZONE, INTO THE NEXT.
YOU'RE IN LUCK! I JUST REPOSSESSED A BRAND NEW PAZZACARINI MARK IX BATTLEWAGON.
THIS LITTLE BABY HAS A MACH III CAPABILITY-- HEAT-SEEKING AND THOUGHT-CONTROLLED AIR-TO-AIR, AIR-TO-SEA, SEA-TO-SEA, AND SEA-TO-AIR. AND YOU GET THE DINETTE SET.
CLANK CLANK
THROW IN YOUR SWORD AND YOU CAN HAVE YOUR PICK OF ANYTHING ELSE ON THE LOT.
OH NO...

SWOOSH

HA!

PLOP

PLOP

BOOT

PLOP?!

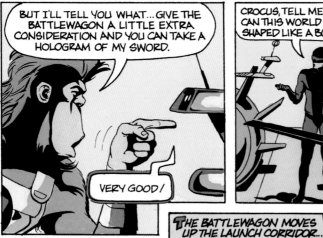

BUT I'LL TELL YOU WHAT... GIVE THE BATTLEWAGON A LITTLE EXTRA CONSIDERATION AND YOU CAN TAKE A HOLOGRAM OF MY SWORD.

VERY GOOD!

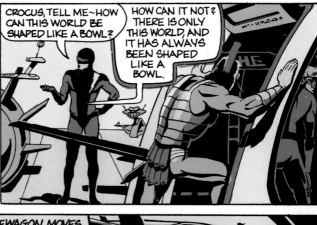

CROCUS, TELL ME~HOW CAN THIS WORLD BE SHAPED LIKE A BOWL?

HOW CAN IT NOT? THERE IS ONLY THIS WORLD, AND IT HAS ALWAYS BEEN SHAPED LIKE A BOWL.

THE BATTLEWAGON MOVES UP THE LAUNCH CORRIDOR...

WE'RE GOING TO BE CHALLENGED AT LEAST A DOZEN TIMES BETWEEN HERE AND THE BORDER...

BUT YOU HAVE AN ADVANCED TECHNOLOGY! HI-TECH ALLOYS! COMPUTERS! DON'T YOU UNDERSTAND THE IMPLICATIONS OF THIS WORLD?

SPEAK NOT TO ME OF THEOLOGY!

GO! GET OUT! GOOD LUCK!

THIS COMPUTER IS ALLEGEDLY STATE-OF-ART. IT'S PROGRAMMED TO CHOOSE A PATH OF LEAST RESISTANCE TO THE NEXT ZONE. WE'LL RETURN FIRE ONLY IF ABSOLUTELY NECESSARY.

THIS WORLD IS ARTIFICIAL! WE ARE LOOKING AT A GENETIC EXPERIMENT THAT BEGGARS THE IMAGINATION! *THINK OF IT!*

THAT LARRY GUY SEEMED PRETTY EAGER TO GET RID OF US. ANYONE NOTICE?

79

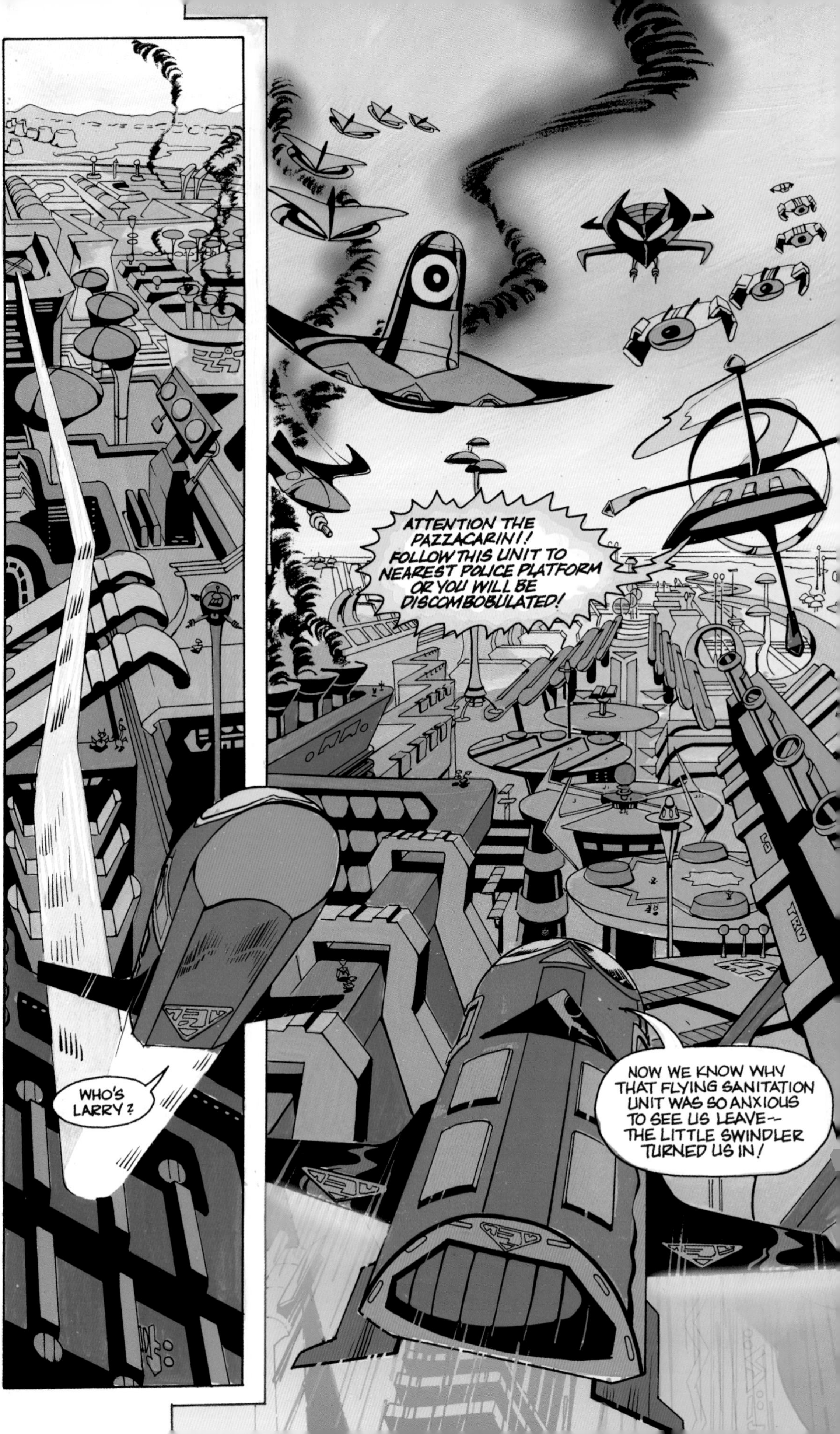
WHO'S LARRY?
ATTENTION THE PAZZACARINI! FOLLOW THIS UNIT TO NEAREST POLICE PLATFORM OR YOU WILL BE DISCOMBOBULATED!
NOW WE KNOW WHY THAT FLYING SANITATION UNIT WAS SO ANXIOUS TO SEE US LEAVE-- THE LITTLE SWINDLER TURNED US IN!

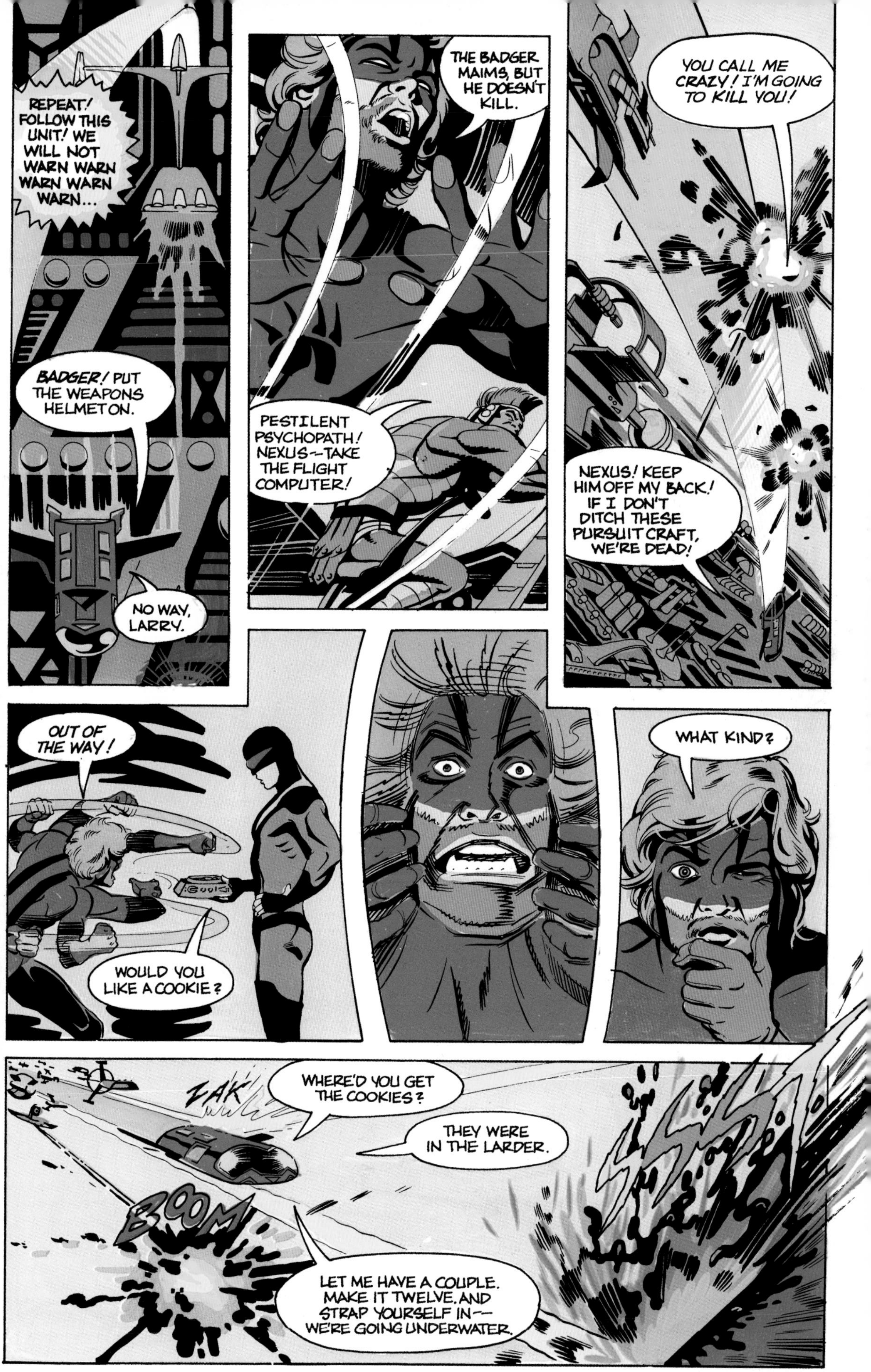
REPEAT! FOLLOW THIS UNIT! WE WILL NOT WARN WARN WARN WARN WARN...
BADGER! PUT THE WEAPONS HELMET ON.
NO WAY, LARRY.
THE BADGER MAIMS, BUT HE DOESN'T KILL.
PESTILENT PSYCHOPATH! NEXUS--TAKE THE FLIGHT COMPUTER!
YOU CALL ME CRAZY! I'M GOING TO KILL YOU!
NEXUS! KEEP HIM OFF MY BACK! IF I DON'T DITCH THESE PURSUIT CRAFT, WE'RE DEAD!
OUT OF THE WAY!
WOULD YOU LIKE A COOKIE?
WHAT KIND?
ZAK
WHERE'D YOU GET THE COOKIES?
THEY WERE IN THE LARDER.
BOOM
LET ME HAVE A COUPLE. MAKE IT TWELVE. AND STRAP YOURSELF IN-- WE'RE GOING UNDERWATER.

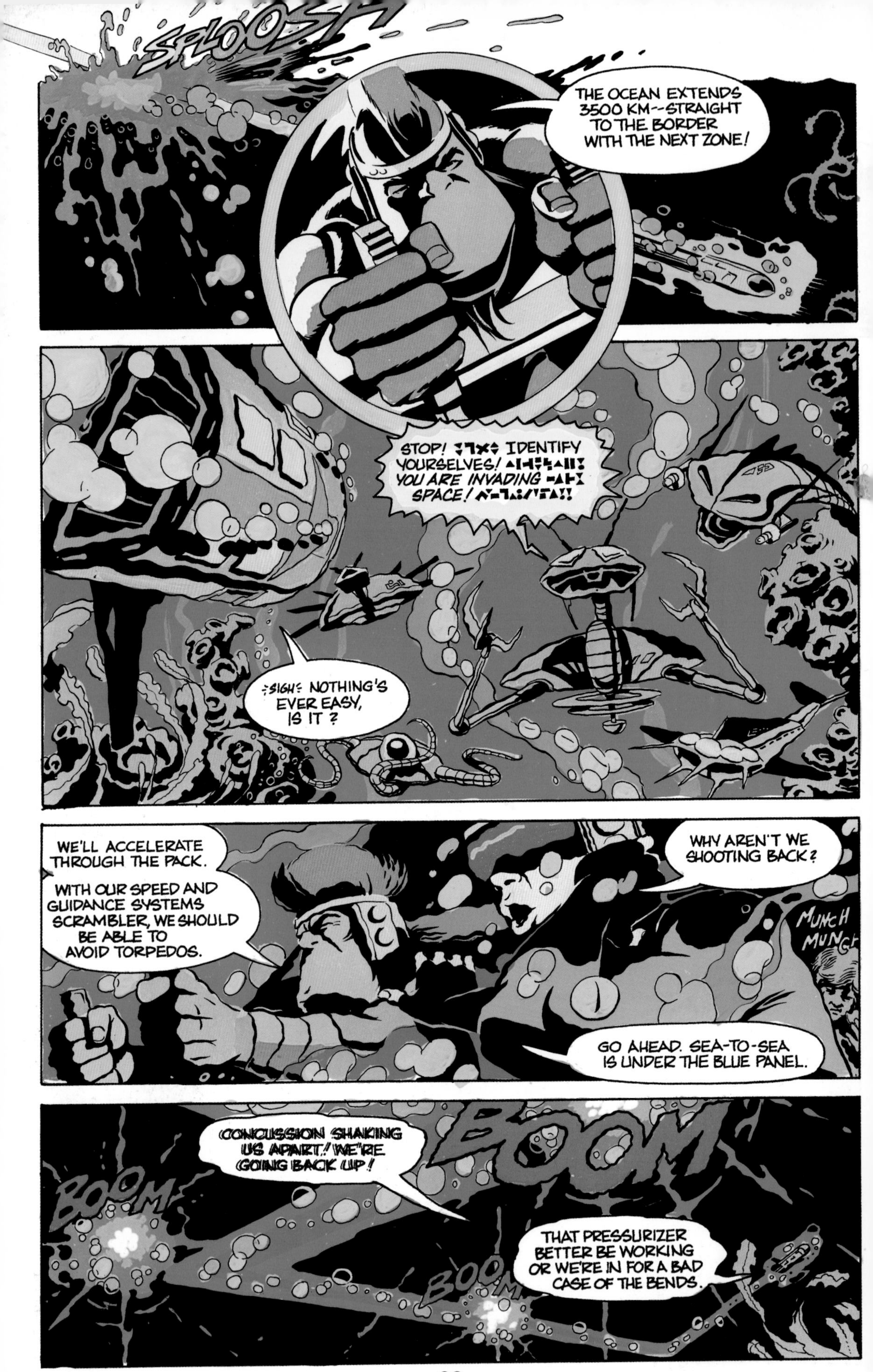
SPLOOSH
THE OCEAN EXTENDS 3500 KM--STRAIGHT TO THE BORDER WITH THE NEXT ZONE!
STOP! IDENTIFY YOURSELVES! YOU ARE INVADING SPACE!
:SIGH: NOTHING'S EVER EASY, IS IT?
WE'LL ACCELERATE THROUGH THE PACK.
WITH OUR SPEED AND GUIDANCE SYSTEMS SCRAMBLER, WE SHOULD BE ABLE TO AVOID TORPEDOS.
WHY AREN'T WE SHOOTING BACK?
MUNCH MUNCH
GO AHEAD. SEA-TO-SEA IS UNDER THE BLUE PANEL.
CONCUSSION SHAKING US APART! WE'RE GOING BACK UP!
BOOM
BOOM
THAT PRESSURIZER BETTER BE WORKING OR WE'RE IN FOR A BAD CASE OF THE BENDS.
BOOM

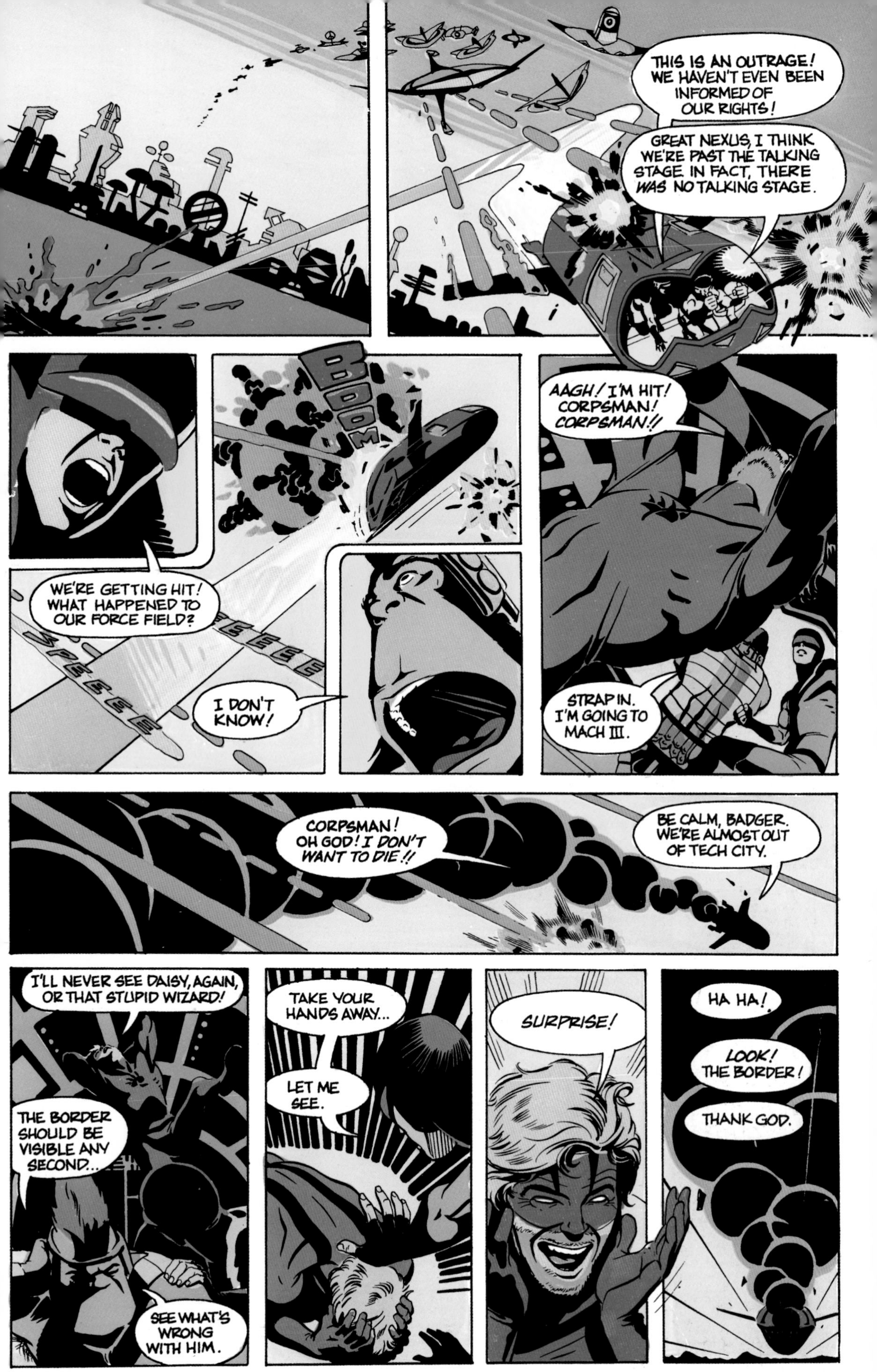
THIS IS AN OUTRAGE! WE HAVEN'T EVEN BEEN INFORMED OF OUR RIGHTS!
GREAT NEXUS, I THINK WE'RE PAST THE TALKING STAGE. IN FACT, THERE WAS NO TALKING STAGE.
BOOM
WE'RE GETTING HIT! WHAT HAPPENED TO OUR FORCE FIELD?
SPEEEE
I DON'T KNOW!
AAGH! I'M HIT! CORPSMAN! CORPSMAN!!
STRAP IN. I'M GOING TO MACH III.
CORPSMAN! OH GOD! I DON'T WANT TO DIE!!
BE CALM, BADGER. WE'RE ALMOST OUT OF TECH CITY.
I'LL NEVER SEE DAISY, AGAIN, OR THAT STUPID WIZARD!
THE BORDER SHOULD BE VISIBLE ANY SECOND...
SEE WHAT'S WRONG WITH HIM.
TAKE YOUR HANDS AWAY...
LET ME SEE.
SURPRISE!
HA HA!
LOOK! THE BORDER!
THANK GOD.

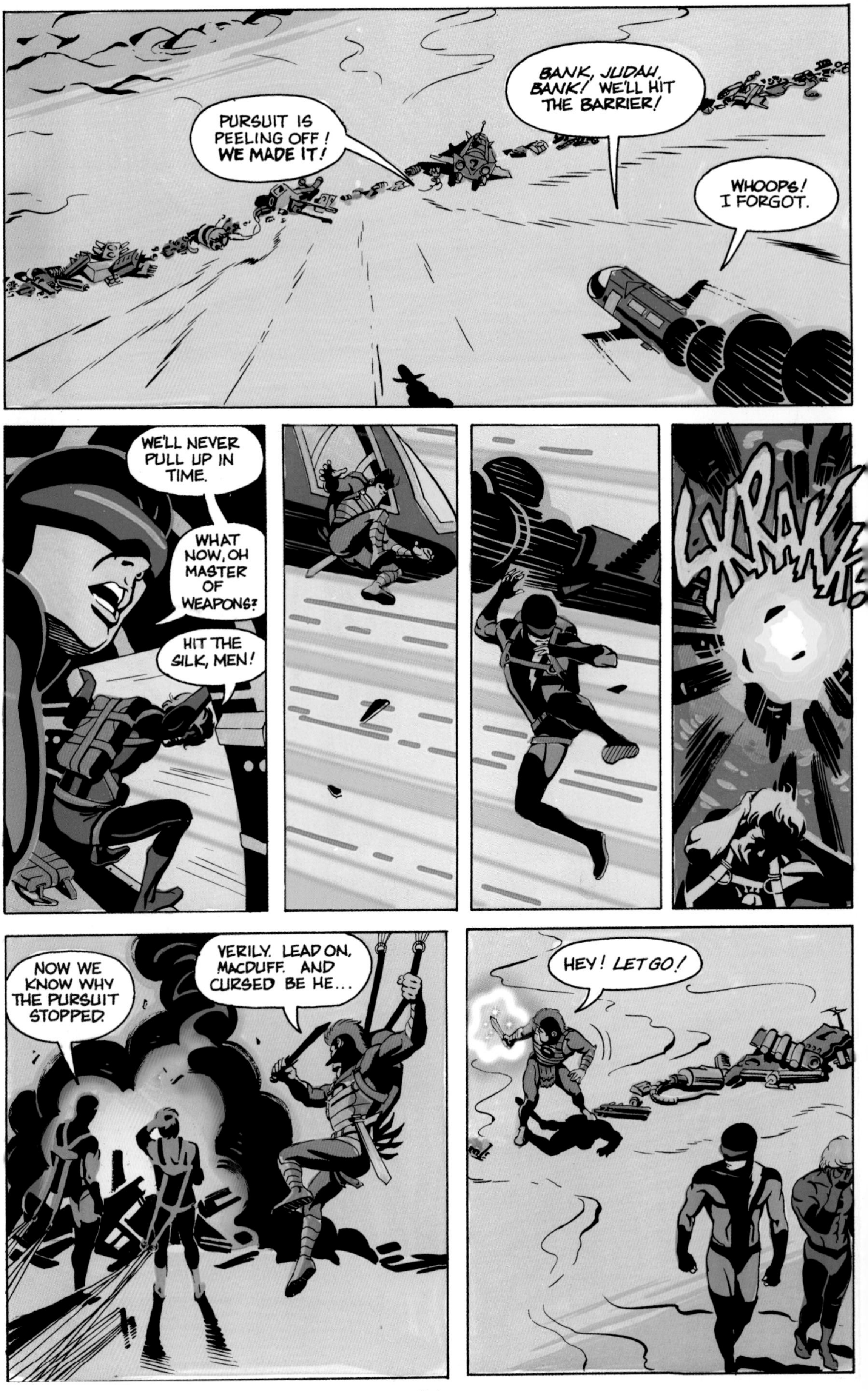
PURSUIT IS PEELING OFF! WE MADE IT!
BANK, JUDAH, BANK! WE'LL HIT THE BARRIER!
WHOOPS! I FORGOT.
WE'LL NEVER PULL UP IN TIME.
WHAT NOW, OH MASTER OF WEAPONS?
HIT THE SILK, MEN!
NOW WE KNOW WHY THE PURSUIT STOPPED.
VERILY. LEAD ON, MACDUFF. AND CURSED BE HE...
HEY! LET GO!

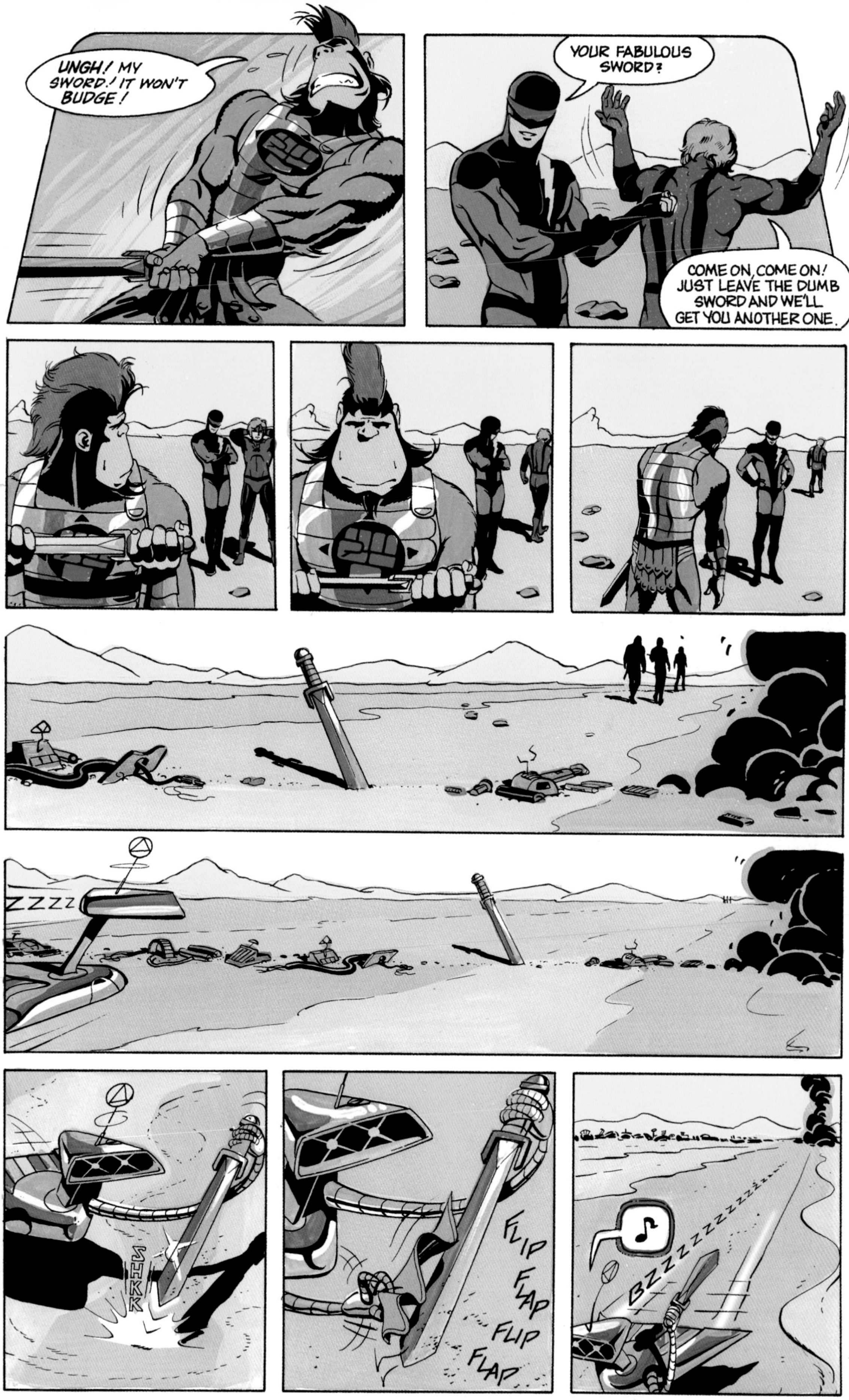
UNGH! MY SWORD! IT WON'T BUDGE!
YOUR FABULOUS SWORD?
COME ON, COME ON! JUST LEAVE THE DUMB SWORD AND WE'LL GET YOU ANOTHER ONE.
ZZZZ
SHKK
FLIP FLAP FLIP FLAP
BZZZZZZZZZZZZZ

IF THIS IS SUNDRA AND JIL, THIS MUST BE YLUM.

THAT'S IT.

COULD BE.

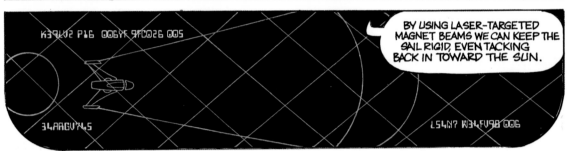

BY USING LASER-TARGETED MAGNET BEAMS WE CAN KEEP THE SAIL RIGID, EVEN TACKING BACK IN TOWARD THE SUN.

THE SAIL DOUBLES AS A SOLAR COLLECTOR, TO POWER THE MAGNETS. NEXT BEST THING TO PERPETUAL MOTION.

S'LONG AS THE BIG BULB KEEPS SHININ' ON. I'LL START PATENT PROCEDURES WITH THE WEB. BUT FIRST WE'LL HAVE TO BUILD A PROTOTYPE.

MAKE SURE THE DARN THING WORKS.

WE'LL NEED AT LEAST ¥500,000 TO PUT 4 OR 5 INTO PRODUCTION...

ARE WE GETTING SERIOUS, OR WHAT?

I BELIEVE WE ARE. SO? WANT TO BUILD SOLAR SAILSHIPS?

I THINK I DO. I GUESS THERE'S ONLY ONE WAY TO FIND OUT.

WE CAN SET UP SHOP RIGHT HERE. AND I'VE FOUND THE PERFECT PRODUCTION SUPERVISOR...

LADIES, EXCUSE PLEASE—

VUTT VUTT VUTT VUTT

HAS EITHER OF YOU SEEN LHASA RANGOON?

NO ONE HAS HEARD FROM HER IN 48 HOURS.

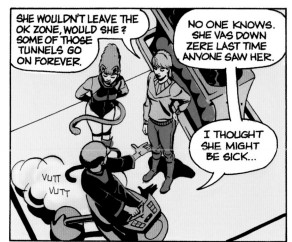

SHE WOULDN'T LEAVE THE OK ZONE, WOULD SHE? SOME OF THOSE TUNNELS GO ON FOREVER.

NO ONE KNOWS. SHE VAS DOWN ZERE LAST TIME ANYONE SAW HER.

I THOUGHT SHE MIGHT BE SICK...

VUTT VUTT

I'LL CHECK WITH DAVE. MAYBE WE CAN FIND HER ON THE MONITORS.

VUTT VU

I HAVEN'T SEEN LHASA IN TWO DAYS. REPEATED SCANS OF THE TUNNELS REVEAL LITTLE.

I DON'T KNOW WHY THEY BOTHERED ME WITH THIS.

AH. YOU ARE PERCEIVED TO BE IN A POSITION OF AUTHORITY BECAUSE OF YOUR PROXIMITY TO NEXUS.

THAT'S RIDICULOUS.

THE DIGS.

NO, WE HAVEN'T SEEN HER HAVE WE, FFASNER? HAVE WE, HUH?

NOPE. NOPE. HAVEN'T SEEN HER. NEED HER BACK.

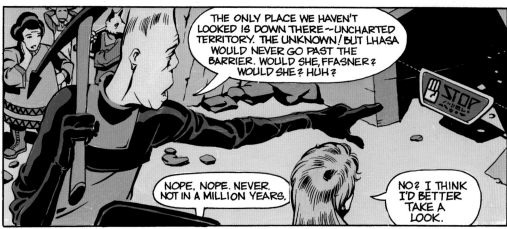

THE ONLY PLACE WE HAVEN'T LOOKED IS DOWN THERE ~ UNCHARTED TERRITORY. THE UNKNOWN! BUT LHASA WOULD NEVER GO PAST THE BARRIER. WOULD SHE, FFASNER? WOULD SHE? HUH?

STOP

NOPE, NOPE. NEVER. NOT IN A MILLION YEARS.

NO? I THINK I'D BETTER TAKE A LOOK.

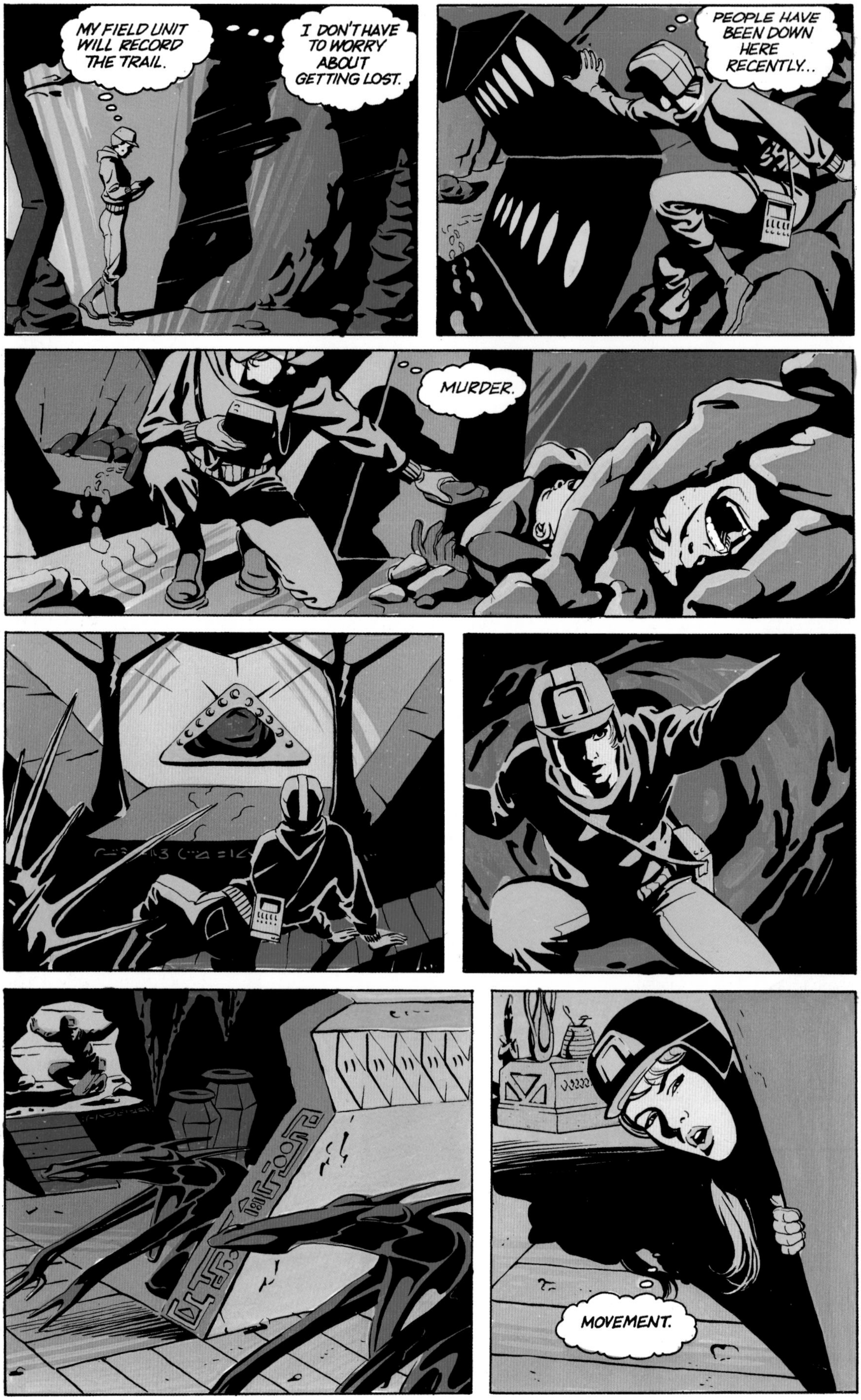
MY FIELD UNIT WILL RECORD THE TRAIL.
I DON'T HAVE TO WORRY ABOUT GETTING LOST.
PEOPLE HAVE BEEN DOWN HERE RECENTLY...
MURDER.
MOVEMENT.

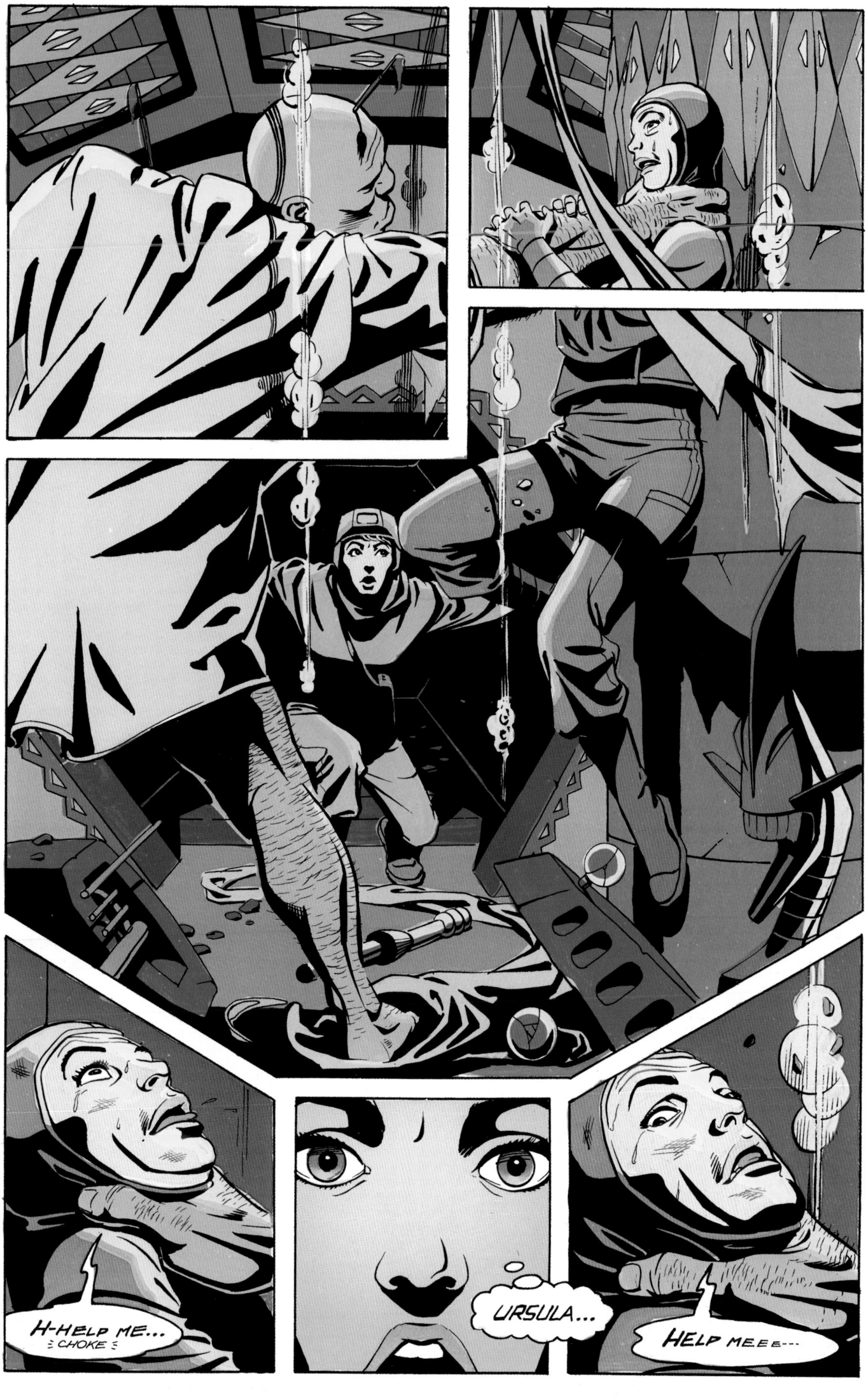
H-HELP ME...
CHOKE
URSULA...
HELP MEEE---

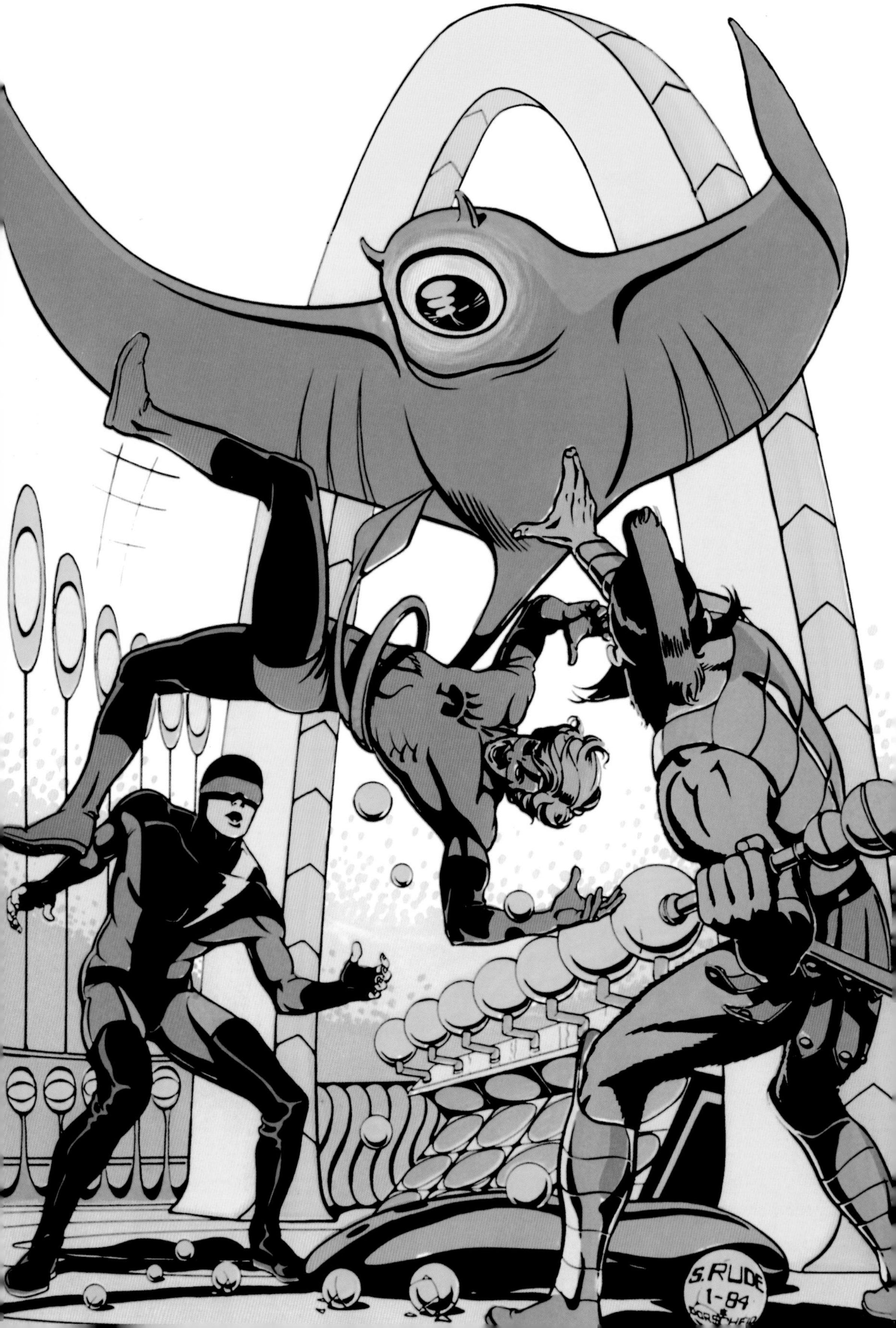
S.RUDE
1-84

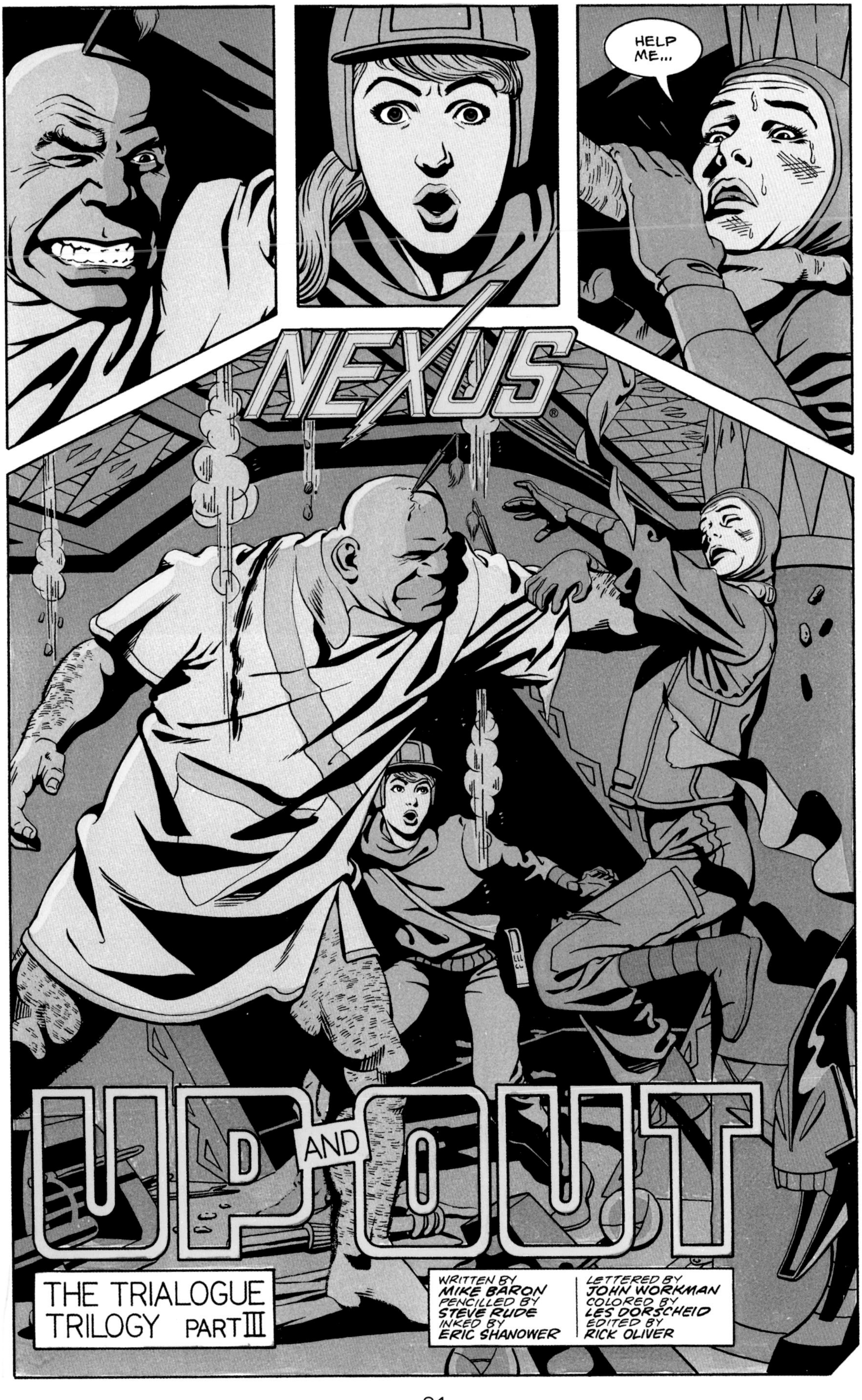
HELP ME...
NEXUS®
UP AND OUT
THE TRIALOGUE TRILOGY PART III
WRITTEN BY MIKE BARON
PENCILLED BY STEVE RUDE
INKED BY ERIC SHANOWER
LETTERED BY JOHN WORKMAN
COLORED BY LES DORSCHEID
EDITED BY RICK OLIVER

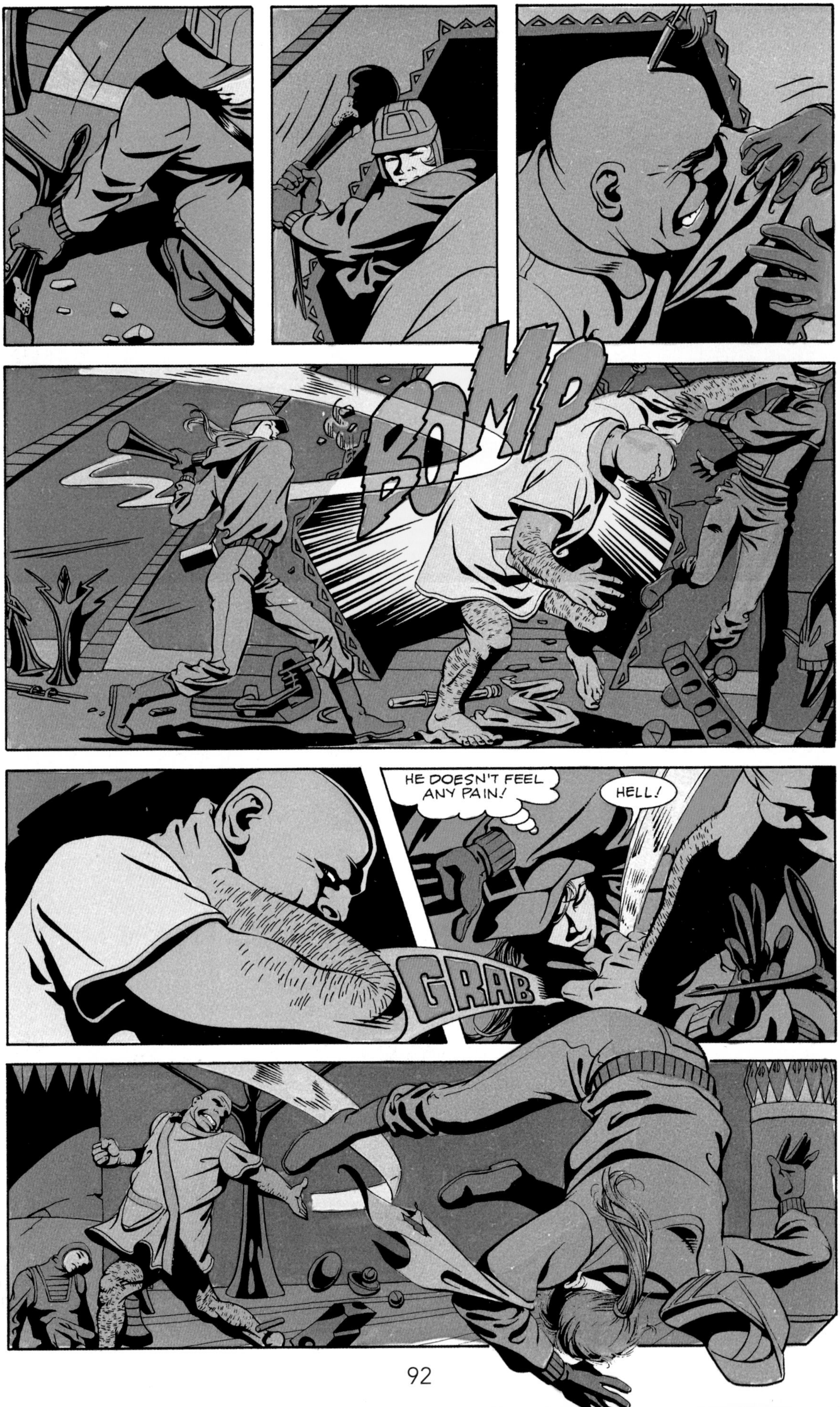
BOMP
HE DOESN'T FEEL ANY PAIN!
HELL!
GRAB

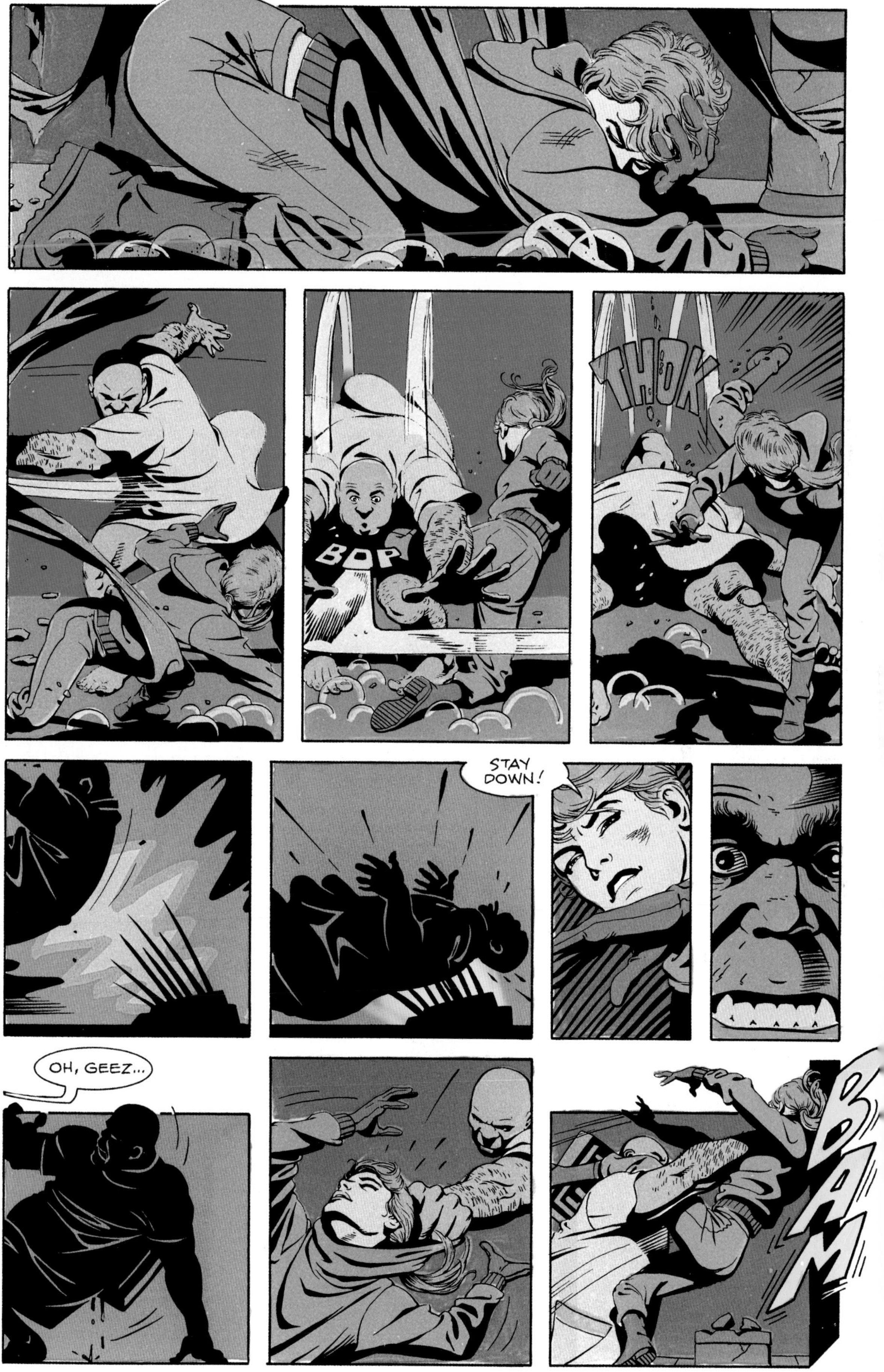
BOP
THOK
STAY DOWN!
OH, GEEZ...
BAM

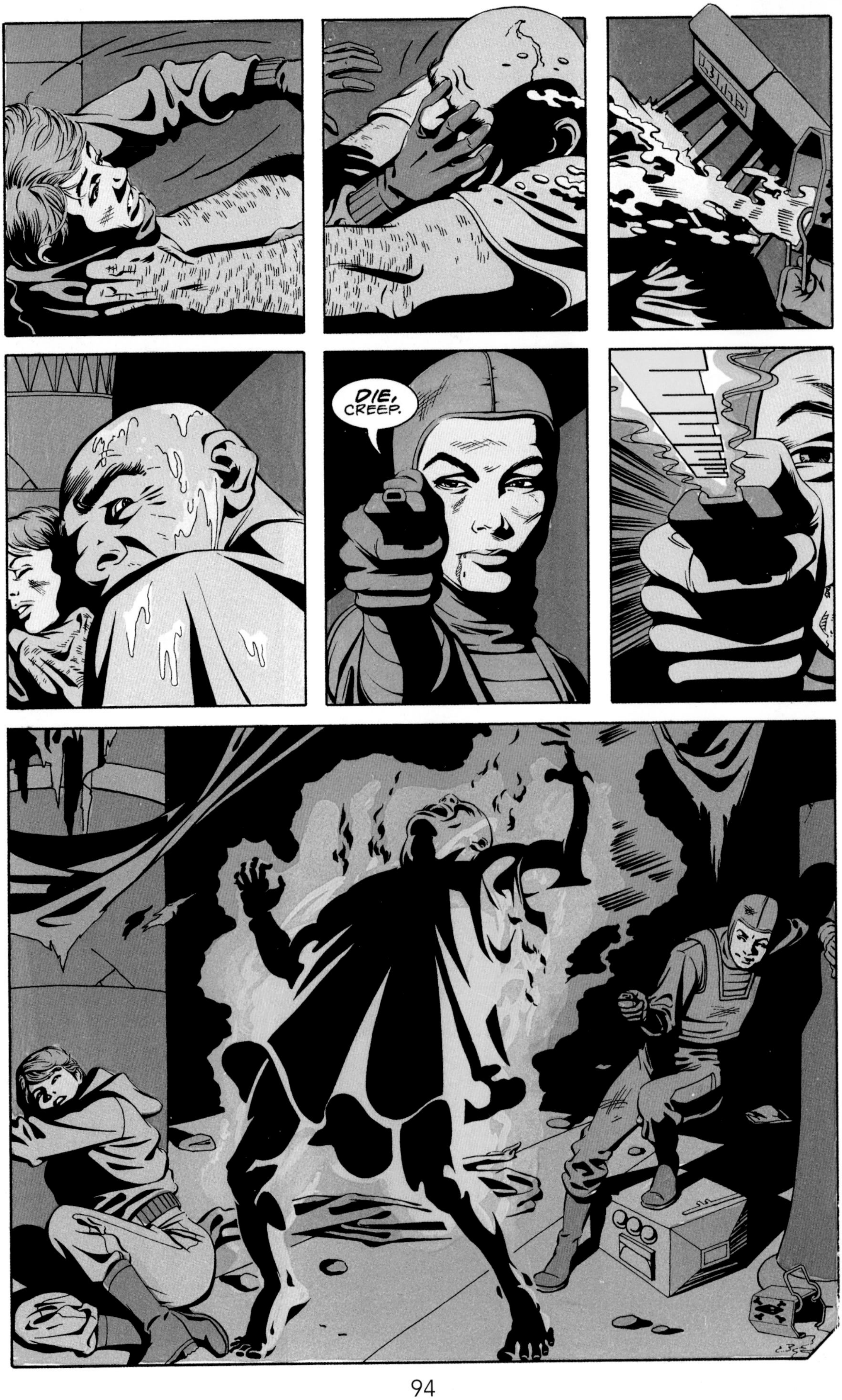
DIE, CREEP.

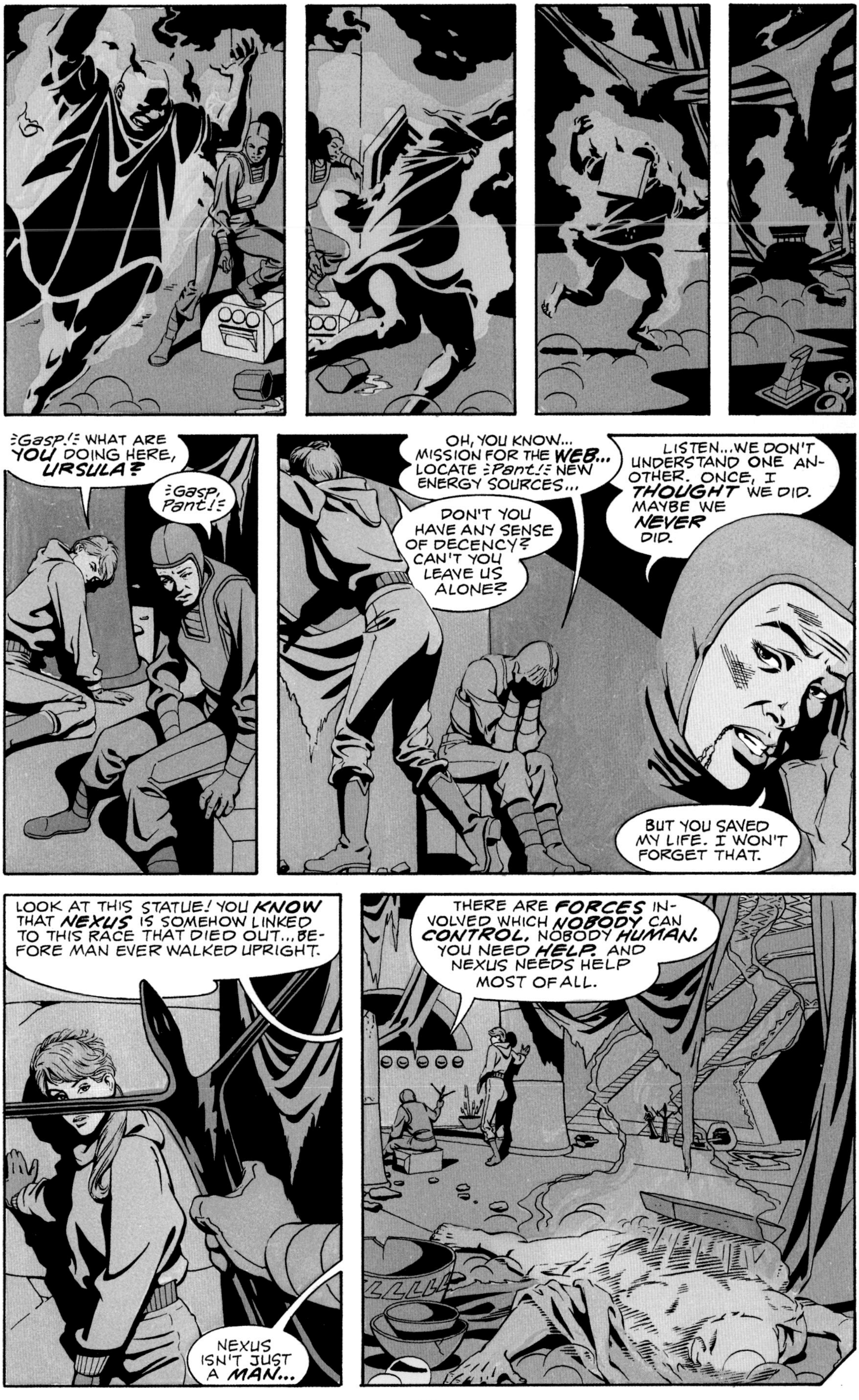

=Gasp!= WHAT ARE YOU DOING HERE, URSULA?
=Gasp, Pant!=
OH, YOU KNOW... MISSION FOR THE WEB... LOCATE =Pant!= NEW ENERGY SOURCES...
DON'T YOU HAVE ANY SENSE OF DECENCY? CAN'T YOU LEAVE US ALONE?
LISTEN...WE DON'T UNDERSTAND ONE AN-OTHER. ONCE, I THOUGHT WE DID. MAYBE WE NEVER DID.
BUT YOU SAVED MY LIFE. I WON'T FORGET THAT.
LOOK AT THIS STATUE! YOU KNOW THAT NEXUS IS SOMEHOW LINKED TO THIS RACE THAT DIED OUT...BE-FORE MAN EVER WALKED UPRIGHT.
NEXUS ISN'T JUST A MAN...
THERE ARE FORCES IN-VOLVED WHICH NOBODY CAN CONTROL. NOBODY HUMAN. YOU NEED HELP. AND NEXUS NEEDS HELP MOST OF ALL.

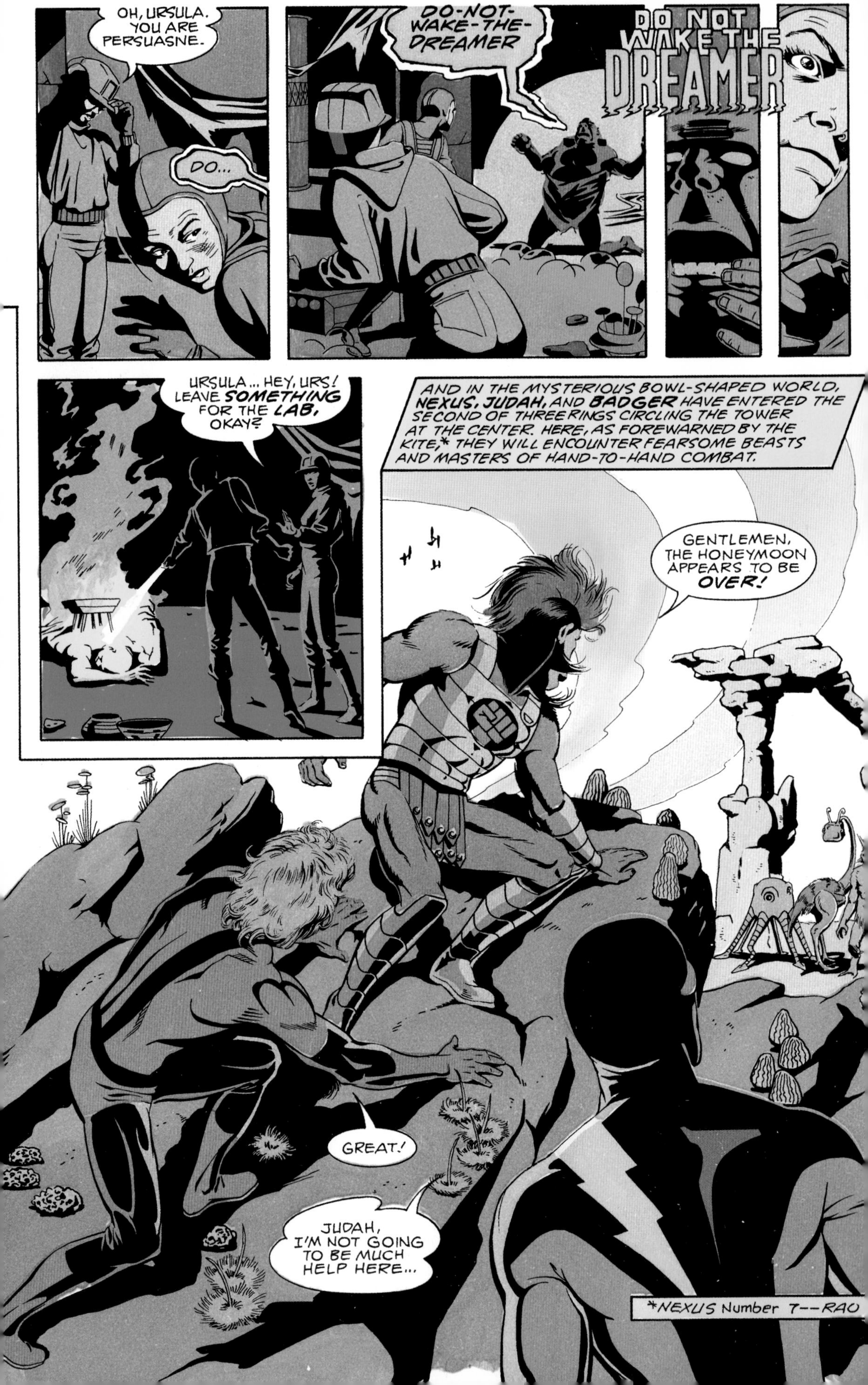
OH, URSULA. YOU ARE PERSUASNE.
DO...
DO-NOT-WAKE-THE-DREAMER
DO NOT WAKE THE DREAMER
URSULA... HEY, URS! LEAVE SOMETHING FOR THE LAB, OKAY?
AND IN THE MYSTERIOUS BOWL-SHAPED WORLD, NEXUS, JUDAH, AND BADGER HAVE ENTERED THE SECOND OF THREE RINGS CIRCLING THE TOWER AT THE CENTER. HERE, AS FOREWARNED BY THE KITE,* THEY WILL ENCOUNTER FEARSOME BEASTS AND MASTERS OF HAND-TO-HAND COMBAT.
GENTLEMEN, THE HONEYMOON APPEARS TO BE OVER!
GREAT!
JUDAH, I'M NOT GOING TO BE MUCH HELP HERE...
*NEXUS Number 7--RAO

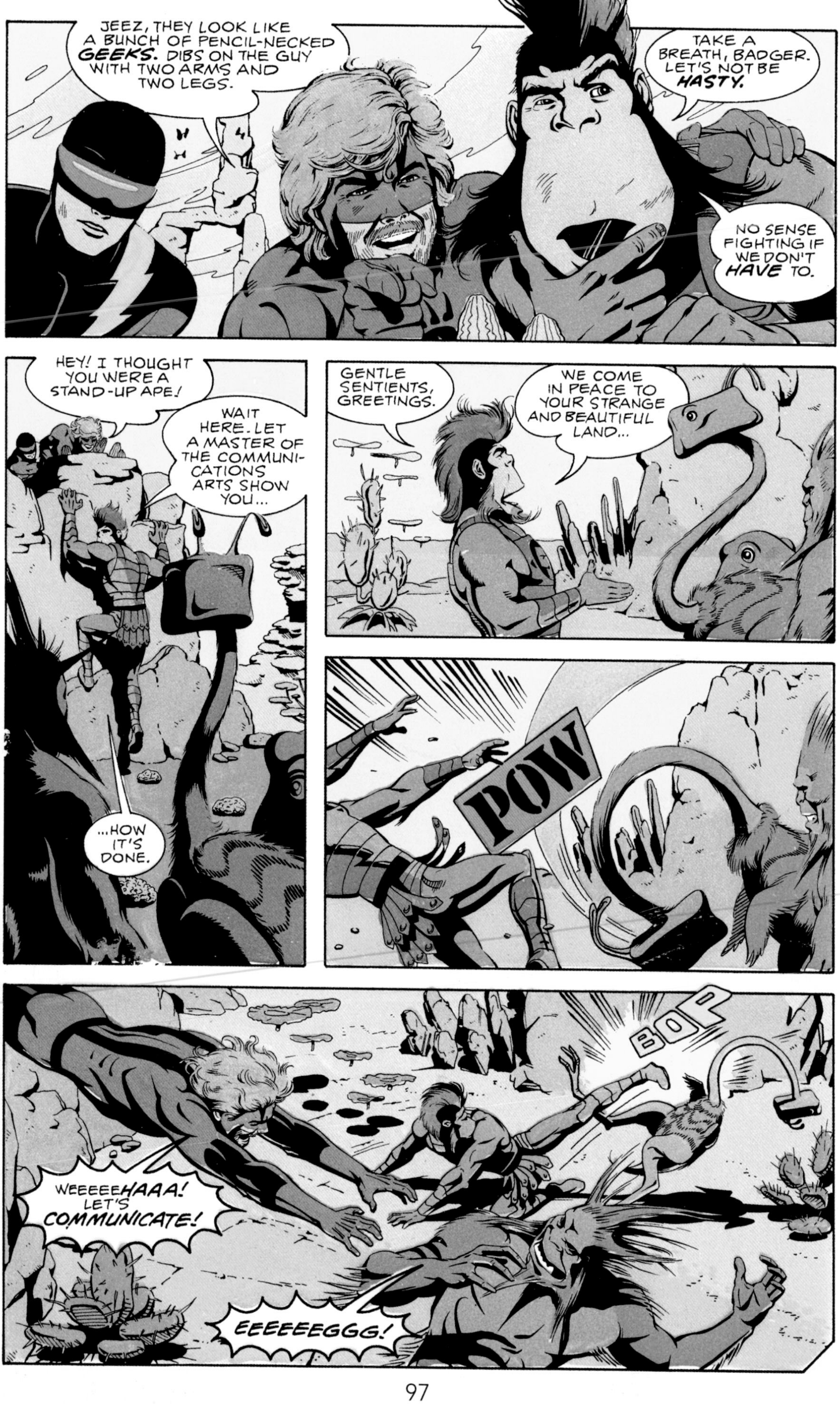
JEEZ, THEY LOOK LIKE A BUNCH OF PENCIL-NECKED GEEKS. DIBS ON THE GUY WITH TWO ARMS AND TWO LEGS.
TAKE A BREATH, BADGER. LET'S NOT BE HASTY.
NO SENSE FIGHTING IF WE DON'T HAVE TO.
HEY! I THOUGHT YOU WERE A STAND-UP APE!
WAIT HERE. LET A MASTER OF THE COMMUNI-CATIONS ARTS SHOW YOU...
...HOW IT'S DONE.
GENTLE SENTIENTS, GREETINGS.
WE COME IN PEACE TO YOUR STRANGE AND BEAUTIFUL LAND...
POW
BOP
WEEEEEHAAA! LET'S COMMUNICATE!
EEEEEEGGG!

I'M NO **GOOD** AT THIS...

KRAKK

BONK!

OUCH!

SWOOSH
SWOOSH
SWOOSH
WOOSH
SWOOSH

NO FAIR! THIS IS **SUP-POSED** TO BE **HAND-TO-HAND!**

THLP THLP THLP
THLP
THLP

BOING

S'LONG, LARRY! WEEEE-**HAAAA!**

ZIPPP

WHAT DO YOU DO FOR AN ACHING BACK?

THEY'RE GONE!

JUDAH...

GREAT GOULES-SARIAN! I **THOUGHT** THAT WAS TOO **EASY.**

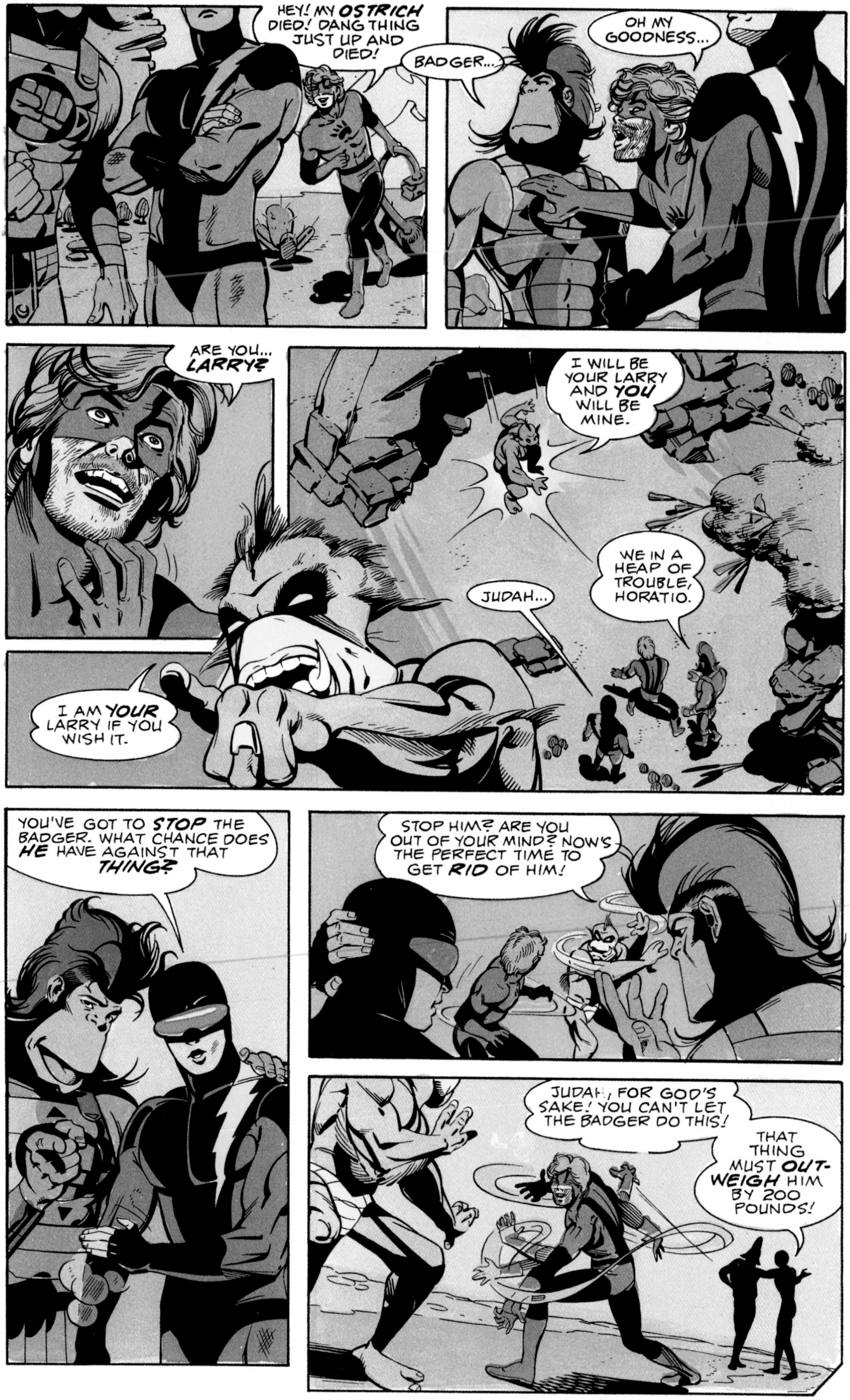
HEY! MY OSTRICH DIED! DANG THING JUST UP AND DIED!
BADGER...
OH MY GOODNESS...
ARE YOU... LARRY?
I WILL BE YOUR LARRY AND YOU WILL BE MINE.
I AM YOUR LARRY IF YOU WISH IT.
JUDAH...
WE IN A HEAP OF TROUBLE, HORATIO.
YOU'VE GOT TO STOP THE BADGER. WHAT CHANCE DOES HE HAVE AGAINST THAT THING?
STOP HIM? ARE YOU OUT OF YOUR MIND? NOW'S THE PERFECT TIME TO GET RID OF HIM!
JUDAH, FOR GOD'S SAKE! YOU CAN'T LET THE BADGER DO THIS!
THAT THING MUST OUT-WEIGH HIM BY 200 POUNDS!

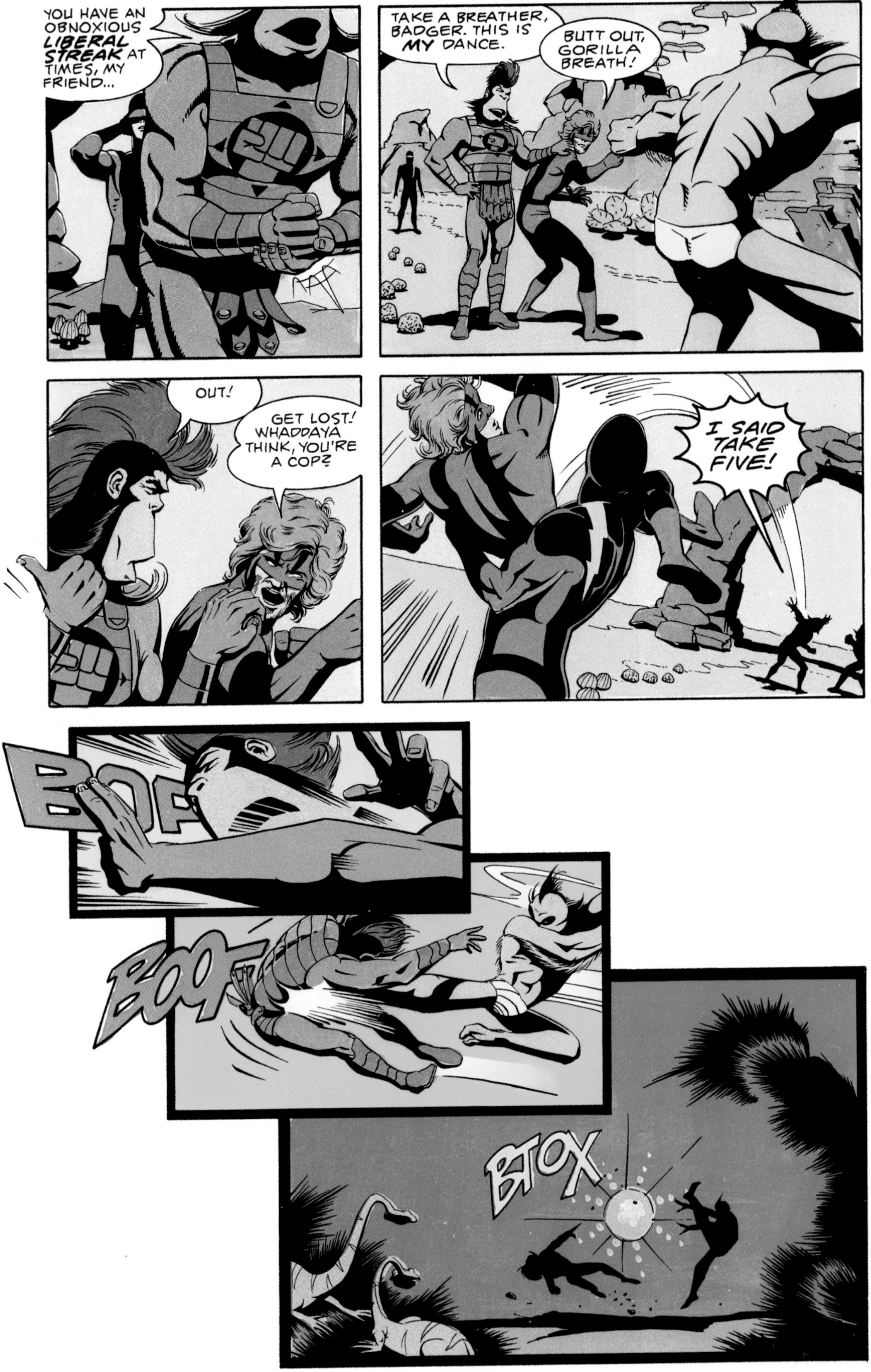
YOU HAVE AN OBNOXIOUS LIBERAL STREAK AT TIMES, MY FRIEND...
TAKE A BREATHER, BADGER. THIS IS MY DANCE.
BUTT OUT, GORILLA BREATH!
OUT!
GET LOST! WHADDAYA THINK, YOU'RE A COP?
I SAID TAKE FIVE!
BOP
BOOF
BTOX

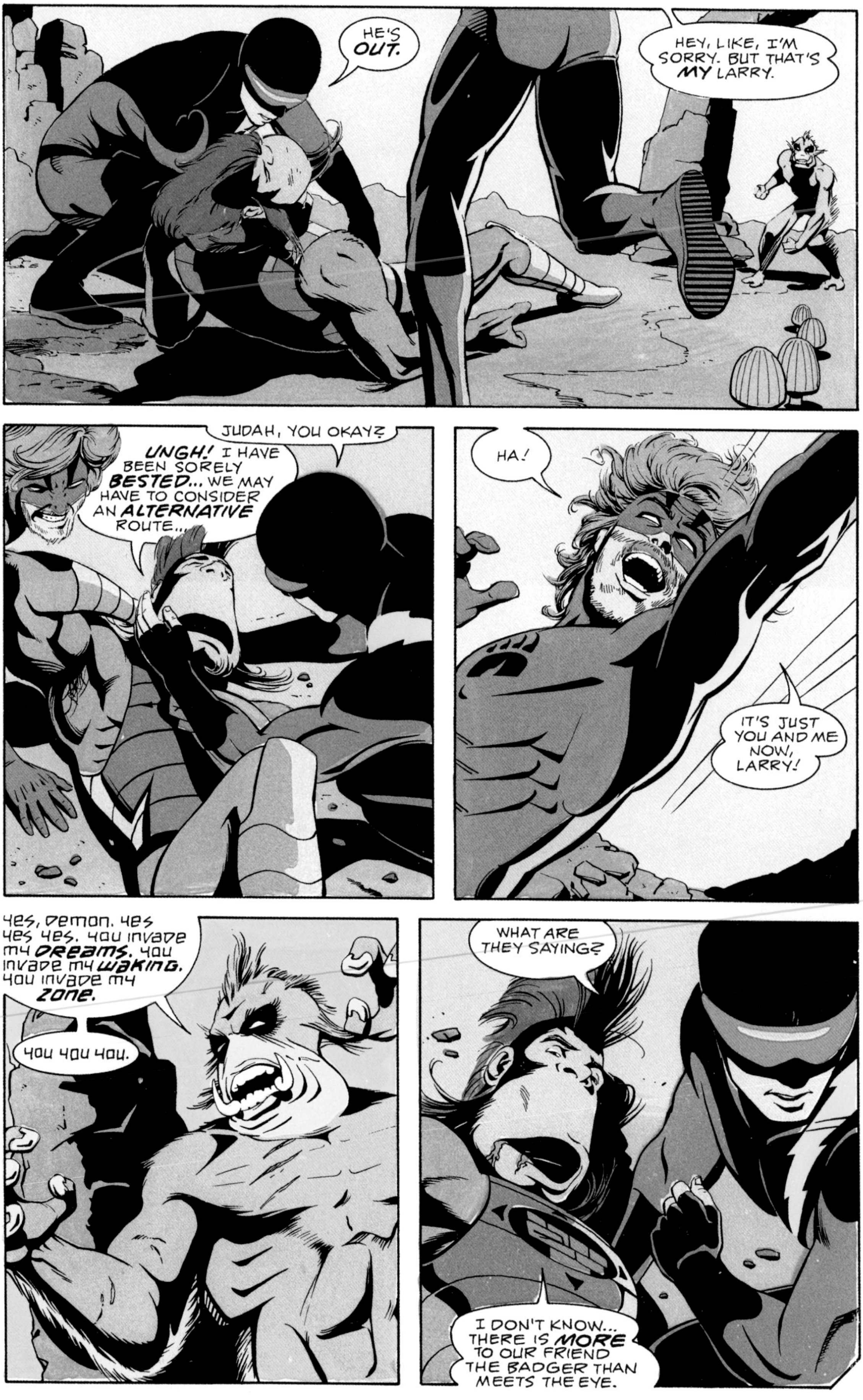
HE'S OUT.
HEY, LIKE, I'M SORRY. BUT THAT'S MY LARRY.
JUDAH, YOU OKAY?
UNGH! I HAVE BEEN SORELY BESTED... WE MAY HAVE TO CONSIDER AN ALTERNATIVE ROUTE...
HA!
IT'S JUST YOU AND ME NOW, LARRY!
YES, DEMON. YES YES YES. YOU INVADE MY DREAMS. YOU INVADE MY WAKING. YOU INVADE MY ZONE.
YOU YOU YOU.
WHAT ARE THEY SAYING?
I DON'T KNOW... THERE IS MORE TO OUR FRIEND THE BADGER THAN MEETS THE EYE.

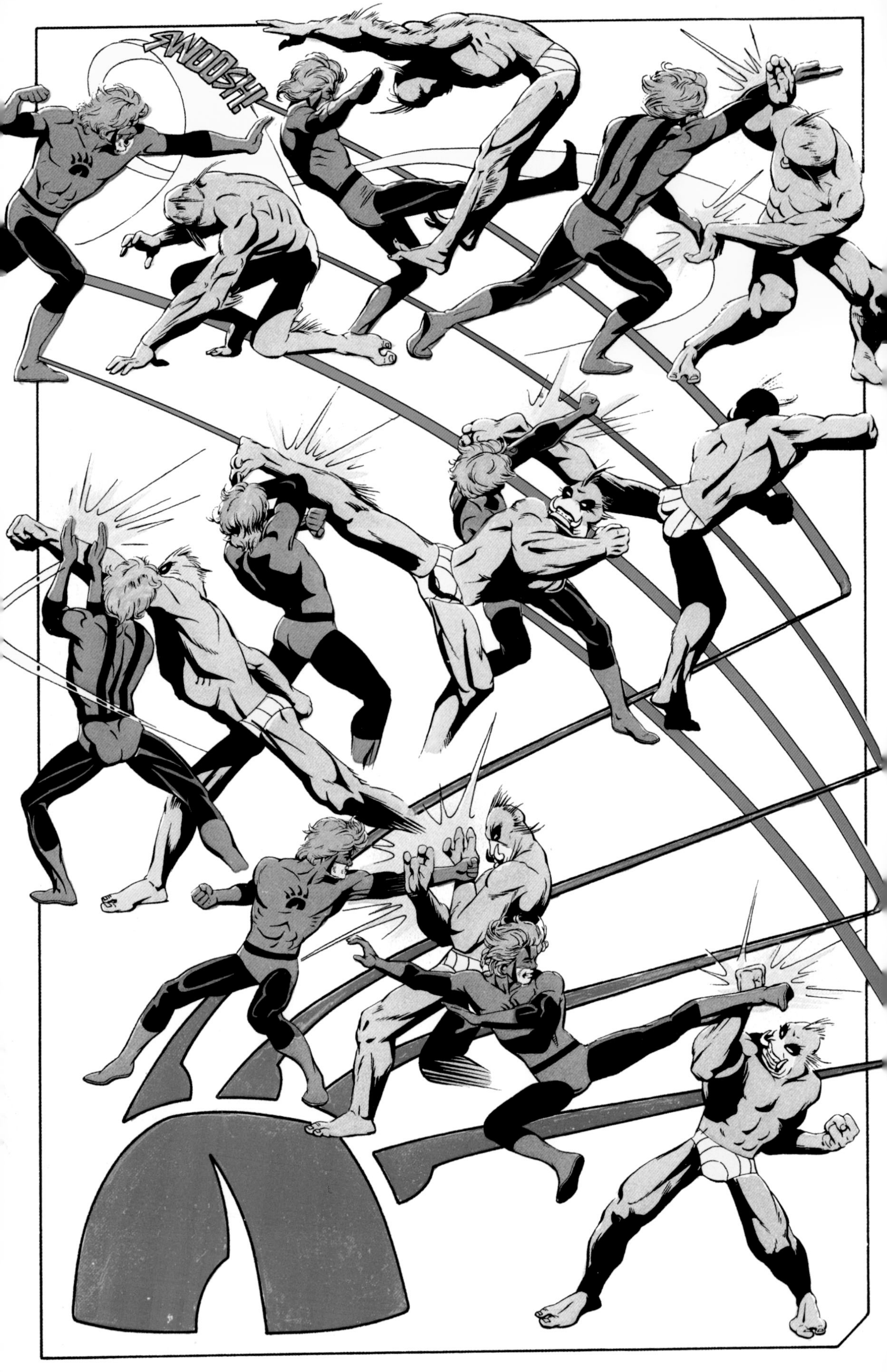
SWOOSH!

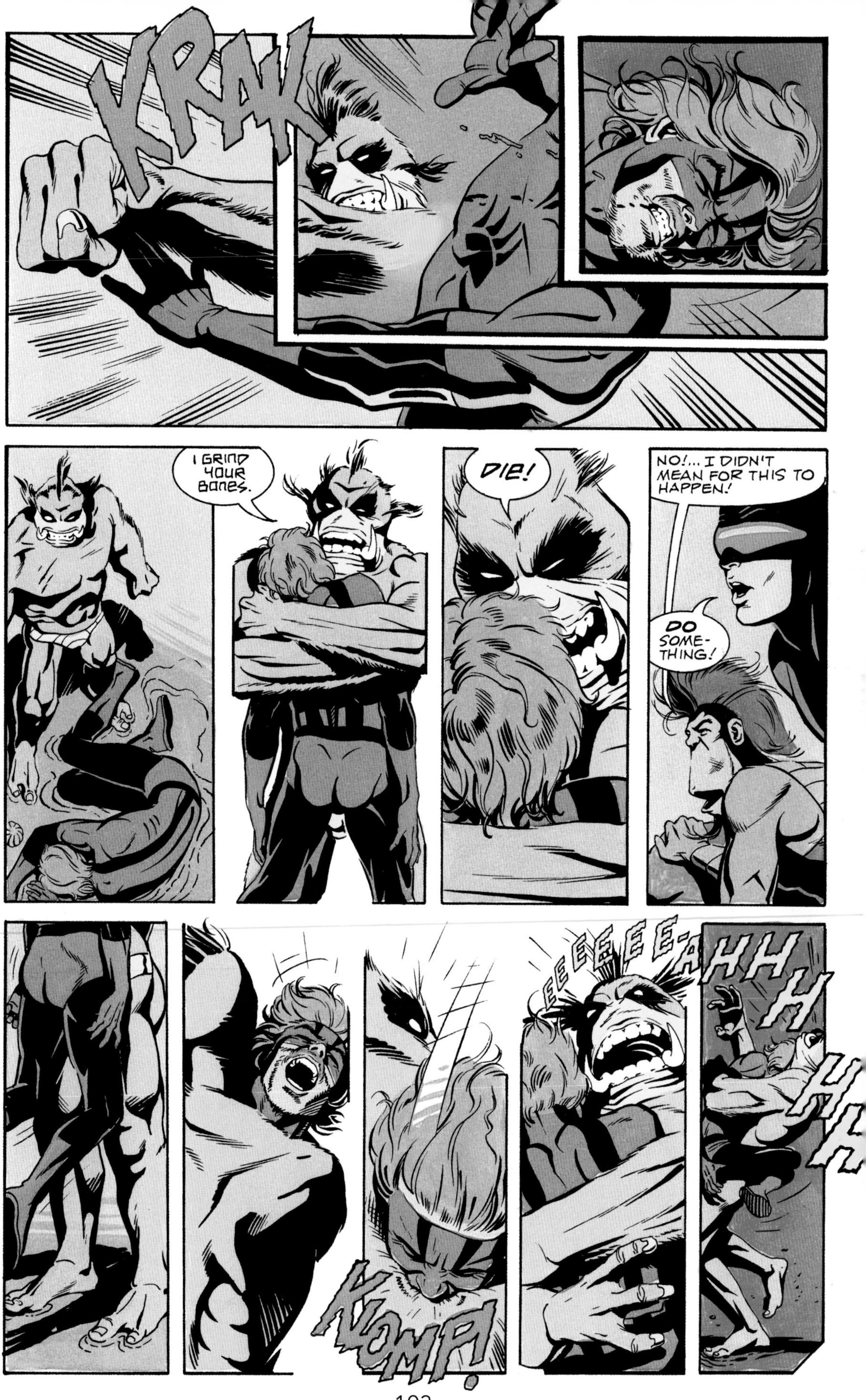
KRAK
I GRIND YOUR BONES.
DIE!
NO!... I DIDN'T MEAN FOR THIS TO HAPPEN!
DO SOMETHING!
EEEEEEE-AHHHHH
KOMP!

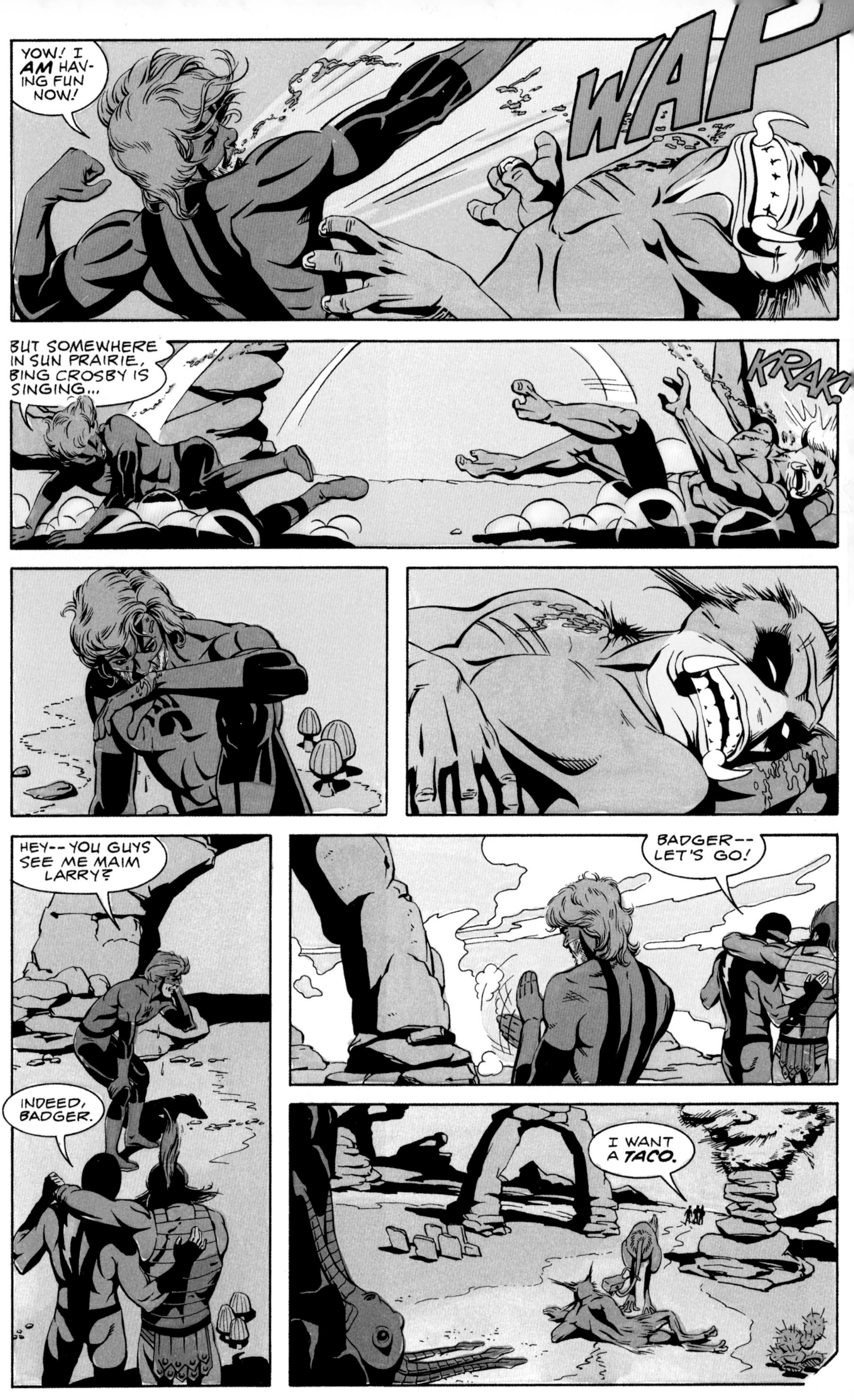
YOW! I AM HAVING FUN NOW!
WAP
BUT SOMEWHERE IN SUN PRAIRIE, BING CROSBY IS SINGING...
KRAK!
HEY--YOU GUYS SEE ME MAIM LARRY?
INDEED, BADGER.
BADGER-- LET'S GO!
I WANT A TACO.

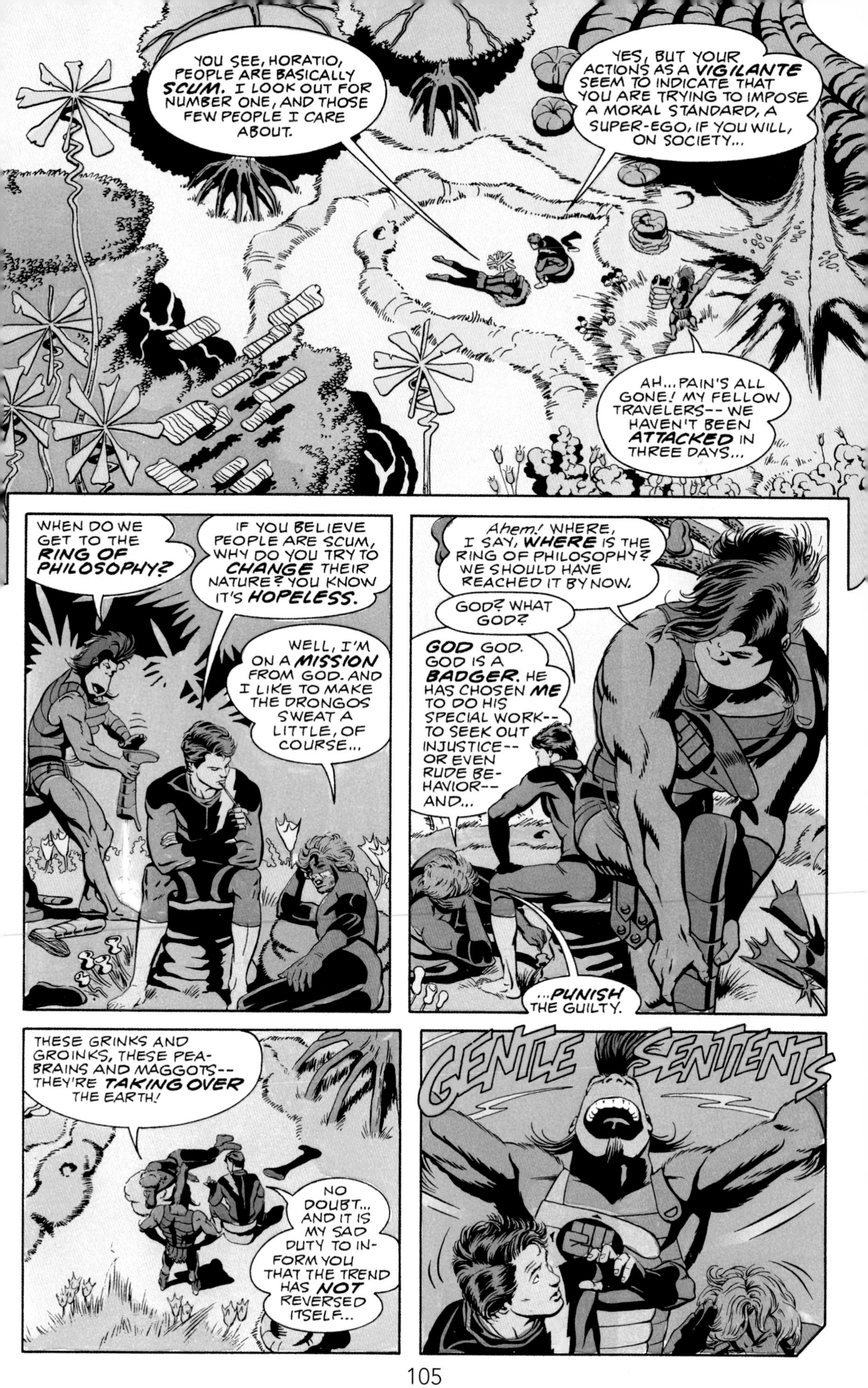
YOU SEE, HORATIO, PEOPLE ARE BASICALLY SCUM. I LOOK OUT FOR NUMBER ONE, AND THOSE FEW PEOPLE I CARE ABOUT.
YES, BUT YOUR ACTIONS AS A VIGILANTE SEEM TO INDICATE THAT YOU ARE TRYING TO IMPOSE A MORAL STANDARD, A SUPER-EGO, IF YOU WILL, ON SOCIETY...
AH... PAIN'S ALL GONE! MY FELLOW TRAVELERS-- WE HAVEN'T BEEN ATTACKED IN THREE DAYS...
WHEN DO WE GET TO THE RING OF PHILOSOPHY?
IF YOU BELIEVE PEOPLE ARE SCUM, WHY DO YOU TRY TO CHANGE THEIR NATURE? YOU KNOW IT'S HOPELESS.
WELL, I'M ON A MISSION FROM GOD. AND I LIKE TO MAKE THE DRONGOS SWEAT A LITTLE, OF COURSE...
Ahem! WHERE, I SAY, WHERE IS THE RING OF PHILOSOPHY? WE SHOULD HAVE REACHED IT BY NOW.
GOD? WHAT GOD?
GOD GOD. GOD IS A BADGER. HE HAS CHOSEN ME TO DO HIS SPECIAL WORK-- TO SEEK OUT INJUSTICE-- OR EVEN RUDE BE-HAVIOR-- AND...
...PUNISH THE GUILTY.
THESE GRINKS AND GROINKS, THESE PEA-BRAINS AND MAGGOTS-- THEY'RE TAKING OVER THE EARTH!
NO DOUBT... AND IT IS MY SAD DUTY TO IN-FORM YOU THAT THE TREND HAS NOT REVERSED ITSELF...
GENTLE SENTIENTS

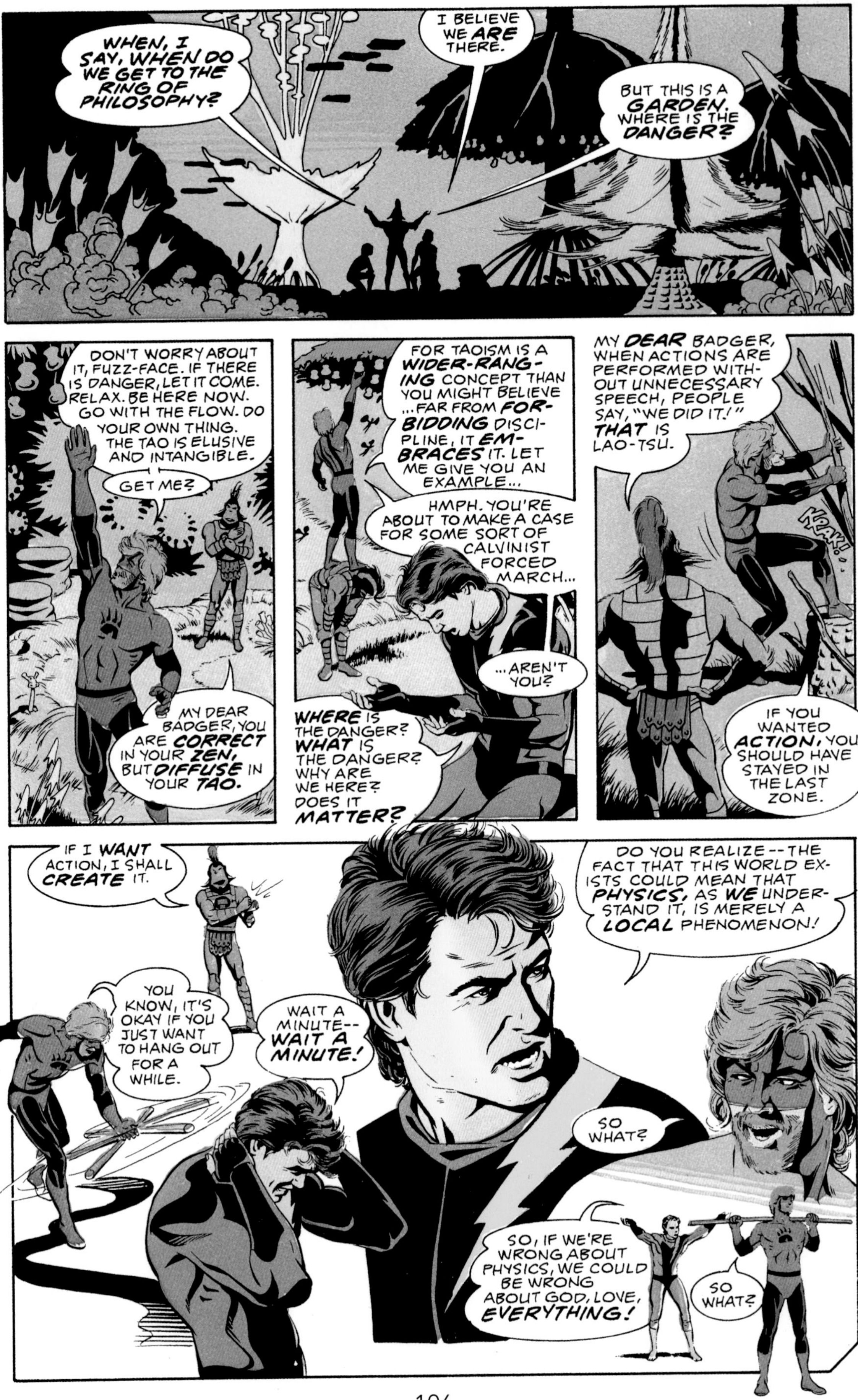

WHEN, I SAY, WHEN DO WE GET TO THE RING OF PHILOSOPHY?
I BELIEVE WE ARE THERE.
BUT THIS IS A GARDEN. WHERE IS THE DANGER?
DON'T WORRY ABOUT IT, FUZZ-FACE. IF THERE IS DANGER, LET IT COME. RELAX. BE HERE NOW. GO WITH THE FLOW. DO YOUR OWN THING. THE TAO IS ELUSIVE AND INTANGIBLE.
GET ME?
MY DEAR BADGER, YOU ARE CORRECT IN YOUR ZEN, BUT DIFFUSE IN YOUR TAO.
FOR TAOISM IS A WIDER-RANGING CONCEPT THAN YOU MIGHT BELIEVE ...FAR FROM FORBIDDING DISCIPLINE, IT EMBRACES IT. LET ME GIVE YOU AN EXAMPLE...
HMPH. YOU'RE ABOUT TO MAKE A CASE FOR SOME SORT OF CALVINIST FORCED MARCH...
...AREN'T YOU?
WHERE IS THE DANGER? WHAT IS THE DANGER? WHY ARE WE HERE? DOES IT MATTER?
MY DEAR BADGER, WHEN ACTIONS ARE PERFORMED WITHOUT UNNECESSARY SPEECH, PEOPLE SAY, "WE DID IT!" THAT IS LAO-TSU.
KRAK!
IF YOU WANTED ACTION, YOU SHOULD HAVE STAYED IN THE LAST ZONE.
IF I WANT ACTION, I SHALL CREATE IT.
YOU KNOW, IT'S OKAY IF YOU JUST WANT TO HANG OUT FOR A WHILE.
WAIT A MINUTE-- WAIT A MINUTE!
DO YOU REALIZE--THE FACT THAT THIS WORLD EXISTS COULD MEAN THAT PHYSICS, AS WE UNDERSTAND IT, IS MERELY A LOCAL PHENOMENON!
SO WHAT?
SO, IF WE'RE WRONG ABOUT PHYSICS, WE COULD BE WRONG ABOUT GOD, LOVE, EVERYTHING!
SO WHAT?

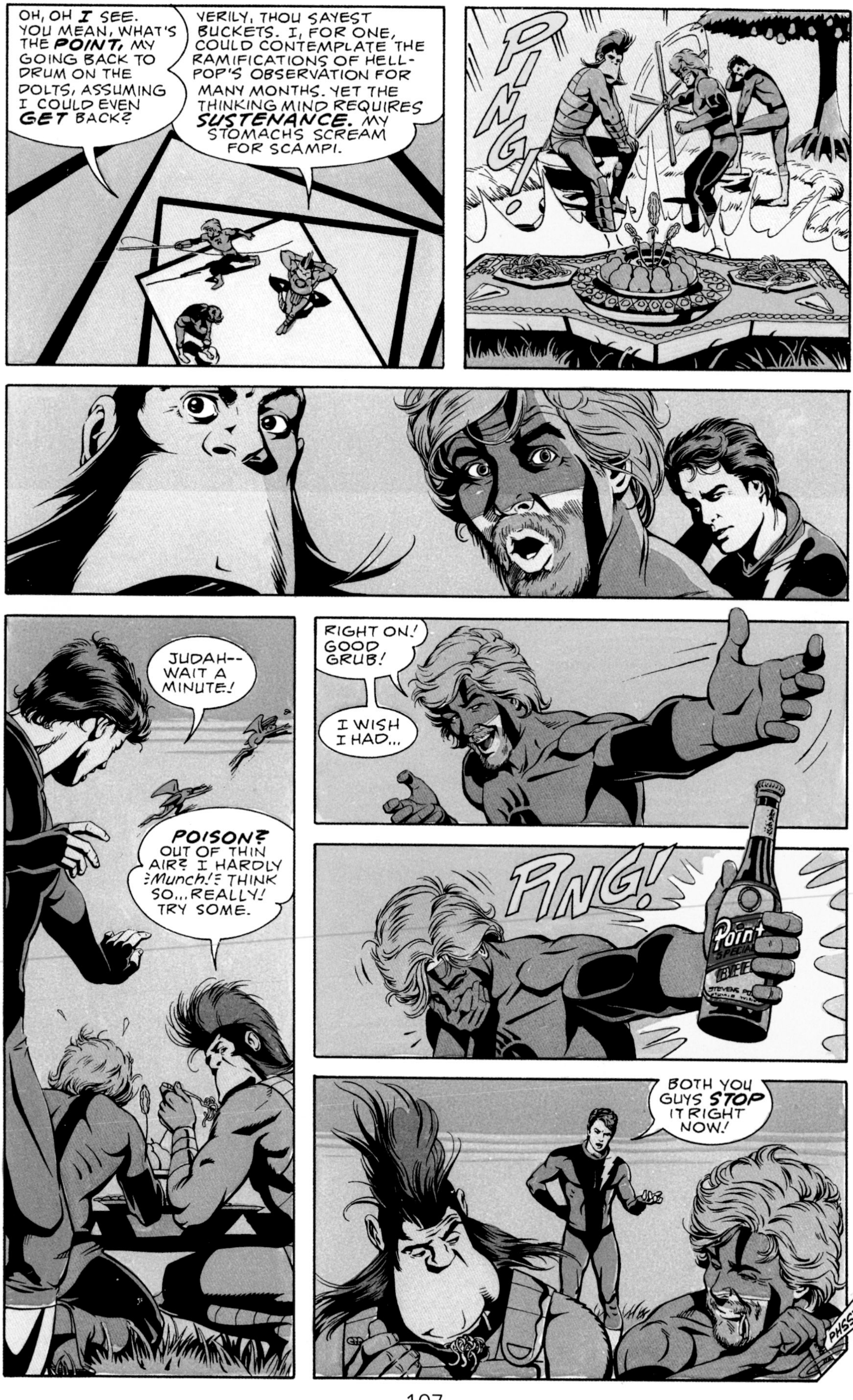
OH, OH **I** SEE. YOU MEAN, WHAT'S THE **POINT,** MY GOING BACK TO DRUM ON THE DOLTS, ASSUMING I COULD EVEN **GET** BACK?
VERILY, THOU SAYEST BUCKETS. I, FOR ONE, COULD CONTEMPLATE THE RAMIFICATIONS OF HELL-POP'S OBSERVATION FOR MANY MONTHS. YET THE THINKING MIND REQUIRES **SUSTENANCE.** MY STOMACHS SCREAM FOR SCAMPI.
PING!
JUDAH-- WAIT A MINUTE!
POISON? OUT OF THIN AIR? I HARDLY *Munch!* THINK SO... REALLY! TRY SOME.
RIGHT ON! GOOD GRUB!
I WISH I HAD...
PING!
Point
SPECIAL
BOTH YOU GUYS **STOP** IT RIGHT NOW!
PHSST

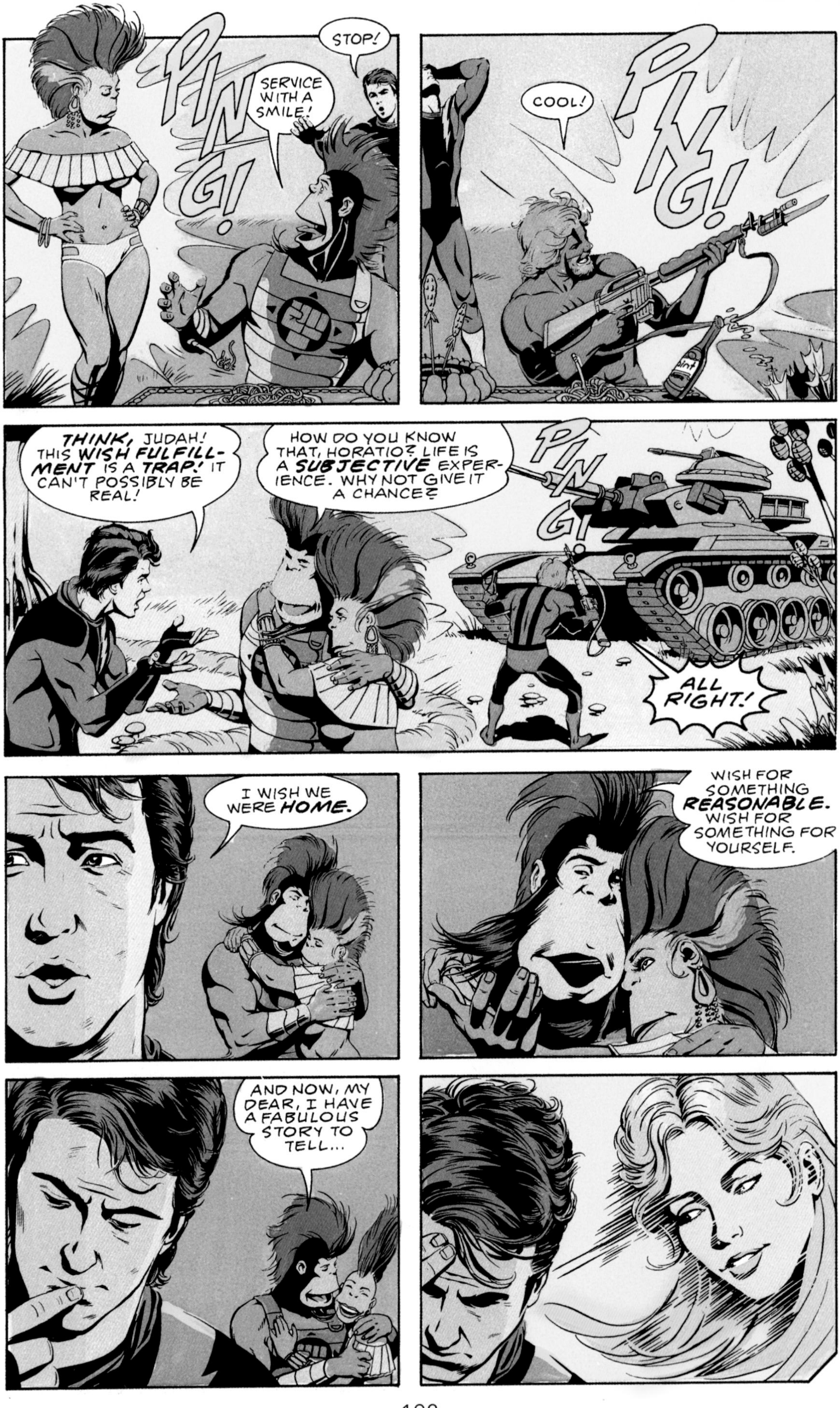

PING!
STOP!
SERVICE WITH A SMILE!
COOL!
PING!
THINK, JUDAH! THIS WISH FULFILL-MENT IS A TRAP! IT CAN'T POSSIBLY BE REAL!
HOW DO YOU KNOW THAT, HORATIO? LIFE IS A SUBJECTIVE EXPER-IENCE. WHY NOT GIVE IT A CHANCE?
PING!
ALL RIGHT!
I WISH WE WERE HOME.
WISH FOR SOMETHING REASONABLE. WISH FOR SOMETHING FOR YOURSELF.
AND NOW, MY DEAR, I HAVE A FABULOUS STORY TO TELL...

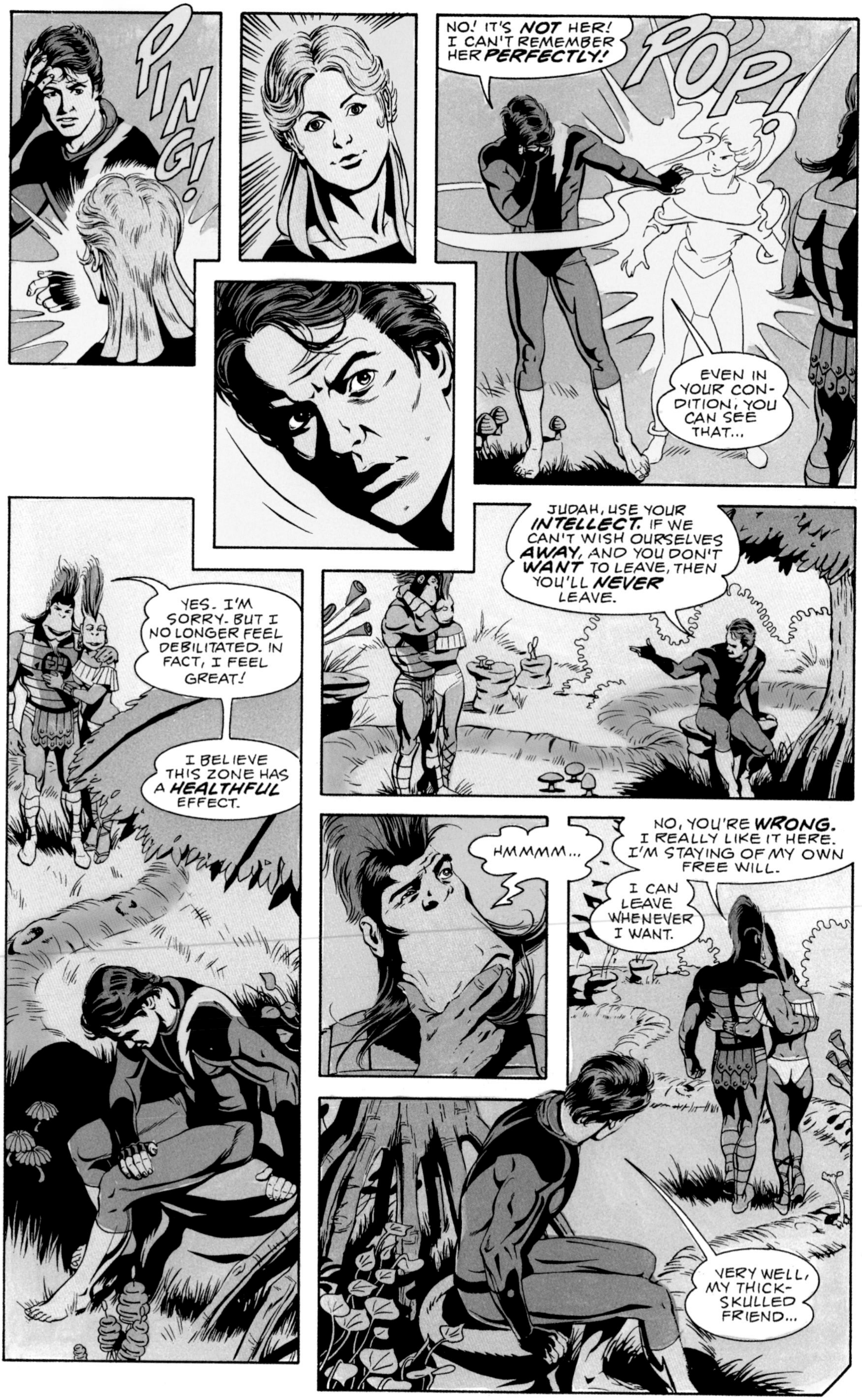
PING!
NO! IT'S NOT HER! I CAN'T REMEMBER HER PERFECTLY!
POP!
EVEN IN YOUR CONDITION, YOU CAN SEE THAT...
YES. I'M SORRY. BUT I NO LONGER FEEL DEBILITATED. IN FACT, I FEEL GREAT!
I BELIEVE THIS ZONE HAS A HEALTHFUL EFFECT.
JUDAH, USE YOUR INTELLECT. IF WE CAN'T WISH OURSELVES AWAY, AND YOU DON'T WANT TO LEAVE, THEN YOU'LL NEVER LEAVE.
HMMMM...
NO, YOU'RE WRONG. I REALLY LIKE IT HERE. I'M STAYING OF MY OWN FREE WILL.
I CAN LEAVE WHENEVER I WANT.
VERY WELL, MY THICK-SKULLED FRIEND...

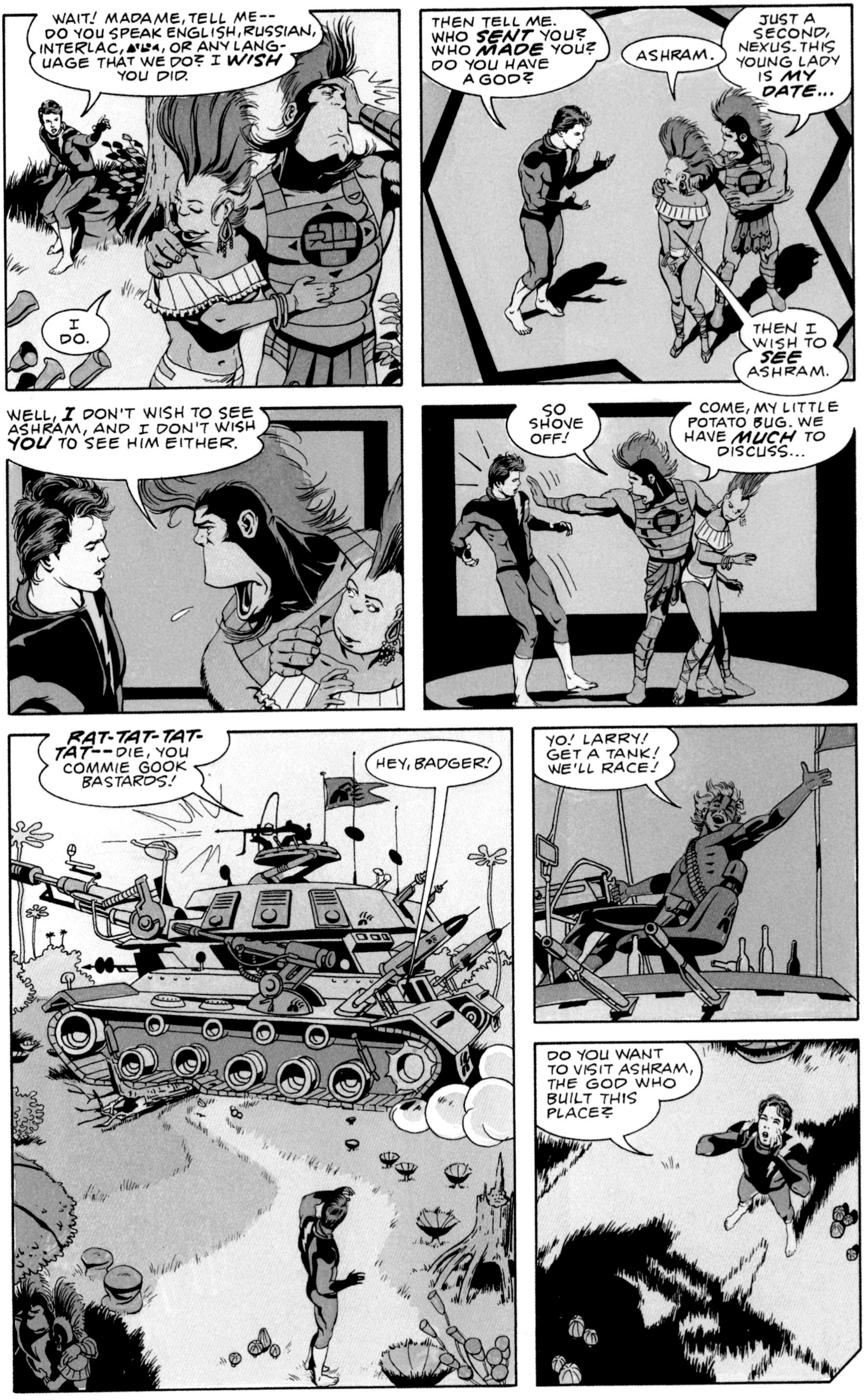
WAIT! MADAME, TELL ME-- DO YOU SPEAK ENGLISH, RUSSIAN, INTERLAC, OR ANY LANGUAGE THAT WE DO? I WISH YOU DID.
I DO.
THEN TELL ME. WHO SENT YOU? WHO MADE YOU? DO YOU HAVE A GOD?
ASHRAM.
JUST A SECOND, NEXUS. THIS YOUNG LADY IS MY DATE...
THEN I WISH TO SEE ASHRAM.
WELL, I DON'T WISH TO SEE ASHRAM, AND I DON'T WISH YOU TO SEE HIM EITHER.
SO SHOVE OFF!
COME, MY LITTLE POTATO BUG. WE HAVE MUCH TO DISCUSS...
RAT-TAT-TAT-TAT--DIE, YOU COMMIE GOOK BASTARDS!
HEY, BADGER!
YO! LARRY! GET A TANK! WE'LL RACE!
DO YOU WANT TO VISIT ASHRAM, THE GOD WHO BUILT THIS PLACE?

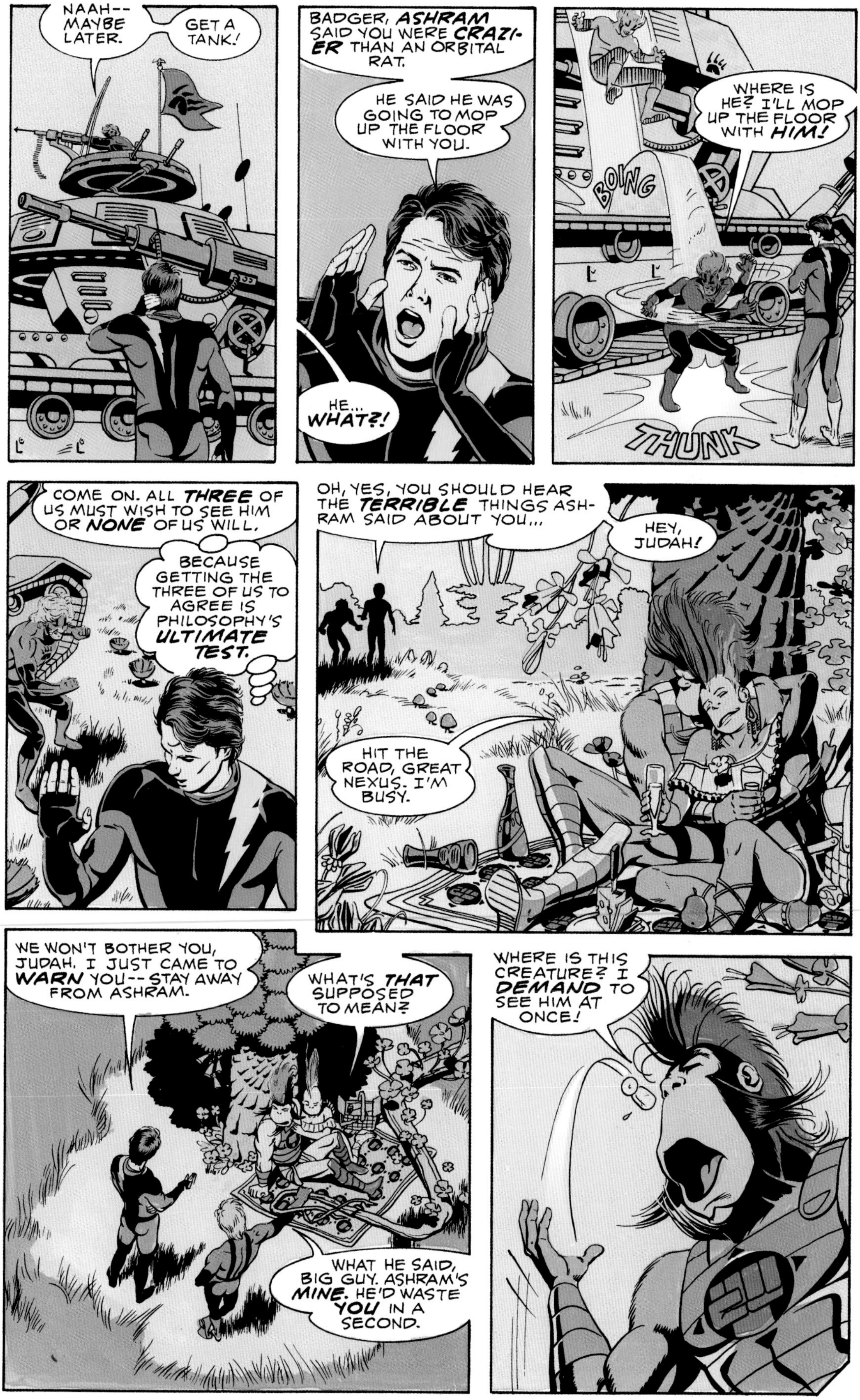
NAAH-- MAYBE LATER.
GET A TANK!
BADGER, ASHRAM SAID YOU WERE CRAZIER THAN AN ORBITAL RAT.
HE SAID HE WAS GOING TO MOP UP THE FLOOR WITH YOU.
HE... WHAT?!
BOING
WHERE IS HE? I'LL MOP UP THE FLOOR WITH HIM!
THUNK
COME ON. ALL THREE OF US MUST WISH TO SEE HIM OR NONE OF US WILL.
BECAUSE GETTING THE THREE OF US TO AGREE IS PHILOSOPHY'S ULTIMATE TEST.
OH, YES, YOU SHOULD HEAR THE TERRIBLE THINGS ASHRAM SAID ABOUT YOU...
HEY, JUDAH!
HIT THE ROAD, GREAT NEXUS. I'M BUSY.
WE WON'T BOTHER YOU, JUDAH. I JUST CAME TO WARN YOU-- STAY AWAY FROM ASHRAM.
WHAT'S THAT SUPPOSED TO MEAN?
WHAT HE SAID, BIG GUY. ASHRAM'S MINE. HE'D WASTE YOU IN A SECOND.
WHERE IS THIS CREATURE? I DEMAND TO SEE HIM AT ONCE!

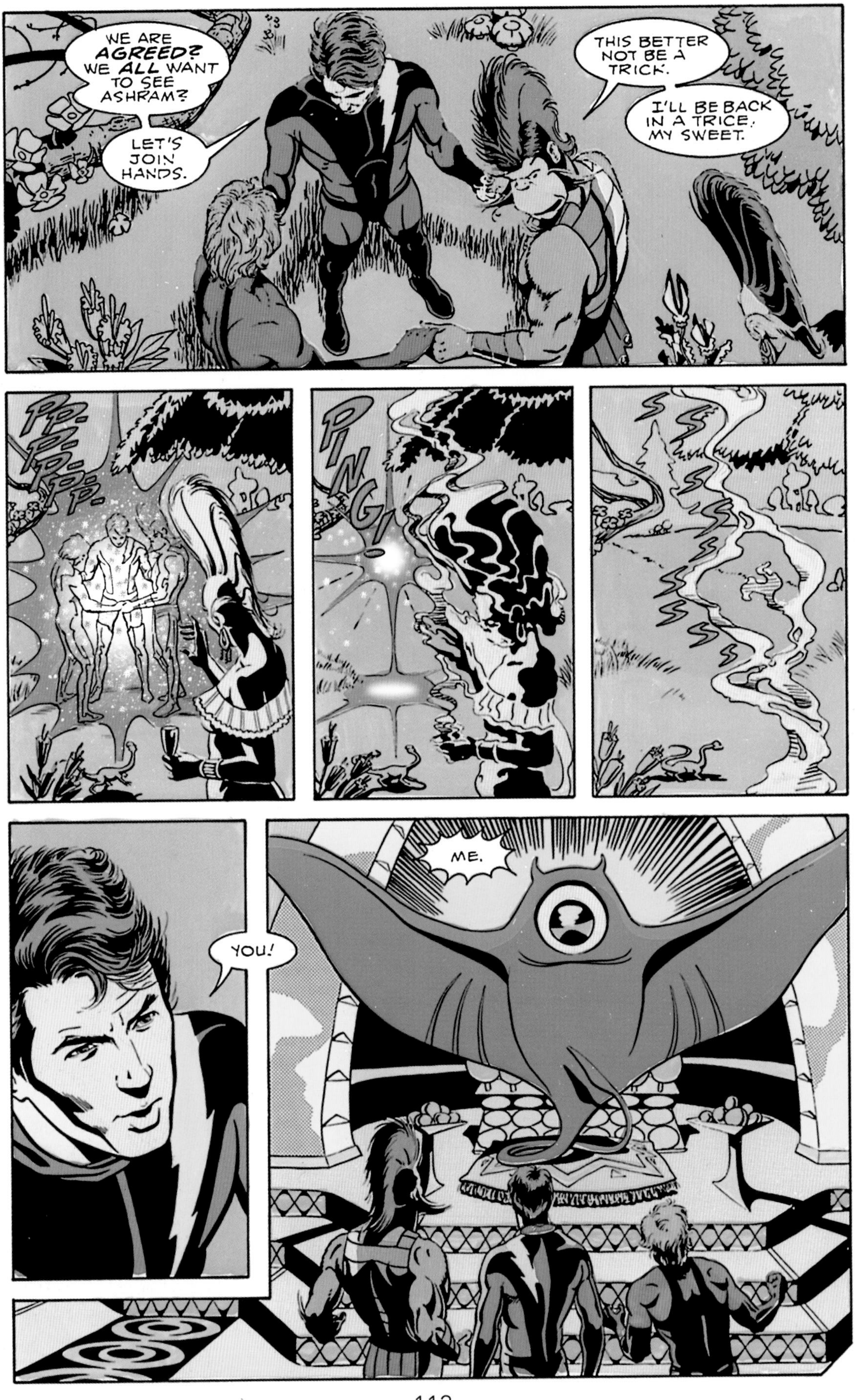

WE ARE AGREED? WE ALL WANT TO SEE ASHRAM?
LET'S JOIN HANDS.
THIS BETTER NOT BE A TRICK.
I'LL BE BACK IN A TRICE, MY SWEET.
PP-P-P-P-
PING!
SSSSSSS
ME.
YOU!

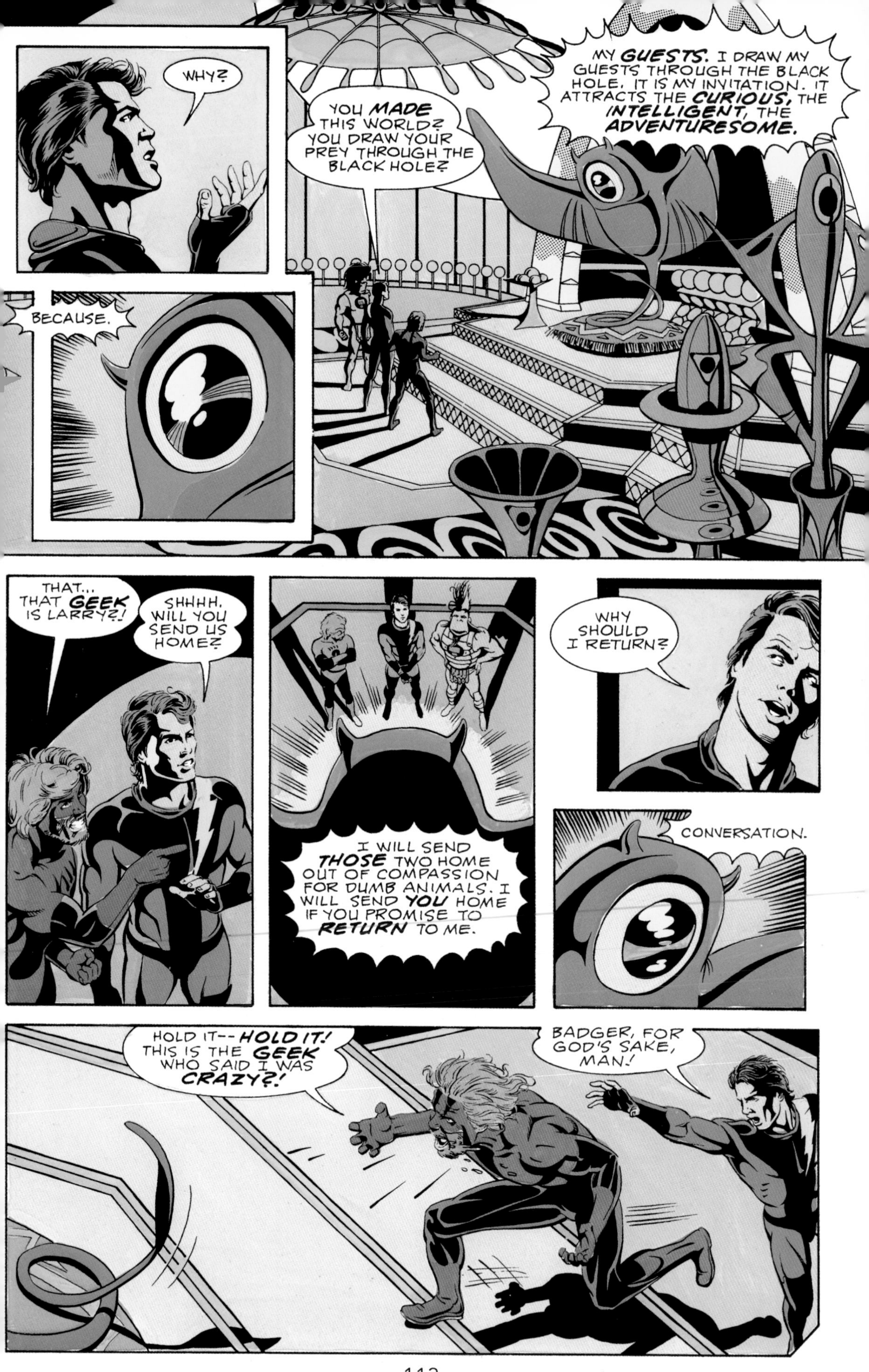
WHY?
YOU MADE THIS WORLD? YOU DRAW YOUR PREY THROUGH THE BLACK HOLE?
MY GUESTS. I DRAW MY GUESTS THROUGH THE BLACK HOLE. IT IS MY INVITATION. IT ATTRACTS THE CURIOUS, THE INTELLIGENT, THE ADVENTURESOME.
BECAUSE.
THAT... THAT GEEK IS LARRY?!
SHHHH. WILL YOU SEND US HOME?
I WILL SEND THOSE TWO HOME OUT OF COMPASSION FOR DUMB ANIMALS. I WILL SEND YOU HOME IF YOU PROMISE TO RETURN TO ME.
WHY SHOULD I RETURN?
CONVERSATION.
HOLD IT-- HOLD IT! THIS IS THE GEEK WHO SAID I WAS CRAZY?!
BADGER, FOR GOD'S SAKE, MAN!

EEEEE-YAA
SWOOOOOSHH
PING!
AND US?
THROUGH THE ARCH, DOWN THE STAIRS, THIRD DOOR ON THE LEFT.

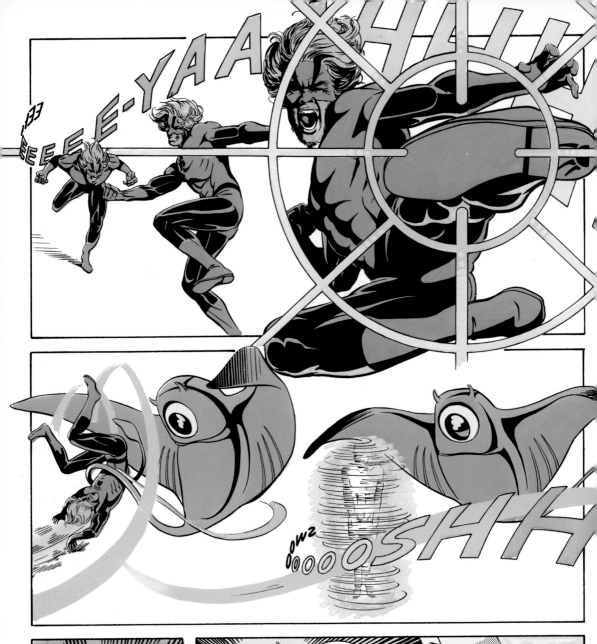

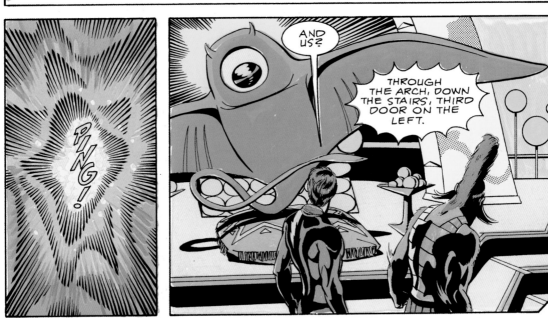

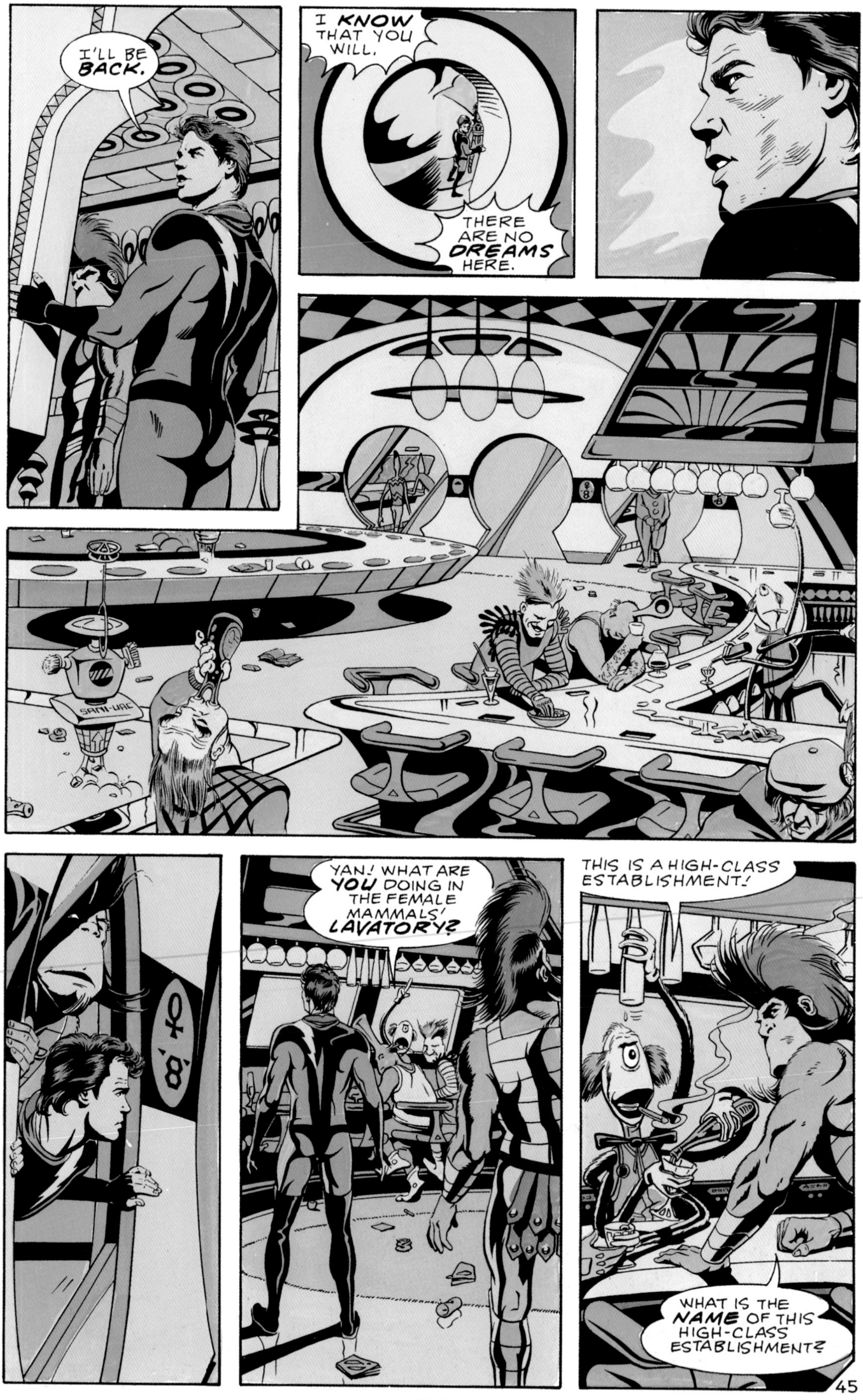
I'LL BE BACK.
I KNOW THAT YOU WILL.
THERE ARE NO DREAMS HERE.
SANI-VAC
YAN! WHAT ARE YOU DOING IN THE FEMALE MAMMALS' LAVATORY?
THIS IS A HIGH-CLASS ESTABLISHMENT!
WHAT IS THE NAME OF THIS HIGH-CLASS ESTABLISHMENT?
45

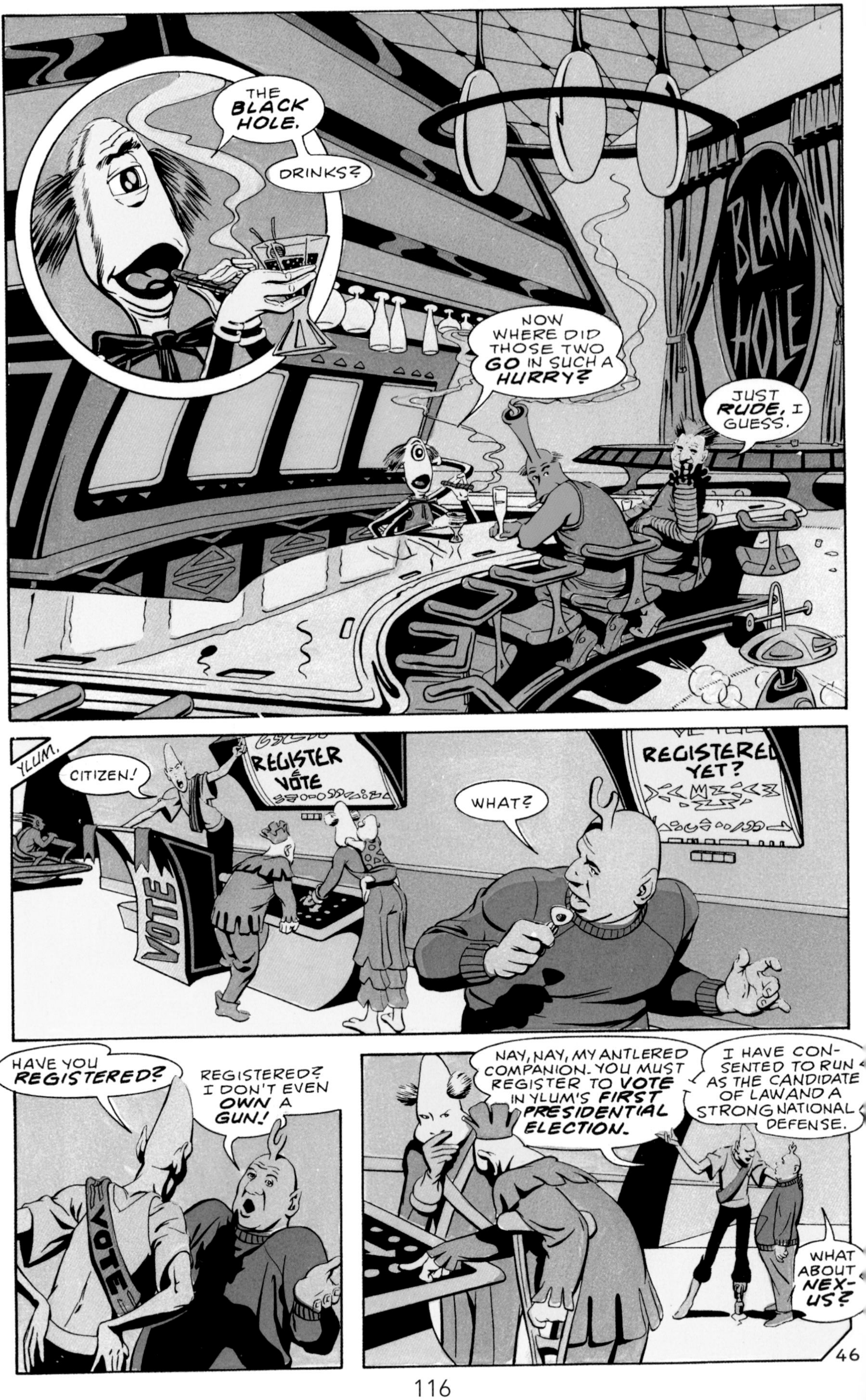
THE BLACK HOLE.
DRINKS?
BLACK HOLE
NOW WHERE DID THOSE TWO GO IN SUCH A HURRY?
JUST RUDE, I GUESS.
YLUM.
CITIZEN!
REGISTER & VOTE
WHAT?
REGISTERED YET?
VOTE
HAVE YOU REGISTERED?
REGISTERED? I DON'T EVEN OWN A GUN!
VOTE
NAY, NAY, MY ANTLERED COMPANION. YOU MUST REGISTER TO VOTE IN YLUM'S FIRST PRESIDENTIAL ELECTION.
I HAVE CON-SENTED TO RUN AS THE CANDIDATE OF LAW AND A STRONG NATIONAL DEFENSE.
WHAT ABOUT NEX-US?
46

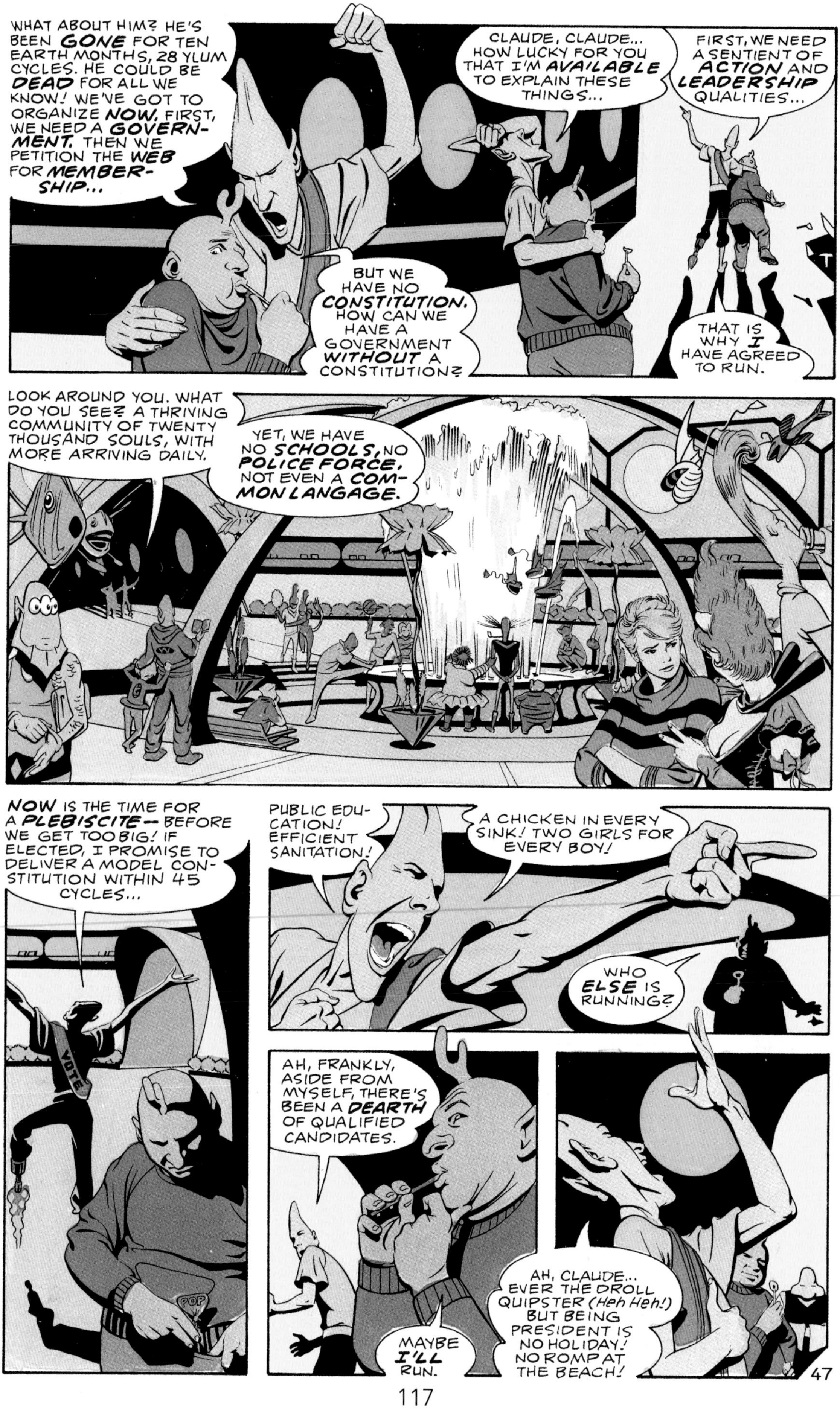
WHAT ABOUT HIM? HE'S BEEN GONE FOR TEN EARTH MONTHS, 28 YLUM CYCLES. HE COULD BE DEAD FOR ALL WE KNOW! WE'VE GOT TO ORGANIZE NOW. FIRST, WE NEED A GOVERNMENT. THEN WE PETITION THE WEB FOR MEMBERSHIP...
BUT WE HAVE NO CONSTITUTION. HOW CAN WE HAVE A GOVERNMENT WITHOUT A CONSTITUTION?
CLAUDE, CLAUDE... HOW LUCKY FOR YOU THAT I'M AVAILABLE TO EXPLAIN THESE THINGS...
FIRST, WE NEED A SENTIENT OF ACTION AND LEADERSHIP QUALITIES...
THAT IS WHY I HAVE AGREED TO RUN.
LOOK AROUND YOU. WHAT DO YOU SEE? A THRIVING COMMUNITY OF TWENTY THOUSAND SOULS, WITH MORE ARRIVING DAILY.
YET, WE HAVE NO SCHOOLS, NO POLICE FORCE, NOT EVEN A COMMON LANGAGE.
NOW IS THE TIME FOR A PLEBISCITE-- BEFORE WE GET TOO BIG! IF ELECTED, I PROMISE TO DELIVER A MODEL CONSTITUTION WITHIN 45 CYCLES...
VOTE
POP
PUBLIC EDUCATION! EFFICIENT SANITATION!
A CHICKEN IN EVERY SINK! TWO GIRLS FOR EVERY BOY!
WHO ELSE IS RUNNING?
AH, FRANKLY, ASIDE FROM MYSELF, THERE'S BEEN A DEARTH OF QUALIFIED CANDIDATES.
MAYBE I'LL RUN.
AH, CLAUDE... EVER THE DROLL QUIPSTER (Heh Heh!) BUT BEING PRESIDENT IS NO HOLIDAY! NO ROMP AT THE BEACH!
47

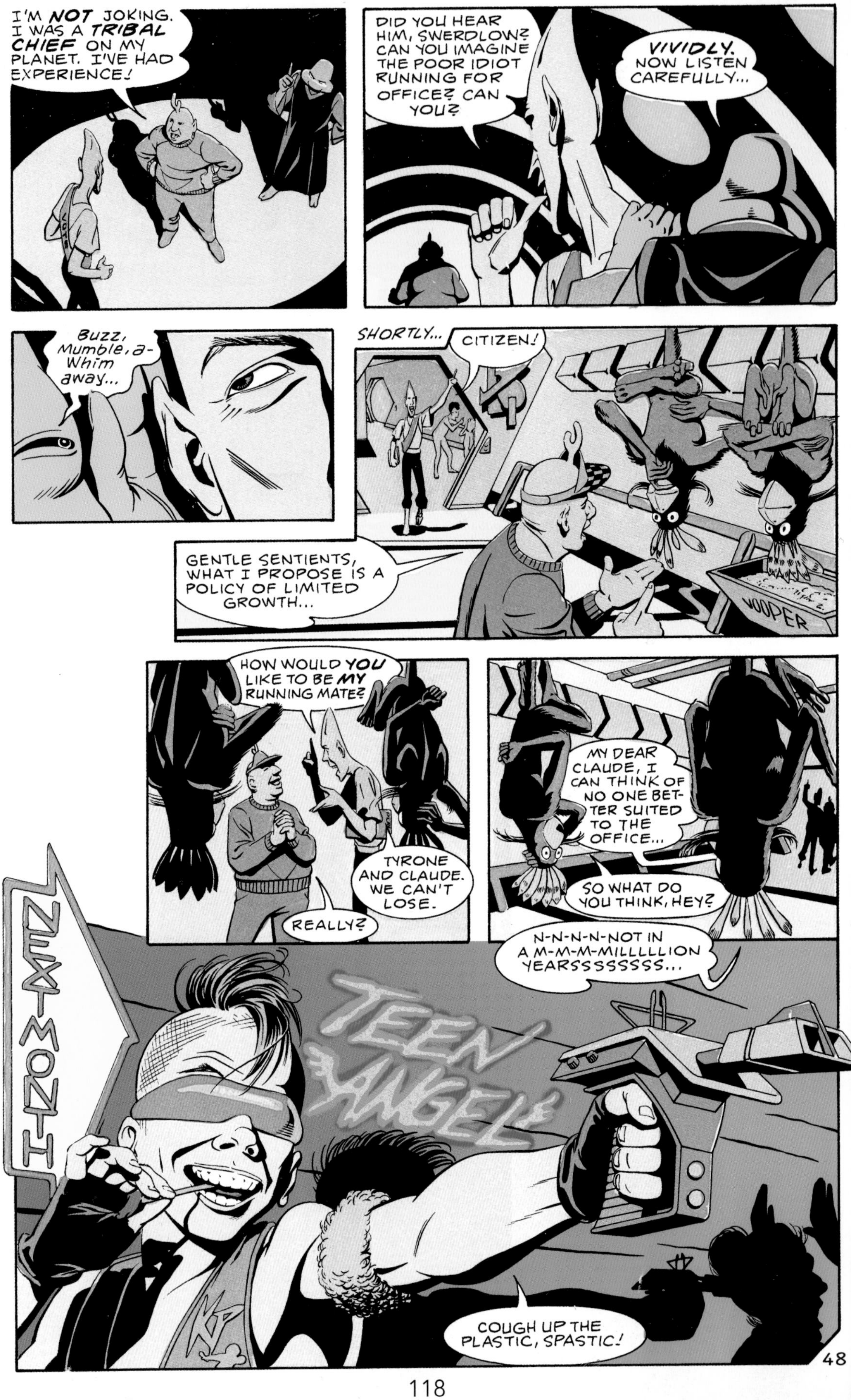
I'M NOT JOKING. I WAS A TRIBAL CHIEF ON MY PLANET. I'VE HAD EXPERIENCE!
DID YOU HEAR HIM, SWERDLOW? CAN YOU IMAGINE THE POOR IDIOT RUNNING FOR OFFICE? CAN YOU?
VIVIDLY. NOW LISTEN CAREFULLY...
Buzz, Mumble, a-Whim away...
SHORTLY...
CITIZEN!
GENTLE SENTIENTS, WHAT I PROPOSE IS A POLICY OF LIMITED GROWTH...
VOOPER
HOW WOULD YOU LIKE TO BE MY RUNNING MATE?
TYRONE AND CLAUDE. WE CAN'T LOSE.
REALLY?
MY DEAR CLAUDE, I CAN THINK OF NO ONE BETTER SUITED TO THE OFFICE...
SO WHAT DO YOU THINK, HEY?
N-N-N-N-NOT IN A M-M-M-MILLLLLION YEARSSSSSSSS...
NEXT MONTH
TEEN ANGELS
COUGH UP THE PLASTIC, SPASTIC!
48

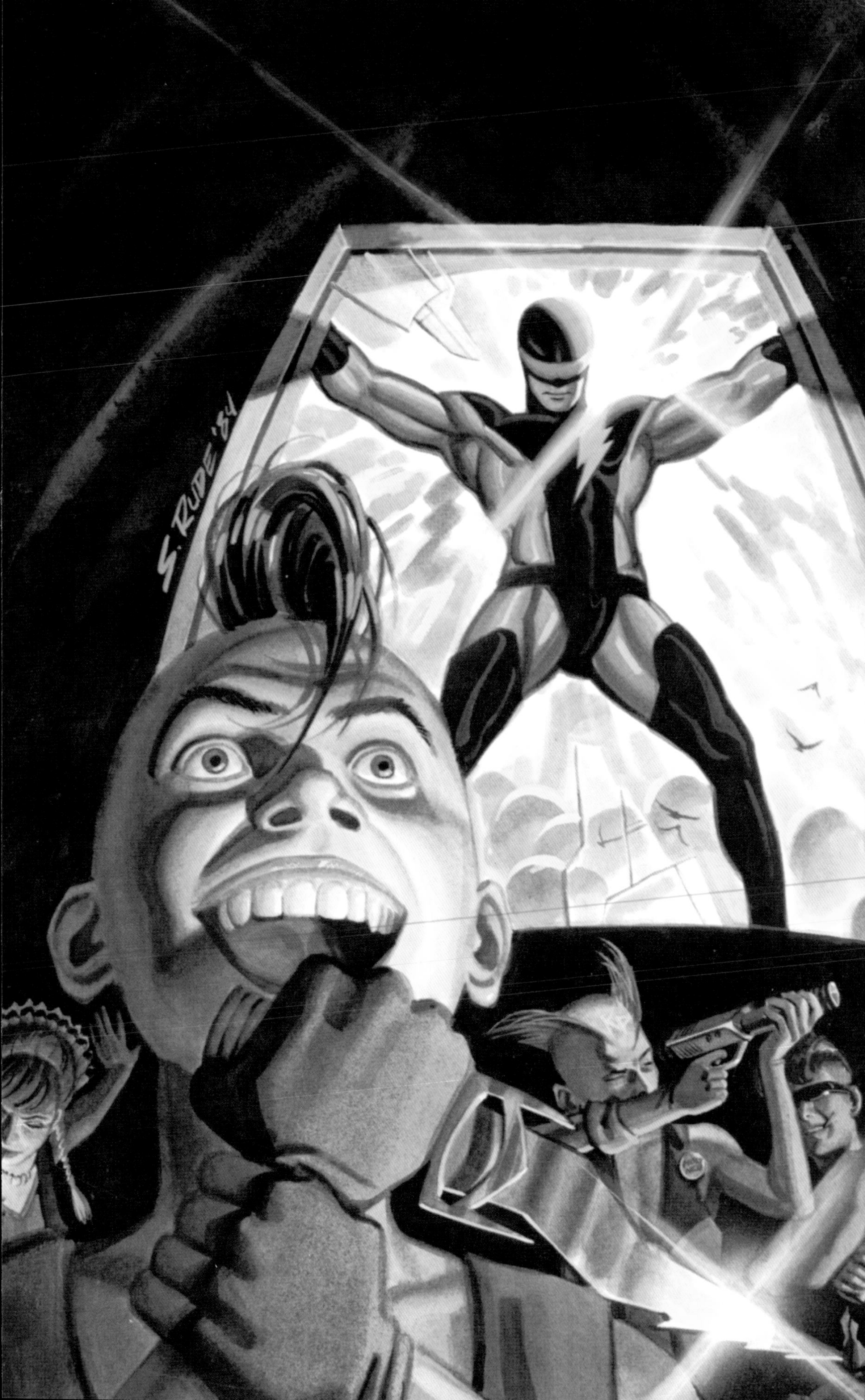
S. RUDE '84

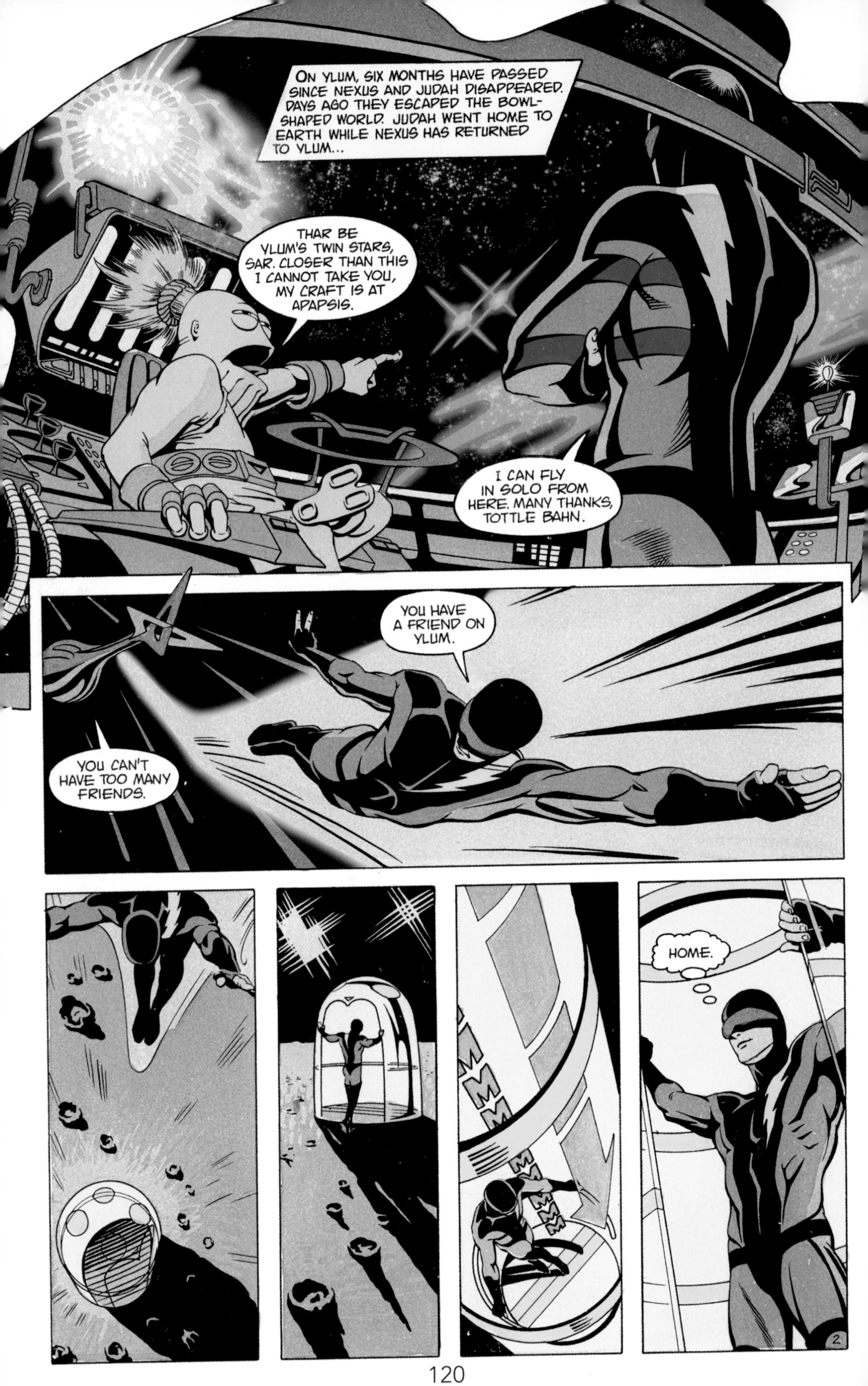
ON YLUM, SIX MONTHS HAVE PASSED SINCE NEXUS AND JUDAH DISAPPEARED. DAYS AGO THEY ESCAPED THE BOWL-SHAPED WORLD. JUDAH WENT HOME TO EARTH WHILE NEXUS HAS RETURNED TO YLUM...
THAR BE YLUM'S TWIN STARS, SAR. CLOSER THAN THIS I CANNOT TAKE YOU, MY CRAFT IS AT APAPSIS.
I CAN FLY IN SOLO FROM HERE. MANY THANKS, TOTTLE BAHN.
YOU HAVE A FRIEND ON YLUM.
YOU CAN'T HAVE TOO MANY FRIENDS.
HOME.

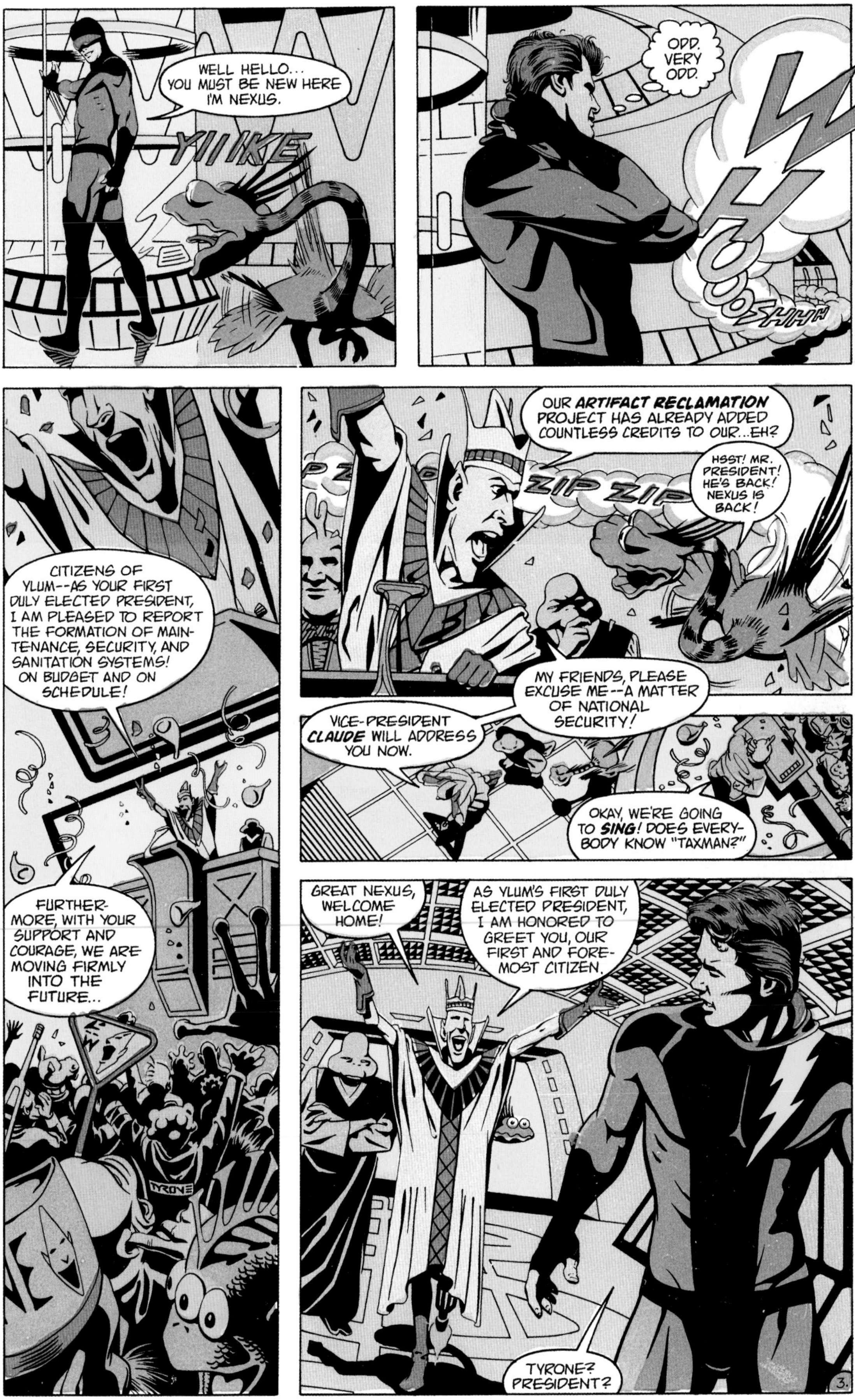
WELL HELLO... YOU MUST BE NEW HERE I'M NEXUS.
YIIIKE
ODD. VERY ODD.
WHOOOSHHH
CITIZENS OF YLUM--AS YOUR FIRST DULY ELECTED PRESIDENT, I AM PLEASED TO REPORT THE FORMATION OF MAINTENANCE, SECURITY, AND SANITATION SYSTEMS! ON BUDGET AND ON SCHEDULE!
FURTHERMORE, WITH YOUR SUPPORT AND COURAGE, WE ARE MOVING FIRMLY INTO THE FUTURE...
TYRONE
OUR ARTIFACT RECLAMATION PROJECT HAS ALREADY ADDED COUNTLESS CREDITS TO OUR...EH?
ZIP ZIP
HSST! MR. PRESIDENT! HE'S BACK! NEXUS IS BACK!
MY FRIENDS, PLEASE EXCUSE ME--A MATTER OF NATIONAL SECURITY!
VICE-PRESIDENT CLAUDE WILL ADDRESS YOU NOW.
OKAY, WE'RE GOING TO SING! DOES EVERYBODY KNOW "TAXMAN?"
GREAT NEXUS, WELCOME HOME!
AS YLUM'S FIRST DULY ELECTED PRESIDENT, I AM HONORED TO GREET YOU, OUR FIRST AND FOREMOST CITIZEN.
TYRONE? PRESIDENT?
3.

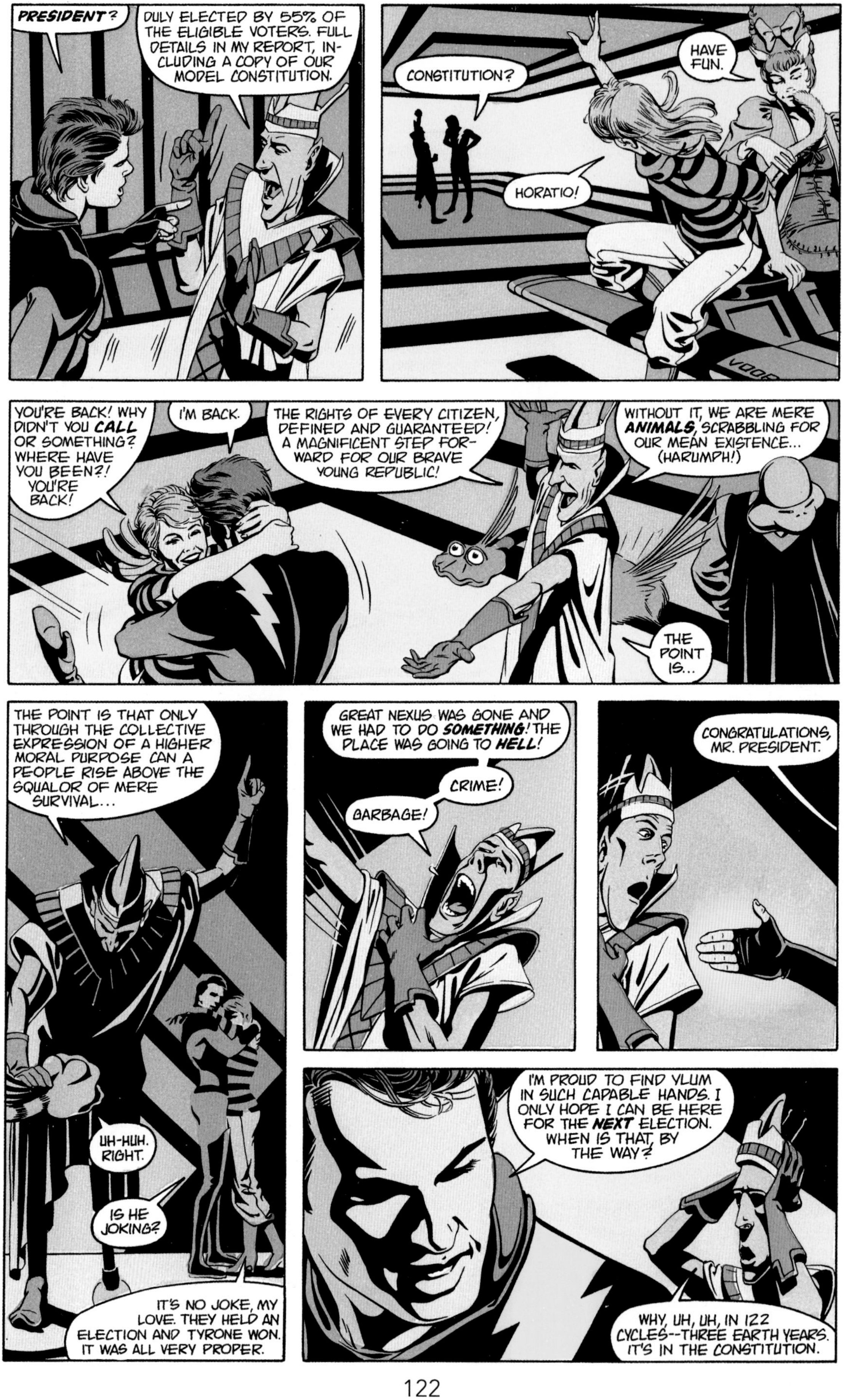
PRESIDENT?
DULY ELECTED BY 55% OF THE ELIGIBLE VOTERS. FULL DETAILS IN MY REPORT, INCLUDING A COPY OF OUR MODEL CONSTITUTION.
CONSTITUTION?
HAVE FUN.
HORATIO!
YOU'RE BACK! WHY DIDN'T YOU CALL OR SOMETHING? WHERE HAVE YOU BEEN?! YOU'RE BACK!
I'M BACK.
THE RIGHTS OF EVERY CITIZEN, DEFINED AND GUARANTEED! A MAGNIFICENT STEP FORWARD FOR OUR BRAVE YOUNG REPUBLIC!
WITHOUT IT, WE ARE MERE ANIMALS, SCRABBLING FOR OUR MEAN EXISTENCE... (HARUMPH!)
THE POINT IS...
THE POINT IS THAT ONLY THROUGH THE COLLECTIVE EXPRESSION OF A HIGHER MORAL PURPOSE CAN A PEOPLE RISE ABOVE THE SQUALOR OF MERE SURVIVAL...
UH-HUH. RIGHT.
IS HE JOKING?
IT'S NO JOKE, MY LOVE. THEY HELD AN ELECTION AND TYRONE WON. IT WAS ALL VERY PROPER.
GREAT NEXUS WAS GONE AND WE HAD TO DO SOMETHING! THE PLACE WAS GOING TO HELL!
CRIME!
GARBAGE!
CONGRATULATIONS, MR. PRESIDENT.
I'M PROUD TO FIND YLUM IN SUCH CAPABLE HANDS. I ONLY HOPE I CAN BE HERE FOR THE NEXT ELECTION. WHEN IS THAT, BY THE WAY?
WHY, UH, UH, IN 122 CYCLES--THREE EARTH YEARS. IT'S IN THE CONSTITUTION.

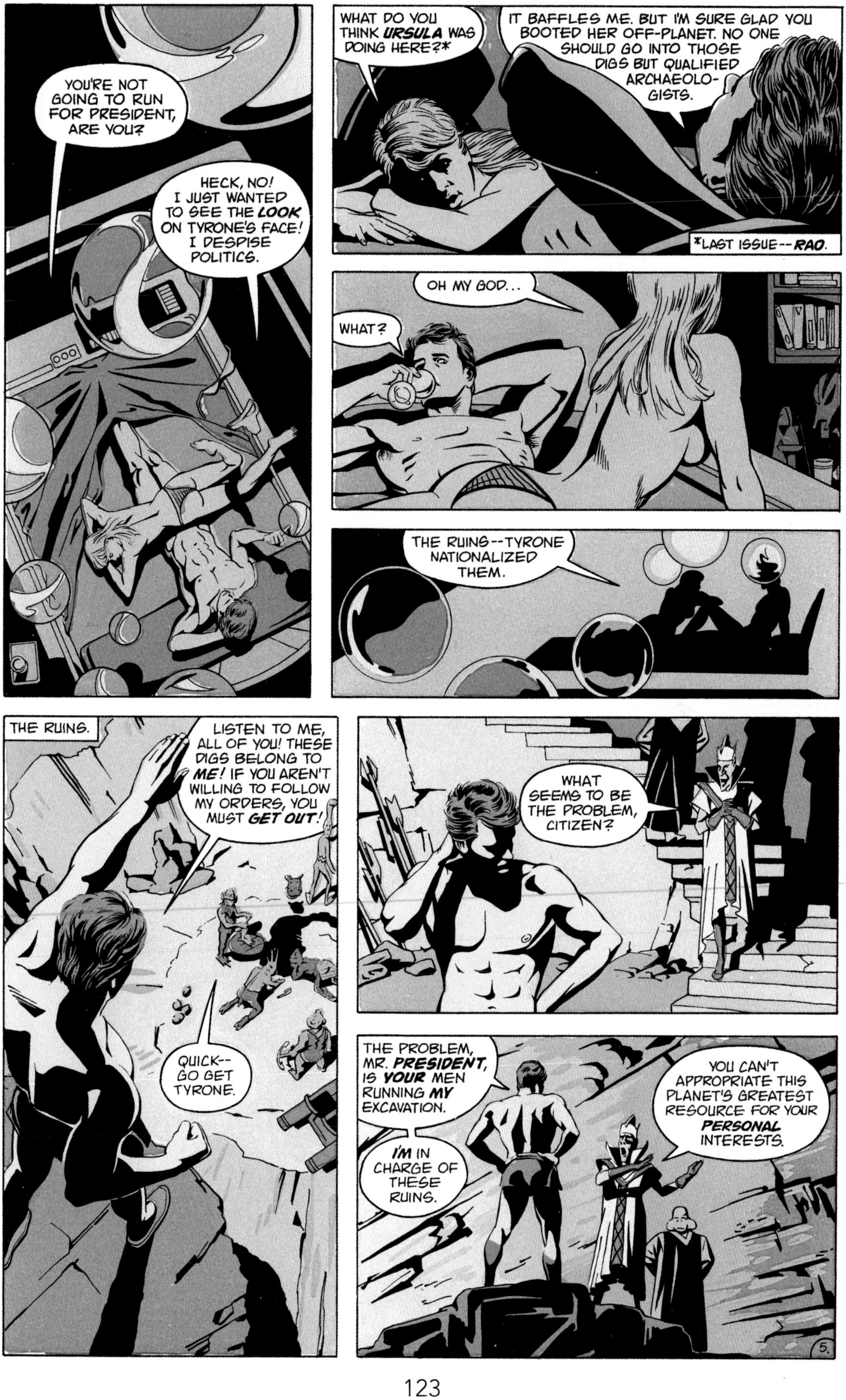
YOU'RE NOT GOING TO RUN FOR PRESIDENT, ARE YOU?
HECK, NO! I JUST WANTED TO SEE THE LOOK ON TYRONE'S FACE! I DESPISE POLITICS.
WHAT DO YOU THINK URSULA WAS DOING HERE?*
IT BAFFLES ME. BUT I'M SURE GLAD YOU BOOTED HER OFF-PLANET. NO ONE SHOULD GO INTO THOSE DIGS BUT QUALIFIED ARCHAEOLOGISTS.
*LAST ISSUE--RAO.
OH MY GOD...
WHAT?
THE RUINS--TYRONE NATIONALIZED THEM.
THE RUINS.
LISTEN TO ME, ALL OF YOU! THESE DIGS BELONG TO ME! IF YOU AREN'T WILLING TO FOLLOW MY ORDERS, YOU MUST GET OUT!
QUICK--GO GET TYRONE.
WHAT SEEMS TO BE THE PROBLEM, CITIZEN?
THE PROBLEM, MR. PRESIDENT, IS YOUR MEN RUNNING MY EXCAVATION.
YOU CAN'T APPROPRIATE THIS PLANET'S GREATEST RESOURCE FOR YOUR PERSONAL INTERESTS.
I'M IN CHARGE OF THESE RUINS.
5.

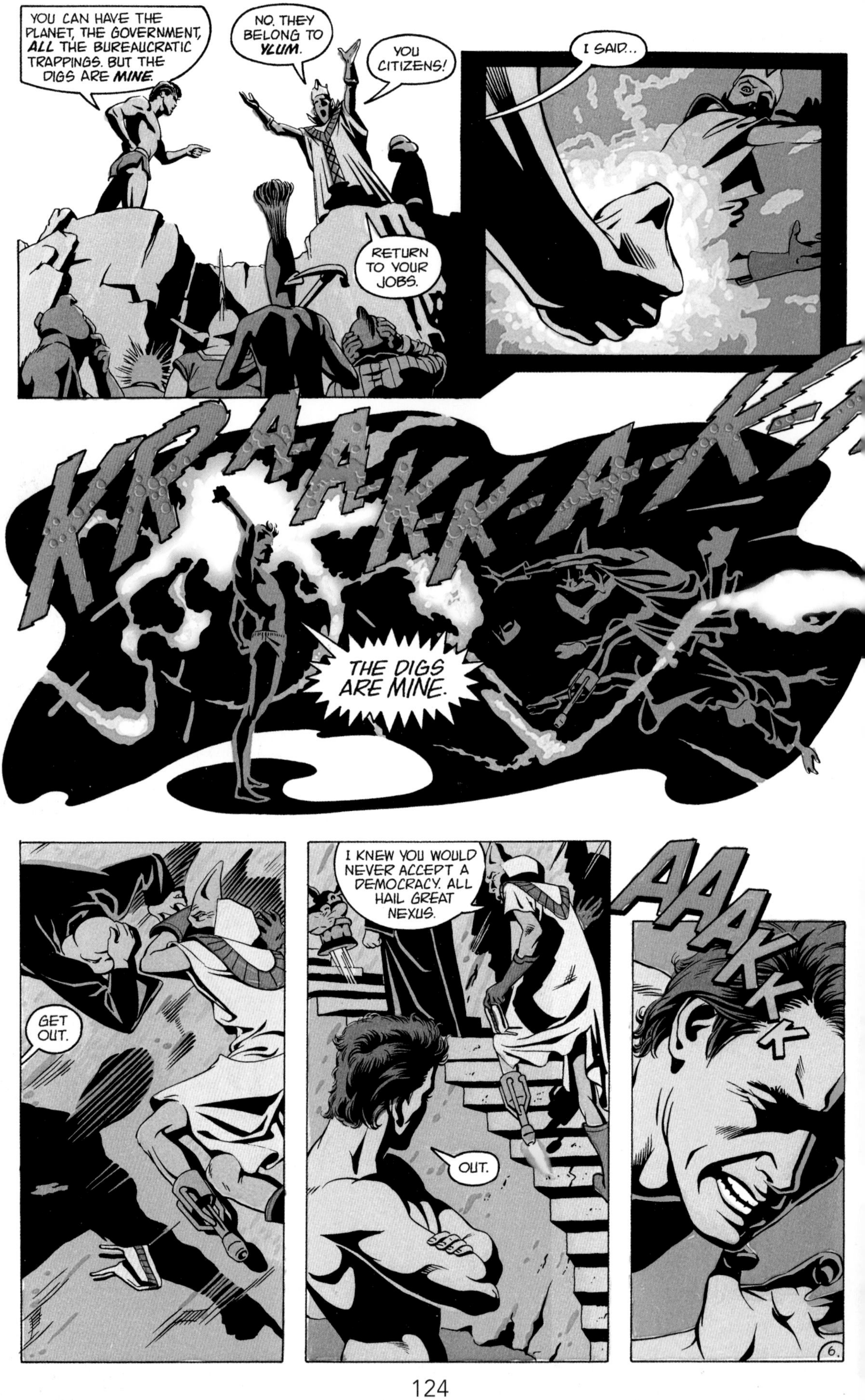
YOU CAN HAVE THE PLANET, THE GOVERNMENT, ALL THE BUREAUCRATIC TRAPPINGS. BUT THE DIGS ARE MINE.
NO. THEY BELONG TO YLUM.
YOU CITIZENS!
RETURN TO YOUR JOBS.
I SAID...
KRAAKK-AAK-KK
THE DIGS ARE MINE.
GET OUT.
I KNEW YOU WOULD NEVER ACCEPT A DEMOCRACY. ALL HAIL GREAT NEXUS.
OUT.
AAAKKK
6.

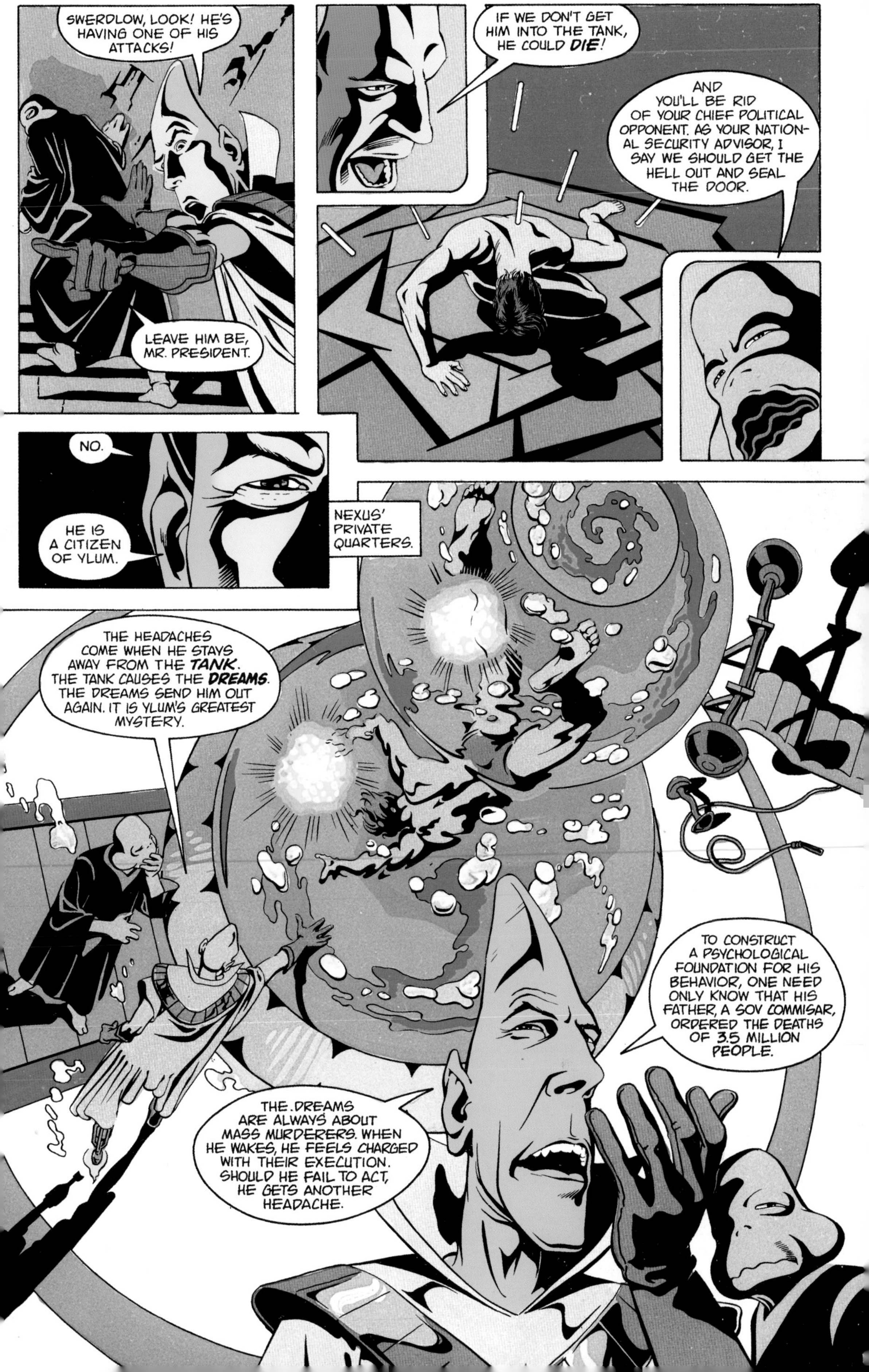
SWERDLOW, LOOK! HE'S HAVING ONE OF HIS ATTACKS!
LEAVE HIM BE, MR. PRESIDENT.
IF WE DON'T GET HIM INTO THE TANK, HE COULD DIE!
AND YOU'LL BE RID OF YOUR CHIEF POLITICAL OPPONENT. AS YOUR NATIONAL SECURITY ADVISOR, I SAY WE SHOULD GET THE HELL OUT AND SEAL THE DOOR.
NO.
HE IS A CITIZEN OF YLUM.
NEXUS' PRIVATE QUARTERS.
THE HEADACHES COME WHEN HE STAYS AWAY FROM THE TANK. THE TANK CAUSES THE DREAMS. THE DREAMS SEND HIM OUT AGAIN. IT IS YLUM'S GREATEST MYSTERY.
TO CONSTRUCT A PSYCHOLOGICAL FOUNDATION FOR HIS BEHAVIOR, ONE NEED ONLY KNOW THAT HIS FATHER, A SOV COMMISAR, ORDERED THE DEATHS OF 3.5 MILLION PEOPLE.
THE DREAMS ARE ALWAYS ABOUT MASS MURDERERS. WHEN HE WAKES, HE FEELS CHARGED WITH THEIR EXECUTION. SHOULD HE FAIL TO ACT, HE GETS ANOTHER HEADACHE.

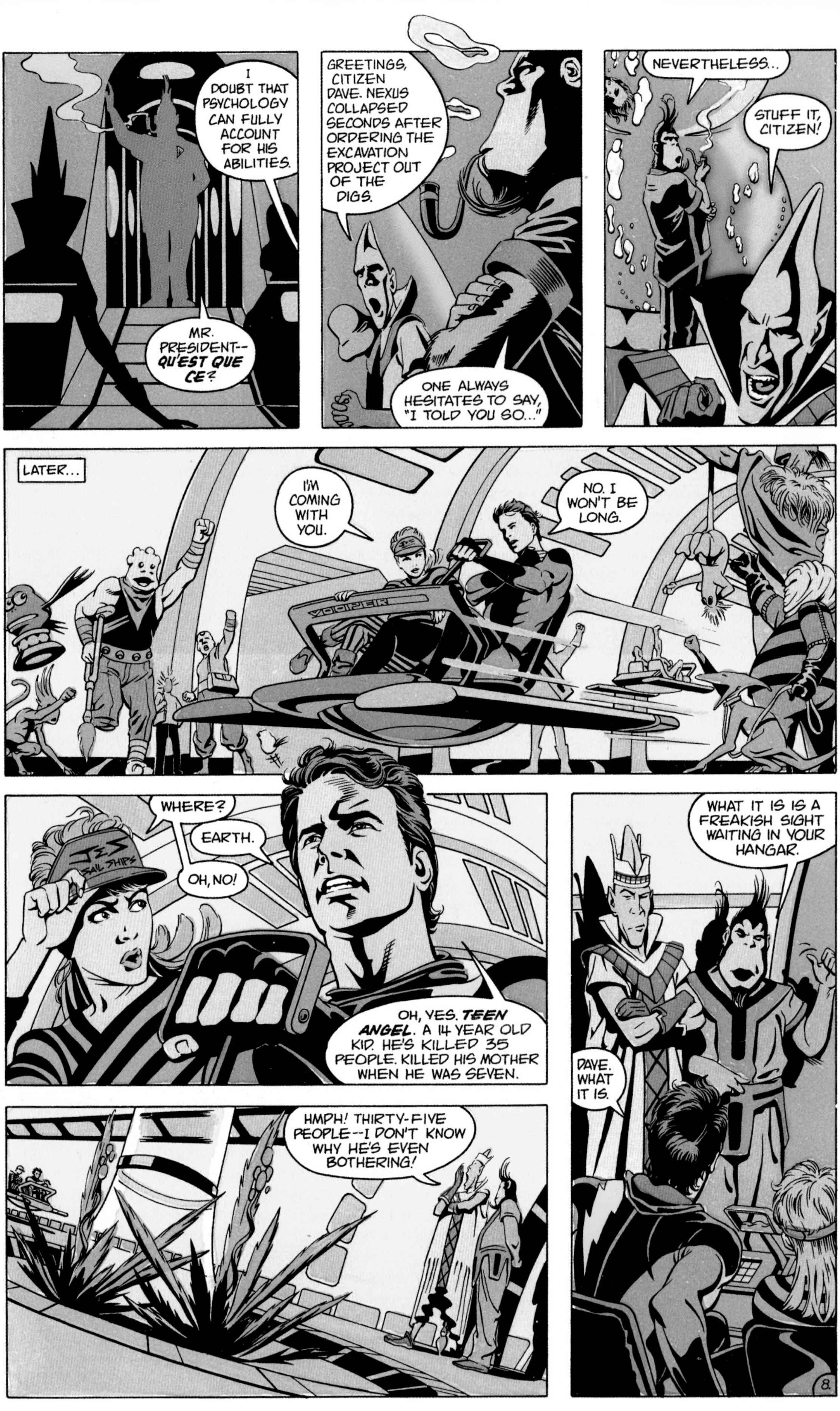
I DOUBT THAT PSYCHOLOGY CAN FULLY ACCOUNT FOR HIS ABILITIES.
MR. PRESIDENT-- QU'EST QUE CE?
GREETINGS, CITIZEN DAVE. NEXUS COLLAPSED SECONDS AFTER ORDERING THE EXCAVATION PROJECT OUT OF THE DIGS.
ONE ALWAYS HESITATES TO SAY, "I TOLD YOU SO..."
NEVERTHELESS...
STUFF IT, CITIZEN!
LATER...
I'M COMING WITH YOU.
NO. I WON'T BE LONG.
WHERE?
EARTH.
OH, NO!
OH, YES. TEEN ANGEL. A 14 YEAR OLD KID. HE'S KILLED 35 PEOPLE. KILLED HIS MOTHER WHEN HE WAS SEVEN.
HMPH! THIRTY-FIVE PEOPLE--I DON'T KNOW WHY HE'S EVEN BOTHERING!
WHAT IT IS IS A FREAKISH SIGHT WAITING IN YOUR HANGAR.
DAVE. WHAT IT IS.
8.

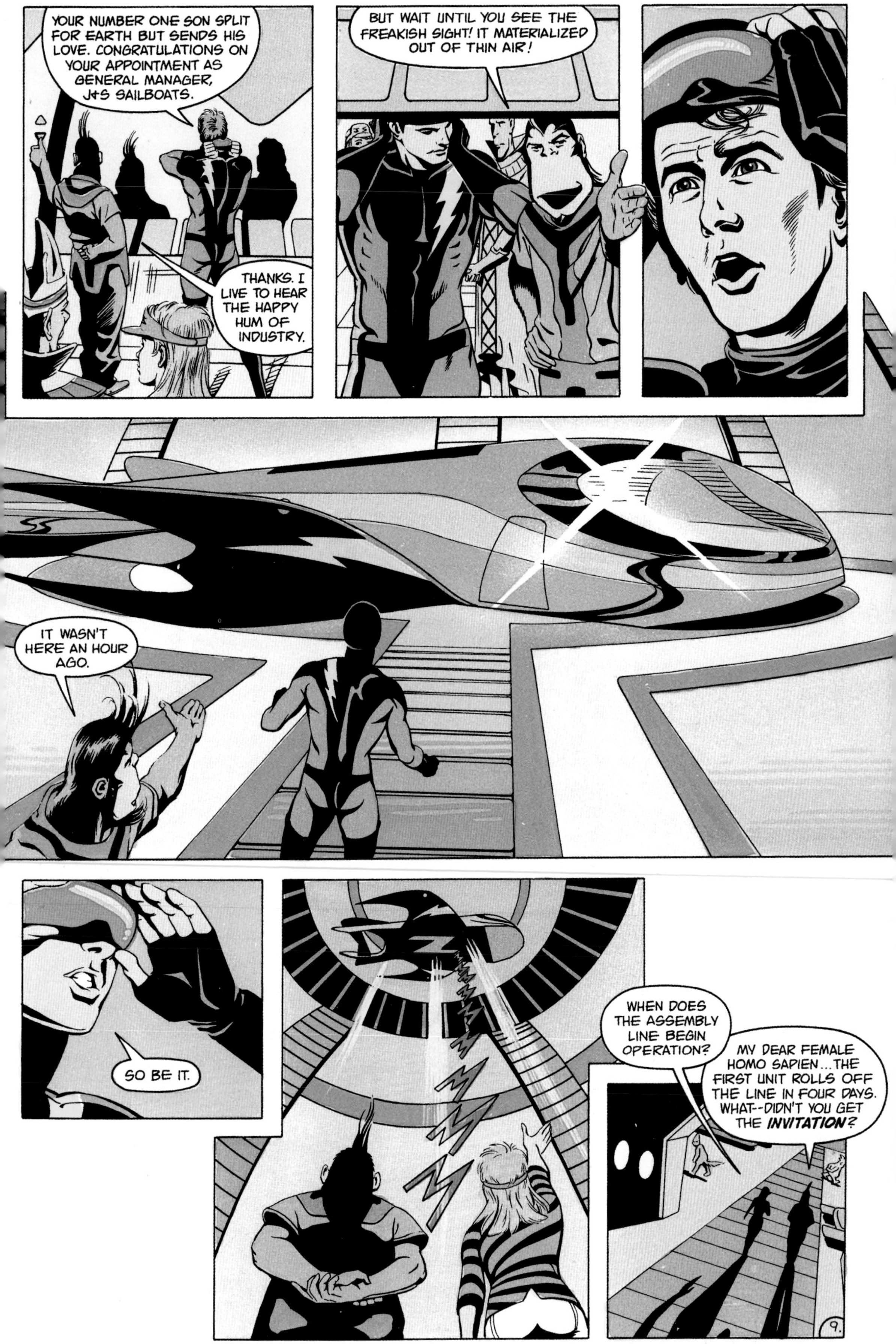
YOUR NUMBER ONE SON SPLIT FOR EARTH BUT SENDS HIS LOVE. CONGRATULATIONS ON YOUR APPOINTMENT AS GENERAL MANAGER, J&S SAILBOATS.
THANKS. I LIVE TO HEAR THE HAPPY HUM OF INDUSTRY.
BUT WAIT UNTIL YOU SEE THE FREAKISH SIGHT! IT MATERIALIZED OUT OF THIN AIR!
IT WASN'T HERE AN HOUR AGO.
SO BE IT.
WHEN DOES THE ASSEMBLY LINE BEGIN OPERATION?
MY DEAR FEMALE HOMO SAPIEN...THE FIRST UNIT ROLLS OFF THE LINE IN FOUR DAYS. WHAT--DIDN'T YOU GET THE *INVITATION*?
9.

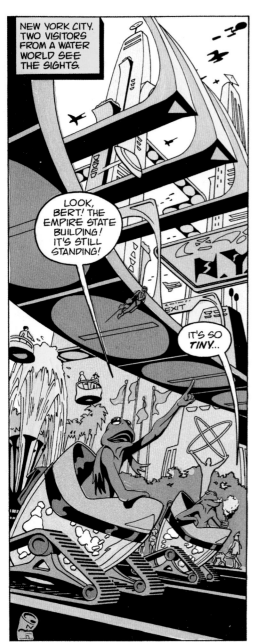

NEW YORK CITY. TWO VISITORS FROM A WATER WORLD SEE THE SIGHTS.

LOOK, BERT! THE EMPIRE STATE BUILDING! IT'S STILL STANDING!

IT'S SO *TINY*...

JAIME! A NATIVE TAD IN DISTRESS!

WHAT'S THE PROBLEM, TADPOLE? CAN WE HELP?

I DROPPED MY MOTHER'S MEDI-CINE IN THE LAKE! IT'S TOO DEEP FOR ME! MY POOR MOTHER WILL *DIE*!

NOT IF *WE* CAN HELP IT! WHERE'S THE LAKE?

OH, THANK YOU, GENTLE SENTIENTS! THANK YOU! THE LAKE'S RIGHT THROUGH HERE...COME ON!

JAIME, IS THIS WISE?

WHO KNOWS?

HEY--THIS IS A *DEAD END*.

WHERE'S THE LAKE?

MAGNESIUM TABLETS.

YAHHH!

YARR! TWO ORDERS OF *BOILED FROG*--COMING UP!

10.

128

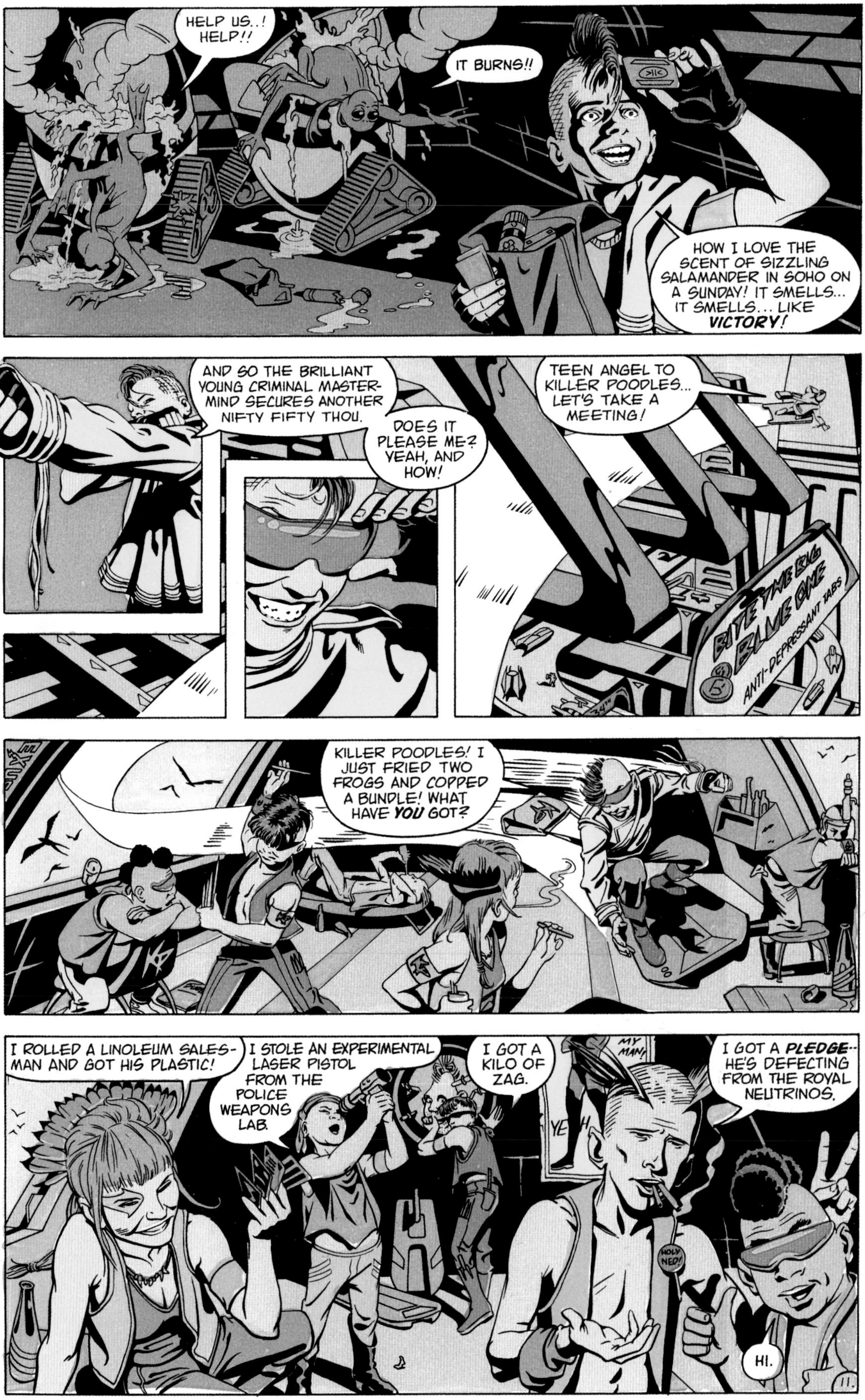
HELP US..! HELP!!
IT BURNS!!
HOW I LOVE THE SCENT OF SIZZLING SALAMANDER IN SOHO ON A SUNDAY! IT SMELLS... IT SMELLS... LIKE **VICTORY**!
AND SO THE BRILLIANT YOUNG CRIMINAL MASTER-MIND SECURES ANOTHER NIFTY FIFTY THOU.
DOES IT PLEASE ME? YEAH, AND HOW!
TEEN ANGEL TO KILLER POODLES... LET'S TAKE A MEETING!
BITE THE BIG BLUE ONE
ANTI-DEPRESSANT TABS
KILLER POODLES! I JUST FRIED TWO FROGS AND COPPED A BUNDLE! WHAT HAVE ***YOU*** GOT?
I ROLLED A LINOLEUM SALES-MAN AND GOT HIS PLASTIC!
I STOLE AN EXPERIMENTAL LASER PISTOL FROM THE POLICE WEAPONS LAB.
I GOT A KILO OF ZAG.
I GOT A ***PLEDGE***-- HE'S DEFECTING FROM THE ROYAL NEUTRINOS.
HI.

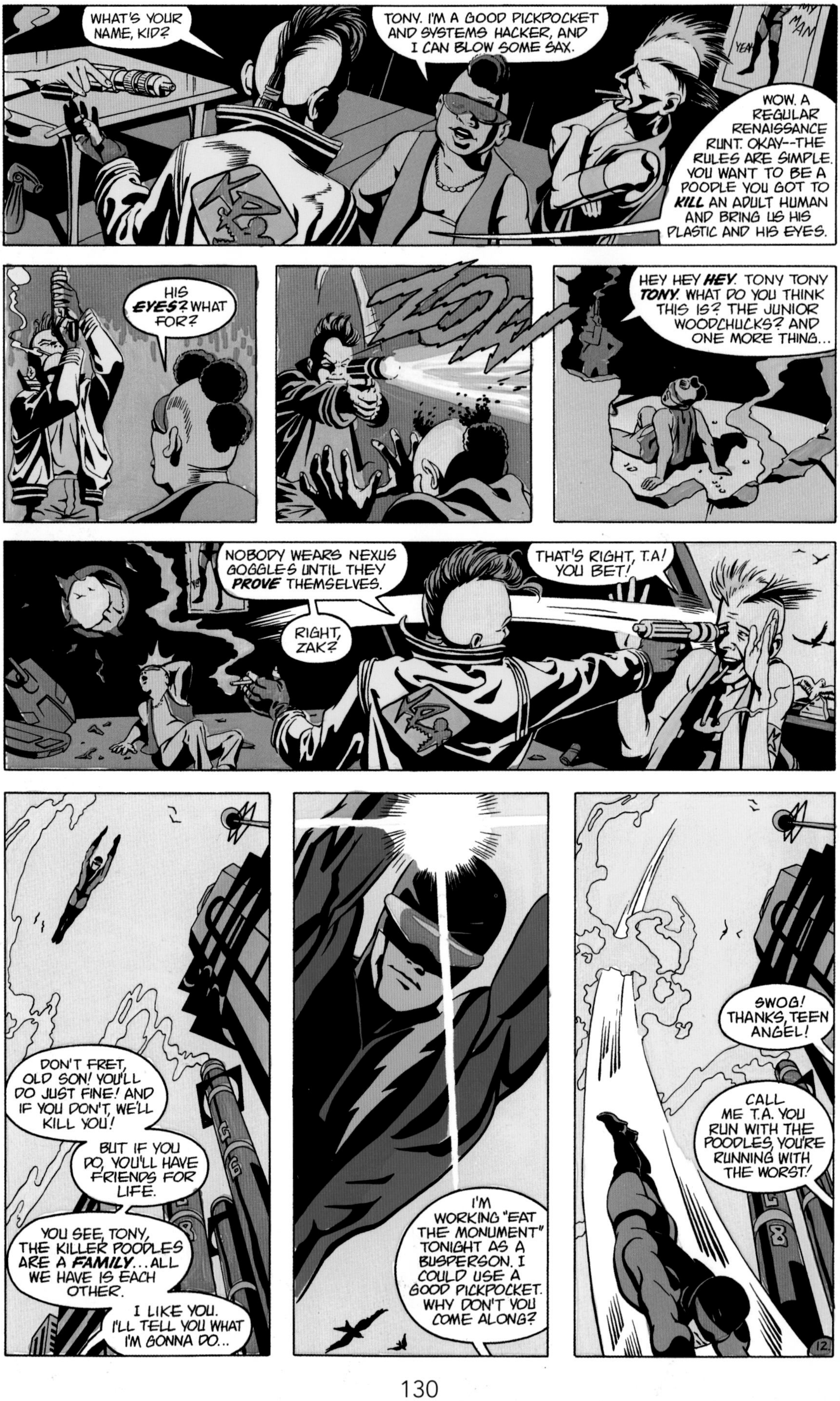

WHAT'S YOUR NAME, KID?
TONY. I'M A GOOD PICKPOCKET AND SYSTEMS HACKER, AND I CAN BLOW SOME SAX.
WOW. A REGULAR RENAISSANCE RUNT. OKAY--THE RULES ARE SIMPLE. YOU WANT TO BE A POODLE YOU GOT TO **KILL** AN ADULT HUMAN AND BRING US HIS PLASTIC AND HIS EYES.
HIS **EYES?** WHAT FOR?
ZOW
HEY HEY **HEY**. TONY TONY **TONY**. WHAT DO YOU THINK THIS IS? THE JUNIOR WOODCHUCKS? AND ONE MORE THING...
NOBODY WEARS NEXUS GOGGLES UNTIL THEY **PROVE** THEMSELVES.
RIGHT, ZAK?
THAT'S RIGHT, T.A! YOU BET!
DON'T FRET, OLD SON! YOU'LL DO JUST FINE! AND IF YOU DON'T, WE'LL KILL YOU!
BUT IF YOU DO, YOU'LL HAVE FRIENDS FOR LIFE.
YOU SEE, TONY, THE KILLER POODLES ARE A **FAMILY**... ALL WE HAVE IS EACH OTHER.
I LIKE YOU. I'LL TELL YOU WHAT I'M GONNA DO...
I'M WORKING "EAT THE MONUMENT" TONIGHT AS A BUSPERSON. I COULD USE A GOOD PICKPOCKET. WHY DON'T YOU COME ALONG?
SWOG! THANKS, TEEN ANGEL!
CALL ME T.A. YOU RUN WITH THE POODLES, YOU'RE RUNNING WITH THE WORST!
12.

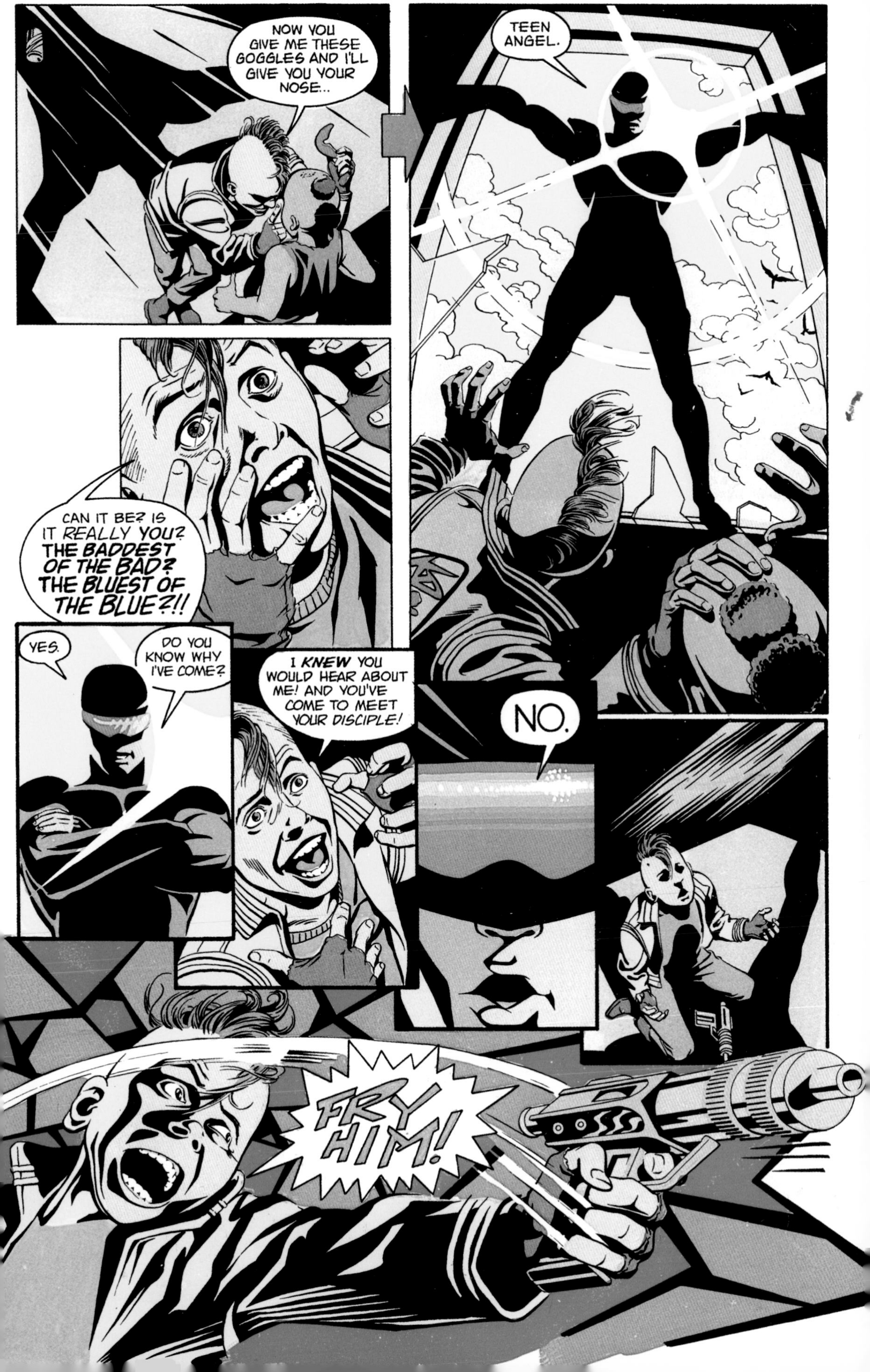
NOW YOU GIVE ME THESE GOGGLES AND I'LL GIVE YOU YOUR NOSE...
TEEN ANGEL.
CAN IT BE? IS IT REALLY YOU? THE BADDEST OF THE BAD? THE BLUEST OF THE BLUE?!!
YES.
DO YOU KNOW WHY I'VE COME?
I KNEW YOU WOULD HEAR ABOUT ME! AND YOU'VE COME TO MEET YOUR DISCIPLE!
NO.
FRY HIM!

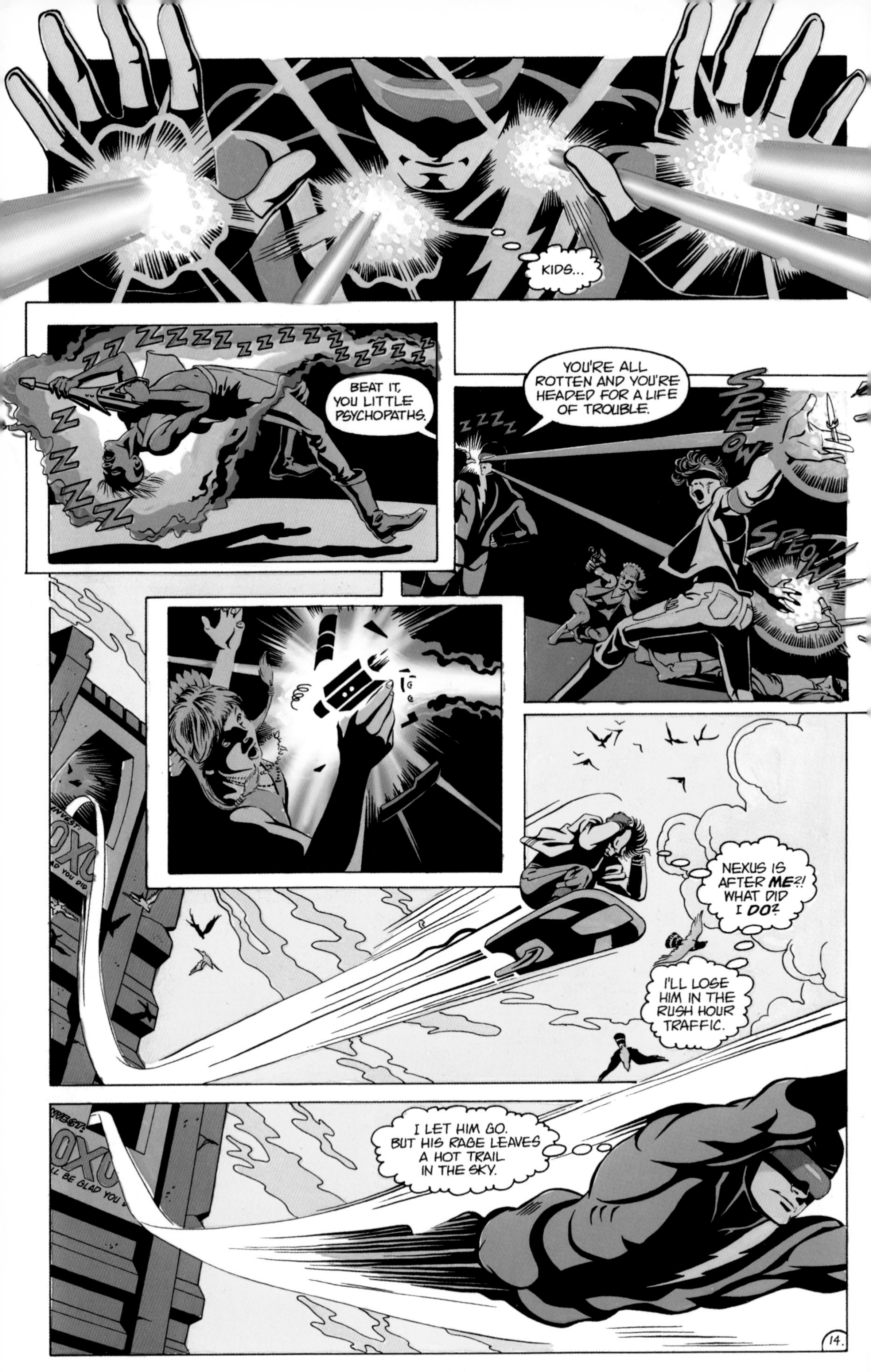
KIDS...
ZZZZZZZZZZZZZZZZ
BEAT IT, YOU LITTLE PSYCHOPATHS.
YOU'RE ALL ROTTEN AND YOU'RE HEADED FOR A LIFE OF TROUBLE.
SPEOW
SPEOW
NEXUS IS AFTER ME?! WHAT DID I DO?
I'LL LOSE HIM IN THE RUSH HOUR TRAFFIC.
I LET HIM GO. BUT HIS RAGE LEAVES A HOT TRAIL IN THE SKY.
14.

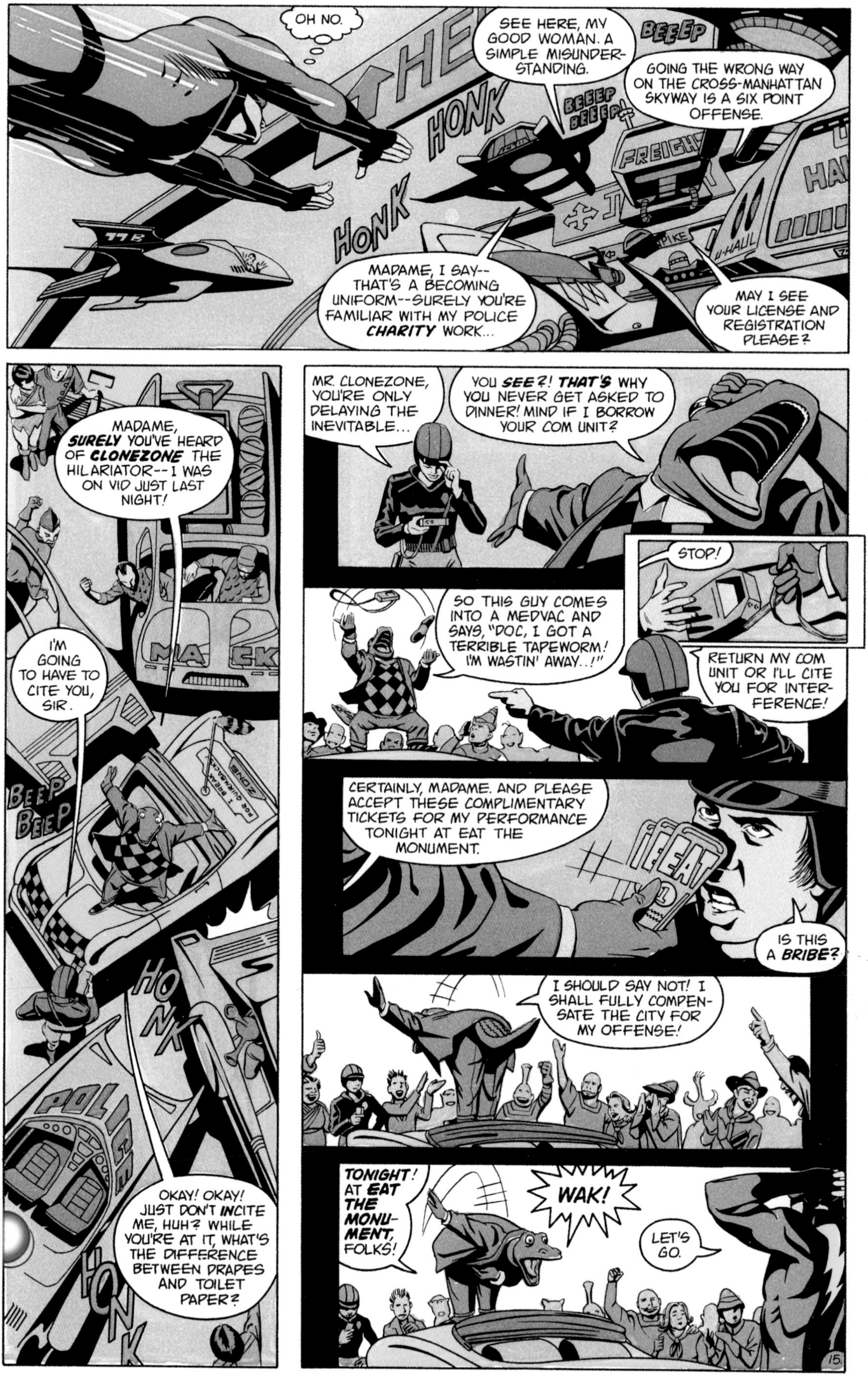
OH NO.
SEE HERE, MY GOOD WOMAN. A SIMPLE MISUNDERSTANDING.
BEEEP
BEEEP BEEEP!
GOING THE WRONG WAY ON THE CROSS-MANHATTAN SKYWAY IS A SIX POINT OFFENSE.
HONK HONK
HONK
FREIGHT
U-HAUL
MADAME, I SAY-- THAT'S A BECOMING UNIFORM--SURELY YOU'RE FAMILIAR WITH MY POLICE CHARITY WORK...
MAY I SEE YOUR LICENSE AND REGISTRATION PLEASE?
MADAME, SURELY YOU'VE HEARD OF CLONEZONE THE HILARIATOR-- I WAS ON VID JUST LAST NIGHT!
I'M GOING TO HAVE TO CITE YOU, SIR.
MACK
BEEP BEEP
HONK
POLICE
OKAY! OKAY! JUST DON'T INCITE ME, HUH? WHILE YOU'RE AT IT, WHAT'S THE DIFFERENCE BETWEEN DRAPES AND TOILET PAPER?
HONK
MR. CLONEZONE, YOU'RE ONLY DELAYING THE INEVITABLE...
YOU SEE?! THAT'S WHY YOU NEVER GET ASKED TO DINNER! MIND IF I BORROW YOUR COM UNIT?
STOP!
SO THIS GUY COMES INTO A MEDVAC AND SAYS, "DOC, I GOT A TERRIBLE TAPEWORM! I'M WASTIN' AWAY..!"
RETURN MY COM UNIT OR I'LL CITE YOU FOR INTERFERENCE!
CERTAINLY, MADAME. AND PLEASE ACCEPT THESE COMPLIMENTARY TICKETS FOR MY PERFORMANCE TONIGHT AT EAT THE MONUMENT.
EAT
IS THIS A BRIBE?
I SHOULD SAY NOT! I SHALL FULLY COMPENSATE THE CITY FOR MY OFFENSE!
TONIGHT! AT EAT THE MONUMENT, FOLKS!
WAK!
LET'S GO.
15.

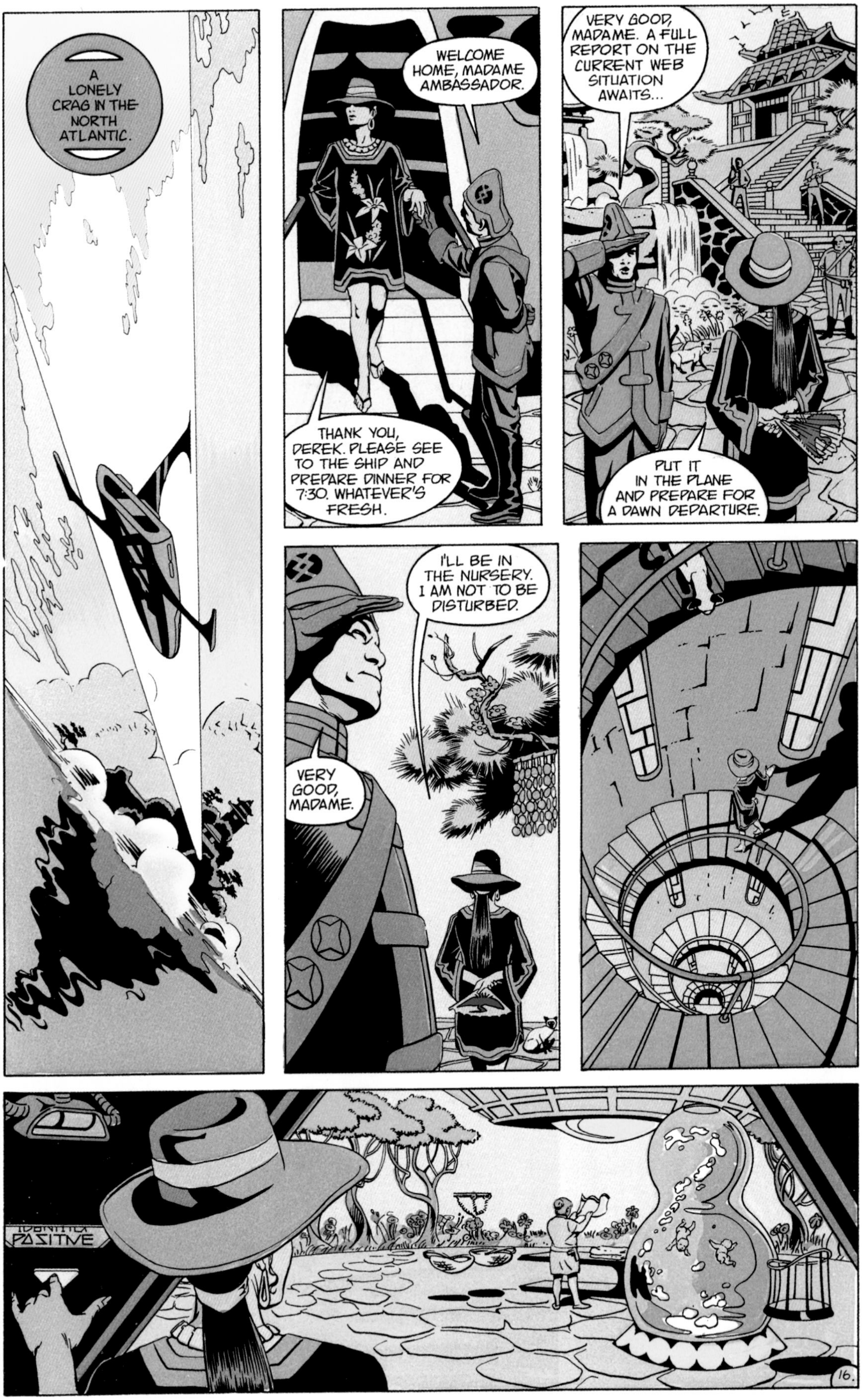
A LONELY CRAG IN THE NORTH ATLANTIC.
WELCOME HOME, MADAME AMBASSADOR.
THANK YOU, DEREK. PLEASE SEE TO THE SHIP AND PREPARE DINNER FOR 7:30. WHATEVER'S FRESH.
VERY GOOD, MADAME. A FULL REPORT ON THE CURRENT WEB SITUATION AWAITS...
PUT IT IN THE PLANE AND PREPARE FOR A DAWN DEPARTURE.
I'LL BE IN THE NURSERY. I AM NOT TO BE DISTURBED.
VERY GOOD, MADAME.
POSITIVE
16.

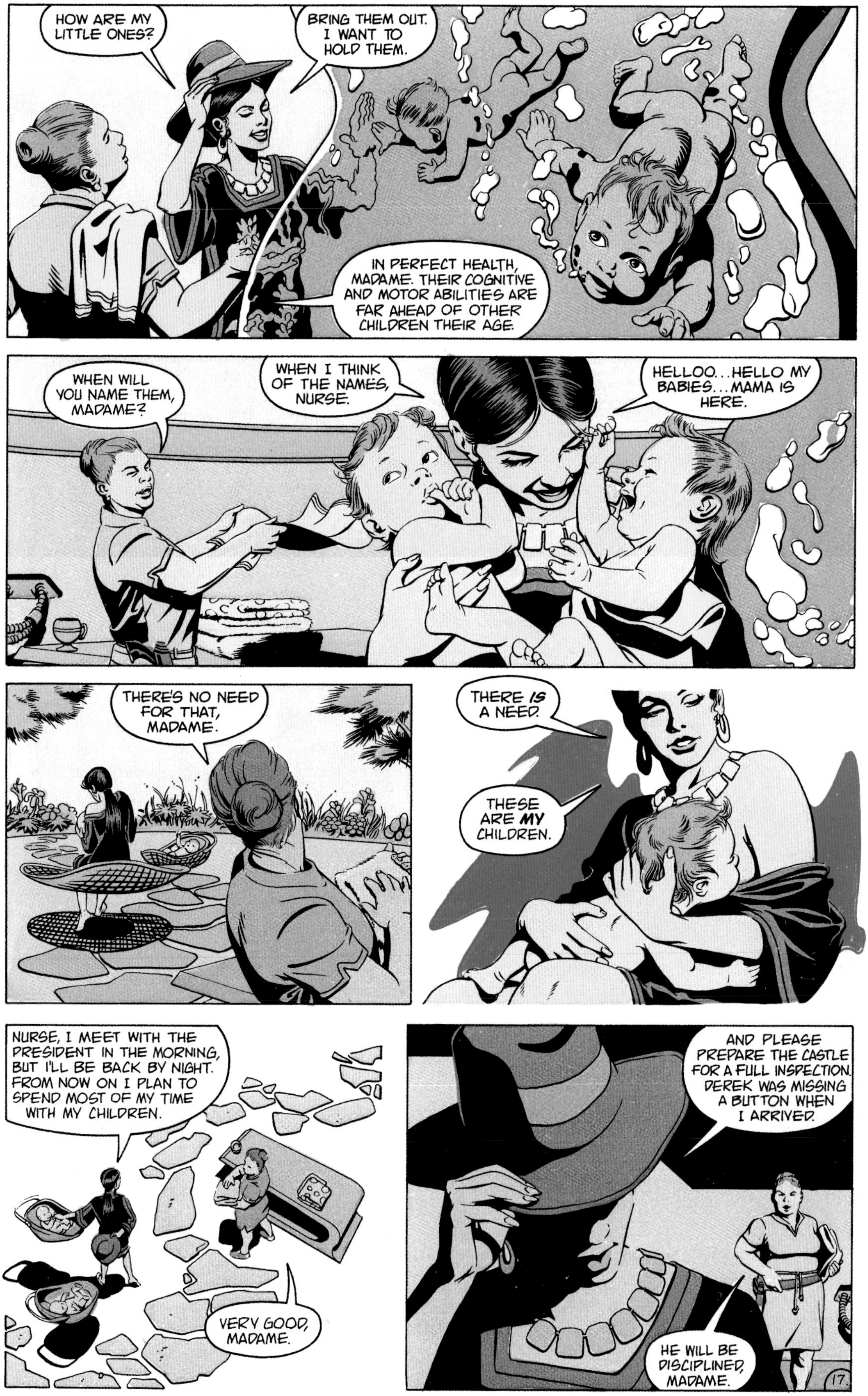
HOW ARE MY LITTLE ONES?
BRING THEM OUT. I WANT TO HOLD THEM.
IN PERFECT HEALTH, MADAME. THEIR COGNITIVE AND MOTOR ABILITIES ARE FAR AHEAD OF OTHER CHILDREN THEIR AGE.
WHEN WILL YOU NAME THEM, MADAME?
WHEN I THINK OF THE NAMES, NURSE.
HELLOO...HELLO MY BABIES...MAMA IS HERE.
THERE'S NO NEED FOR THAT, MADAME.
THERE *IS* A NEED.
THESE ARE **MY** CHILDREN.
NURSE, I MEET WITH THE PRESIDENT IN THE MORNING, BUT I'LL BE BACK BY NIGHT. FROM NOW ON I PLAN TO SPEND MOST OF MY TIME WITH MY CHILDREN.
VERY GOOD, MADAME.
AND PLEASE PREPARE THE CASTLE FOR A FULL INSPECTION. DEREK WAS MISSING A BUTTON WHEN I ARRIVED.
HE WILL BE DISCIPLINED, MADAME.
17

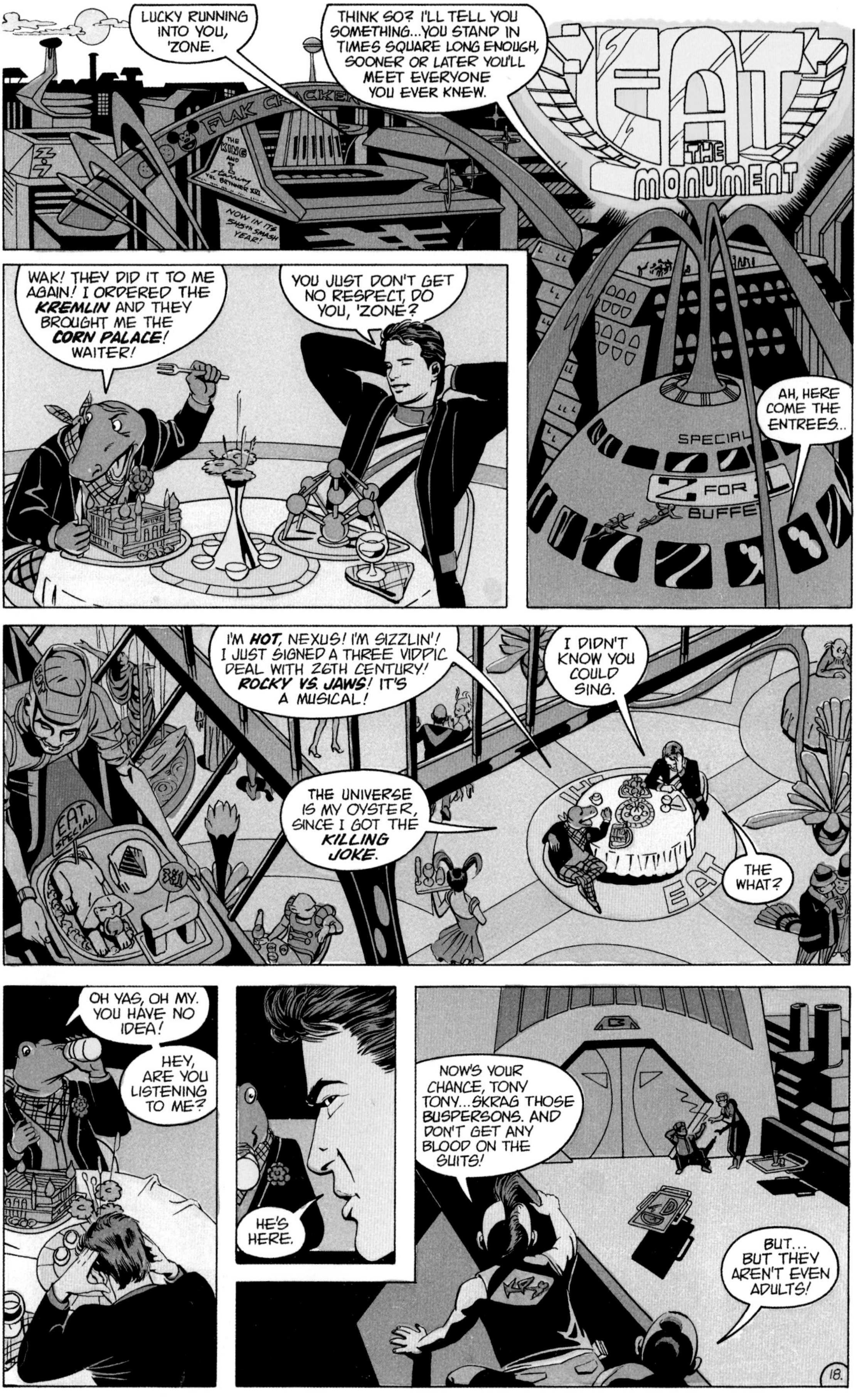
LUCKY RUNNING INTO YOU, 'ZONE.
THINK SO? I'LL TELL YOU SOMETHING...YOU STAND IN TIMES SQUARE LONG ENOUGH, SOONER OR LATER YOU'LL MEET EVERYONE YOU EVER KNEW.
FLAK CRACKER
THE KING AND I starring YUL BRYNNER XXII
NOW IN ITS 545th SMASH YEAR!
EAT THE MONUMENT
WAK! THEY DID IT TO ME AGAIN! I ORDERED THE **KREMLIN** AND THEY BROUGHT ME THE **CORN PALACE**! WAITER!
YOU JUST DON'T GET NO RESPECT, DO YOU, 'ZONE?
AH, HERE COME THE ENTREES...
SPECIAL
Z FOR 1
BUFFET
I'M **HOT**, NEXUS! I'M SIZZLIN'! I JUST SIGNED A THREE VIDPIC DEAL WITH 26TH CENTURY! **ROCKY VS. JAWS**! IT'S A MUSICAL!
I DIDN'T KNOW YOU COULD SING.
THE UNIVERSE IS MY OYSTER, SINCE I GOT THE **KILLING JOKE**.
THE WHAT?
EAT SPECIAL
OH YAS, OH MY. YOU HAVE NO IDEA!
HEY, ARE YOU LISTENING TO ME?
HE'S HERE.
NOW'S YOUR CHANCE, TONY TONY...SKRAG THOSE BUSPERSONS. AND DON'T GET ANY BLOOD ON THE SUITS!
BUT... BUT THEY AREN'T EVEN ADULTS!
18.

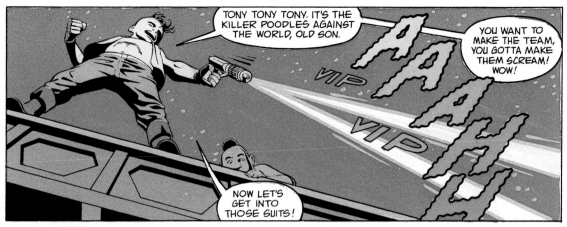

TONY TONY TONY. IT'S THE KILLER POODLES AGAINST THE WORLD, OLD SON.

YOU WANT TO MAKE THE TEAM, YOU GOTTA MAKE THEM SCREAM! WOW!

AAAHH!

VIP

VIP

NOW LET'S GET INTO THOSE SUITS!

WHO'S HERE?

HE WHOM I SEEK.

NEXUS BABY, *SWEETHEART*--I GOT A *SHOW* HERE TONIGHT..! YOU'RE NOT GOING TO EM-BARASS ME, ARE YOU?

THE LIGHTS IN MY HEAD...THE ADUMBRATION OF AGONY...

YOU WANT A PAIN KILLER?

MR. CLONEZONE, SIR, YOUR KREMLIN HAS ARRIVED!

THANKS, KID!

EAT

EAT

IS EVERYTHING SATISFACTORY, SIR?

AH, THE SWEET AROMA OF BOILED CABBAGE!

ANGEL. PSSST! ANGEL! WHAT ARE YOU STARING AT?

E

19.

137

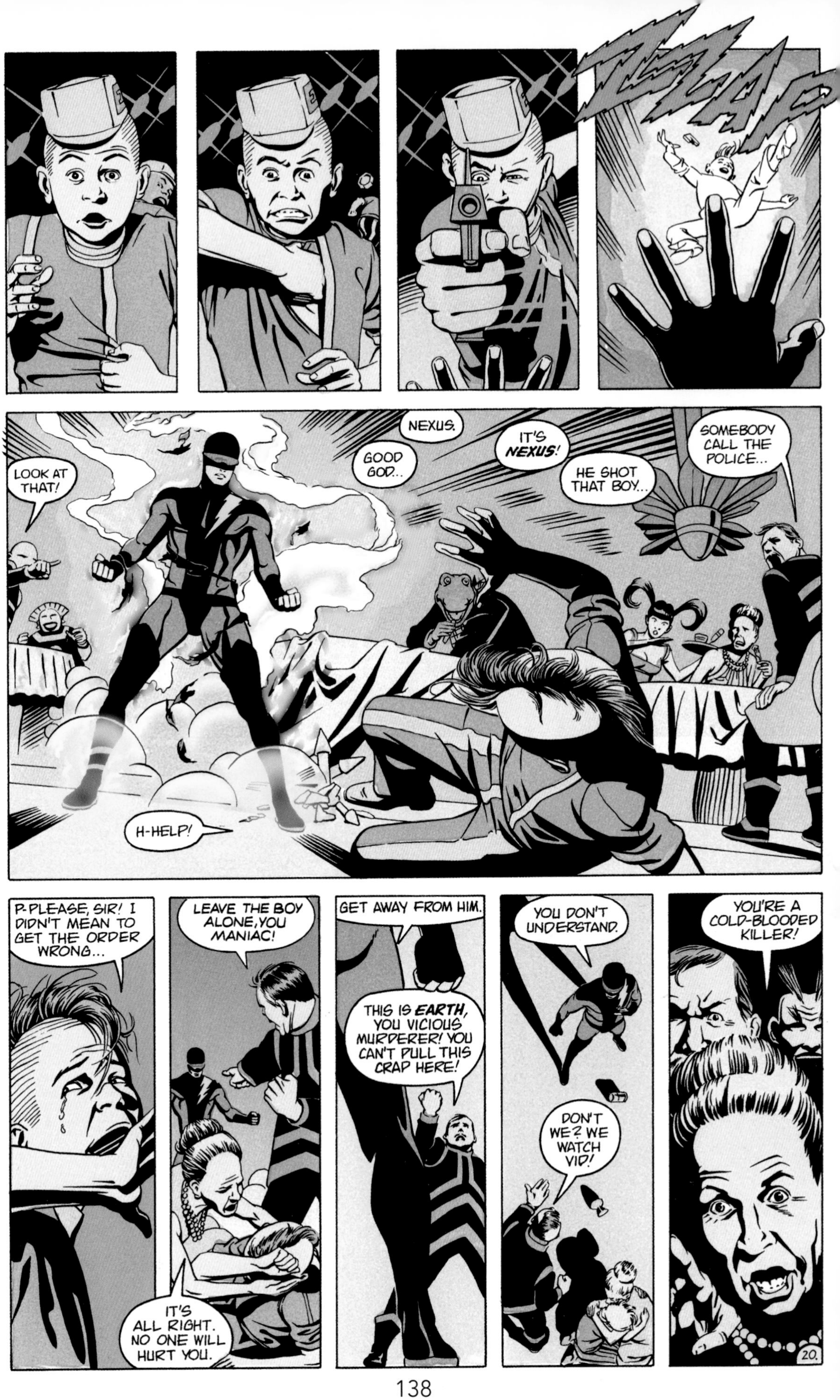
ZZZAP
LOOK AT THAT!
GOOD GOD...
NEXUS.
IT'S NEXUS!
HE SHOT THAT BOY...
SOMEBODY CALL THE POLICE...
H-HELP!
P-PLEASE, SIR! I DIDN'T MEAN TO GET THE ORDER WRONG...
LEAVE THE BOY ALONE, YOU MANIAC!
IT'S ALL RIGHT. NO ONE WILL HURT YOU.
GET AWAY FROM HIM.
THIS IS EARTH, YOU VICIOUS MURDERER! YOU CAN'T PULL THIS CRAP HERE!
YOU DON'T UNDERSTAND.
DON'T WE? WE WATCH VID!
YOU'RE A COLD-BLOODED KILLER!
20.

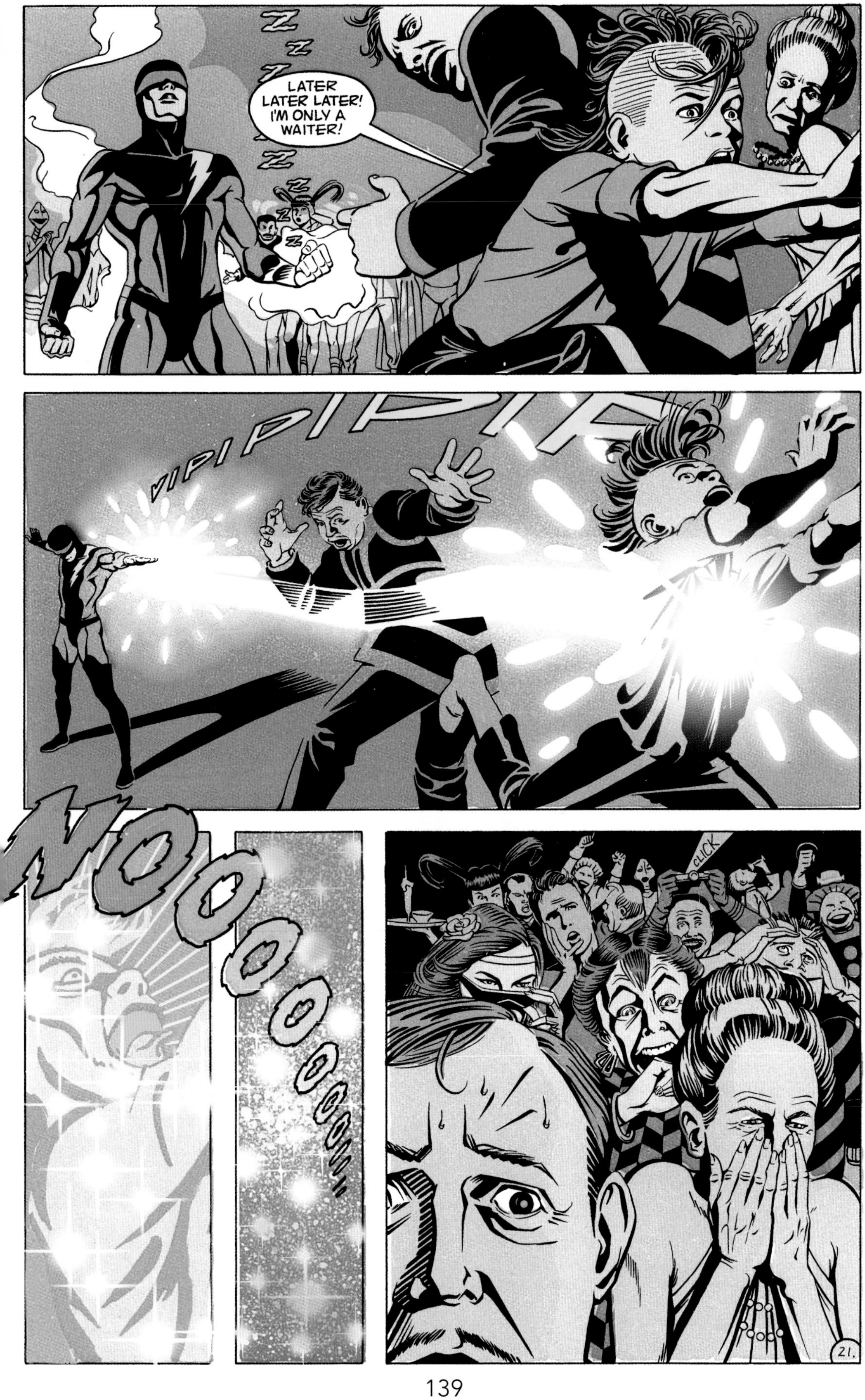
Z Z Z
LATER LATER LATER! I'M ONLY A WAITER!
VIPIPIPIPIR
NOOOOOOOOOO
CLICK
21.

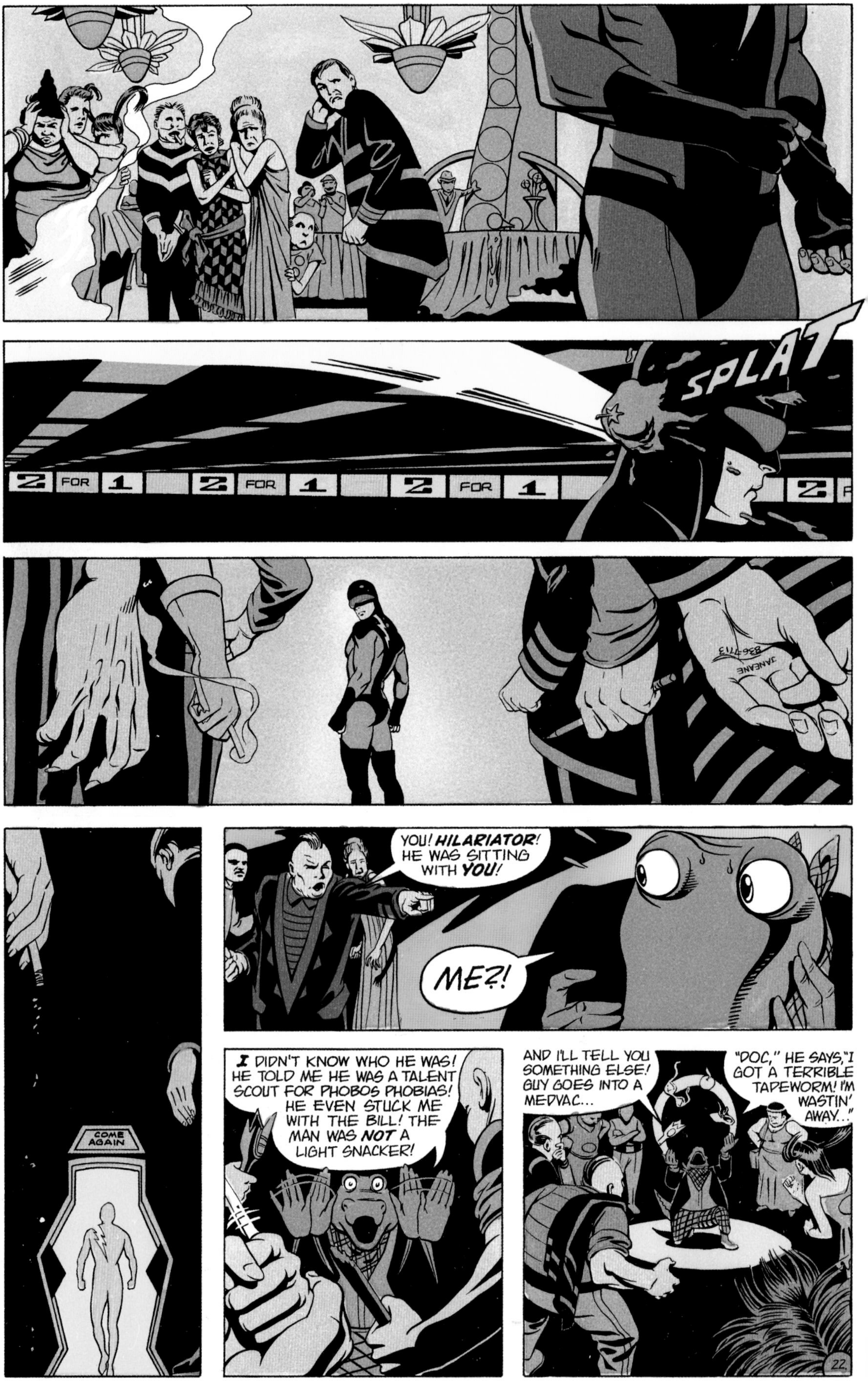
SPLAT
2 FOR 1 2 FOR 1 2 FOR 1
YOU! **HILARIATOR**! HE WAS SITTING WITH **YOU**!
ME?!
COME AGAIN
I DIDN'T KNOW WHO HE WAS! HE TOLD ME HE WAS A TALENT SCOUT FOR PHOBOS PHOBIAS! HE EVEN STUCK ME WITH THE BILL! THE MAN WAS **NOT** A LIGHT SNACKER!
AND I'LL TELL YOU SOMETHING ELSE! GUY GOES INTO A MEDVAC...
"DOC," HE SAYS, "I GOT A TERRIBLE TAPEWORM! I'M WASTIN' AWAY..."
22

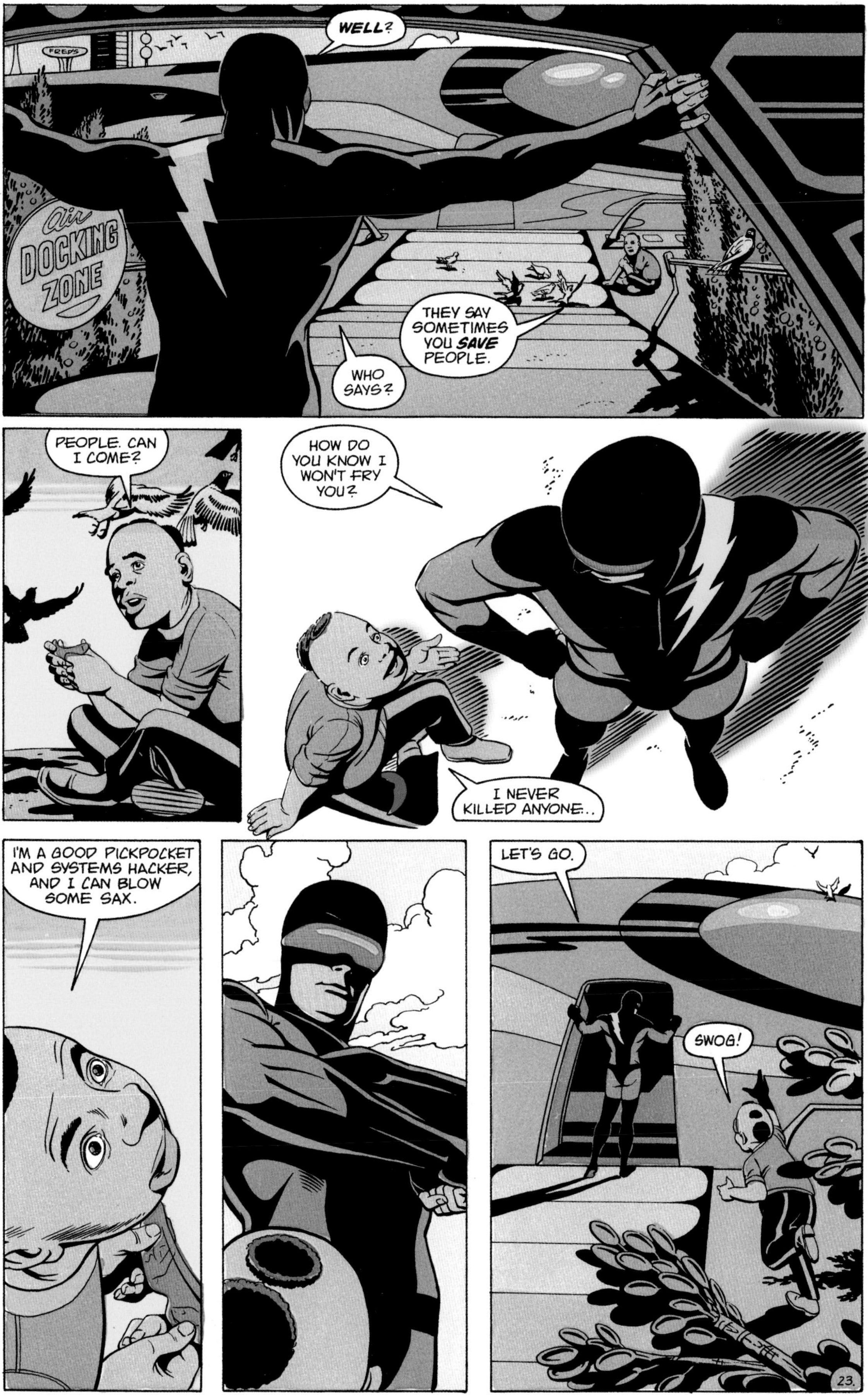

FRED'S
WELL?
AIR DOCKING ZONE
THEY SAY SOMETIMES YOU SAVE PEOPLE.
WHO SAYS?
PEOPLE. CAN I COME?
HOW DO YOU KNOW I WON'T FRY YOU?
I NEVER KILLED ANYONE...
I'M A GOOD PICKPOCKET AND SYSTEMS HACKER, AND I CAN BLOW SOME SAX.
LET'S GO.
SWOG!
23.

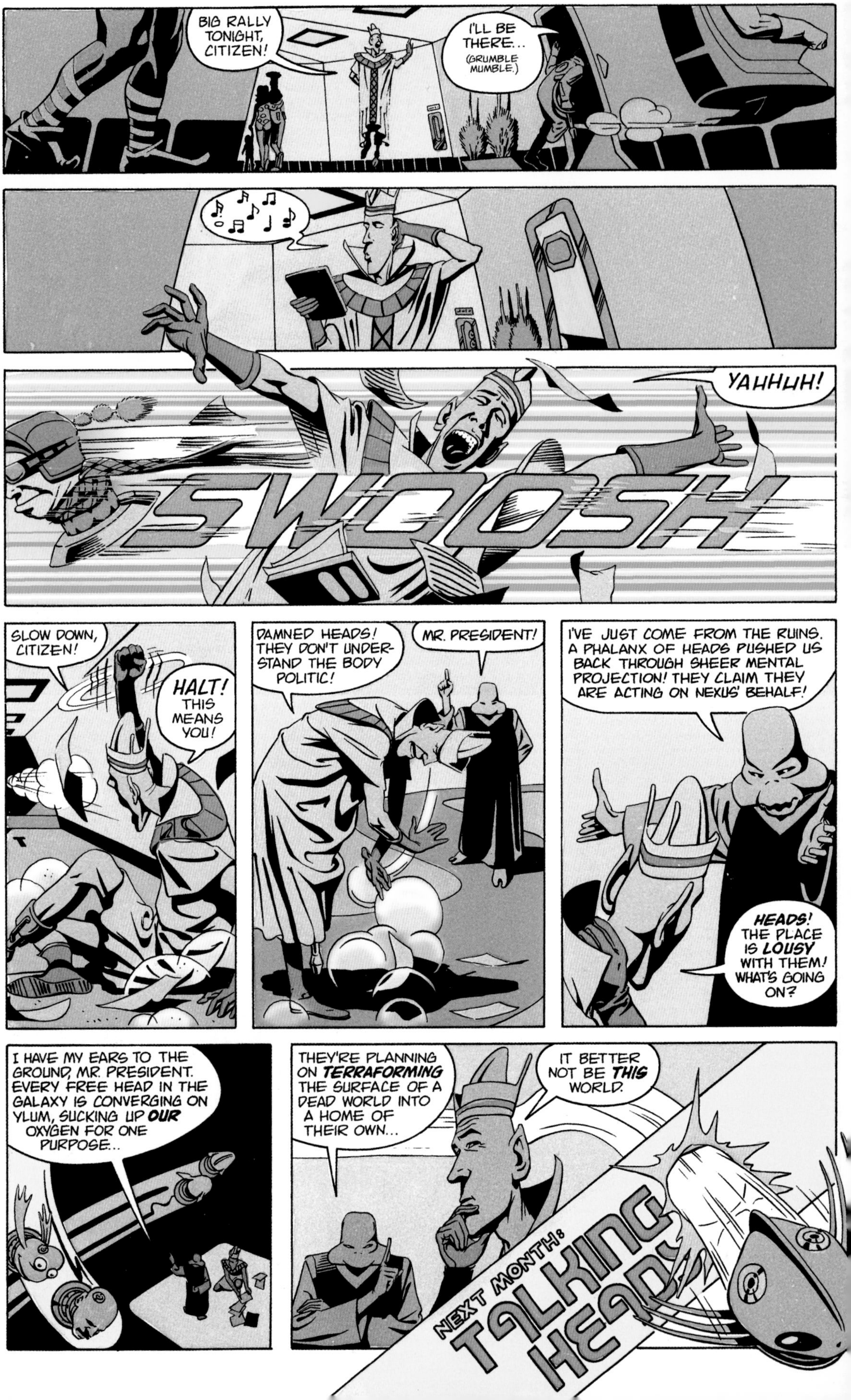
BIG RALLY TONIGHT, CITIZEN!
I'LL BE THERE... (GRUMBLE MUMBLE.)
YAHHUH!
SWOOSH
SLOW DOWN, CITIZEN!
HALT! THIS MEANS YOU!
DAMNED HEADS! THEY DON'T UNDERSTAND THE BODY POLITIC!
MR. PRESIDENT!
I'VE JUST COME FROM THE RUINS. A PHALANX OF HEADS PUSHED US BACK THROUGH SHEER MENTAL PROJECTION! THEY CLAIM THEY ARE ACTING ON NEXUS' BEHALF!
HEADS! THE PLACE IS LOUSY WITH THEM! WHAT'S GOING ON?
I HAVE MY EARS TO THE GROUND, MR. PRESIDENT. EVERY FREE HEAD IN THE GALAXY IS CONVERGING ON YLUM, SUCKING UP OUR OXYGEN FOR ONE PURPOSE...
THEY'RE PLANNING ON TERRAFORMING THE SURFACE OF A DEAD WORLD INTO A HOME OF THEIR OWN...
IT BETTER NOT BE THIS WORLD.
NEXT MONTH: TALKING HEADS

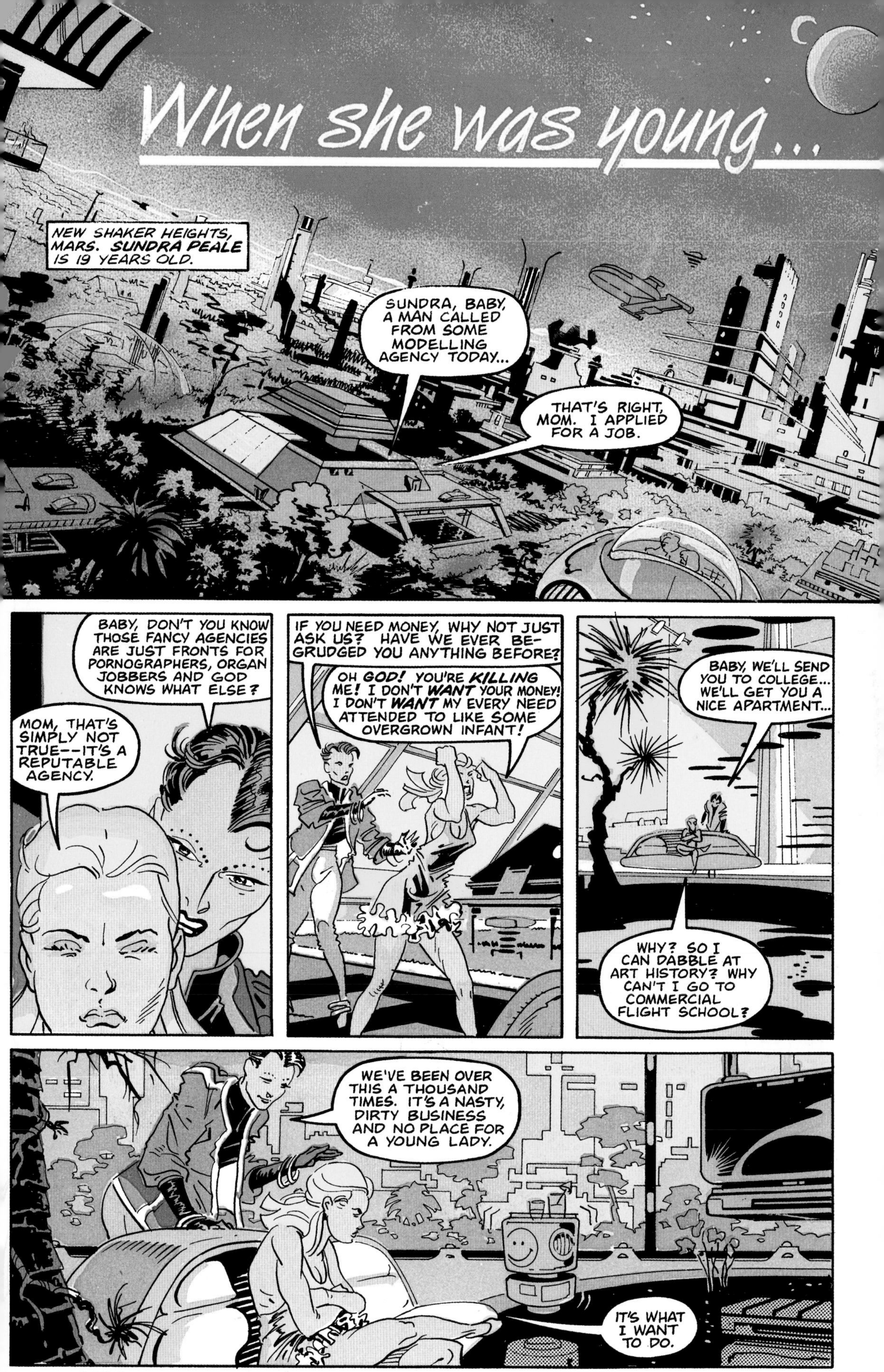
When she was young...
NEW SHAKER HEIGHTS, MARS. SUNDRA PEALE IS 19 YEARS OLD.
SUNDRA, BABY, A MAN CALLED FROM SOME MODELLING AGENCY TODAY...
THAT'S RIGHT, MOM. I APPLIED FOR A JOB.
BABY, DON'T YOU KNOW THOSE FANCY AGENCIES ARE JUST FRONTS FOR PORNOGRAPHERS, ORGAN JOBBERS AND GOD KNOWS WHAT ELSE?
MOM, THAT'S SIMPLY NOT TRUE--IT'S A REPUTABLE AGENCY.
IF YOU NEED MONEY, WHY NOT JUST ASK US? HAVE WE EVER BE-GRUDGED YOU ANYTHING BEFORE?
OH GOD! YOU'RE KILLING ME! I DON'T WANT YOUR MONEY! I DON'T WANT MY EVERY NEED ATTENDED TO LIKE SOME OVERGROWN INFANT!
BABY, WE'LL SEND YOU TO COLLEGE... WE'LL GET YOU A NICE APARTMENT...
WHY? SO I CAN DABBLE AT ART HISTORY? WHY CAN'T I GO TO COMMERCIAL FLIGHT SCHOOL?
WE'VE BEEN OVER THIS A THOUSAND TIMES. IT'S A NASTY, DIRTY BUSINESS AND NO PLACE FOR A YOUNG LADY.
IT'S WHAT I WANT TO DO.

SCRIPT **MIKE BARON** ART & COLORS **GEORGE FREEMAN** LETTERS **STEVE HAYNIE** EDITOR **RICK OLIVER**

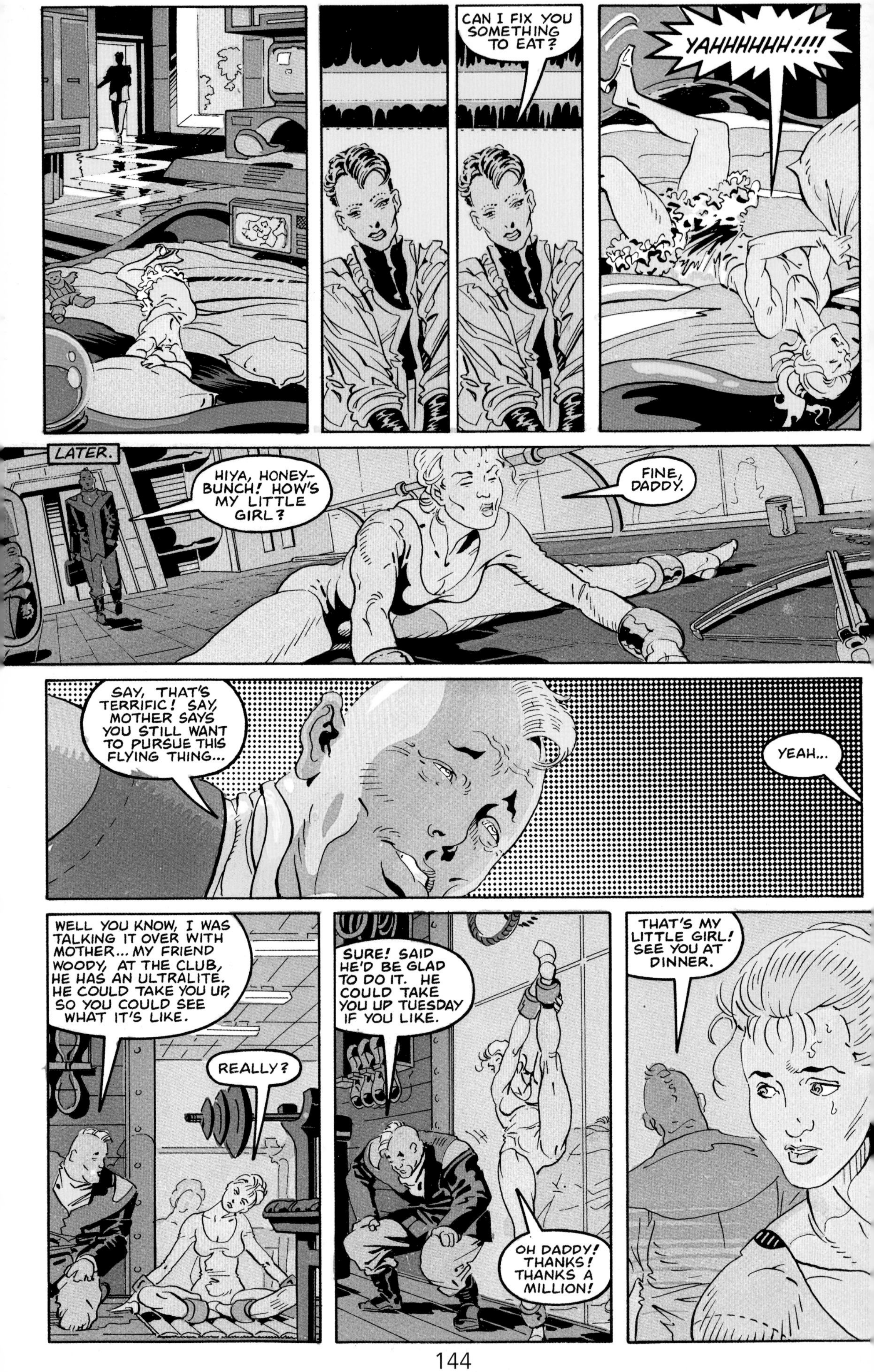

CAN I FIX YOU SOMETHING TO EAT?
YAHHHHHH!!!!
LATER.
HIYA, HONEY-BUNCH! HOW'S MY LITTLE GIRL?
FINE, DADDY.
SAY, THAT'S TERRIFIC! SAY, MOTHER SAYS YOU STILL WANT TO PURSUE THIS FLYING THING...
YEAH...
WELL YOU KNOW, I WAS TALKING IT OVER WITH MOTHER... MY FRIEND WOODY, AT THE CLUB, HE HAS AN ULTRALITE. HE COULD TAKE YOU UP, SO YOU COULD SEE WHAT IT'S LIKE.
REALLY?
SURE! SAID HE'D BE GLAD TO DO IT. HE COULD TAKE YOU UP TUESDAY IF YOU LIKE.
OH DADDY! THANKS! THANKS A MILLION!
THAT'S MY LITTLE GIRL! SEE YOU AT DINNER.

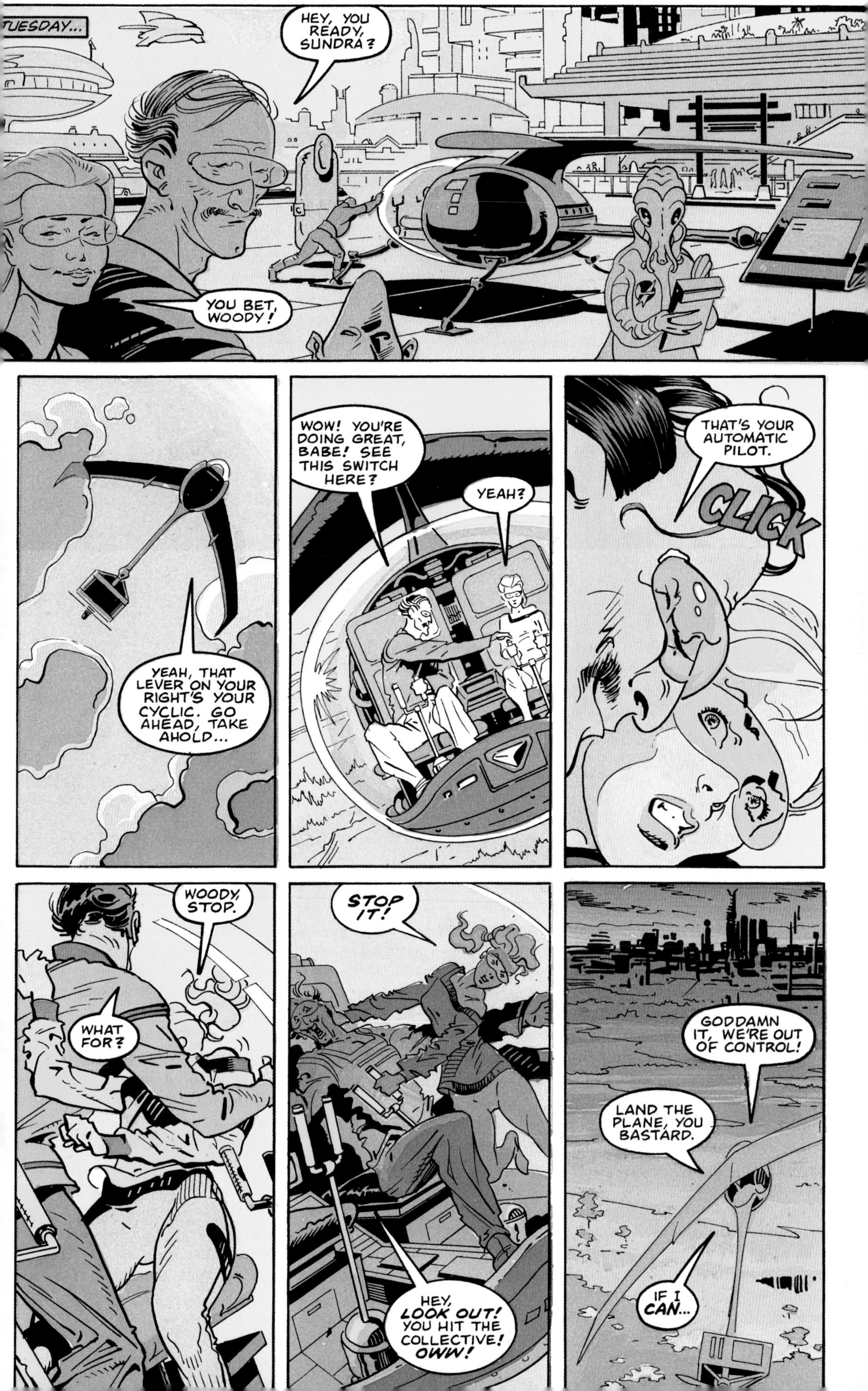
TUESDAY...
HEY, YOU READY, SUNDRA?
YOU BET, WOODY!
YEAH, THAT LEVER ON YOUR RIGHT'S YOUR CYCLIC. GO AHEAD, TAKE AHOLD...
WOW! YOU'RE DOING GREAT, BABE! SEE THIS SWITCH HERE?
YEAH?
THAT'S YOUR AUTOMATIC PILOT.
CLICK
WOODY, STOP.
WHAT FOR?
STOP IT!
HEY, LOOK OUT! YOU HIT THE COLLECTIVE! OWW!
GODDAMN IT, WE'RE OUT OF CONTROL!
LAND THE PLANE, YOU BASTARD.
IF I CAN...

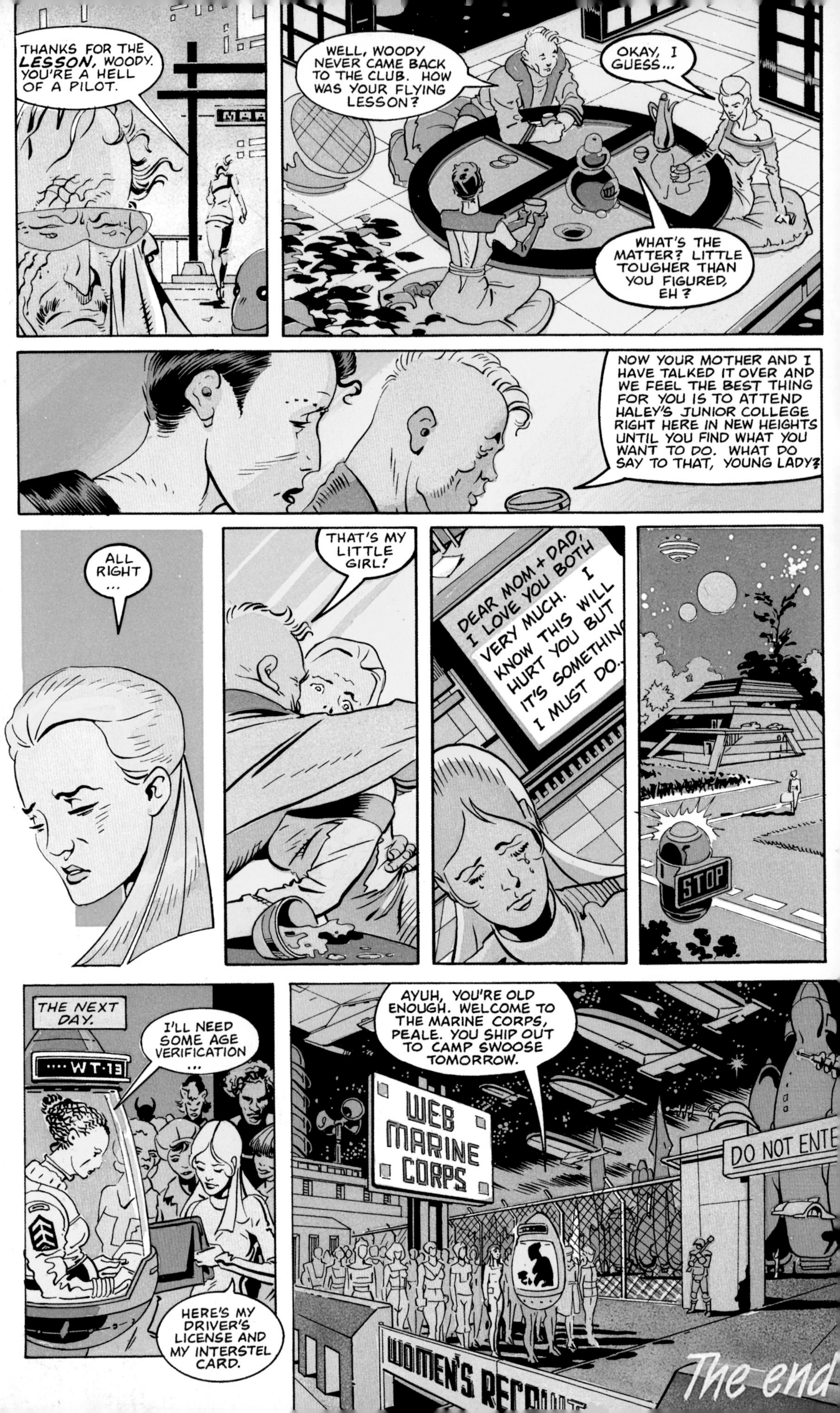
THANKS FOR THE LESSON, WOODY. YOU'RE A HELL OF A PILOT.
WELL, WOODY NEVER CAME BACK TO THE CLUB. HOW WAS YOUR FLYING LESSON?
OKAY, I GUESS...
WHAT'S THE MATTER? LITTLE TOUGHER THAN YOU FIGURED, EH?
NOW YOUR MOTHER AND I HAVE TALKED IT OVER AND WE FEEL THE BEST THING FOR YOU IS TO ATTEND HALEY'S JUNIOR COLLEGE RIGHT HERE IN NEW HEIGHTS UNTIL YOU FIND WHAT YOU WANT TO DO. WHAT DO SAY TO THAT, YOUNG LADY?
ALL RIGHT ...
THAT'S MY LITTLE GIRL!
DEAR MOM + DAD, I LOVE YOU BOTH VERY MUCH. I KNOW THIS WILL HURT YOU BUT IT'S SOMETHING I MUST DO...
STOP
THE NEXT DAY.
WT-13
I'LL NEED SOME AGE VERIFICATION ...
HERE'S MY DRIVER'S LICENSE AND MY INTERSTEL CARD.
AYUH, YOU'RE OLD ENOUGH. WELCOME TO THE MARINE CORPS, PEALE. YOU SHIP OUT TO CAMP SWOOSE TOMORROW.
WEB MARINE CORPS
DO NOT ENTE
WOMEN'S RECRUIT
The end

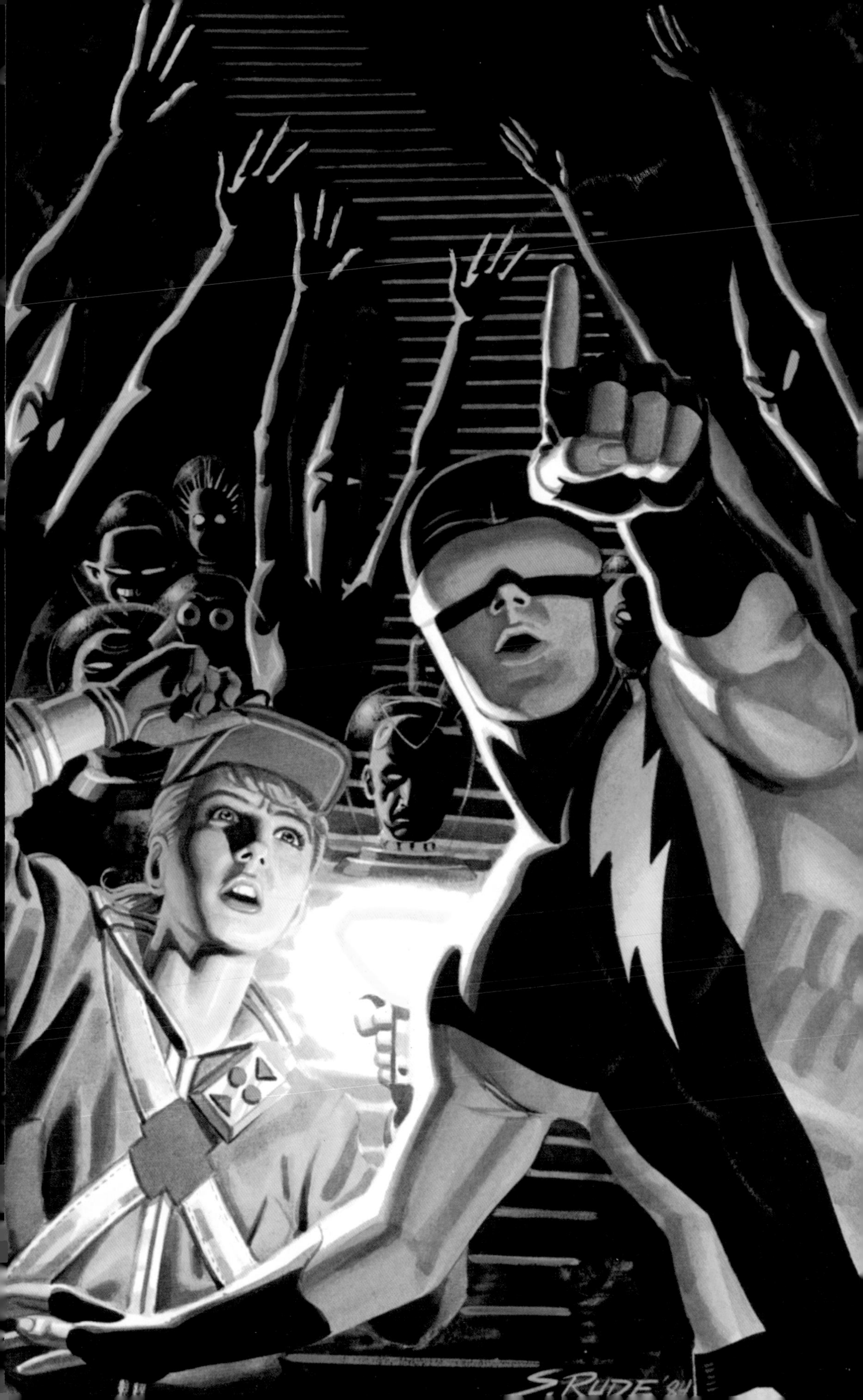
S.RUDE '84

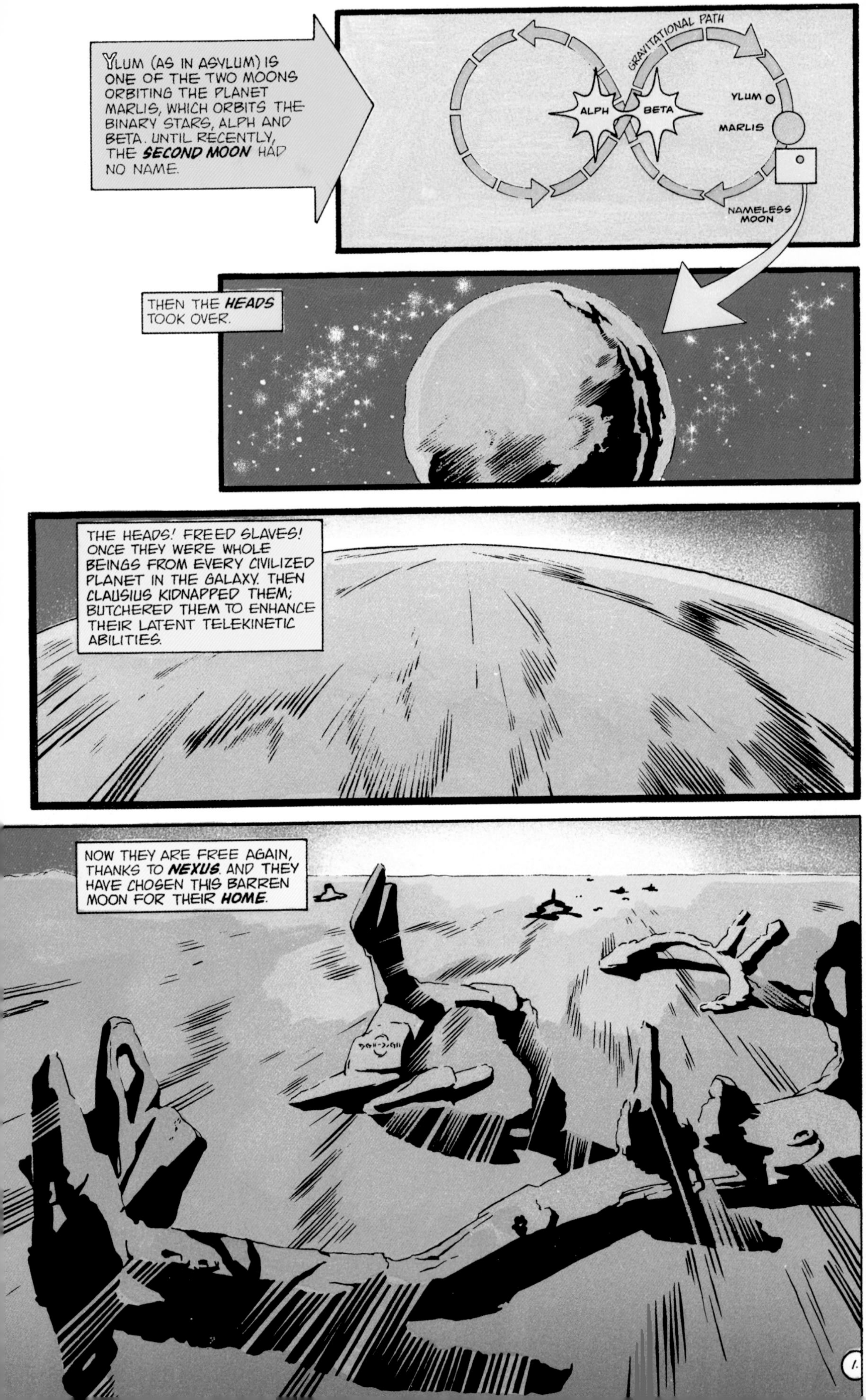
YLUM (AS IN ASYLUM) IS ONE OF THE TWO MOONS ORBITING THE PLANET MARLIS, WHICH ORBITS THE BINARY STARS, ALPH AND BETA. UNTIL RECENTLY, THE SECOND MOON HAD NO NAME.
GRAVITATIONAL PATH
ALPH
BETA
YLUM
MARLIS
NAMELESS MOON
THEN THE HEADS TOOK OVER.
THE HEADS! FREED SLAVES! ONCE THEY WERE WHOLE BEINGS FROM EVERY CIVILIZED PLANET IN THE GALAXY. THEN CLAUSIUS KIDNAPPED THEM; BUTCHERED THEM TO ENHANCE THEIR LATENT TELEKINETIC ABILITIES.
NOW THEY ARE FREE AGAIN, THANKS TO NEXUS. AND THEY HAVE CHOSEN THIS BARREN MOON FOR THEIR HOME.

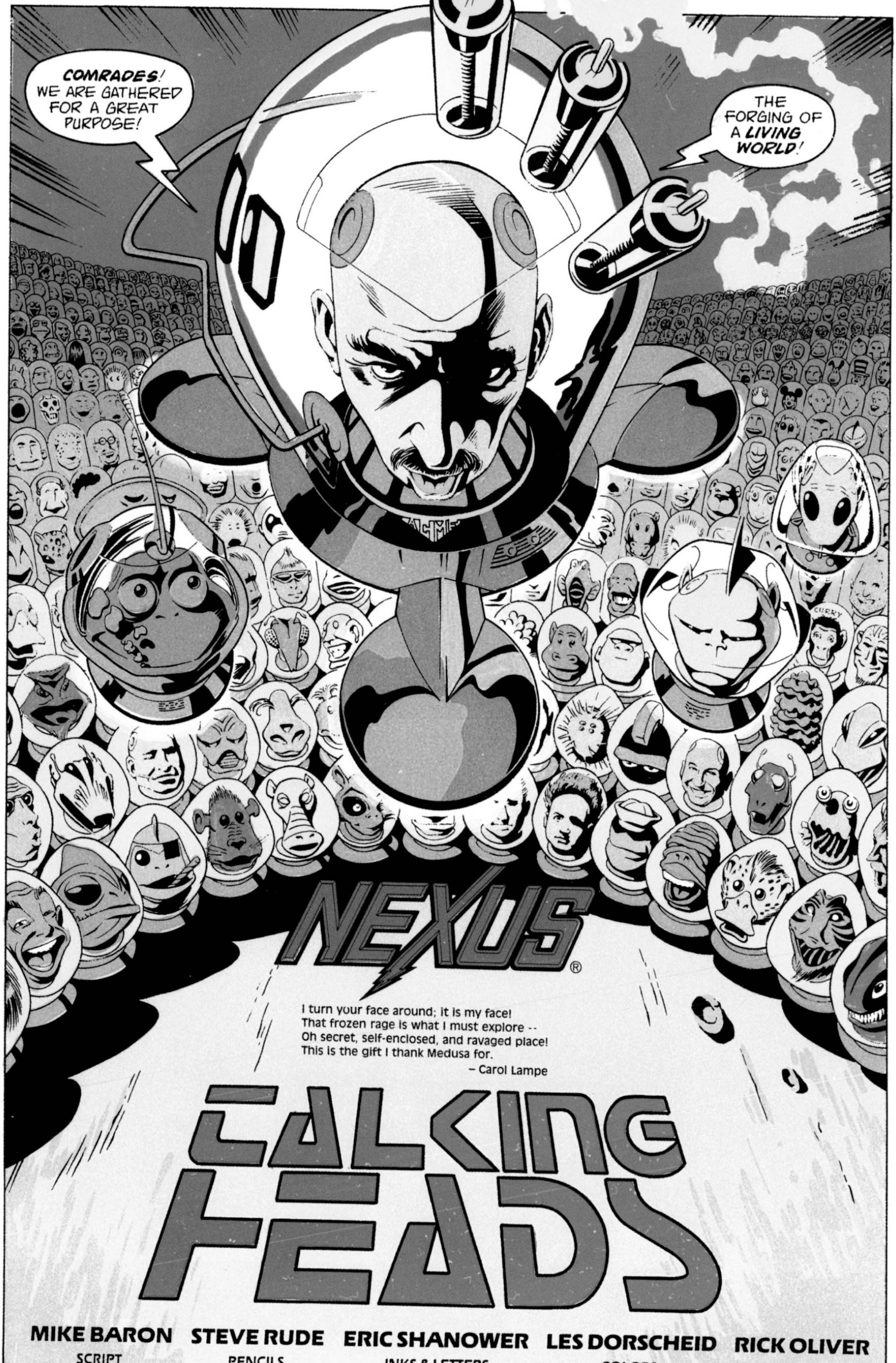
COMRADES! WE ARE GATHERED FOR A GREAT PURPOSE!
THE FORGING OF A LIVING WORLD!
CURRY
NEXUS®
I turn your face around; it is my face!
That frozen rage is what I must explore --
Oh secret, self-enclosed, and ravaged place!
This is the gift I thank Medusa for.
– Carol Lampe
TALKING HEADS
MIKE BARON SCRIPT
STEVE RUDE PENCILS
ERIC SHANOWER INKS & LETTERS
LES DORSCHEID COLORS
RICK OLIVER EDITS

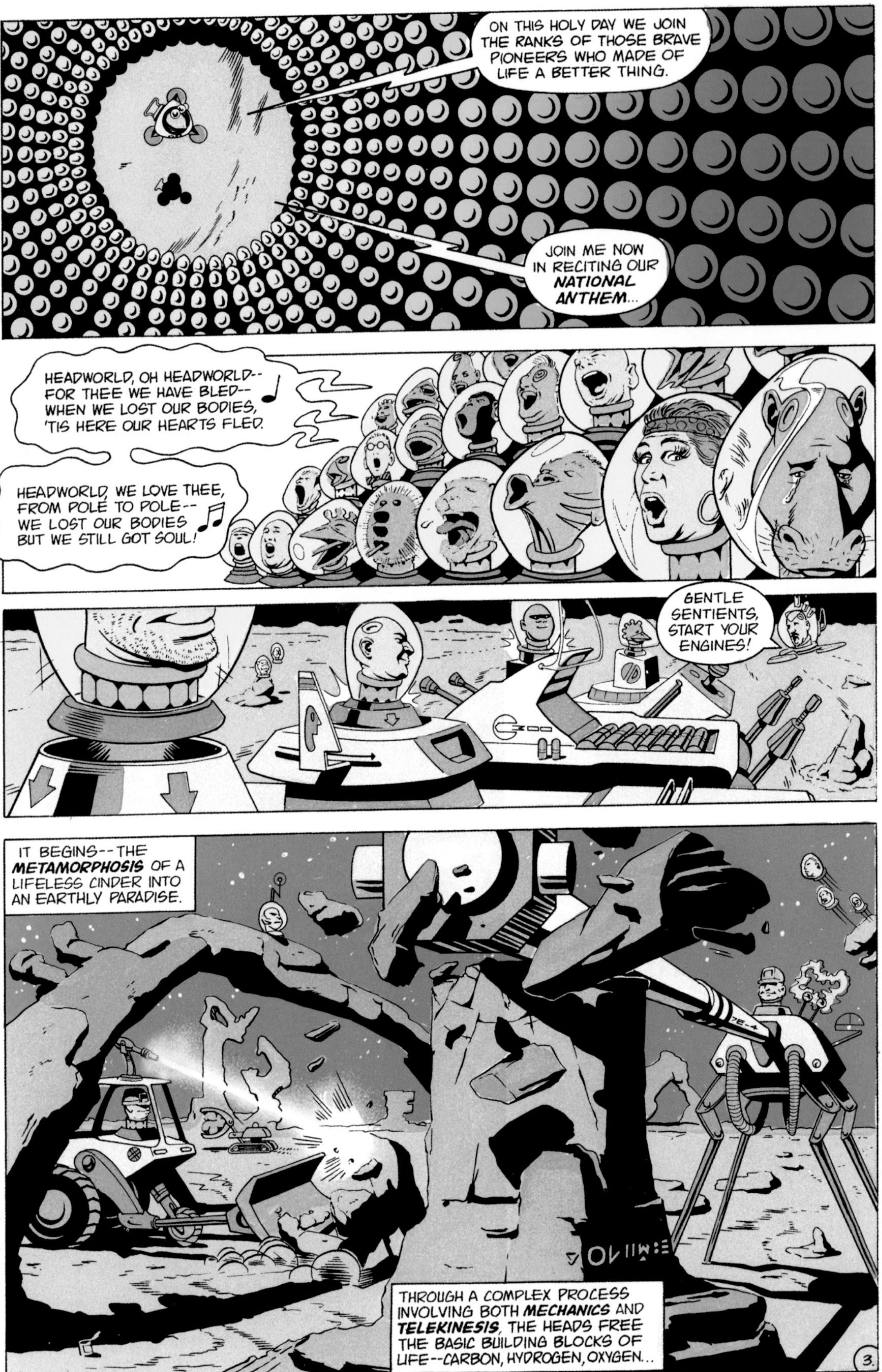
ON THIS HOLY DAY WE JOIN THE RANKS OF THOSE BRAVE PIONEERS WHO MADE OF LIFE A BETTER THING.
JOIN ME NOW IN RECITING OUR NATIONAL ANTHEM...
HEADWORLD, OH HEADWORLD-- FOR THEE WE HAVE BLED-- WHEN WE LOST OUR BODIES, 'TIS HERE OUR HEARTS FLED.
HEADWORLD, WE LOVE THEE, FROM POLE TO POLE-- WE LOST OUR BODIES BUT WE STILL GOT SOUL!
GENTLE SENTIENTS, START YOUR ENGINES!
IT BEGINS--THE METAMORPHOSIS OF A LIFELESS CINDER INTO AN EARTHLY PARADISE.
THROUGH A COMPLEX PROCESS INVOLVING BOTH MECHANICS AND TELEKINESIS, THE HEADS FREE THE BASIC BUILDING BLOCKS OF LIFE--CARBON, HYDROGEN, OXYGEN...
3.

CLUNK
AMPHIGORY TO RAUL! AMPHIGORY TO RAUL! SHAG LOBES OVER HERE, FELLA-- YOU GOTTA SEE THIS!
I'LL BE PICKLED! WHAT DO YOU MAKE OF THIS, AMPHIGORY?
RUINS... EVIDENCE OF A CIVILIZATION...
THE MARKINGS ARE SIMILAR TO THOSE FOUND ON YLUM.
ATTENTION, BLUE TEAM! FORM ON ME!
COMRADES, LINK UP. WE'VE GOT TO SEND A MESSAGE TO YLUM.
WITH PERFECT CONCENTRATION THE HEADS COMBINE THEIR TELEPATHIC ABILITIES INTO A SINGLE CONCENTRATED BEAM...
ON YLUM, SOME REMAIN TO SERVE HEADWORLD FROM AFAR.
HEADS LIKE HIPOLYTE...
WHAP
MESSAGE RECEIVED! I SHALL NOTIFY HIM AT ONCE!
4.

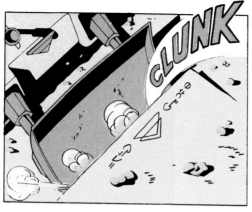

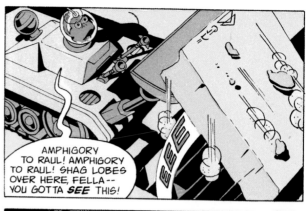

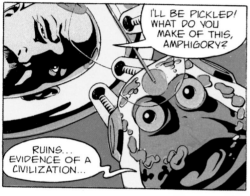

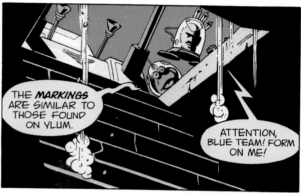

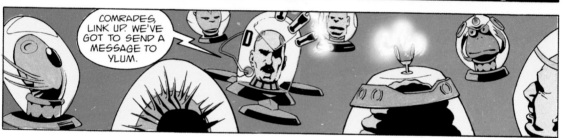

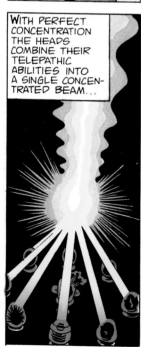

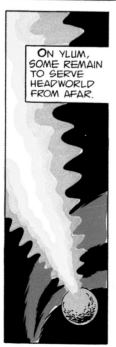

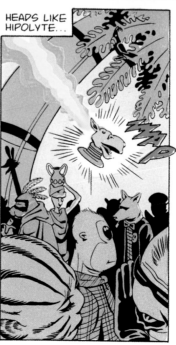

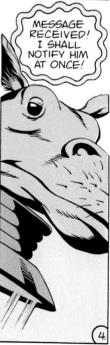

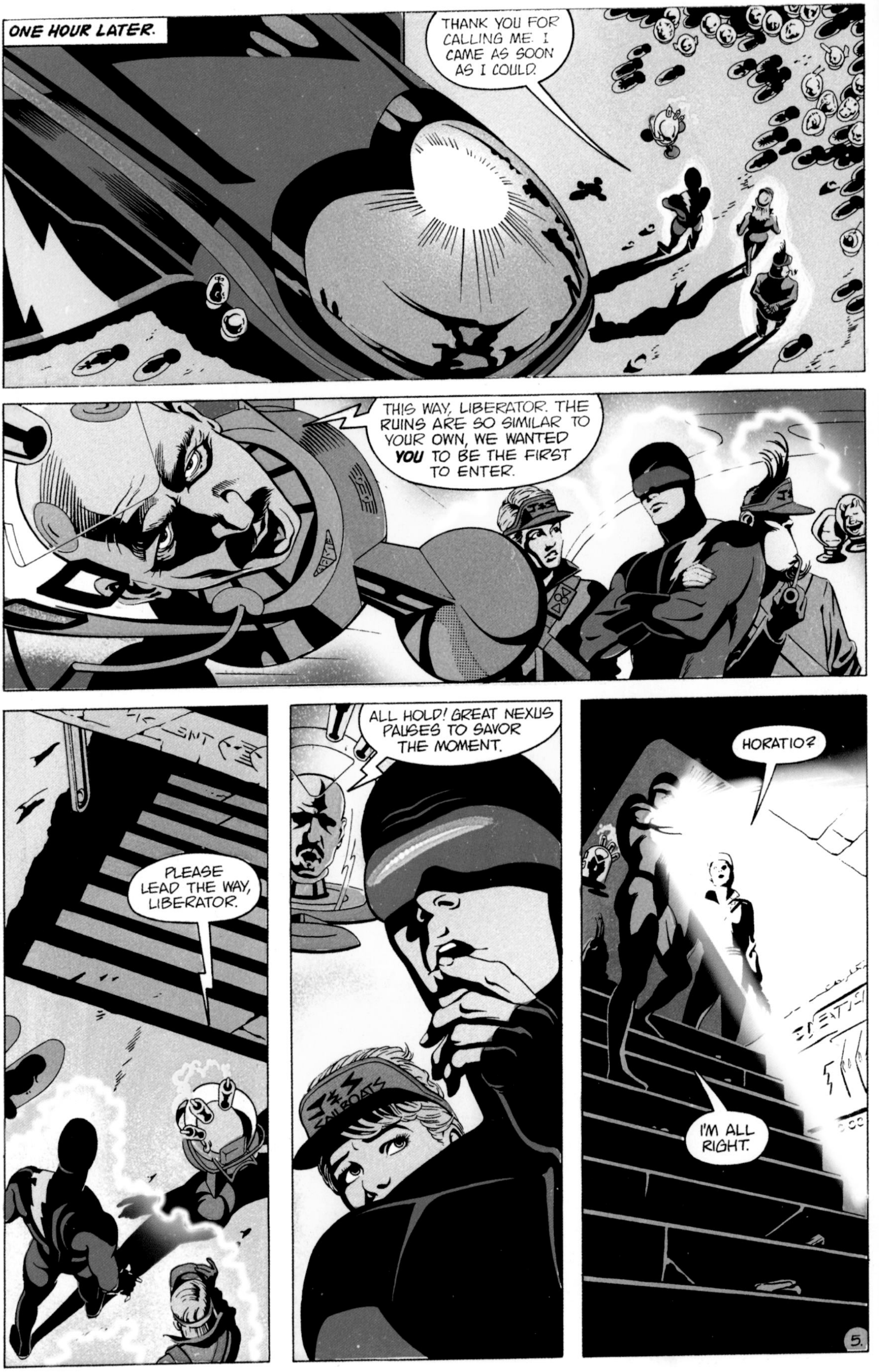
ONE HOUR LATER.
THANK YOU FOR CALLING ME. I CAME AS SOON AS I COULD.
THIS WAY, LIBERATOR. THE RUINS ARE SO SIMILAR TO YOUR OWN, WE WANTED YOU TO BE THE FIRST TO ENTER.
PLEASE LEAD THE WAY, LIBERATOR.
ALL HOLD! GREAT NEXUS PAUSES TO SAVOR THE MOMENT.
HORATIO?
I'M ALL RIGHT.
5.

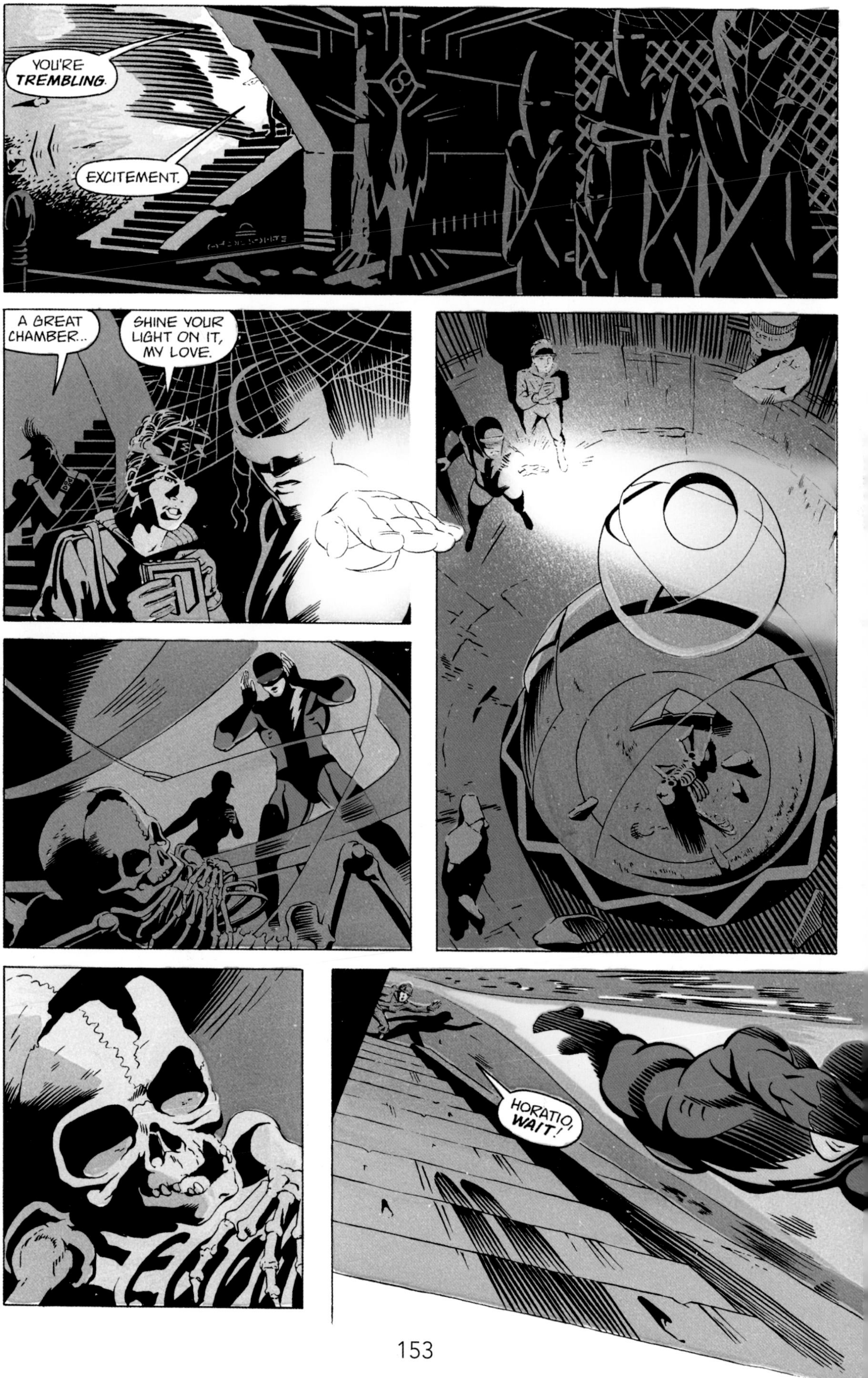
YOU'RE TREMBLING.
EXCITEMENT.
A GREAT CHAMBER...
SHINE YOUR LIGHT ON IT, MY LOVE.
HORATIO, WAIT!

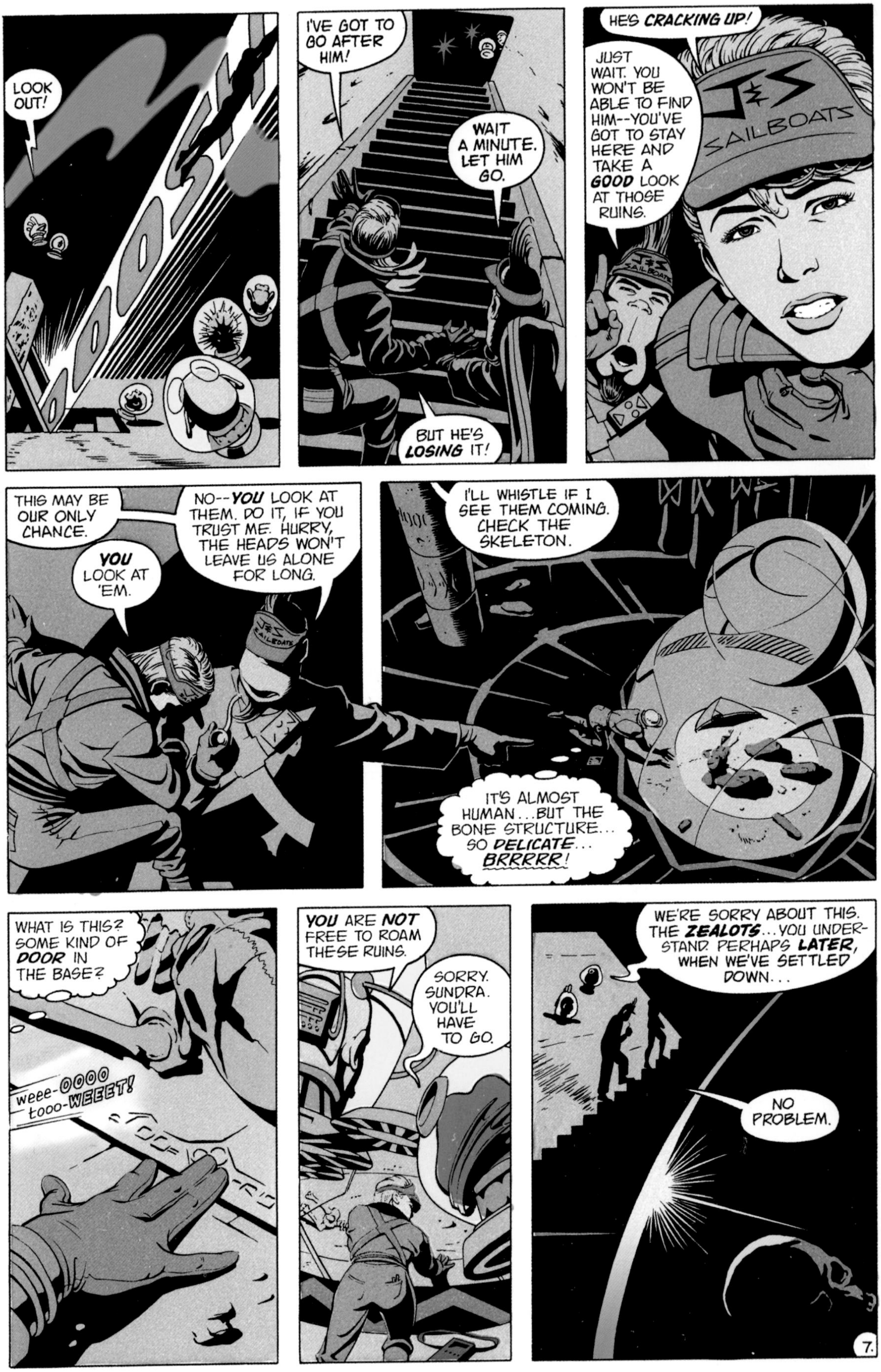
LOOK OUT!
WHOOSH
I'VE GOT TO GO AFTER HIM!
WAIT A MINUTE. LET HIM GO.
BUT HE'S LOSING IT!
HE'S CRACKING UP!
JUST WAIT. YOU WON'T BE ABLE TO FIND HIM--YOU'VE GOT TO STAY HERE AND TAKE A GOOD LOOK AT THOSE RUINS.
J&S SAILBOATS
THIS MAY BE OUR ONLY CHANCE.
NO--YOU LOOK AT THEM. DO IT, IF YOU TRUST ME. HURRY, THE HEADS WON'T LEAVE US ALONE FOR LONG.
YOU LOOK AT 'EM.
I'LL WHISTLE IF I SEE THEM COMING. CHECK THE SKELETON.
IT'S ALMOST HUMAN...BUT THE BONE STRUCTURE... SO DELICATE... BRRRRR!
WHAT IS THIS? SOME KIND OF DOOR IN THE BASE?
weee-OOOO tooo-WEEET!
YOU ARE NOT FREE TO ROAM THESE RUINS.
SORRY. SUNDRA. YOU'LL HAVE TO GO.
WE'RE SORRY ABOUT THIS. THE ZEALOTS...YOU UNDERSTAND. PERHAPS LATER, WHEN WE'VE SETTLED DOWN...
NO PROBLEM.
7.

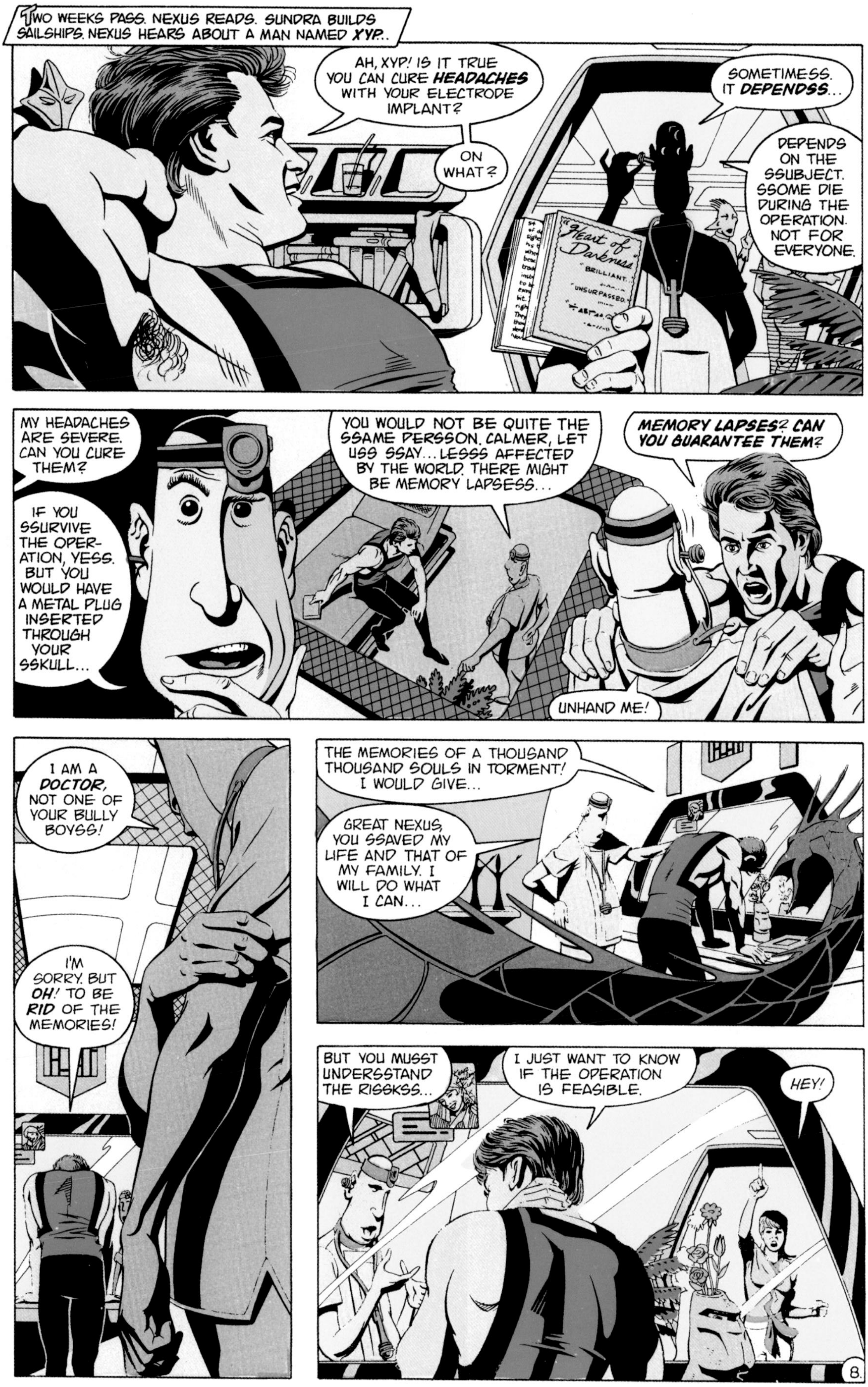
TWO WEEKS PASS. NEXUS READS. SUNDRA BUILDS SAILSHIPS. NEXUS HEARS ABOUT A MAN NAMED XYP..
AH, XYP! IS IT TRUE YOU CAN CURE HEADACHES WITH YOUR ELECTRODE IMPLANT?
SOMETIMESS. IT DEPENDSS...
ON WHAT?
DEPENDS ON THE SSUBJECT. SSOME DIE DURING THE OPERATION. NOT FOR EVERYONE.
Heart of Darkness
BRILLIANT.
UNSURPASSED.
MY HEADACHES ARE SEVERE. CAN YOU CURE THEM?
IF YOU SSURVIVE THE OPERATION, YESS. BUT YOU WOULD HAVE A METAL PLUG INSERTED THROUGH YOUR SSKULL...
YOU WOULD NOT BE QUITE THE SSAME PERSSON. CALMER, LET USS SSAY... LESSS AFFECTED BY THE WORLD. THERE MIGHT BE MEMORY LAPSESS...
MEMORY LAPSES? CAN YOU GUARANTEE THEM?
UNHAND ME!
I AM A DOCTOR, NOT ONE OF YOUR BULLY BOYSS!
I'M SORRY. BUT OH! TO BE RID OF THE MEMORIES!
THE MEMORIES OF A THOUSAND THOUSAND SOULS IN TORMENT! I WOULD GIVE...
GREAT NEXUS, YOU SSAVED MY LIFE AND THAT OF MY FAMILY. I WILL DO WHAT I CAN...
BUT YOU MUSST UNDERSSTAND THE RISSKSS...
I JUST WANT TO KNOW IF THE OPERATION IS FEASIBLE.
HEY!
8.

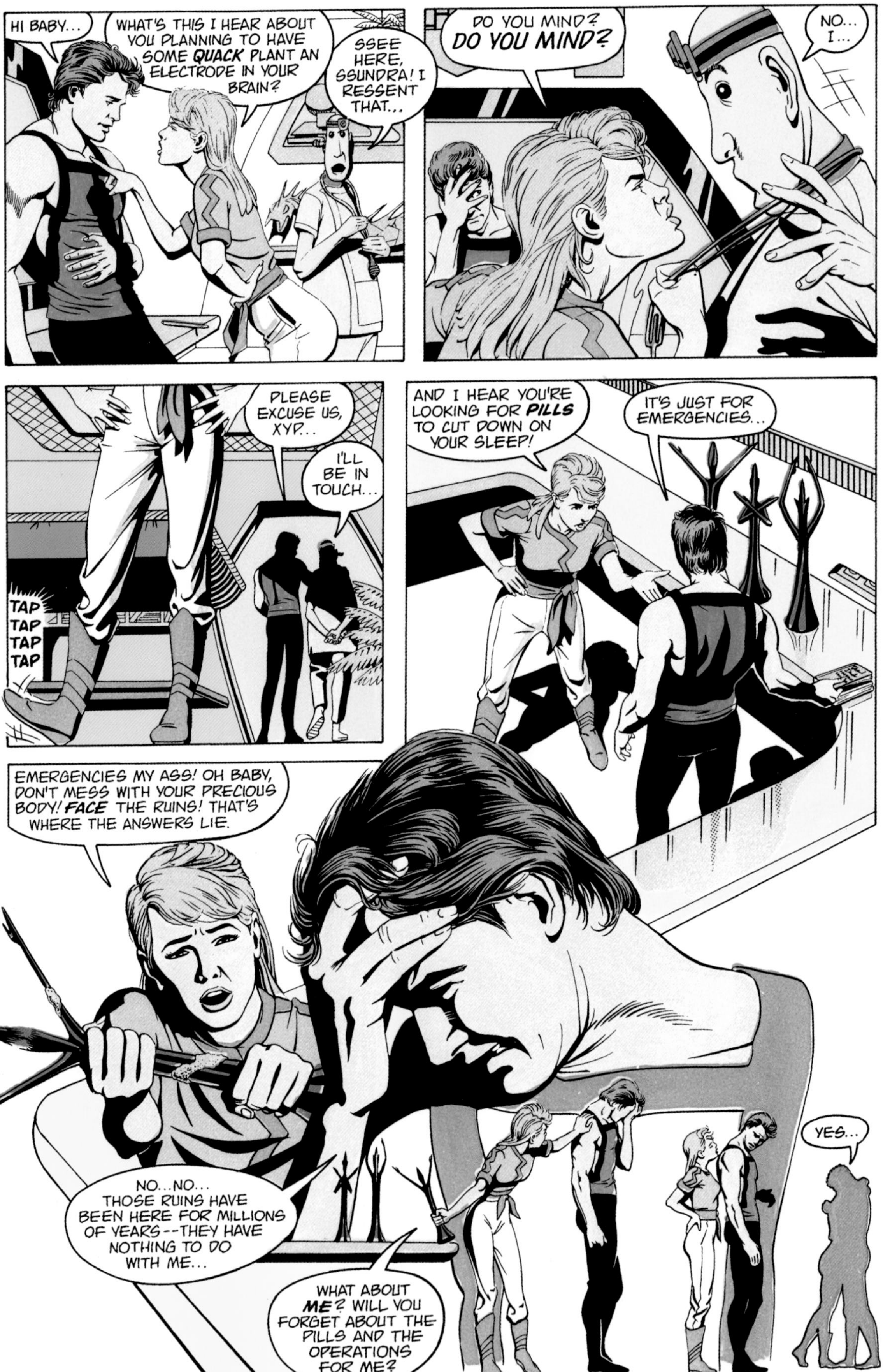
HI BABY...
WHAT'S THIS I HEAR ABOUT YOU PLANNING TO HAVE SOME QUACK PLANT AN ELECTRODE IN YOUR BRAIN?
SSEE HERE, SSUNDRA! I RESSENT THAT...
DO YOU MIND? DO YOU MIND?
NO... I...
PLEASE EXCUSE US, XYP...
I'LL BE IN TOUCH...
TAP TAP TAP TAP
AND I HEAR YOU'RE LOOKING FOR PILLS TO CUT DOWN ON YOUR SLEEP!
IT'S JUST FOR EMERGENCIES...
EMERGENCIES MY ASS! OH BABY, DON'T MESS WITH YOUR PRECIOUS BODY! FACE THE RUINS! THAT'S WHERE THE ANSWERS LIE.
NO...NO... THOSE RUINS HAVE BEEN HERE FOR MILLIONS OF YEARS--THEY HAVE NOTHING TO DO WITH ME...
WHAT ABOUT ME? WILL YOU FORGET ABOUT THE PILLS AND THE OPERATIONS FOR ME?
YES...

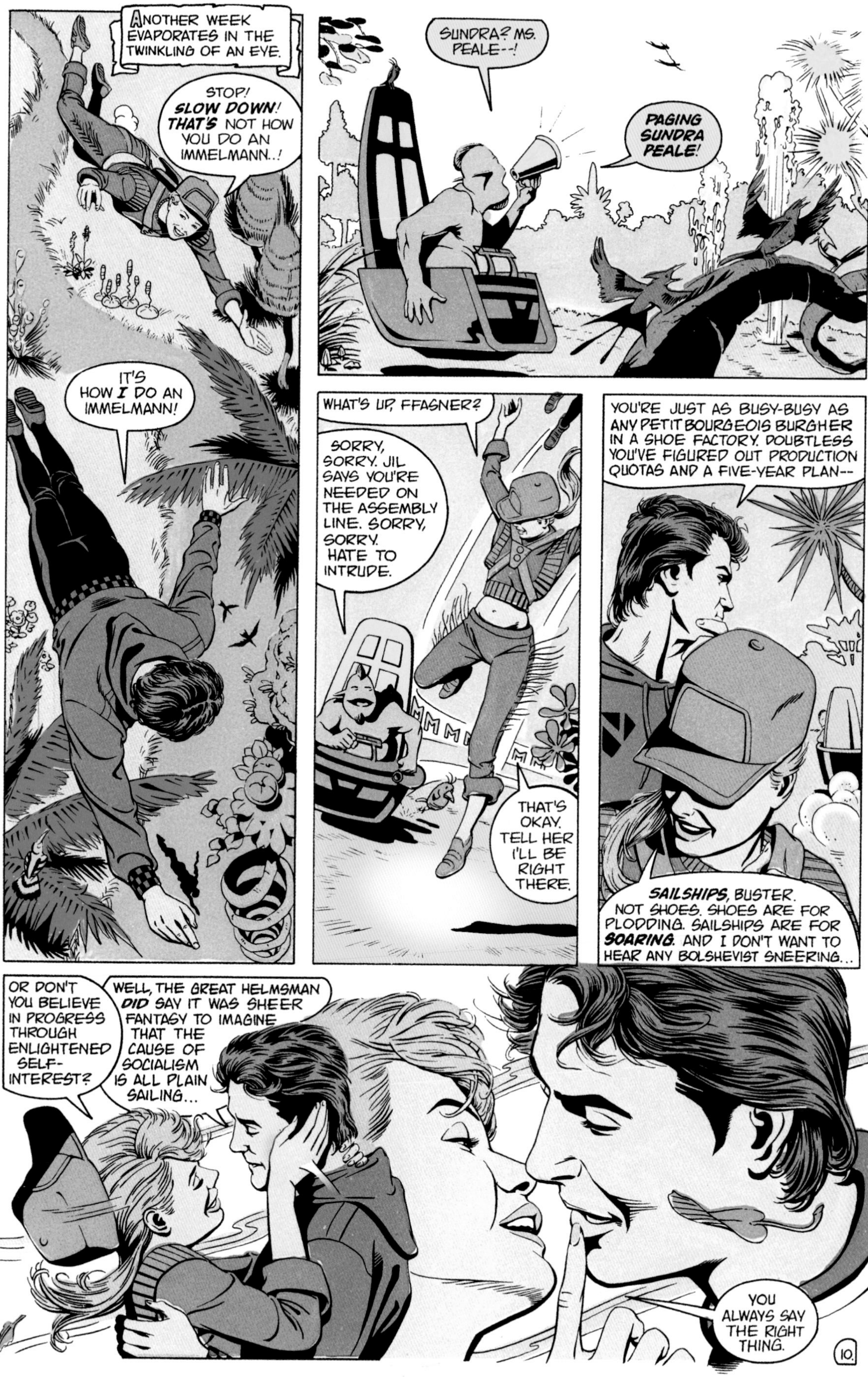
ANOTHER WEEK EVAPORATES IN THE TWINKLING OF AN EYE.
STOP! SLOW DOWN! THAT'S NOT HOW YOU DO AN IMMELMANN..!
IT'S HOW I DO AN IMMELMANN!
SUNDRA? MS. PEALE--!
PAGING SUNDRA PEALE!
WHAT'S UP, FFASNER?
SORRY, SORRY. JIL SAYS YOU'RE NEEDED ON THE ASSEMBLY LINE. SORRY, SORRY. HATE TO INTRUDE.
THAT'S OKAY. TELL HER I'LL BE RIGHT THERE.
YOU'RE JUST AS BUSY-BUSY AS ANY PETIT BOURGEOIS BURGHER IN A SHOE FACTORY. DOUBTLESS YOU'VE FIGURED OUT PRODUCTION QUOTAS AND A FIVE-YEAR PLAN--
SAILSHIPS, BUSTER. NOT SHOES. SHOES ARE FOR PLODDING. SAILSHIPS ARE FOR SOARING. AND I DON'T WANT TO HEAR ANY BOLSHEVIST SNEERING...
OR DON'T YOU BELIEVE IN PROGRESS THROUGH ENLIGHTENED SELF-INTEREST?
WELL, THE GREAT HELMSMAN DID SAY IT WAS SHEER FANTASY TO IMAGINE THAT THE CAUSE OF SOCIALISM IS ALL PLAIN SAILING...
YOU ALWAYS SAY THE RIGHT THING.
10

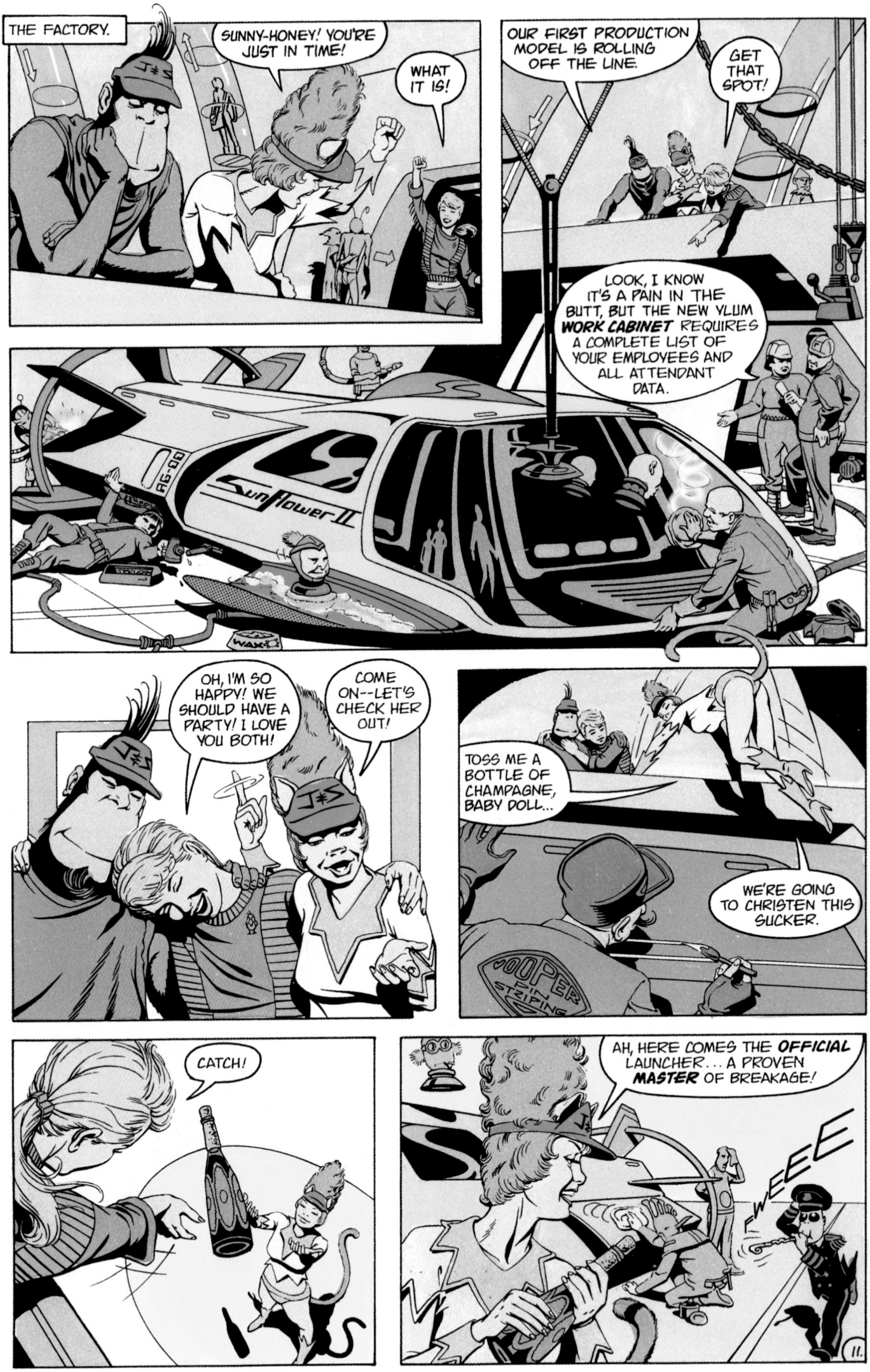
THE FACTORY.
SUNNY-HONEY! YOU'RE JUST IN TIME!
WHAT IT IS!
OUR FIRST PRODUCTION MODEL IS ROLLING OFF THE LINE.
GET THAT SPOT!
LOOK, I KNOW IT'S A PAIN IN THE BUTT, BUT THE NEW YLUM WORK CABINET REQUIRES A COMPLETE LIST OF YOUR EMPLOYEES AND ALL ATTENDANT DATA.
AG-00
SunFlower II
WAX
OH, I'M SO HAPPY! WE SHOULD HAVE A PARTY! I LOVE YOU BOTH!
COME ON--LET'S CHECK HER OUT!
TOSS ME A BOTTLE OF CHAMPAGNE, BABY DOLL...
WE'RE GOING TO CHRISTEN THIS SUCKER.
JOOPER PIN STRIPING
CATCH!
AH, HERE COMES THE OFFICIAL LAUNCHER... A PROVEN MASTER OF BREAKAGE!
FWEEEE
11.

 I CHRISTEN THEE--

 SUNFLOWER TOO! YAYYYY SMASH

OUR NEXT ORDER OF BUSINESS--WE DRAW STRAWS TO SEE WHO TAKES HER ON THE SHAKEDOWN...

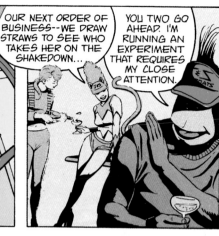 YOU TWO GO AHEAD. I'M RUNNING AN EXPERIMENT THAT REQUIRES MY CLOSE ATTENTION.

 GOOD OLD DAVE! HE DOESN'T HAVE ANY "EXPERIMENT!" HE JUST WANTS US TO GO FIRST!

WELL, WE SHOULD, SUN. IT WAS OUR IDEA TO BEGIN WITH. GET YOUR FLIGHT SUIT AND MEET ME HERE 'IN AN HOUR.

 SO? WHERE IS HE?

CALM DOWN, MR. PRESIDENT.

 I DON'T LIKE IT! RAUL WAS SUPPOSED TO BE HERE 15 MINUTES AGO.

RELAX, MR. PRESIDENT. AS HEAD HEAD, RAUL MUST BE ACCORDED CERTAIN PRIVILEGES...

 IT'S A SIGN OF DISCOURTESY! THAT'S WHAT IT IS!

NOT AT ALL. RAUL AGREED TO COME TO YLUM. THAT SHOWS THEIR RESPECT FOR US.

 HMM. WELL, I WON'T LET A TRIFLE LIKE THIS...

BZZ! MR. PRESIDENT-- THE REPRESENT- ATIVE FROM HEADWORLD HAS ARRIVED.

EXCELLENT. SHOW HIM IN.

 HELLO, HELLO, HELLO! ♪ MY NAME IS LANCE AND I AM YOUR AMBASSADOR FROM HEADWORLD. I'M SIMPLY THRILLED TO BE HERE!

12.

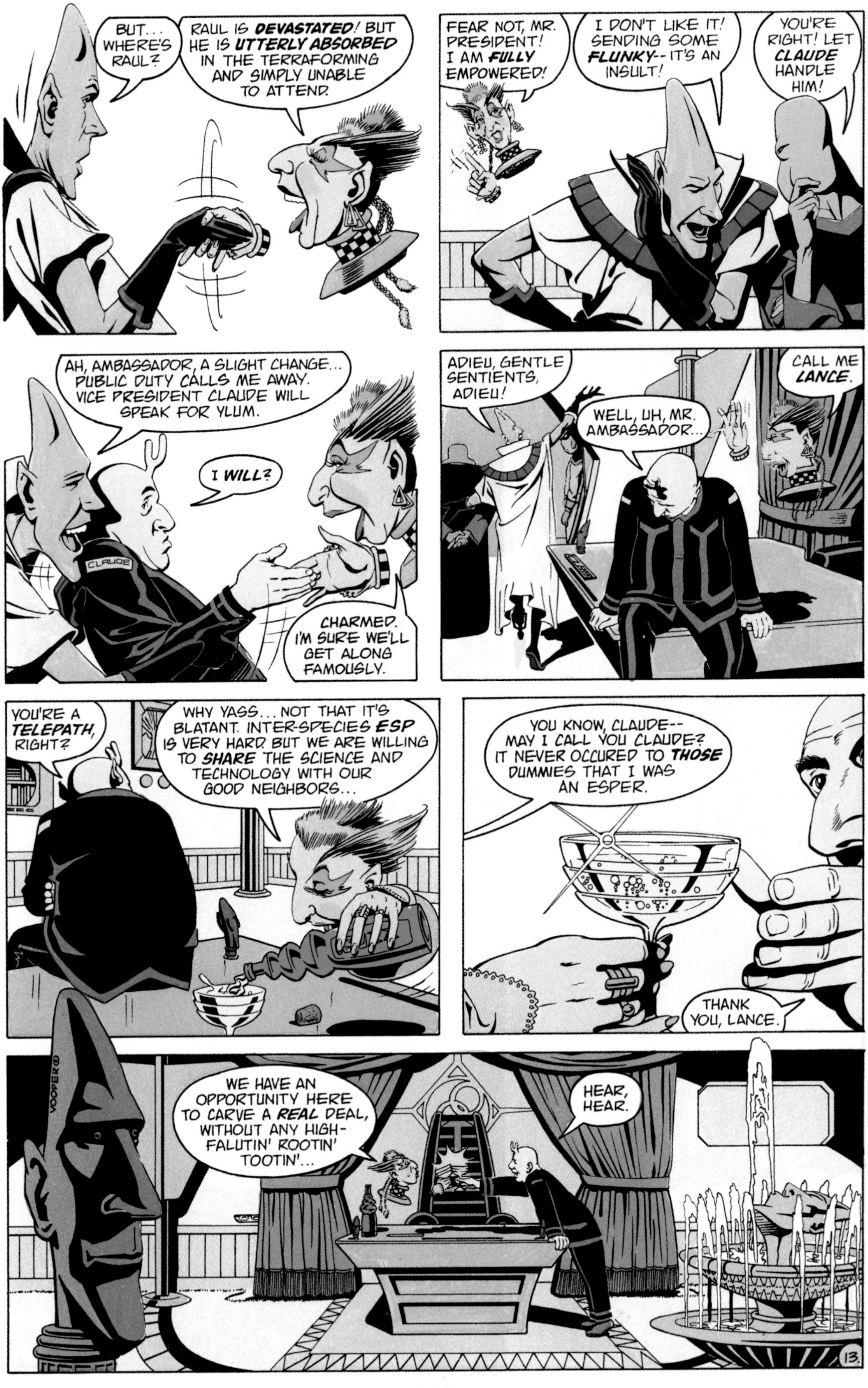

BUT... WHERE'S RAUL?
RAUL IS DEVASTATED! BUT HE IS UTTERLY ABSORBED IN THE TERRAFORMING AND SIMPLY UNABLE TO ATTEND.
FEAR NOT, MR. PRESIDENT! I AM FULLY EMPOWERED!
I DON'T LIKE IT! SENDING SOME FLUNKY-- IT'S AN INSULT!
YOU'RE RIGHT! LET CLAUDE HANDLE HIM!
AH, AMBASSADOR, A SLIGHT CHANGE... PUBLIC DUTY CALLS ME AWAY. VICE PRESIDENT CLAUDE WILL SPEAK FOR YLUM.
I WILL?
CLAUDE
CHARMED. I'M SURE WE'LL GET ALONG FAMOUSLY.
ADIEU, GENTLE SENTIENTS, ADIEU!
WELL, UH, MR. AMBASSADOR...
CALL ME LANCE.
YOU'RE A TELEPATH, RIGHT?
WHY YASS... NOT THAT IT'S BLATANT. INTER-SPECIES ESP IS VERY HARD. BUT WE ARE WILLING TO SHARE THE SCIENCE AND TECHNOLOGY WITH OUR GOOD NEIGHBORS...
YOU KNOW, CLAUDE-- MAY I CALL YOU CLAUDE? IT NEVER OCCURED TO THOSE DUMMIES THAT I WAS AN ESPER.
THANK YOU, LANCE.
WE HAVE AN OPPORTUNITY HERE TO CARVE A REAL DEAL, WITHOUT ANY HIGH-FALUTIN' ROOTIN' TOOTIN'...
HEAR, HEAR.
13.

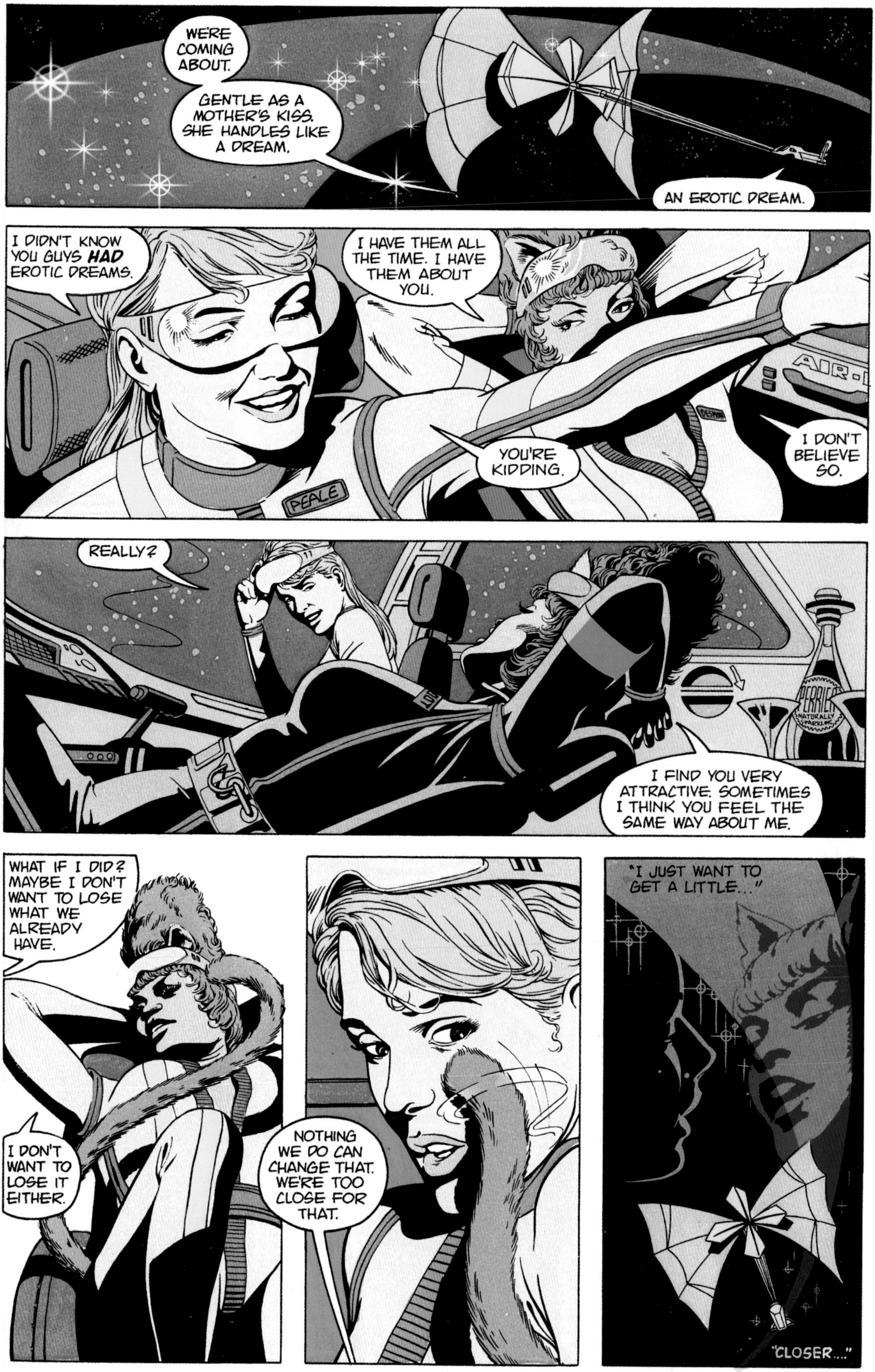
WE'RE COMING ABOUT.
GENTLE AS A MOTHER'S KISS. SHE HANDLES LIKE A DREAM.
AN EROTIC DREAM.
I DIDN'T KNOW YOU GUYS HAD EROTIC DREAMS.
I HAVE THEM ALL THE TIME. I HAVE THEM ABOUT YOU.
YOU'RE KIDDING.
I DON'T BELIEVE SO.
PEALE
REALLY?
I FIND YOU VERY ATTRACTIVE. SOMETIMES I THINK YOU FEEL THE SAME WAY ABOUT ME.
WHAT IF I DID? MAYBE I DON'T WANT TO LOSE WHAT WE ALREADY HAVE.
I DON'T WANT TO LOSE IT EITHER.
NOTHING WE DO CAN CHANGE THAT. WE'RE TOO CLOSE FOR THAT.
"I JUST WANT TO GET A LITTLE..."
"CLOSER..."

HELLO, JUDAH. IF YOU DON'T GET THIS SPHERE BY APRIL, LET ME KNOW SO I CAN SWITCH TO ANOTHER CARRIER.

WELL, SON, IT'S BEEN AWHILE SINCE WE SPOKE. YOUR FRIENDS THE HEADS ARE *TERRAFORMING* A NEW HOME. THE SAILBOATS ARE ROLLING. BIT OF TROUBLE WITH *NEXUS*, I'M AFRAID...

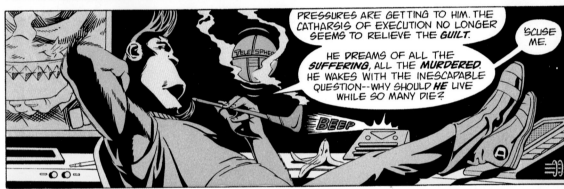

PRESSURES ARE GETTING TO HIM. THE CATHARSIS OF EXECUTION NO LONGER SEEMS TO RELIEVE THE *GUILT*.

HE DREAMS OF ALL THE *SUFFERING*, ALL THE *MURDERED*. HE WAKES WITH THE INESCAPABLE QUESTION--WHY SHOULD *HE* LIVE WHILE SO MANY DIE?

'SCUSE ME.

BEEP

AH, *DUKE*. WHAT NEWS?

YOU'RE RIGHT: THOSE *CALLS* WERE *ALL* MADE BY THE PARTY IN JK20.09. HE'S BEEN HERE FOR THREE EARTH YEARS.

EUREKA! THANK YOU, DUKE!

JUDAH! HOT NEWS! I'VE FOUND THE *SPY!* THE SPY WHO SQUEALED TO CLAUSIUS, SUTTA LEBERQ, AND GOULESSARIAN KNOWS WHO ELSE...*

GOT TO TELL NEXUS. WE'LL CHAT AGAIN LATER.

*SEE *NEXUS* VOL. I, #1-3, IF YOU CAN FIND 'EM. --RAO.

MR. PRESIDENT!

AH, DUKE! WHAT NEWS?

MOMENTS LATER.

I HOPE WE'RE IN TIME! I'VE JUST LEARNED THAT THE SPY *BOLTED*, HEADING FOR ONE OF THE HANGARS. SOMEONE MUST HAVE TIPPED HIM OFF.

HE WON'T GET FAR. I WANT TO ASK THIS CHARACTER SOME QUESTIONS... NOTHING BUGS ME MORE THAN AN INVASION OF PRIVACY!

15.

162

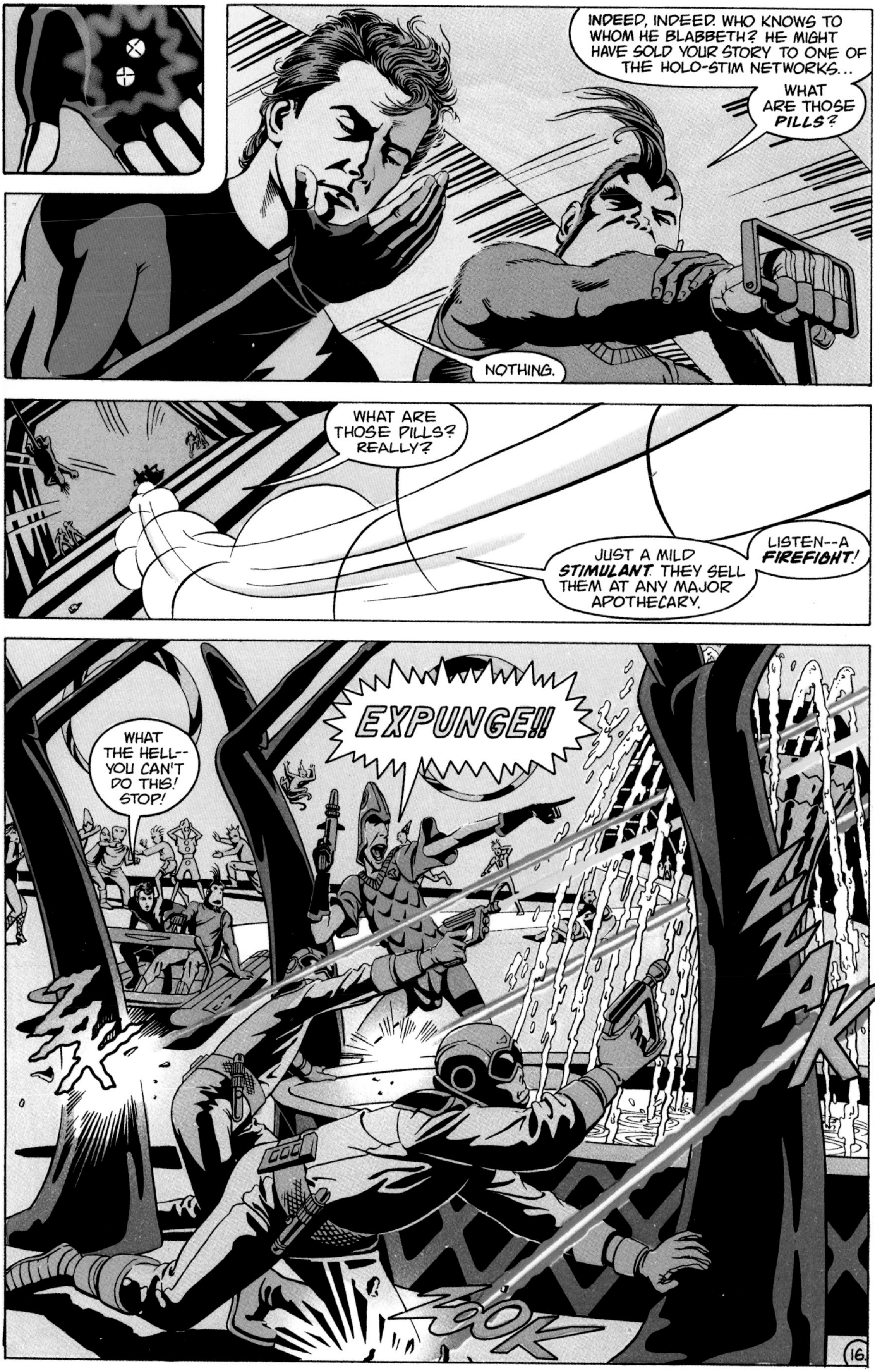
INDEED, INDEED. WHO KNOWS TO WHOM HE BLABBETH? HE MIGHT HAVE SOLD YOUR STORY TO ONE OF THE HOLO-STIM NETWORKS...
WHAT ARE THOSE PILLS?
NOTHING.
WHAT ARE THOSE PILLS? REALLY?
JUST A MILD STIMULANT. THEY SELL THEM AT ANY MAJOR APOTHECARY.
LISTEN--A FIREFIGHT!
WHAT THE HELL-- YOU CAN'T DO THIS! STOP!
EXPUNGE!!
ZZAK
ZZZAK
ZOOK
16.

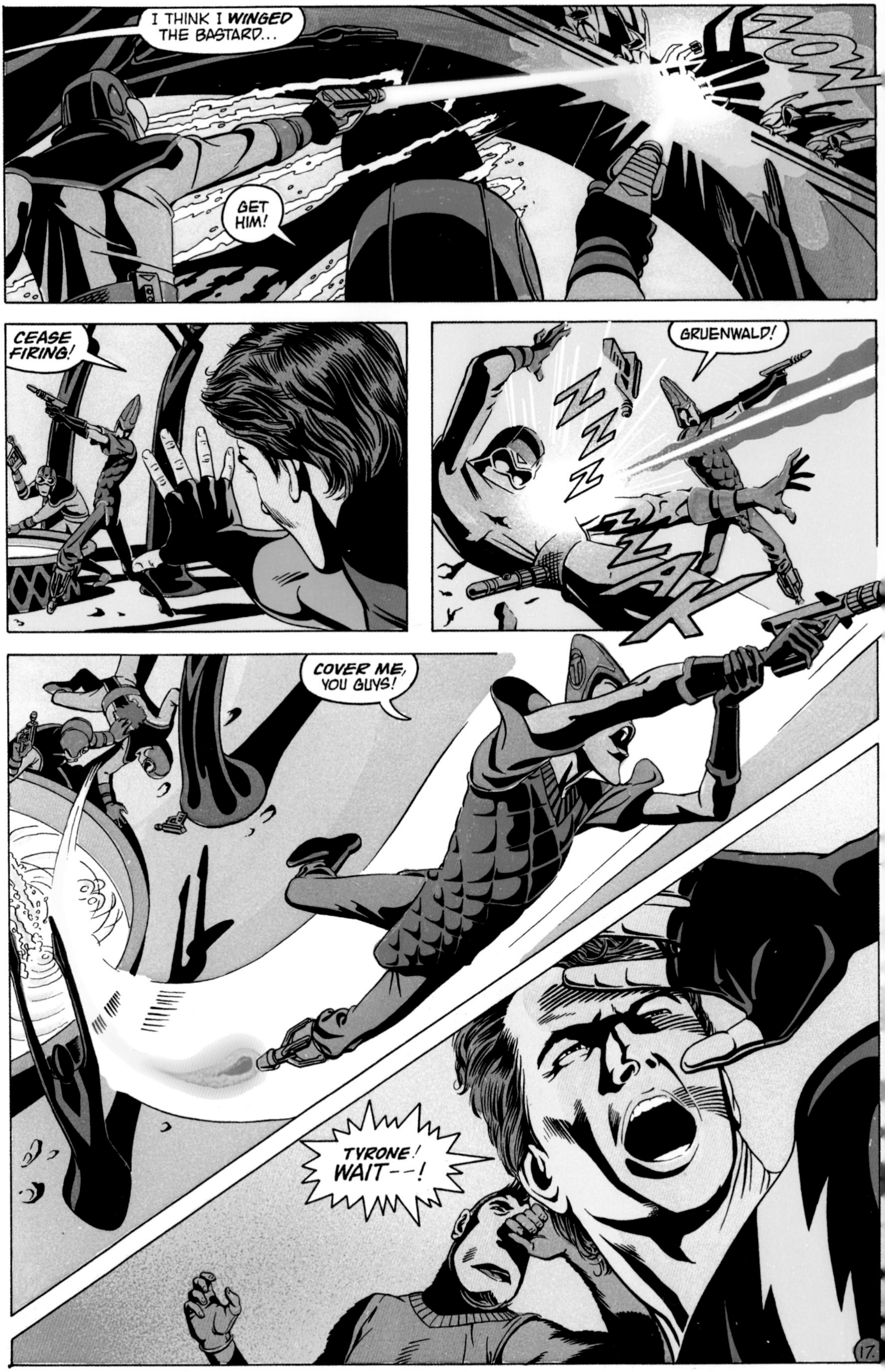
I THINK I WINGED THE BASTARD...
ZOW
GET HIM!
CEASE FIRING!
GRUENWALD!
ZZZ
ZZAK
COVER ME, YOU GUYS!
TYRONE! WAIT--!
17.

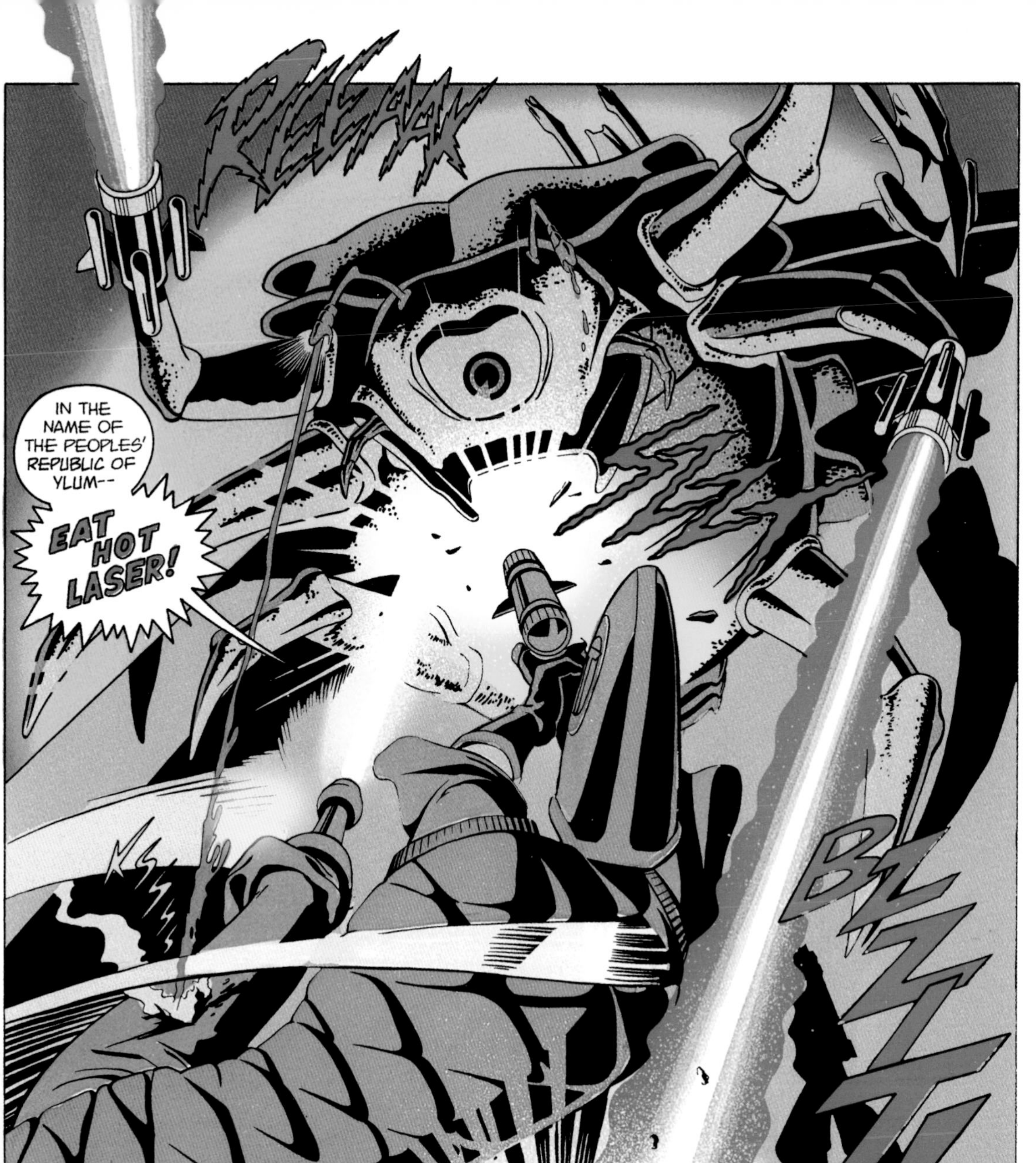
RKEAAK
IN THE NAME OF THE PEOPLES' REPUBLIC OF YLUM--
EAT HOT LASER!
BZZZT!

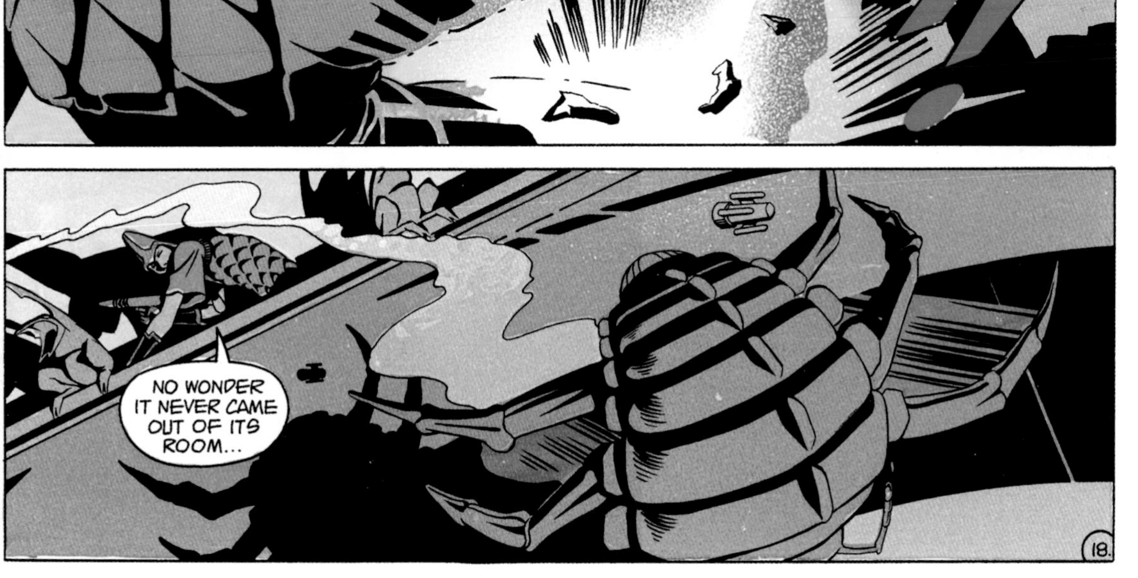
NO WONDER IT NEVER CAME OUT OF ITS ROOM...
18.

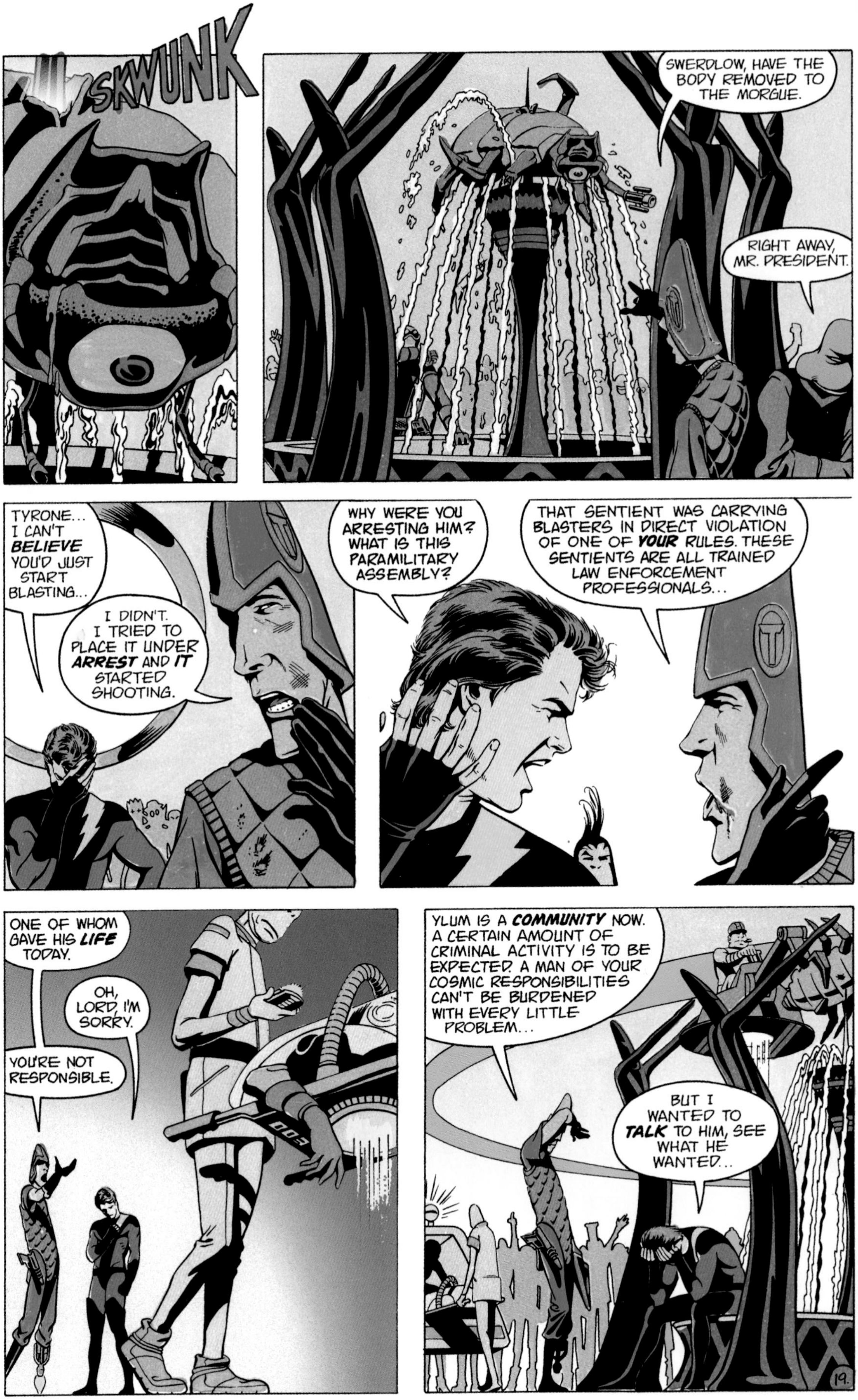
SKWUNK
SWERDLOW, HAVE THE BODY REMOVED TO THE MORGUE.
RIGHT AWAY, MR. PRESIDENT.
TYRONE... I CAN'T BELIEVE YOU'D JUST START BLASTING...
I DIDN'T. I TRIED TO PLACE IT UNDER ARREST AND IT STARTED SHOOTING.
WHY WERE YOU ARRESTING HIM? WHAT IS THIS PARAMILITARY ASSEMBLY?
THAT SENTIENT WAS CARRYING BLASTERS IN DIRECT VIOLATION OF ONE OF YOUR RULES. THESE SENTIENTS ARE ALL TRAINED LAW ENFORCEMENT PROFESSIONALS...
ONE OF WHOM GAVE HIS LIFE TODAY.
OH, LORD, I'M SORRY.
YOU'RE NOT RESPONSIBLE.
YLUM IS A COMMUNITY NOW. A CERTAIN AMOUNT OF CRIMINAL ACTIVITY IS TO BE EXPECTED. A MAN OF YOUR COSMIC RESPONSIBILITIES CAN'T BE BURDENED WITH EVERY LITTLE PROBLEM...
BUT I WANTED TO TALK TO HIM, SEE WHAT HE WANTED...
19.

I'M SORRY. I HAD NO CHOICE. I REALIZE YOU COULD HAVE APPREHENDED THE CREATURE, BUT WHAT'S DONE IS DONE. WE HAVE A POLICE FORCE NOW, EMPOWERED BY A POPULAR VOTE.

YES... I SEE...

CARRY ON, MR. PRESIDENT.

RIGHT ON, CITIZEN!

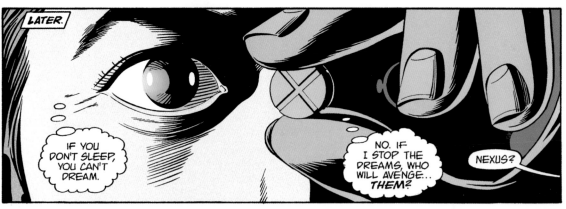

LATER.

IF YOU DON'T SLEEP, YOU CAN'T DREAM.

NO. IF I STOP THE DREAMS, WHO WILL AVENGE... THEM?

NEXUS?

YOU WISHED TO BE INFORMED--

YOU'RE READY?

WE ARE READY TO CONDUCT TESTSS-- TO SSEE IF IT CAN BE DONE.

LEAD THE WAY.

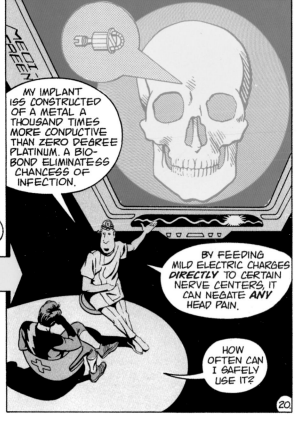

MY IMPLANT ISS CONSTRUCTED OF A METAL A THOUSAND TIMES MORE CONDUCTIVE THAN ZERO DEGREE PLATINUM. A BIO-BOND ELIMINATESS CHANCESS OF INFECTION.

BY FEEDING MILD ELECTRIC CHARGES DIRECTLY TO CERTAIN NERVE CENTERS, IT CAN NEGATE ANY HEAD PAIN.

HOW OFTEN CAN I SAFELY USE IT?

20.

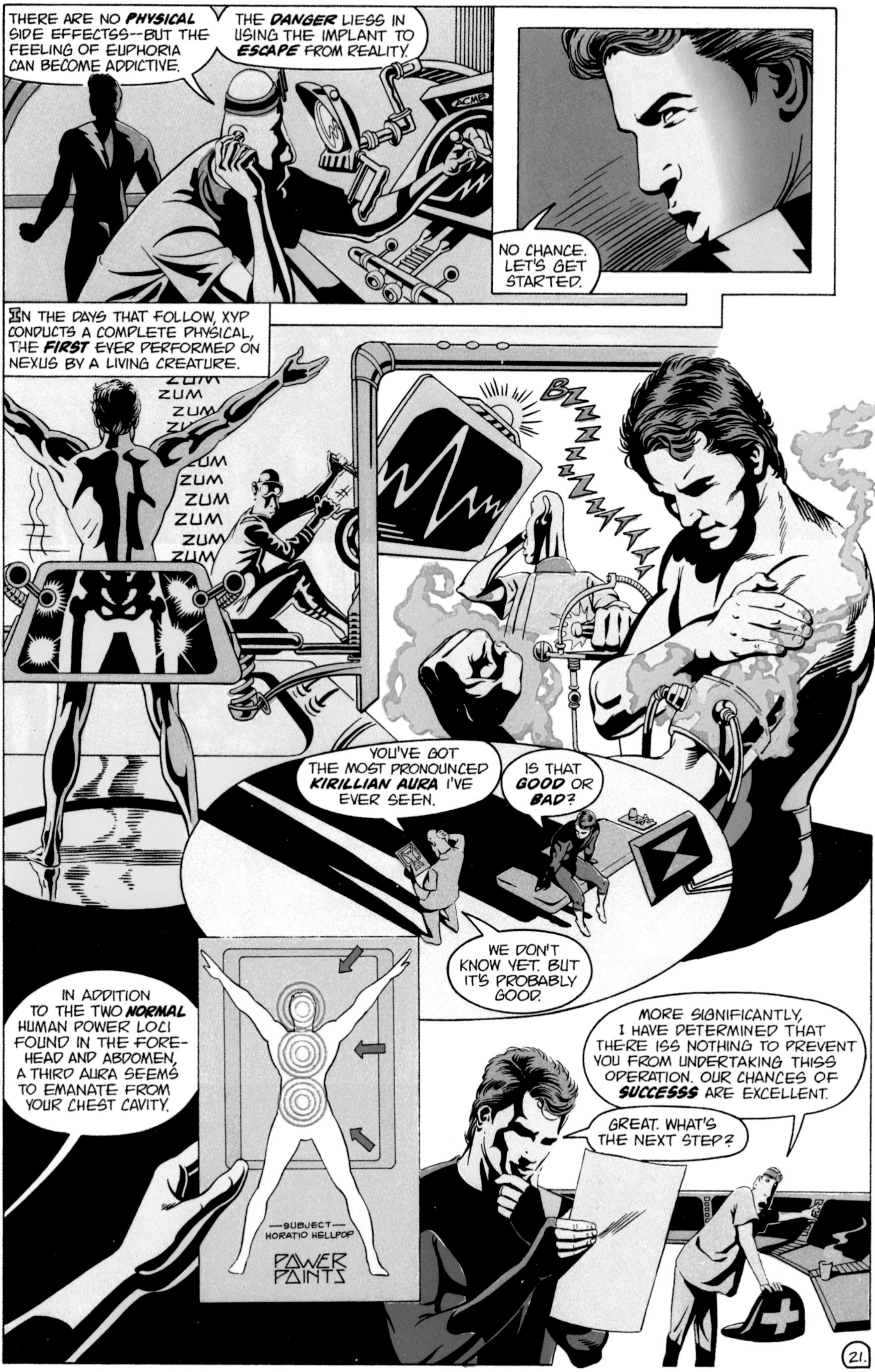
THERE ARE NO PHYSICAL SIDE EFFECTSS--BUT THE FEELING OF EUPHORIA CAN BECOME ADDICTIVE.
THE DANGER LIESS IN USING THE IMPLANT TO ESCAPE FROM REALITY.
ACME
NO CHANCE. LET'S GET STARTED.
IN THE DAYS THAT FOLLOW, XYP CONDUCTS A COMPLETE PHYSICAL, THE FIRST EVER PERFORMED ON NEXUS BY A LIVING CREATURE.
ZUM ZUM ZUM ZUM ZUM ZUM ZUM ZUM ZUM ZUM
BZZZZZZZZZZZZZ
YOU'VE GOT THE MOST PRONOUNCED KIRILLIAN AURA I'VE EVER SEEN.
IS THAT GOOD OR BAD?
WE DON'T KNOW YET. BUT IT'S PROBABLY GOOD.
IN ADDITION TO THE TWO NORMAL HUMAN POWER LOCI FOUND IN THE FORE-HEAD AND ABDOMEN, A THIRD AURA SEEMS TO EMANATE FROM YOUR CHEST CAVITY.
—SUBJECT— HORATIO HELLPOP
POWER POINTS
MORE SIGNIFICANTLY, I HAVE DETERMINED THAT THERE ISS NOTHING TO PREVENT YOU FROM UNDERTAKING THISS OPERATION. OUR CHANCES OF SUCCESSS ARE EXCELLENT.
GREAT. WHAT'S THE NEXT STEP?
21.

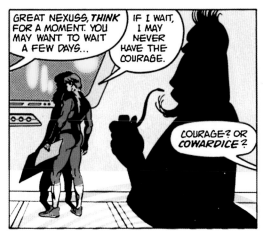

GREAT NEXUSS, *THINK* FOR A MOMENT. YOU MAY WANT TO WAIT A FEW DAYS...

IF I WAIT, I MAY NEVER HAVE THE COURAGE.

COURAGE? OR *COWARDICE*?

HAVE I NOT SHOWN *ENOUGH* COURAGE?

BUT I FEAR THE LOSS OF THE MAN I HAVE KNOWN.

I WON'T CHANGE...

WHAT'S WRONG?

I HAVE WAITED... *TOO LONG*...!

WHERE'S HORATIO?

IN THE TANK.

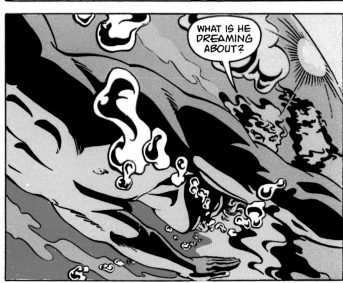

WHAT IS HE DREAMING ABOUT?

SOMEONE HUMAN. SOMEONE AWFUL.

22

169

ON HEADWORLD ONLY A MONTH HAS PASSED. FROM *ANCIENT ASHES*, THE HEADS HAVE CARVED A TINY POCKET OF *PARADISE*, BUBBLE ATMOSPHERE PRESERVED BY FORCE FIELD.

PARADISE VALLEY IS OPEN FOR OCCUPATION. WE INTRODUCE THE INSECTS TOMORROW.

ARE THE INSECTS REALLY NECESSARY?

BUT OF COURSE. WE WANT A FULLY *SELF-SUSTAINING* BIO-SPHERE. THAT MEANS INSECTS TO SPREAD POLLEN.

BRRR. I *HATE* MOSQUITOES!

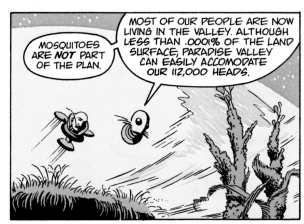

MOSQUITOES ARE *NOT* PART OF THE PLAN.

MOST OF OUR PEOPLE ARE NOW LIVING IN THE VALLEY. ALTHOUGH LESS THAN .0001% OF THE LAND SURFACE, PARADISE VALLEY CAN EASILY ACCOMODATE OUR 112,000 HEADS.

AFTER THE HORRORS WE HAVE SUFFERED, IT IS ONLY *JUST* THAT WE ENJOY THIS PLACE OF REST.

YET WE MUST REMAIN EVER VIGILANT, FOR WE HEADS CONSTITUTE A GREAT SOURCE OF POTENTIAL POWER AND WEALTH...

23.

UNTIL OUR *DEFENSES* ARE COMPLETE, WE WILL PROVE TEMPTING TO OUR ENEMIES, THE *SLAVERS*...

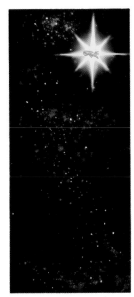

JUST LOOK AT IT, JACQUES.

THOUSANDS OF THEM, RIPE FOR PLUCKING!

AND THE BEAUTY OF IT IS THEY'VE ALREADY BEEN *PROCESSED*. THEY'RE READY TO GO *ON LINE!*

OUR SHIELDS KEEP US HIDDEN FROM THEIR SWEEPS. NEXUS IS OUT TO LUNCH.

ARE YOU READY TO ROCK?

OH, CAPTAIN, MY CAPTAIN, OUR SITES ARE ON THE BUBBLE. BUT HEED MY WORDS-- *FORGET* THOSE BIRDS! THE HEADS ARE TROUBLE.

EXQUISITE, JACQUES. WHAT A *GIFT*. NOW PLEASE PRIME THE TRACTOR BEAMS WE'RE GOING DOWN.

TO BE CONTINUED...

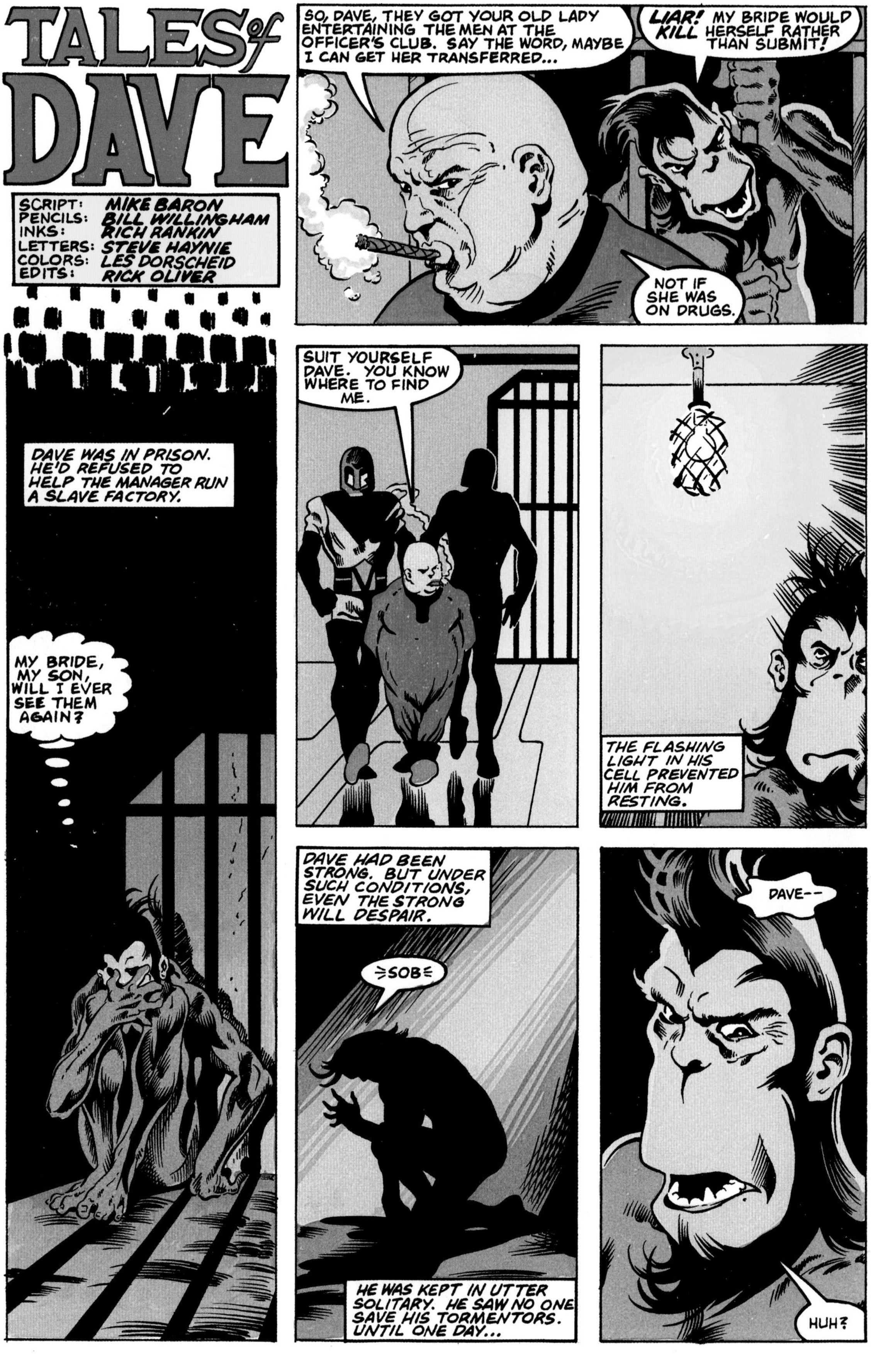
TALES of DAVE
SCRIPT: MIKE BARON
PENCILS: BILL WILLINGHAM
INKS: RICH RANKIN
LETTERS: STEVE HAYNIE
COLORS: LES DORSCHEID
EDITS: RICK OLIVER
SO, DAVE, THEY GOT YOUR OLD LADY ENTERTAINING THE MEN AT THE OFFICER'S CLUB. SAY THE WORD, MAYBE I CAN GET HER TRANSFERRED...
LIAR! MY BRIDE WOULD KILL HERSELF RATHER THAN SUBMIT!
NOT IF SHE WAS ON DRUGS.
DAVE WAS IN PRISON. HE'D REFUSED TO HELP THE MANAGER RUN A SLAVE FACTORY.
MY BRIDE, MY SON, WILL I EVER SEE THEM AGAIN?
SUIT YOURSELF DAVE. YOU KNOW WHERE TO FIND ME.
THE FLASHING LIGHT IN HIS CELL PREVENTED HIM FROM RESTING.
DAVE HAD BEEN STRONG. BUT UNDER SUCH CONDITIONS, EVEN THE STRONG WILL DESPAIR.
SOB
HE WAS KEPT IN UTTER SOLITARY. HE SAW NO ONE SAVE HIS TORMENTORS. UNTIL ONE DAY...
DAVE--
HUH?

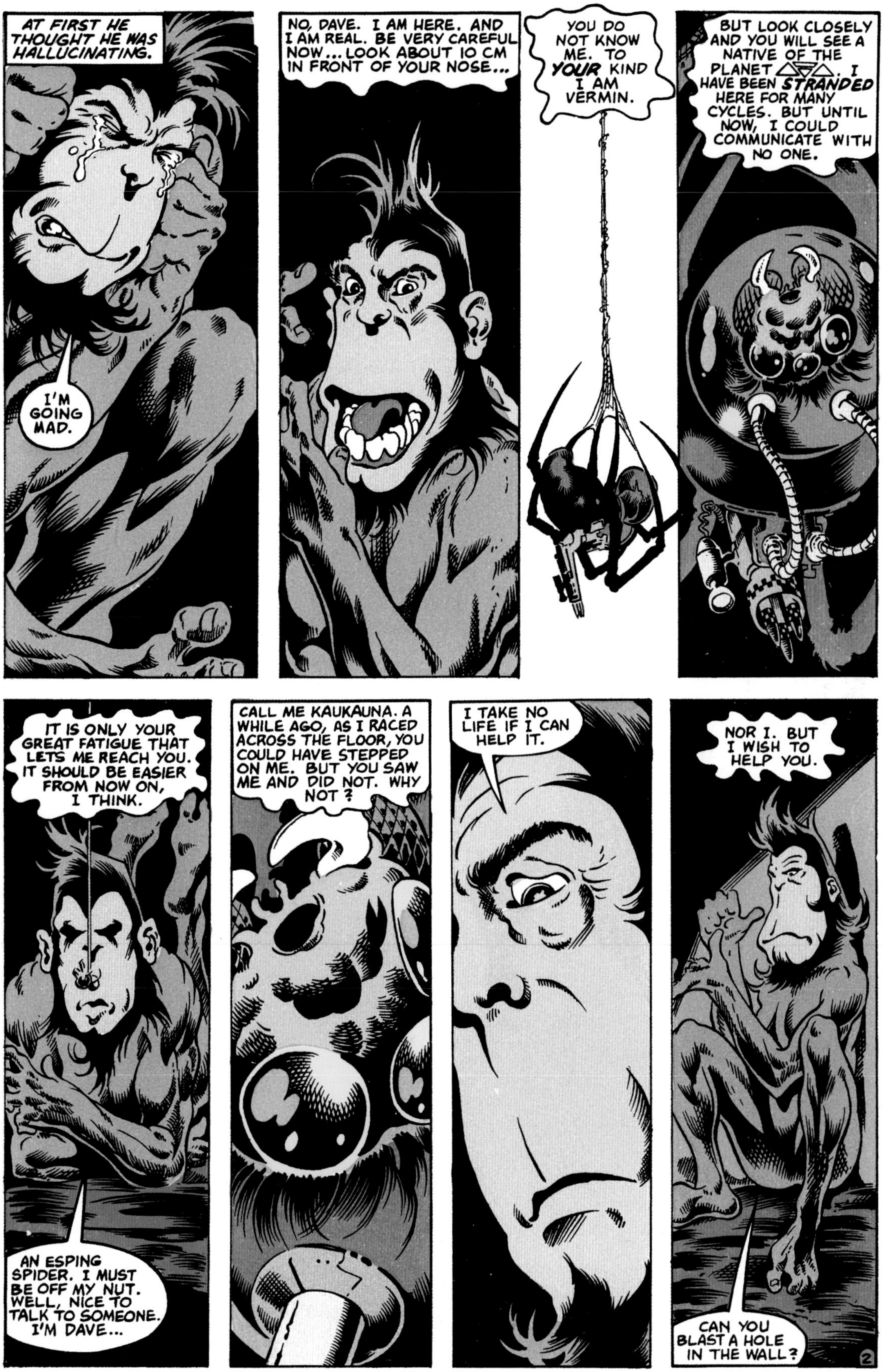
AT FIRST HE THOUGHT HE WAS HALLUCINATING.
I'M GOING MAD.
NO, DAVE. I AM HERE. AND I AM REAL. BE VERY CAREFUL NOW... LOOK ABOUT 10 CM IN FRONT OF YOUR NOSE...
YOU DO NOT KNOW ME. TO YOUR KIND I AM VERMIN.
BUT LOOK CLOSELY AND YOU WILL SEE A NATIVE OF THE PLANET △▽△. I HAVE BEEN STRANDED HERE FOR MANY CYCLES. BUT UNTIL NOW, I COULD COMMUNICATE WITH NO ONE.
IT IS ONLY YOUR GREAT FATIGUE THAT LETS ME REACH YOU. IT SHOULD BE EASIER FROM NOW ON, I THINK.
AN ESPING SPIDER. I MUST BE OFF MY NUT. WELL, NICE TO TALK TO SOMEONE. I'M DAVE...
CALL ME KAUKAUNA. A WHILE AGO, AS I RACED ACROSS THE FLOOR, YOU COULD HAVE STEPPED ON ME. BUT YOU SAW ME AND DID NOT. WHY NOT?
I TAKE NO LIFE IF I CAN HELP IT.
NOR I. BUT I WISH TO HELP YOU.
CAN YOU BLAST A HOLE IN THE WALL?
2

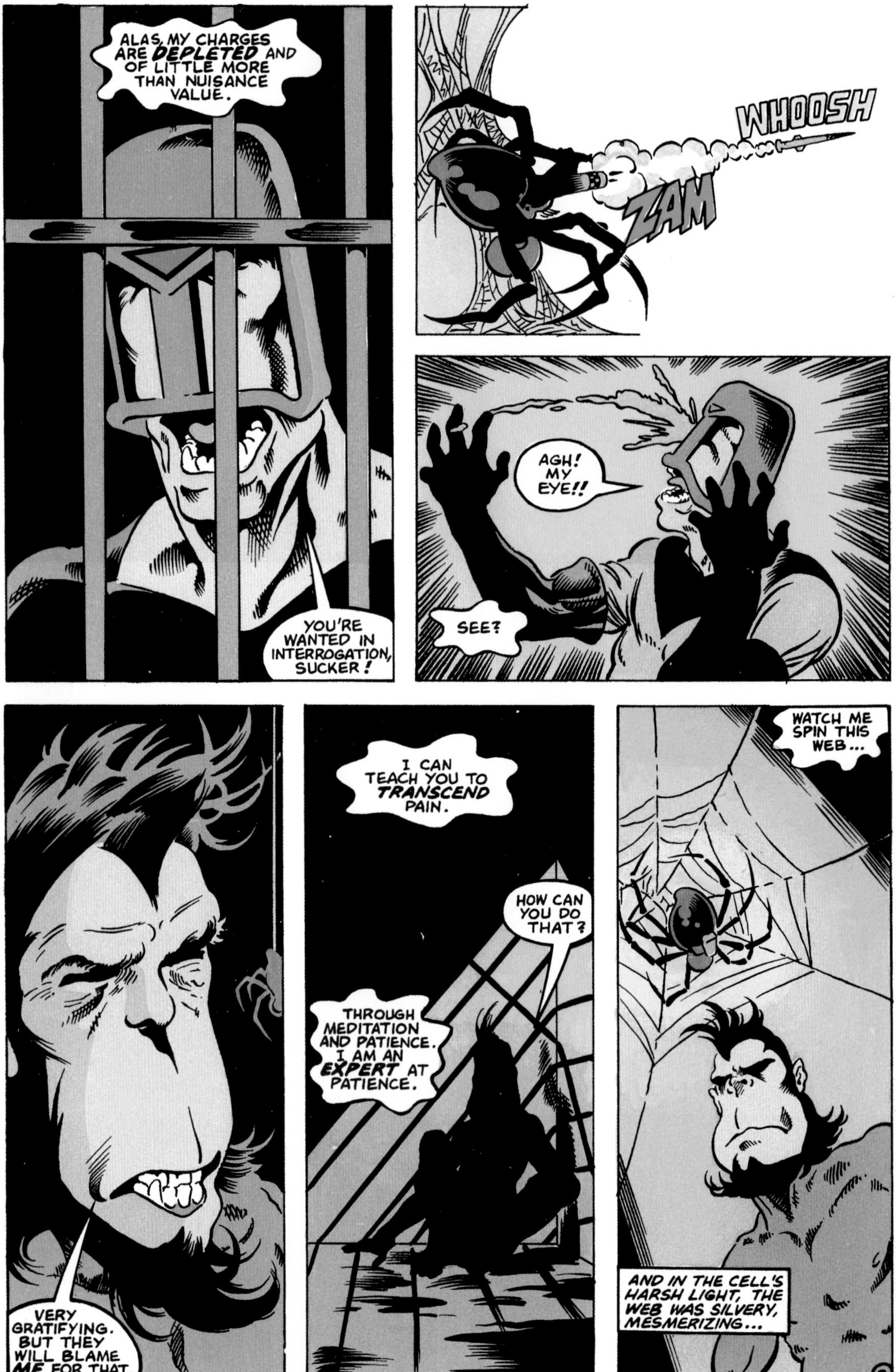
ALAS, MY CHARGES ARE DEPLETED AND OF LITTLE MORE THAN NUISANCE VALUE.
YOU'RE WANTED IN INTERROGATION, SUCKER!
WHOOSH
ZAM
AGH! MY EYE!!
SEE?
VERY GRATIFYING. BUT THEY WILL BLAME ME FOR THAT.
I CAN TEACH YOU TO TRANSCEND PAIN.
HOW CAN YOU DO THAT?
THROUGH MEDITATION AND PATIENCE. I AM AN EXPERT AT PATIENCE.
WATCH ME SPIN THIS WEB...
AND IN THE CELL'S HARSH LIGHT, THE WEB WAS SILVERY, MESMERIZING...
3

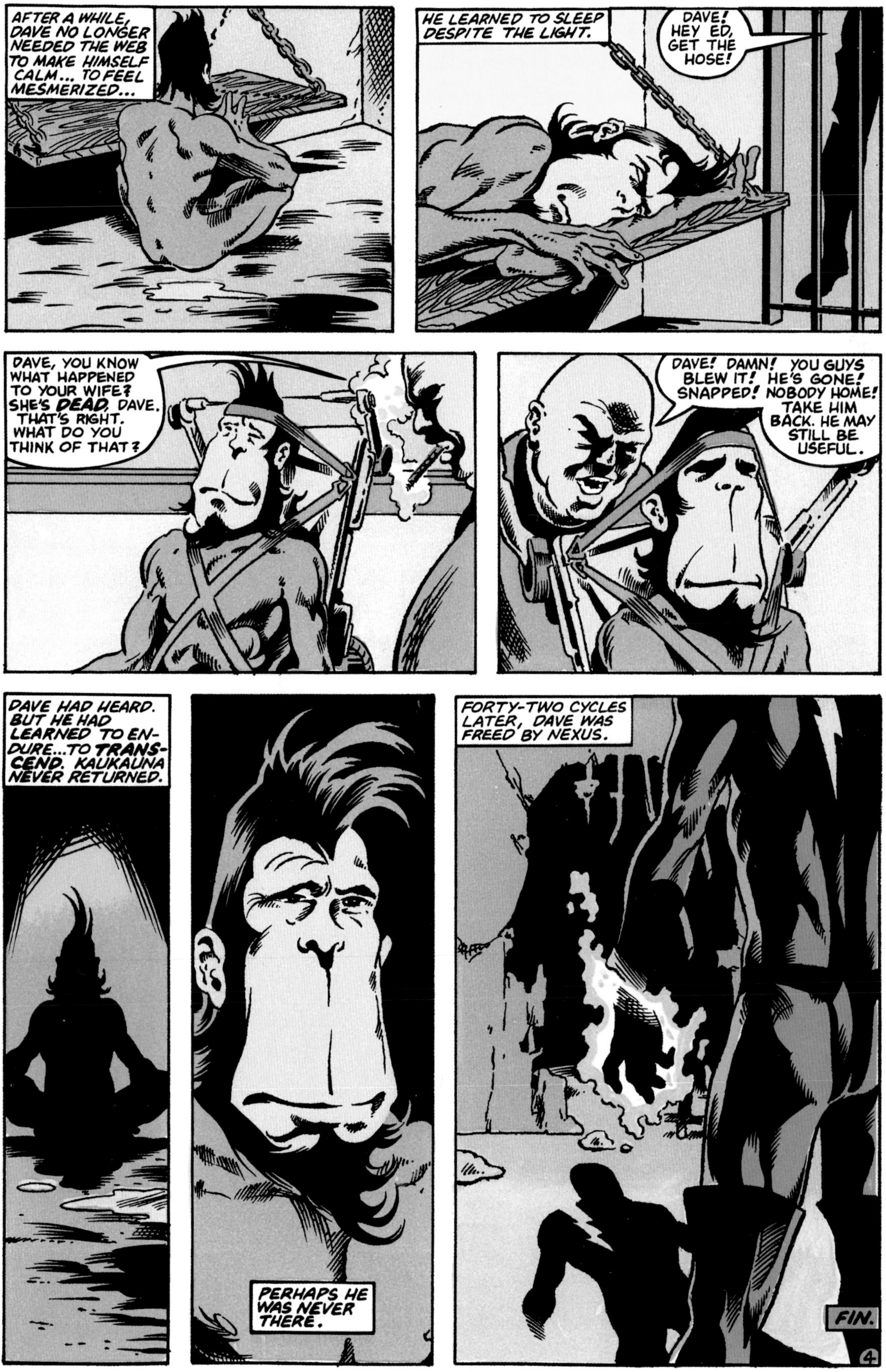
AFTER A WHILE, DAVE NO LONGER NEEDED THE WEB TO MAKE HIMSELF CALM... TO FEEL MESMERIZED...
HE LEARNED TO SLEEP DESPITE THE LIGHT.
DAVE! HEY ED, GET THE HOSE!
DAVE, YOU KNOW WHAT HAPPENED TO YOUR WIFE? SHE'S DEAD, DAVE. THAT'S RIGHT. WHAT DO YOU THINK OF THAT?
DAVE! DAMN! YOU GUYS BLEW IT! HE'S GONE! SNAPPED! NOBODY HOME! TAKE HIM BACK. HE MAY STILL BE USEFUL.
DAVE HAD HEARD. BUT HE HAD LEARNED TO ENDURE...TO TRANSCEND. KAUKAUNA NEVER RETURNED.
PERHAPS HE WAS NEVER THERE.
FORTY-TWO CYCLES LATER, DAVE WAS FREED BY NEXUS.
FIN.
4

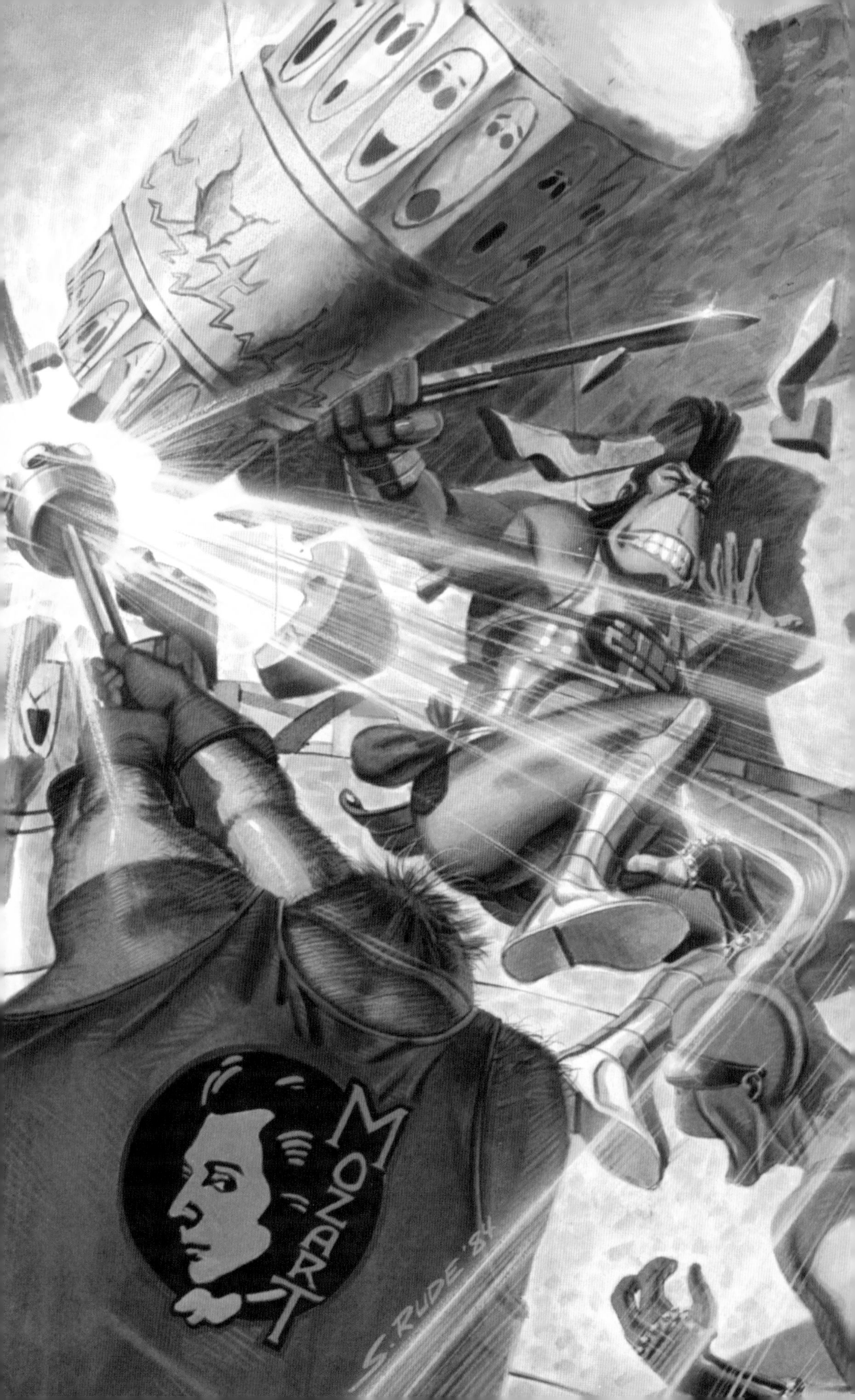
MOZART
S. RUDE '84

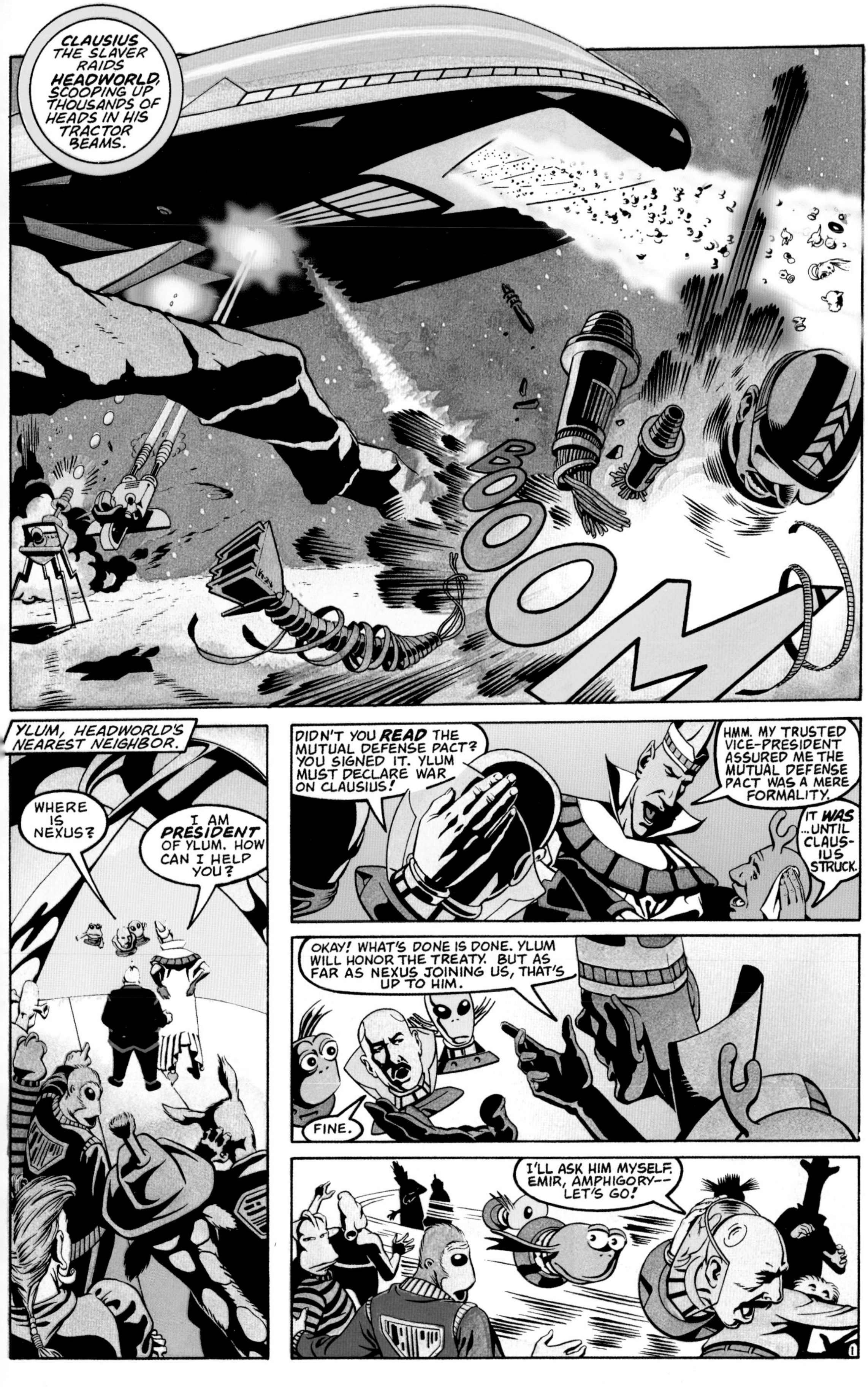
CLAUSIUS THE SLAVER RAIDS HEADWORLD, SCOOPING UP THOUSANDS OF HEADS IN HIS TRACTOR BEAMS.
BOOOOM
YLUM, HEADWORLD'S NEAREST NEIGHBOR.
WHERE IS NEXUS?
I AM PRESIDENT OF YLUM. HOW CAN I HELP YOU?
DIDN'T YOU READ THE MUTUAL DEFENSE PACT? YOU SIGNED IT. YLUM MUST DECLARE WAR ON CLAUSIUS!
HMM. MY TRUSTED VICE-PRESIDENT ASSURED ME THE MUTUAL DEFENSE PACT WAS A MERE FORMALITY.
IT WAS ...UNTIL CLAUSIUS STRUCK.
OKAY! WHAT'S DONE IS DONE. YLUM WILL HONOR THE TREATY. BUT AS FAR AS NEXUS JOINING US, THAT'S UP TO HIM.
FINE.
I'LL ASK HIM MYSELF. EMIR, AMPHIGORY-- LET'S GO!

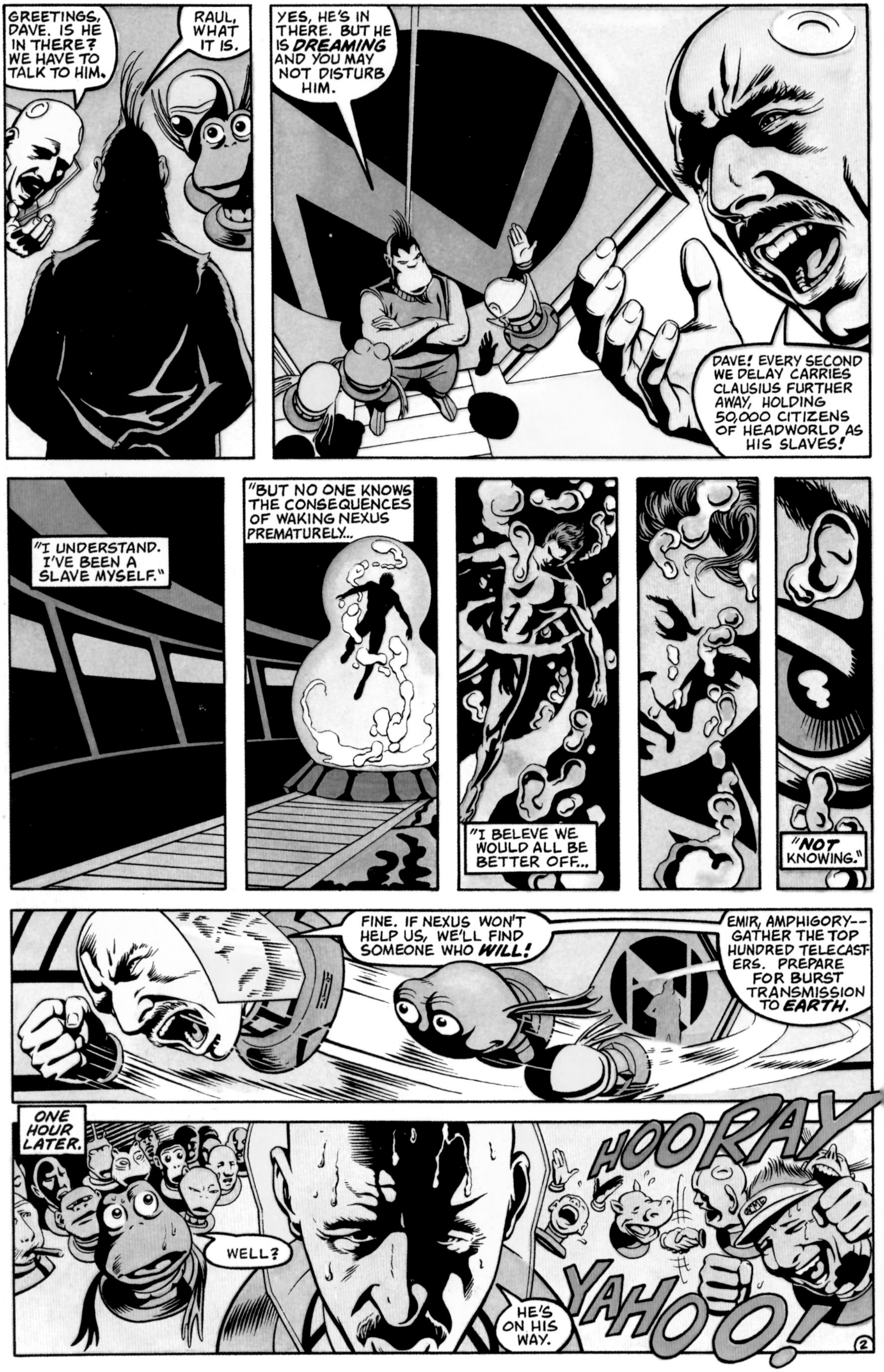
GREETINGS, DAVE. IS HE IN THERE? WE HAVE TO TALK TO HIM.
RAUL, WHAT IT IS.
YES, HE'S IN THERE. BUT HE IS DREAMING AND YOU MAY NOT DISTURB HIM.
DAVE! EVERY SECOND WE DELAY CARRIES CLAUSIUS FURTHER AWAY, HOLDING 50,000 CITIZENS OF HEADWORLD AS HIS SLAVES!
"I UNDERSTAND. I'VE BEEN A SLAVE MYSELF."
"BUT NO ONE KNOWS THE CONSEQUENCES OF WAKING NEXUS PREMATURELY...
"I BELEVE WE WOULD ALL BE BETTER OFF...
"NOT KNOWING."
FINE. IF NEXUS WON'T HELP US, WE'LL FIND SOMEONE WHO WILL!
EMIR, AMPHIGORY-- GATHER THE TOP HUNDRED TELECAST-ERS. PREPARE FOR BURST TRANSMISSION TO EARTH.
ONE HOUR LATER.
HOORAY
WELL?
HE'S ON HIS WAY.
YAHOOO!
2

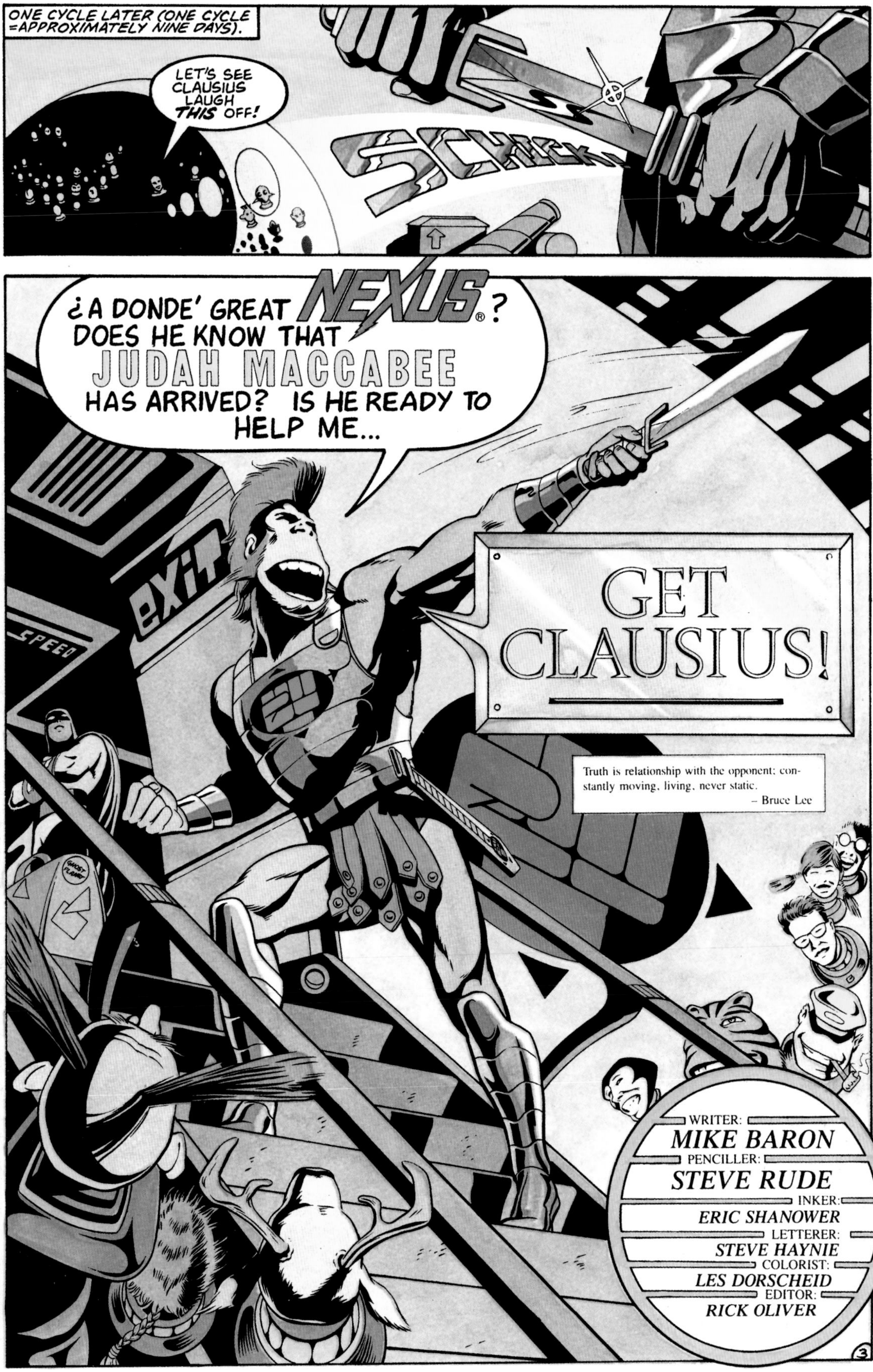
ONE CYCLE LATER (ONE CYCLE =APPROXIMATELY NINE DAYS).
LET'S SEE CLAUSIUS LAUGH THIS OFF!
SCHICK!
¿A DONDE' GREAT NEXUS®? DOES HE KNOW THAT JUDAH MACCABEE HAS ARRIVED? IS HE READY TO HELP ME...
exit
SPEED
GET CLAUSIUS!
Truth is relationship with the opponent: constantly moving, living, never static.
– Bruce Lee
WRITER: MIKE BARON
PENCILLER: STEVE RUDE
INKER: ERIC SHANOWER
LETTERER: STEVE HAYNIE
COLORIST: LES DORSCHEID
EDITOR: RICK OLIVER
3

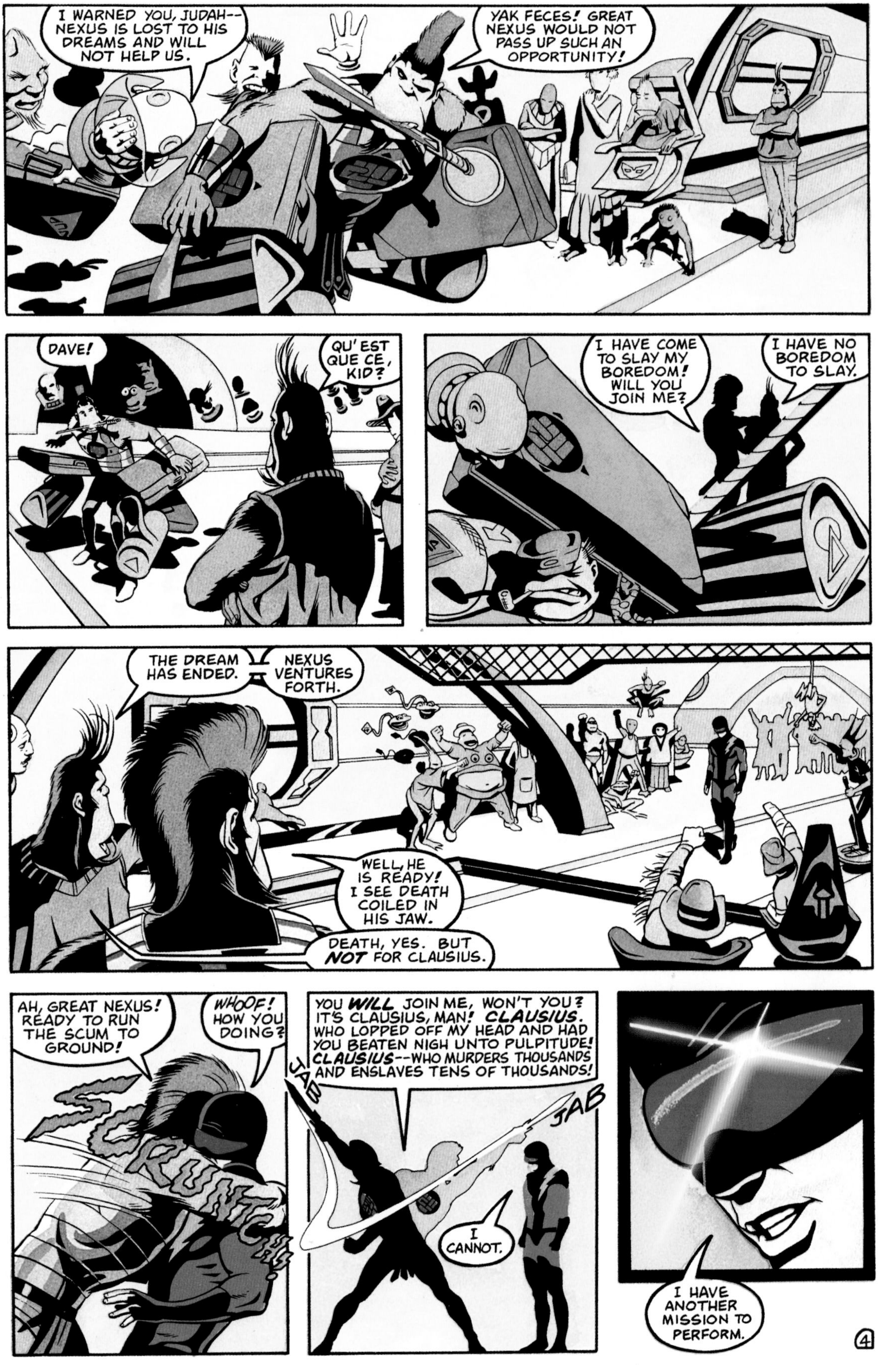
I WARNED YOU, JUDAH--NEXUS IS LOST TO HIS DREAMS AND WILL NOT HELP US.
YAK FECES! GREAT NEXUS WOULD NOT PASS UP SUCH AN OPPORTUNITY!
DAVE!
QU'EST QUE CE, KID?
I HAVE COME TO SLAY MY BOREDOM! WILL YOU JOIN ME?
I HAVE NO BOREDOM TO SLAY.
THE DREAM HAS ENDED.
NEXUS VENTURES FORTH.
WELL, HE IS READY! I SEE DEATH COILED IN HIS JAW.
DEATH, YES. BUT NOT FOR CLAUSIUS.
AH, GREAT NEXUS! READY TO RUN THE SCUM TO GROUND!
WHOOF! HOW YOU DOING?
SCRUNCH
YOU WILL JOIN ME, WON'T YOU? IT'S CLAUSIUS, MAN! CLAUSIUS. WHO LOPPED OFF MY HEAD AND HAD YOU BEATEN NIGH UNTO PULPITUDE! CLAUSIUS--WHO MURDERS THOUSANDS AND ENSLAVES TENS OF THOUSANDS!
JAB
JAB
I CANNOT.
I HAVE ANOTHER MISSION TO PERFORM.
4

YOU SEE? HE WILL NOT COME.

I SEE *MORE* THAN YOU, RAUL. HE *CANNOT* COME. AND WE OWE HIM OUR LIVES. SO LET US BE ABOUT OUR BUSINESS--AND LET NEXUS BE ABOUT HIS.

I KNEW YOU WOULD UNDERSTAND. PLEASE EXCUSE ME FOR BEING SHORT WITH YOU, MY DEAR COMRADE. BUT I MUST LEAVE *NOW.*

GO. I WILL GREET YOU UPON YOUR RETURN.

MAY THE HAMMER POUND CLAUSIUS INTO BUTTER.

FATHER--WHAT IS HIS URGENCY?

I BELIEVE HE IS IN PAIN. I BELIEVE HE SEEKS A QUICK RESOLUTION SO HE CAN RACE BACK HERE AND HAVE HIMSELF ALTERED AGAINST THE PAIN.

"ALTERED?"

AN ELECTRODE IMPLANT. THE IMPLICATIONS ARE UNFORTUNATE.

YOU HEARD NEXUS! EVERY SECOND WE DELAY CARRIES CLAUSIUS FURTHER AWAY!

ALL RIGHT, ALREADY! LET'S GET IT ON!

POK

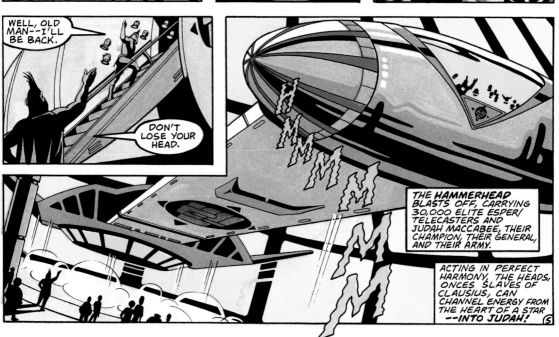

WELL, OLD MAN--I'LL BE BACK.

DON'T LOSE YOUR HEAD.

THE *HAMMERHEAD* BLASTS OFF, CARRYING 30,000 ELITE ESPER/ TELECASTERS AND JUDAH MACCABEE, THEIR CHAMPION, THEIR GENERAL, AND THEIR ARMY.

ACTING IN PERFECT HARMONY, THE HEADS, ONCES SLAVES OF CLAUSIUS, CAN CHANNEL ENERGY FROM THE HEART OF A STAR --INTO JUDAH!

5

181

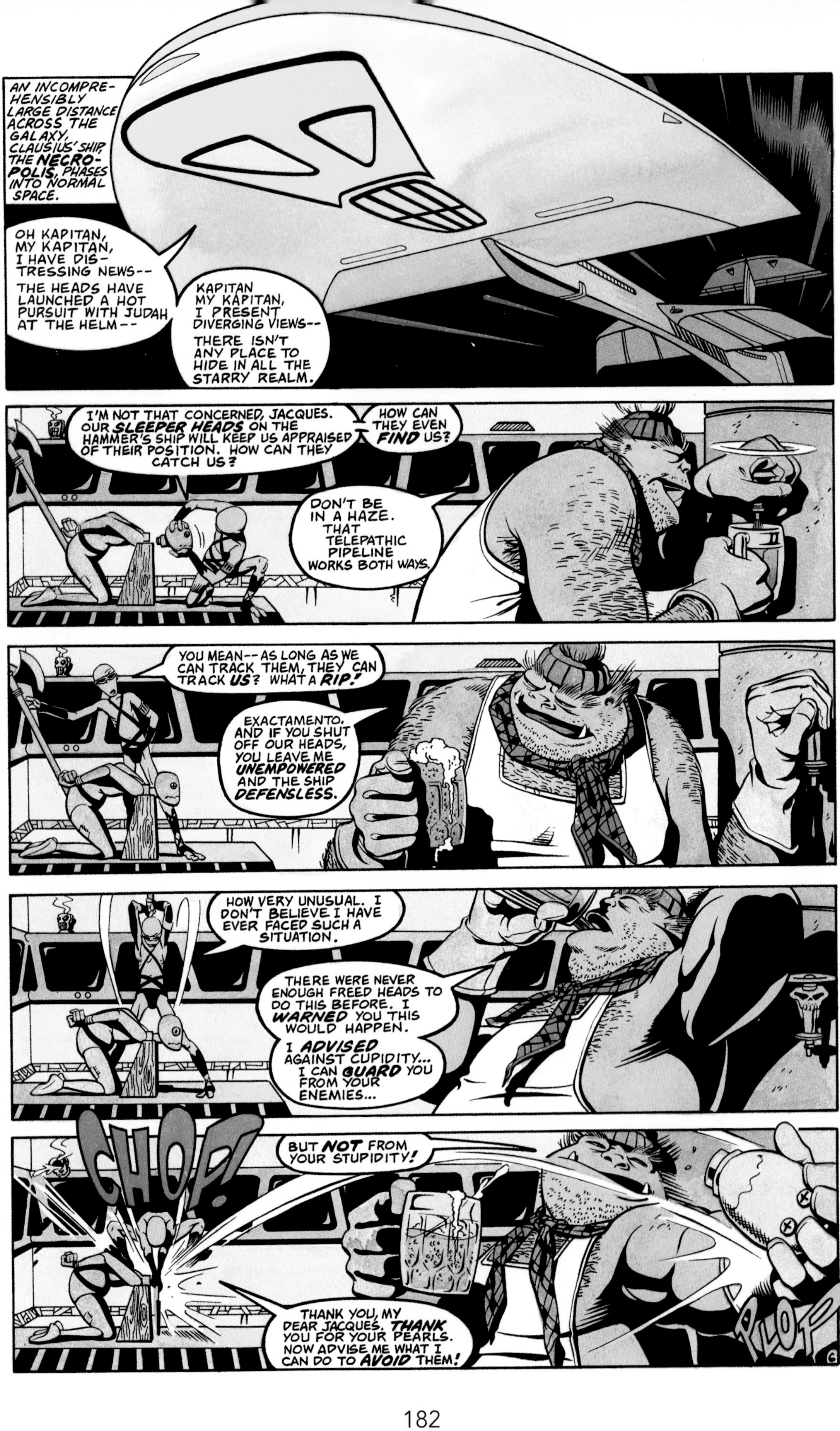
AN INCOMPREHENSIBLY LARGE DISTANCE ACROSS THE GALAXY, CLAUSIUS' SHIP, THE NECROPOLIS, PHASES INTO NORMAL SPACE.
OH KAPITAN, MY KAPITAN, I HAVE DISTRESSING NEWS--
THE HEADS HAVE LAUNCHED A HOT PURSUIT WITH JUDAH AT THE HELM--
KAPITAN MY KAPITAN, I PRESENT DIVERGING VIEWS--
THERE ISN'T ANY PLACE TO HIDE IN ALL THE STARRY REALM.
I'M NOT THAT CONCERNED, JACQUES. OUR SLEEPER HEADS ON THE HAMMER'S SHIP WILL KEEP US APPRAISED OF THEIR POSITION. HOW CAN THEY CATCH US?
HOW CAN THEY EVEN FIND US?
DON'T BE IN A HAZE. THAT TELEPATHIC PIPELINE WORKS BOTH WAYS.
YOU MEAN--AS LONG AS WE CAN TRACK THEM, THEY CAN TRACK US? WHAT A RIP!
EXACTAMENTO. AND IF YOU SHUT OFF OUR HEADS, YOU LEAVE ME UNEMPOWERED AND THE SHIP DEFENSLESS.
HOW VERY UNUSUAL. I DON'T BELIEVE I HAVE EVER FACED SUCH A SITUATION.
THERE WERE NEVER ENOUGH FREED HEADS TO DO THIS BEFORE. I WARNED YOU THIS WOULD HAPPEN.
I ADVISED AGAINST CUPIDITY... I CAN GUARD YOU FROM YOUR ENEMIES...
CHOP!
BUT NOT FROM YOUR STUPIDITY!
THANK YOU, MY DEAR JACQUES. THANK YOU FOR YOUR PEARLS. NOW ADVISE ME WHAT I CAN DO TO AVOID THEM!
PLOP

SPACE IS VAST AND VASTER STILL. WITHOUT THE LINK THEY'D NEVER FIND US. BUT SINCE THE MENTAL FLOWS BOTH WAYS-- I SUSPECT THEY'RE RIGHT BEHIND US.

STOP RHYMING-- *STOP IT RIGHT NOW!* GIVE ME A *PLAN!* OH! I CAN'T *CONCENTRATE!* WHY CAN'T THINGS EVER GO *SMOOTHLY?*

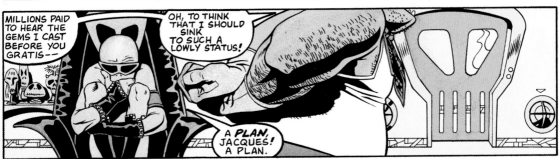

MILLIONS PAID TO HEAR THE GEMS I CAST BEFORE YOU GRATIS--

OH, TO THINK THAT I SHOULD SINK TO SUCH A LOWLY STATUS!

A *PLAN*, JACQUES! A PLAN.

WE COULD TRY TO FRY YOUR SLEEPERS. BUT I THINK WE'RE ALREADY TOO LATE. BY NOW, RAUL'S GOT A FIX ON US VIA HIS FREE HEADS. THEY ARE IMMUNE AT THIS DISTANCE.

WHAT ABOUT A MIND SCREEN?

BEE DEEP
DEEP
BEE DEEP

THAT REQUIRES *UNFETTERED* MINDS. OURS HAVE FETTERS.

WE CAN KEEP PHASING AHEAD OF THEM. BUT I CAN'T PHASE FOR-EVER!

I HAVE *CLIENTS!* RESPONSIBILITIES!

BEE DEEP
BEE DEEP
BEE DEEP
BEE DEEP

I KNOW THE HAMMER--KNOW HIM WELL. I FOUGHT HIM IN THE RING.

HE WON'T GIVE UP UNTIL HE HAS OUR ASSES IN A SLING.

SNIFF

GIVE ME A *PLAN*, YOU VERBAL CHAINSAW BUTCHER! IN THE MEANTIME, WE *PHASE*. WE'LL STAY ONE JUMP AHEAD OF THEM.

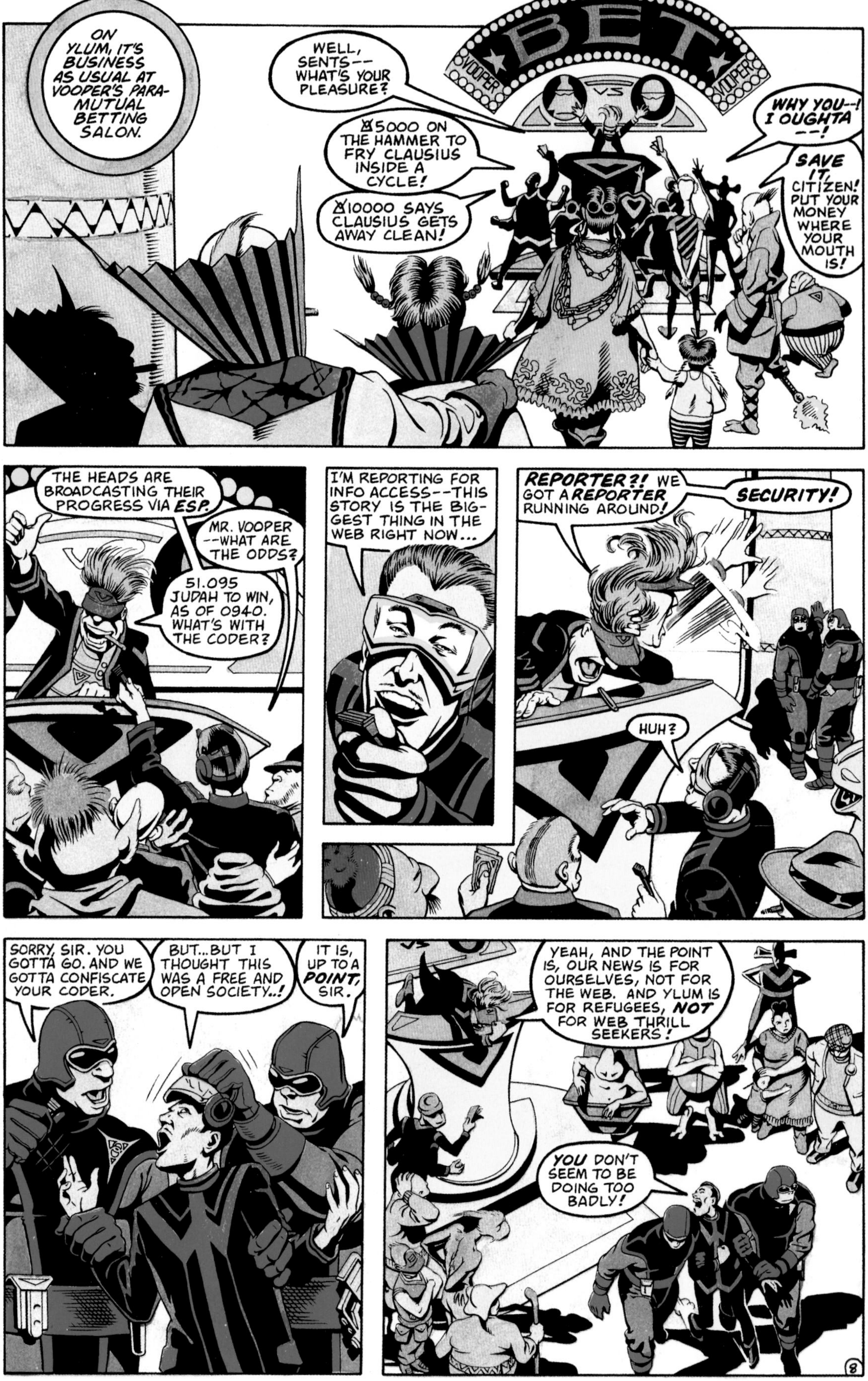
ON YLUM, IT'S BUSINESS AS USUAL AT VOOPER'S PARA-MUTUAL BETTING SALON.
BET
VOOPER
VS
VOOPER
WELL, SENTS-- WHAT'S YOUR PLEASURE?
5000 ON THE HAMMER TO FRY CLAUSIUS INSIDE A CYCLE!
10000 SAYS CLAUSIUS GETS AWAY CLEAN!
WHY YOU--! I OUGHTA --!
SAVE IT, CITIZEN! PUT YOUR MONEY WHERE YOUR MOUTH IS!
THE HEADS ARE BROADCASTING THEIR PROGRESS VIA ESP.
MR. VOOPER --WHAT ARE THE ODDS?
51.095 JUDAH TO WIN, AS OF 0940. WHAT'S WITH THE CODER?
I'M REPORTING FOR INFO ACCESS--THIS STORY IS THE BIGGEST THING IN THE WEB RIGHT NOW...
REPORTER?! WE GOT A REPORTER RUNNING AROUND!
SECURITY!
HUH?
SORRY, SIR. YOU GOTTA GO. AND WE GOTTA CONFISCATE YOUR CODER.
BUT...BUT I THOUGHT THIS WAS A FREE AND OPEN SOCIETY..!
IT IS, UP TO A POINT, SIR.
YEAH, AND THE POINT IS, OUR NEWS IS FOR OURSELVES, NOT FOR THE WEB. AND YLUM IS FOR REFUGEES, NOT FOR WEB THRILL SEEKERS!
YOU DON'T SEEM TO BE DOING TOO BADLY!
8

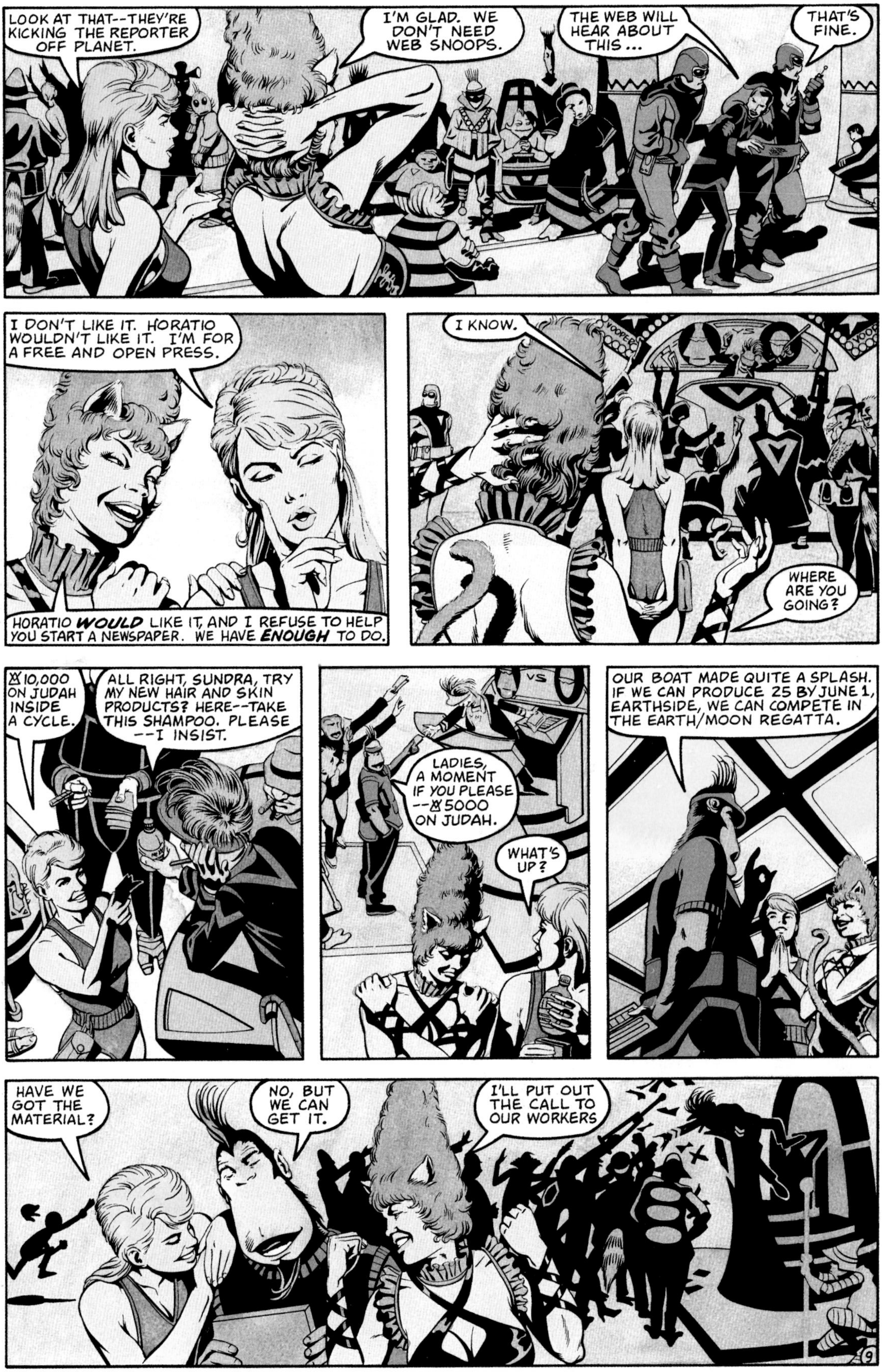
LOOK AT THAT--THEY'RE KICKING THE REPORTER OFF PLANET.
I'M GLAD. WE DON'T NEED WEB SNOOPS.
THE WEB WILL HEAR ABOUT THIS ...
THAT'S FINE.
I DON'T LIKE IT. HORATIO WOULDN'T LIKE IT. I'M FOR A FREE AND OPEN PRESS.
HORATIO **WOULD** LIKE IT, AND I REFUSE TO HELP YOU START A NEWSPAPER. WE HAVE **ENOUGH** TO DO.
I KNOW.
WHERE ARE YOU GOING?
10,000 ON JUDAH INSIDE A CYCLE.
ALL RIGHT, SUNDRA, TRY MY NEW HAIR AND SKIN PRODUCTS? HERE--TAKE THIS SHAMPOO. PLEASE --I INSIST.
LADIES, A MOMENT IF YOU PLEASE --5000 ON JUDAH.
WHAT'S UP?
OUR BOAT MADE QUITE A SPLASH. IF WE CAN PRODUCE 25 BY JUNE 1, EARTHSIDE, WE CAN COMPETE IN THE EARTH/MOON REGATTA.
HAVE WE GOT THE MATERIAL?
NO, BUT WE CAN GET IT.
I'LL PUT OUT THE CALL TO OUR WORKERS
9

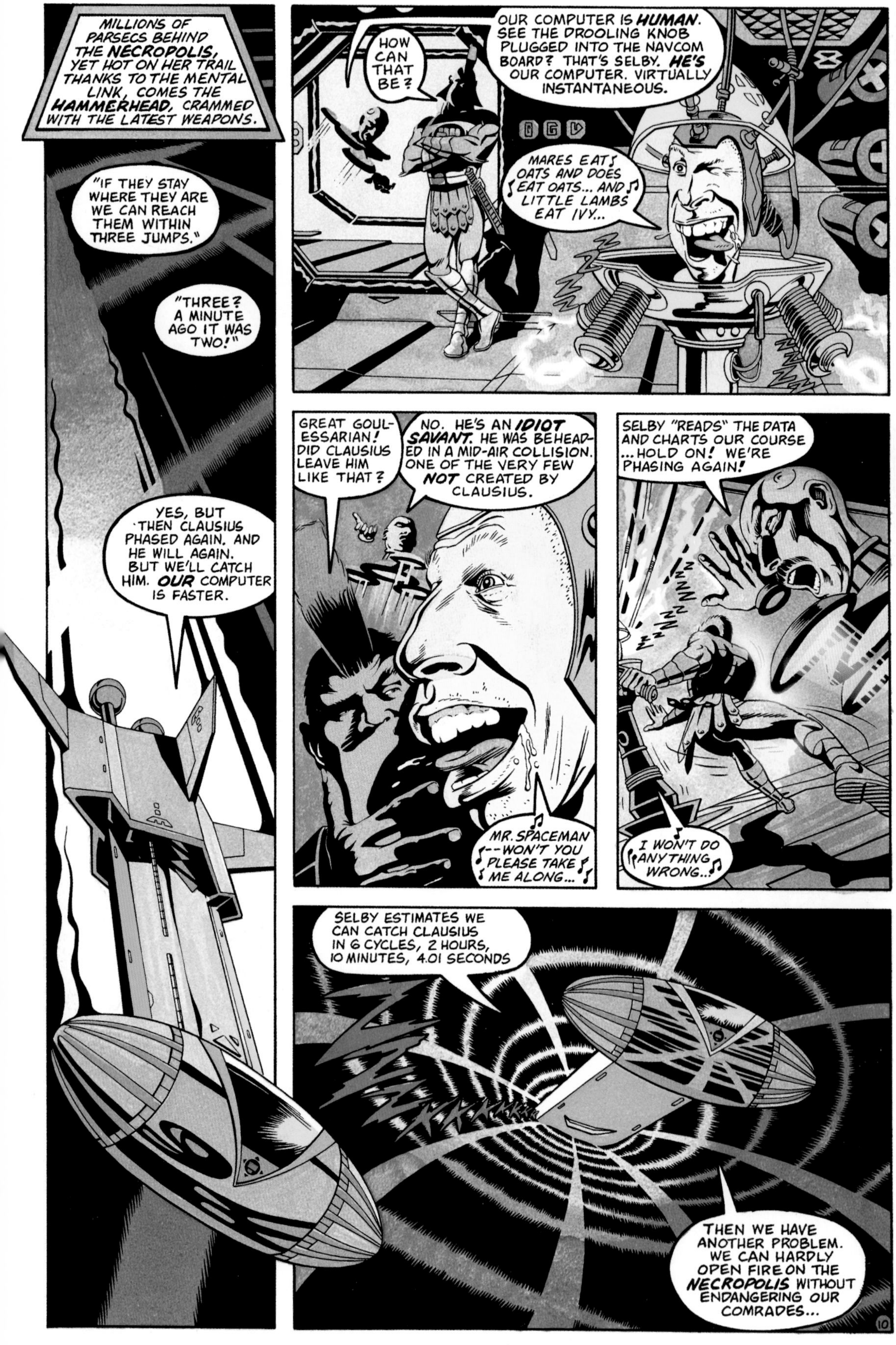

MILLIONS OF PARSECS BEHIND THE NECROPOLIS, YET HOT ON HER TRAIL THANKS TO THE MENTAL LINK, COMES THE HAMMERHEAD, CRAMMED WITH THE LATEST WEAPONS.
"IF THEY STAY WHERE THEY ARE WE CAN REACH THEM WITHIN THREE JUMPS."
"THREE? A MINUTE AGO IT WAS TWO!"
YES, BUT THEN CLAUSIUS PHASED AGAIN. AND HE WILL AGAIN. BUT WE'LL CATCH HIM. OUR COMPUTER IS FASTER.
HOW CAN THAT BE?
OUR COMPUTER IS HUMAN. SEE THE DROOLING KNOB PLUGGED INTO THE NAVCOM BOARD? THAT'S SELBY. HE'S OUR COMPUTER. VIRTUALLY INSTANTANEOUS.
MARES EAT OATS AND DOES EAT OATS... AND LITTLE LAMBS EAT IVY...
GREAT GOUL-ESSARIAN! DID CLAUSIUS LEAVE HIM LIKE THAT?
NO. HE'S AN IDIOT SAVANT. HE WAS BEHEADED IN A MID-AIR COLLISION. ONE OF THE VERY FEW NOT CREATED BY CLAUSIUS.
MR. SPACEMAN--WON'T YOU PLEASE TAKE ME ALONG...
SELBY "READS" THE DATA AND CHARTS OUR COURSE ...HOLD ON! WE'RE PHASING AGAIN!
I WON'T DO ANYTHING WRONG...
SELBY ESTIMATES WE CAN CATCH CLAUSIUS IN 6 CYCLES, 2 HOURS, 10 MINUTES, 4.01 SECONDS
THEN WE HAVE ANOTHER PROBLEM. WE CAN HARDLY OPEN FIRE ON THE NECROPOLIS WITHOUT ENDANGERING OUR COMRADES...
10

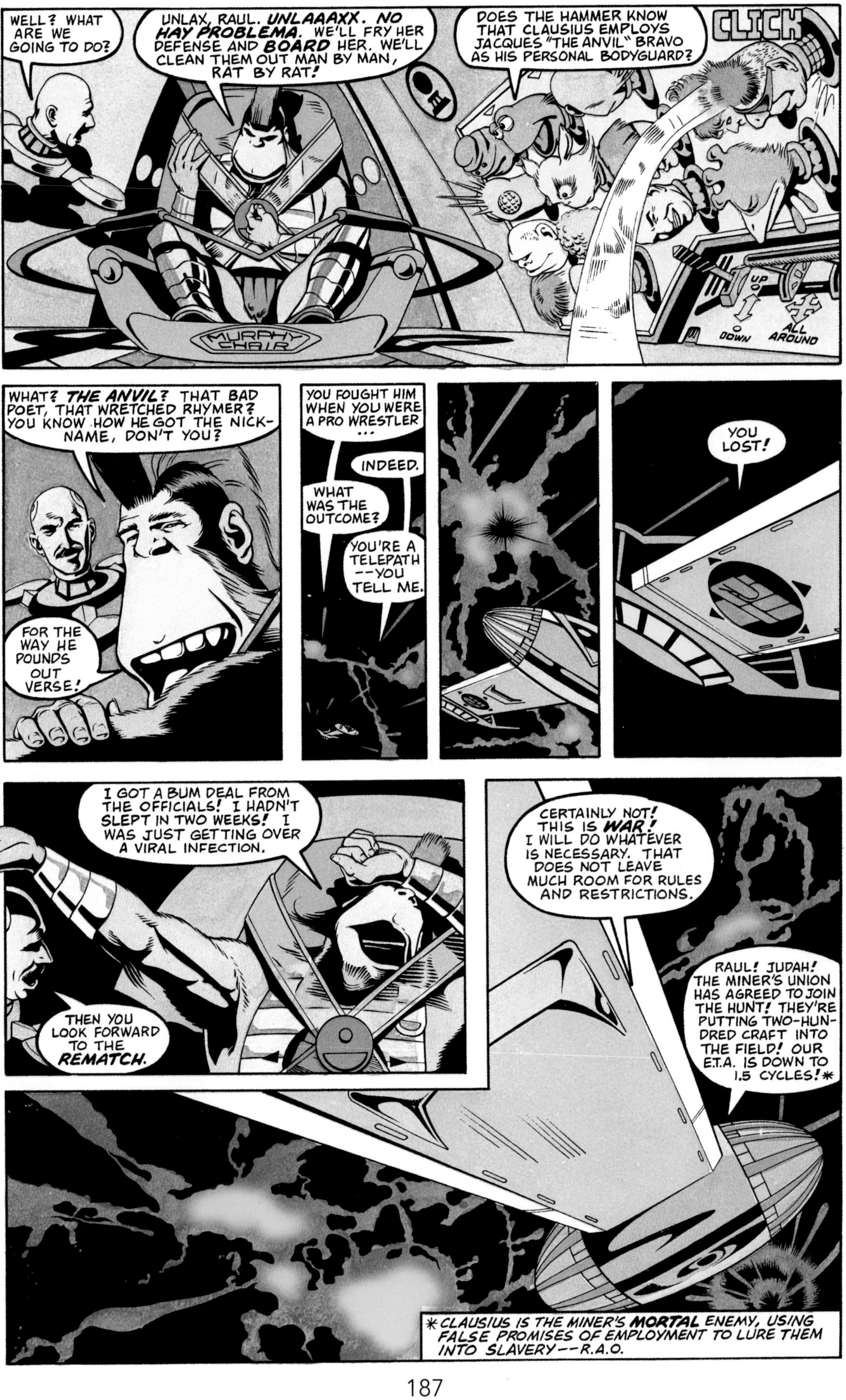
WELL? WHAT ARE WE GOING TO DO?
UNLAX, RAUL. UNLAAAXX. NO HAY PROBLEMA. WE'LL FRY HER DEFENSE AND BOARD HER. WE'LL CLEAN THEM OUT MAN BY MAN, RAT BY RAT!
DOES THE HAMMER KNOW THAT CLAUSIUS EMPLOYS JACQUES "THE ANVIL" BRAVO AS HIS PERSONAL BODYGUARD?
CLICK
MURPHY CHAIR
UP
DOWN
ALL AROUND
WHAT? THE ANVIL? THAT BAD POET, THAT WRETCHED RHYMER? YOU KNOW HOW HE GOT THE NICK-NAME, DON'T YOU?
FOR THE WAY HE POUNDS OUT VERSE!
YOU FOUGHT HIM WHEN YOU WERE A PRO WRESTLER ...
INDEED.
WHAT WAS THE OUTCOME?
YOU'RE A TELEPATH --YOU TELL ME.
YOU LOST!
I GOT A BUM DEAL FROM THE OFFICIALS! I HADN'T SLEPT IN TWO WEEKS! I WAS JUST GETTING OVER A VIRAL INFECTION.
THEN YOU LOOK FORWARD TO THE REMATCH.
CERTAINLY NOT! THIS IS WAR! I WILL DO WHATEVER IS NECESSARY. THAT DOES NOT LEAVE MUCH ROOM FOR RULES AND RESTRICTIONS.
RAUL! JUDAH! THE MINER'S UNION HAS AGREED TO JOIN THE HUNT! THEY'RE PUTTING TWO-HUNDRED CRAFT INTO THE FIELD! OUR E.T.A. IS DOWN TO 1.5 CYCLES!*
*CLAUSIUS IS THE MINER'S MORTAL ENEMY, USING FALSE PROMISES OF EMPLOYMENT TO LURE THEM INTO SLAVERY--R.A.O.

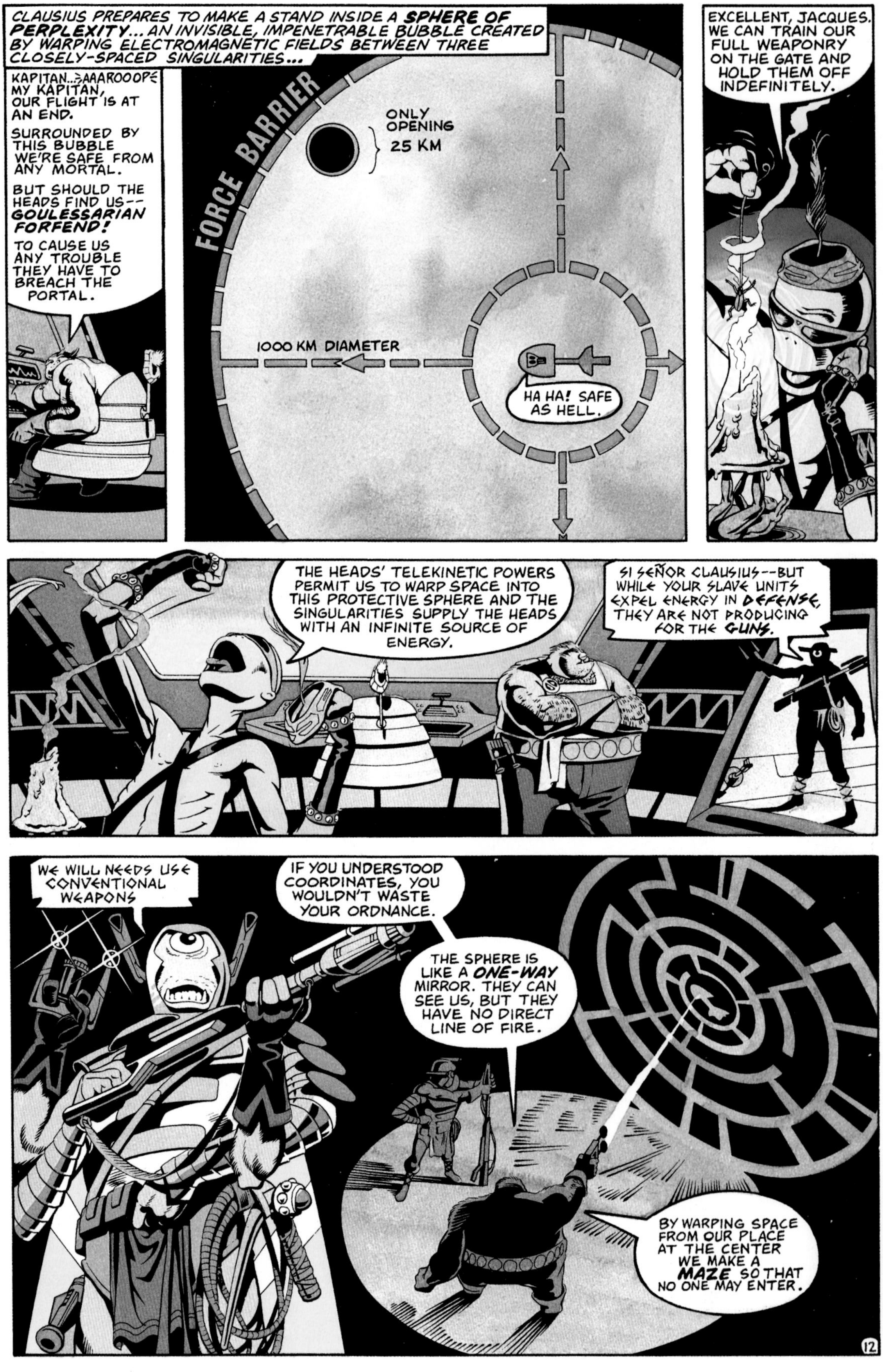
CLAUSIUS PREPARES TO MAKE A STAND INSIDE A SPHERE OF PERPLEXITY... AN INVISIBLE, IMPENETRABLE BUBBLE CREATED BY WARPING ELECTROMAGNETIC FIELDS BETWEEN THREE CLOSELY-SPACED SINGULARITIES...
KAPITAN...AAAROOOP MY KAPITAN, OUR FLIGHT IS AT AN END.
SURROUNDED BY THIS BUBBLE WE'RE SAFE FROM ANY MORTAL.
BUT SHOULD THE HEADS FIND US-- GOULESSARIAN FORFEND!
TO CAUSE US ANY TROUBLE THEY HAVE TO BREACH THE PORTAL.
FORCE BARRIER
ONLY OPENING 25 KM
1000 KM DIAMETER
HA HA! SAFE AS HELL.
EXCELLENT, JACQUES. WE CAN TRAIN OUR FULL WEAPONRY ON THE GATE AND HOLD THEM OFF INDEFINITELY.
THE HEADS' TELEKINETIC POWERS PERMIT US TO WARP SPACE INTO THIS PROTECTIVE SPHERE AND THE SINGULARITIES SUPPLY THE HEADS WITH AN INFINITE SOURCE OF ENERGY.
SI SEÑOR CLAUSIUS--BUT WHILE YOUR SLAVE UNITS EXPEL ENERGY IN DEFENSE, THEY ARE NOT PRODUCING FOR THE GUNS.
WE WILL NEEDS USE CONVENTIONAL WEAPONS
IF YOU UNDERSTOOD COORDINATES, YOU WOULDN'T WASTE YOUR ORDNANCE.
THE SPHERE IS LIKE A ONE-WAY MIRROR. THEY CAN SEE US, BUT THEY HAVE NO DIRECT LINE OF FIRE.
BY WARPING SPACE FROM OUR PLACE AT THE CENTER WE MAKE A MAZE SO THAT NO ONE MAY ENTER.
12

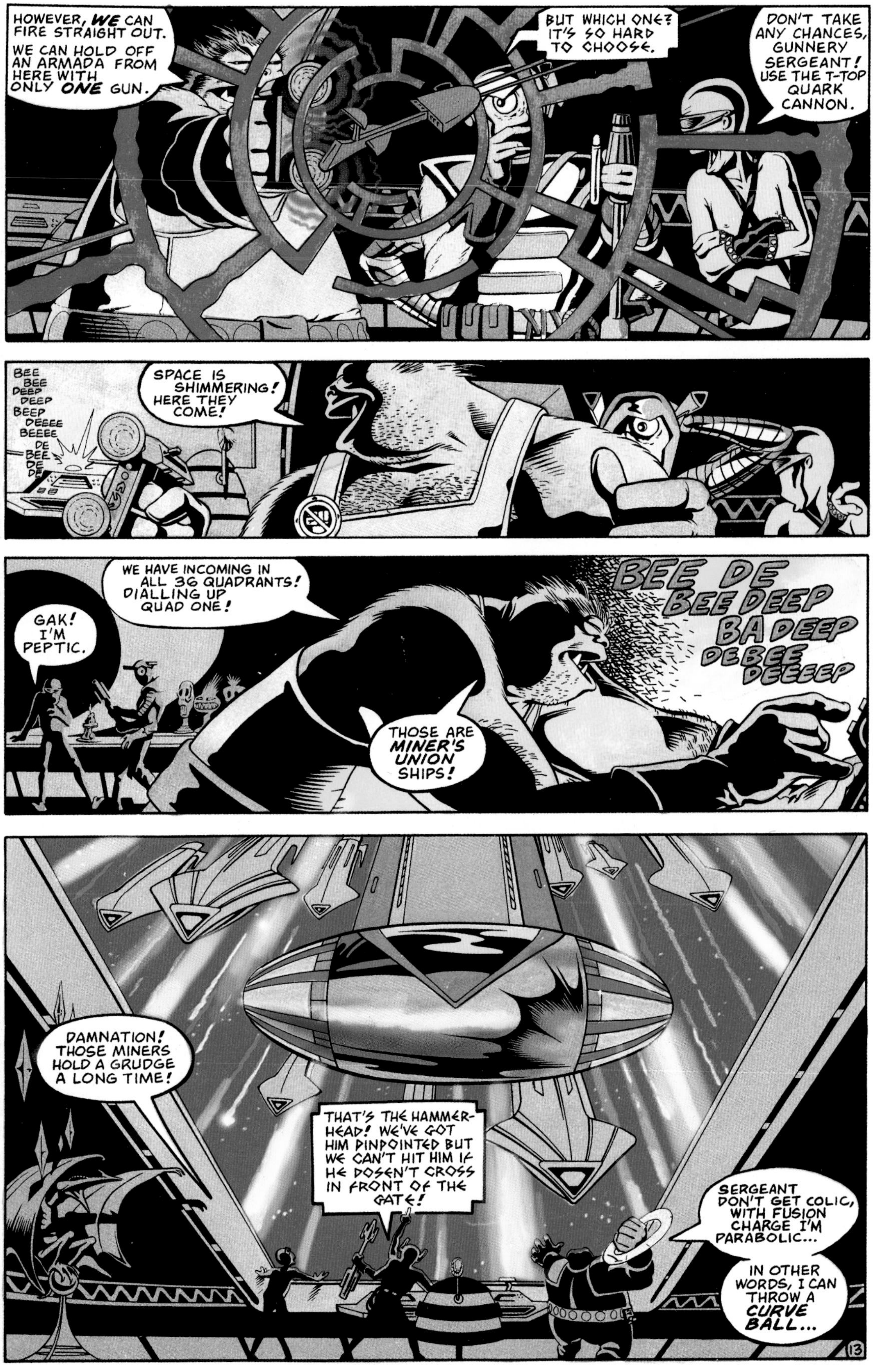
HOWEVER, WE CAN FIRE STRAIGHT OUT.
WE CAN HOLD OFF AN ARMADA FROM HERE WITH ONLY ONE GUN.
BUT WHICH ONE? IT'S SO HARD TO CHOOSE.
DON'T TAKE ANY CHANCES, GUNNERY SERGEANT! USE THE T-TOP QUARK CANNON.
BEE BEE DEEP DEEP BEEP DEEEE BEEEE DE BEE DE DE
SPACE IS SHIMMERING! HERE THEY COME!
WE HAVE INCOMING IN ALL 36 QUADRANTS! DIALLING UP QUAD ONE!
BEE DE BEE DEEP BA DEEP DEBEE DEEEEP
GAK! I'M PEPTIC.
THOSE ARE MINER'S UNION SHIPS!
DAMNATION! THOSE MINERS HOLD A GRUDGE A LONG TIME!
THAT'S THE HAMMER-HEAD! WE'VE GOT HIM PINPOINTED BUT WE CAN'T HIT HIM IF HE DOSEN'T CROSS IN FRONT OF THE GATE!
SERGEANT DON'T GET COLIC, WITH FUSION CHARGE I'M PARABOLIC...
IN OTHER WORDS, I CAN THROW A CURVE BALL...
13

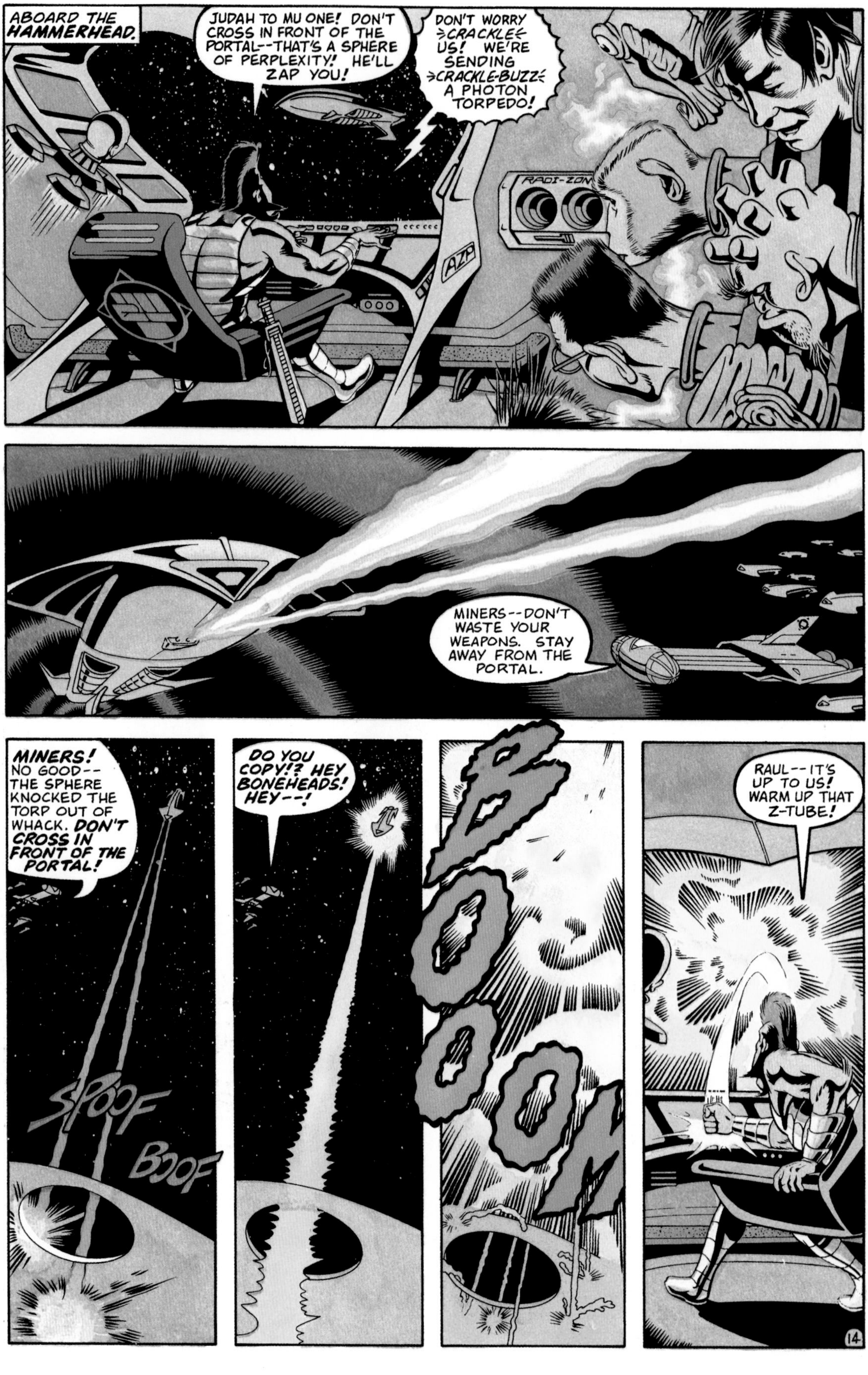

ABOARD THE HAMMERHEAD.
JUDAH TO MU ONE! DON'T CROSS IN FRONT OF THE PORTAL--THAT'S A SPHERE OF PERPLEXITY! HE'LL ZAP YOU!
DON'T WORRY ≡CRACKLE≡ US! WE'RE SENDING ≡CRACKLE-BUZZ≡ A PHOTON TORPEDO!
RADI-ZON
AZP
MINERS--DON'T WASTE YOUR WEAPONS. STAY AWAY FROM THE PORTAL.
MINERS! NO GOOD-- THE SPHERE KNOCKED THE TORP OUT OF WHACK. DON'T CROSS IN FRONT OF THE PORTAL!
SPOOF
BOOF
DO YOU COPY!? HEY BONEHEADS! HEY--!
BOOOOM
RAUL--IT'S UP TO US! WARM UP THAT Z-TUBE!
14

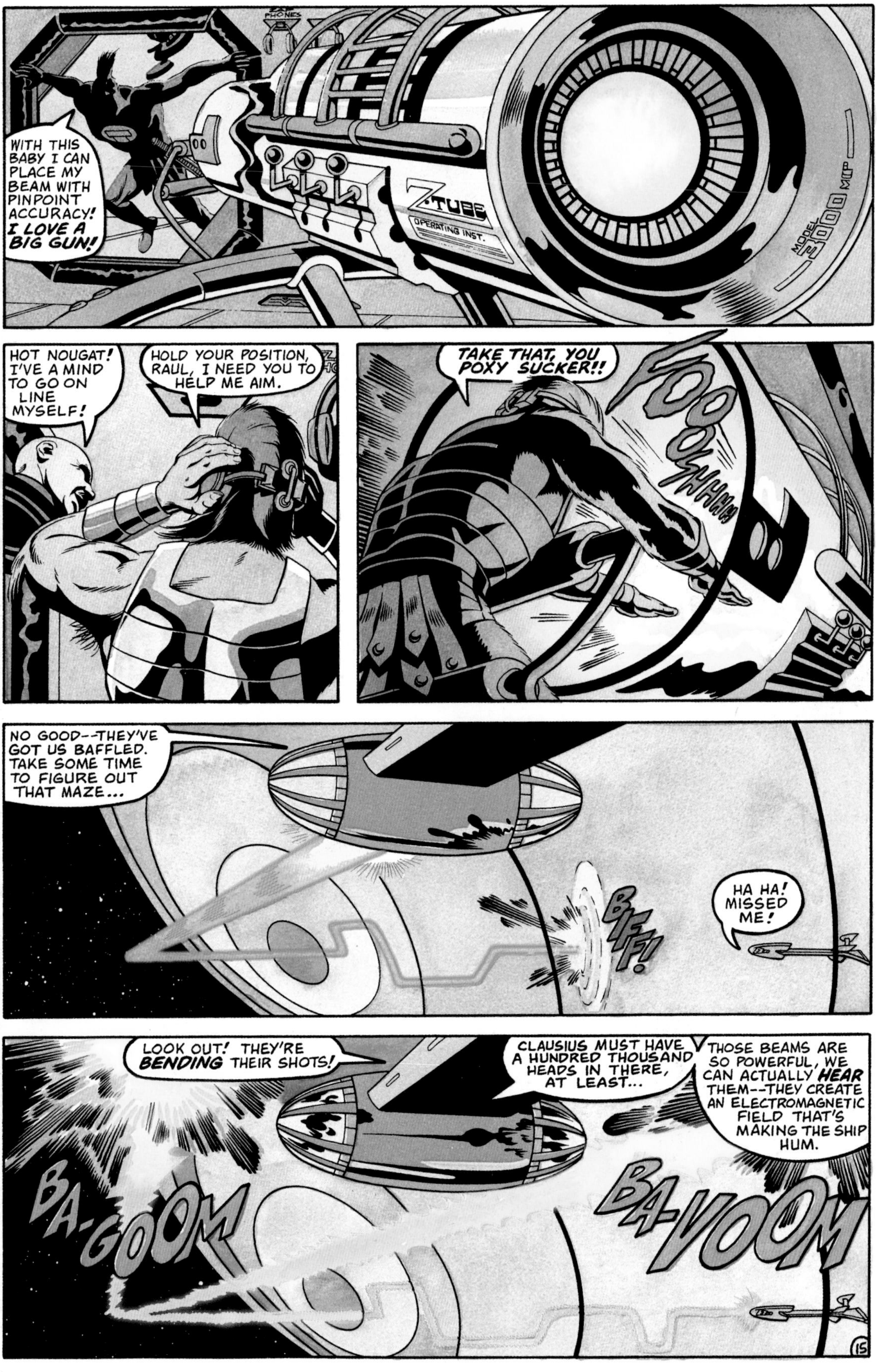
WITH THIS BABY I CAN PLACE MY BEAM WITH PINPOINT ACCURACY! I LOVE A BIG GUN!
Z-TUBE
OPERATING INST.
HOT NOUGAT! I'VE A MIND TO GO ON LINE MYSELF!
HOLD YOUR POSITION, RAUL, I NEED YOU TO HELP ME AIM.
TAKE THAT, YOU POXY SUCKER!!
YOOOOSHHHH
NO GOOD--THEY'VE GOT US BAFFLED. TAKE SOME TIME TO FIGURE OUT THAT MAZE...
BIFF!
HA HA! MISSED ME!
LOOK OUT! THEY'RE BENDING THEIR SHOTS!
CLAUSIUS MUST HAVE A HUNDRED THOUSAND HEADS IN THERE, AT LEAST...
THOSE BEAMS ARE SO POWERFUL, WE CAN ACTUALLY HEAR THEM--THEY CREATE AN ELECTROMAGNETIC FIELD THAT'S MAKING THE SHIP HUM.
BA-GOOM
BA-VOOM
15

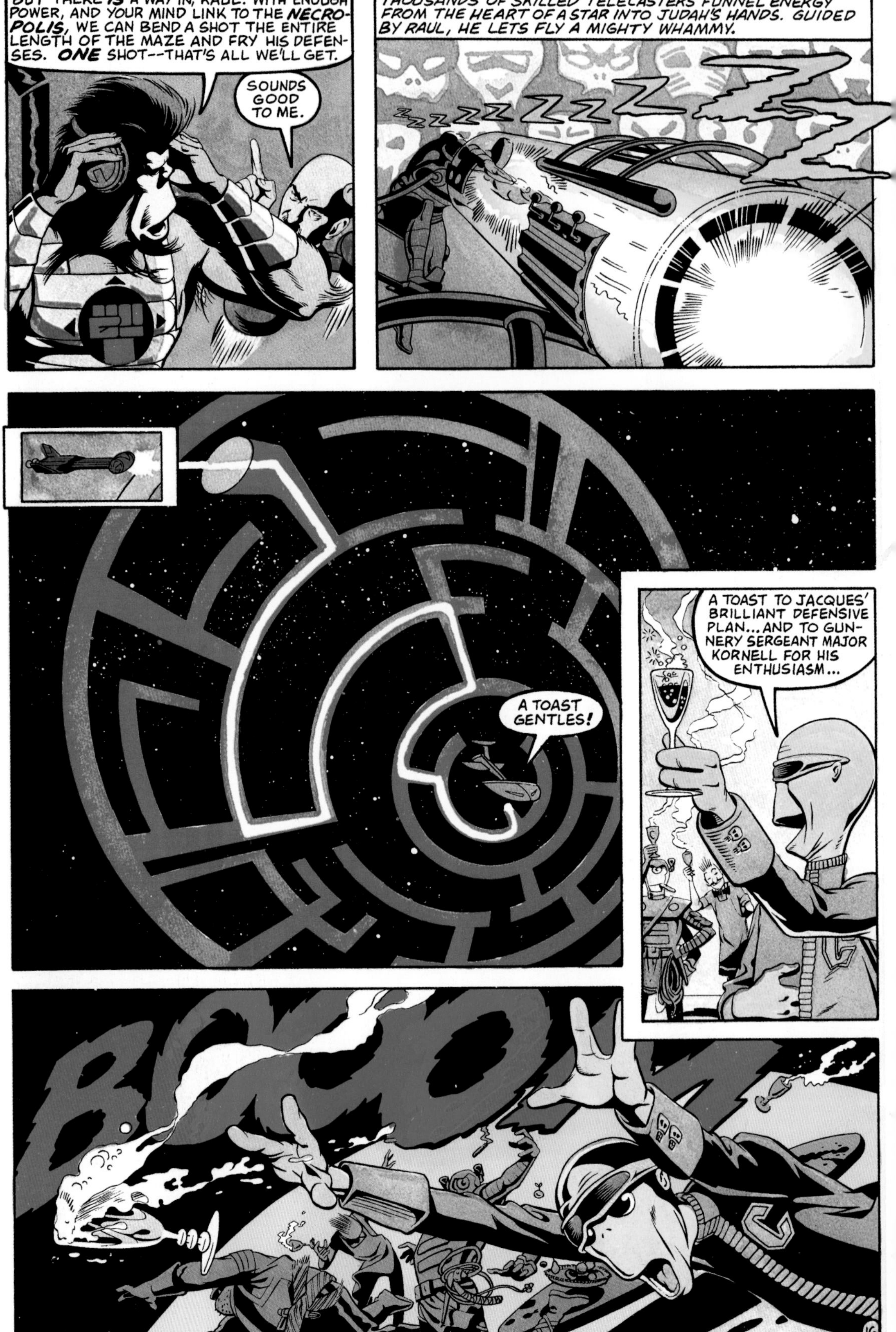
BUT THERE IS A WAY IN, RAUL. WITH ENOUGH POWER, AND YOUR MIND LINK TO THE NECROPOLIS, WE CAN BEND A SHOT THE ENTIRE LENGTH OF THE MAZE AND FRY HIS DEFENSES. ONE SHOT--THAT'S ALL WE'LL GET.
SOUNDS GOOD TO ME.
THOUSANDS OF SKILLED TELECASTERS FUNNEL ENERGY FROM THE HEART OF A STAR INTO JUDAH'S HANDS. GUIDED BY RAUL, HE LETS FLY A MIGHTY WHAMMY.
ZZZZZZZZZ
A TOAST GENTLES!
A TOAST TO JACQUES' BRILLIANT DEFENSIVE PLAN...AND TO GUNNERY SERGEANT MAJOR KORNELL FOR HIS ENTHUSIASM...
BOOOM
16

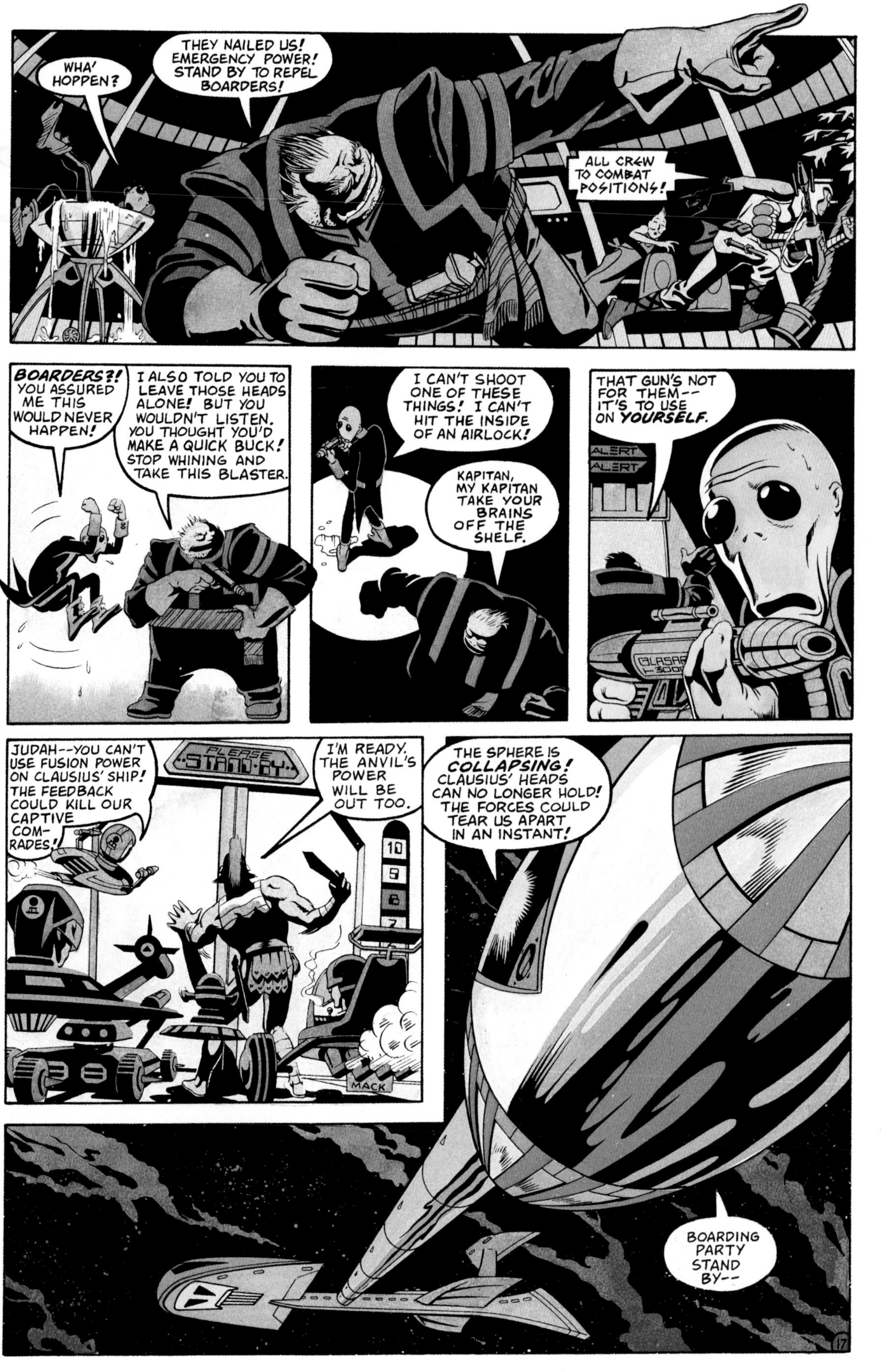

WHA' HOPPEN?
THEY NAILED US! EMERGENCY POWER! STAND BY TO REPEL BOARDERS!
ALL CREW TO COMBAT POSITIONS!
BOARDERS?! YOU ASSURED ME THIS WOULD NEVER HAPPEN!
I ALSO TOLD YOU TO LEAVE THOSE HEADS ALONE! BUT YOU WOULDN'T LISTEN. YOU THOUGHT YOU'D MAKE A QUICK BUCK! STOP WHINING AND TAKE THIS BLASTER.
I CAN'T SHOOT ONE OF THESE THINGS! I CAN'T HIT THE INSIDE OF AN AIRLOCK!
KAPITAN, MY KAPITAN TAKE YOUR BRAINS OFF THE SHELF.
THAT GUN'S NOT FOR THEM-- IT'S TO USE ON YOURSELF.
ALERT
ALERT
JUDAH--YOU CAN'T USE FUSION POWER ON CLAUSIUS' SHIP! THE FEEDBACK COULD KILL OUR CAPTIVE COM-RADES!
PLEASE STAND-BY
I'M READY. THE ANVIL'S POWER WILL BE OUT TOO.
10
9
8
7
MACK
THE SPHERE IS COLLAPSING! CLAUSIUS' HEADS CAN NO LONGER HOLD! THE FORCES COULD TEAR US APART IN AN INSTANT!
BOARDING PARTY STAND BY--
17

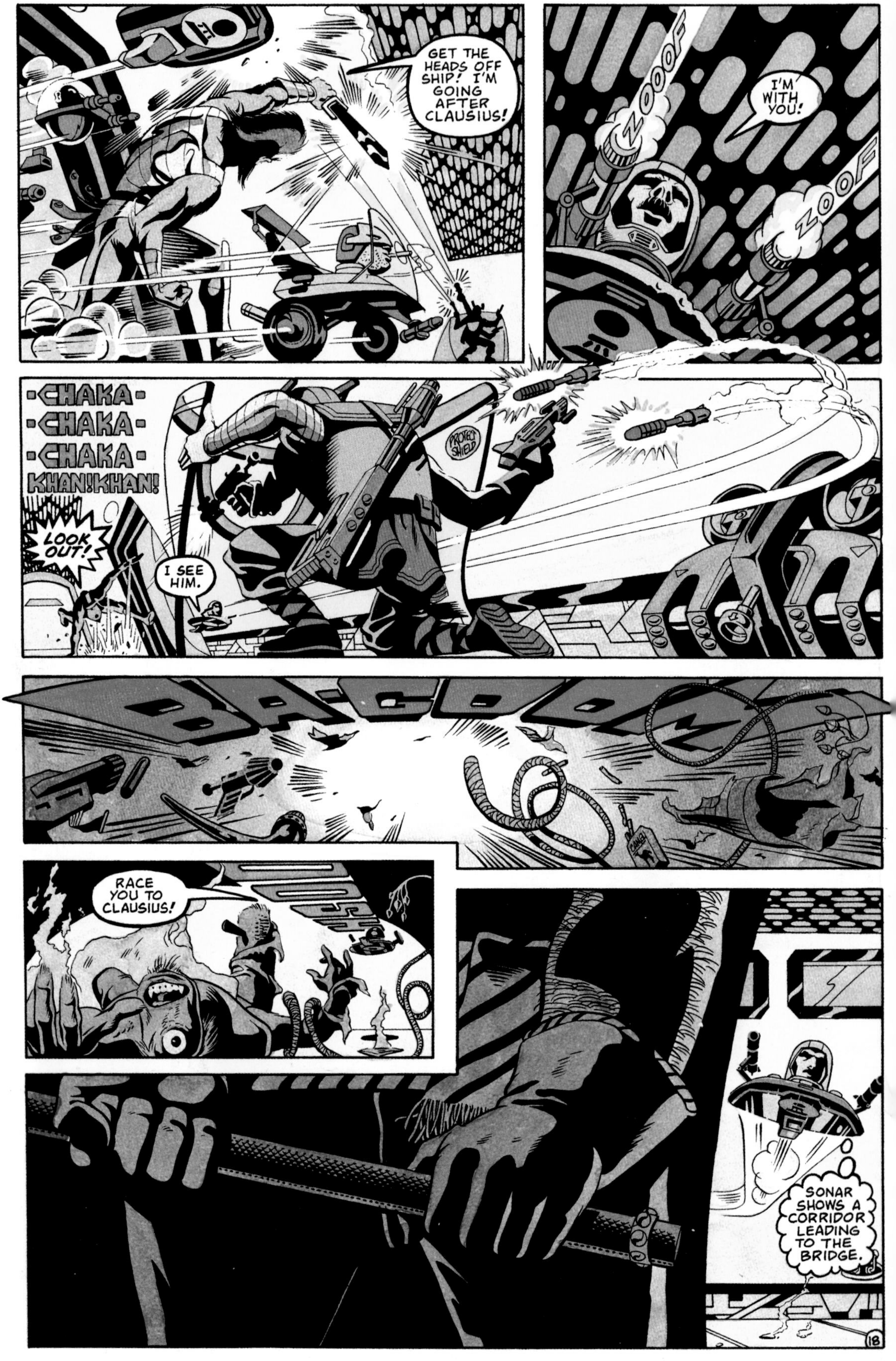
GET THE HEADS OFF SHIP! I'M GOING AFTER CLAUSIUS!
ZOOF
I'M WITH YOU!
ZOOF
-CHAKA-
-CHAKA-
-CHAKA-
KHAN! KHAN!
LOOK OUT!
I SEE HIM.
PROTECT SHIELD
BA-DOOM
RACE YOU TO CLAUSIUS!
SONAR SHOWS A CORRIDOR LEADING TO THE BRIDGE.
18

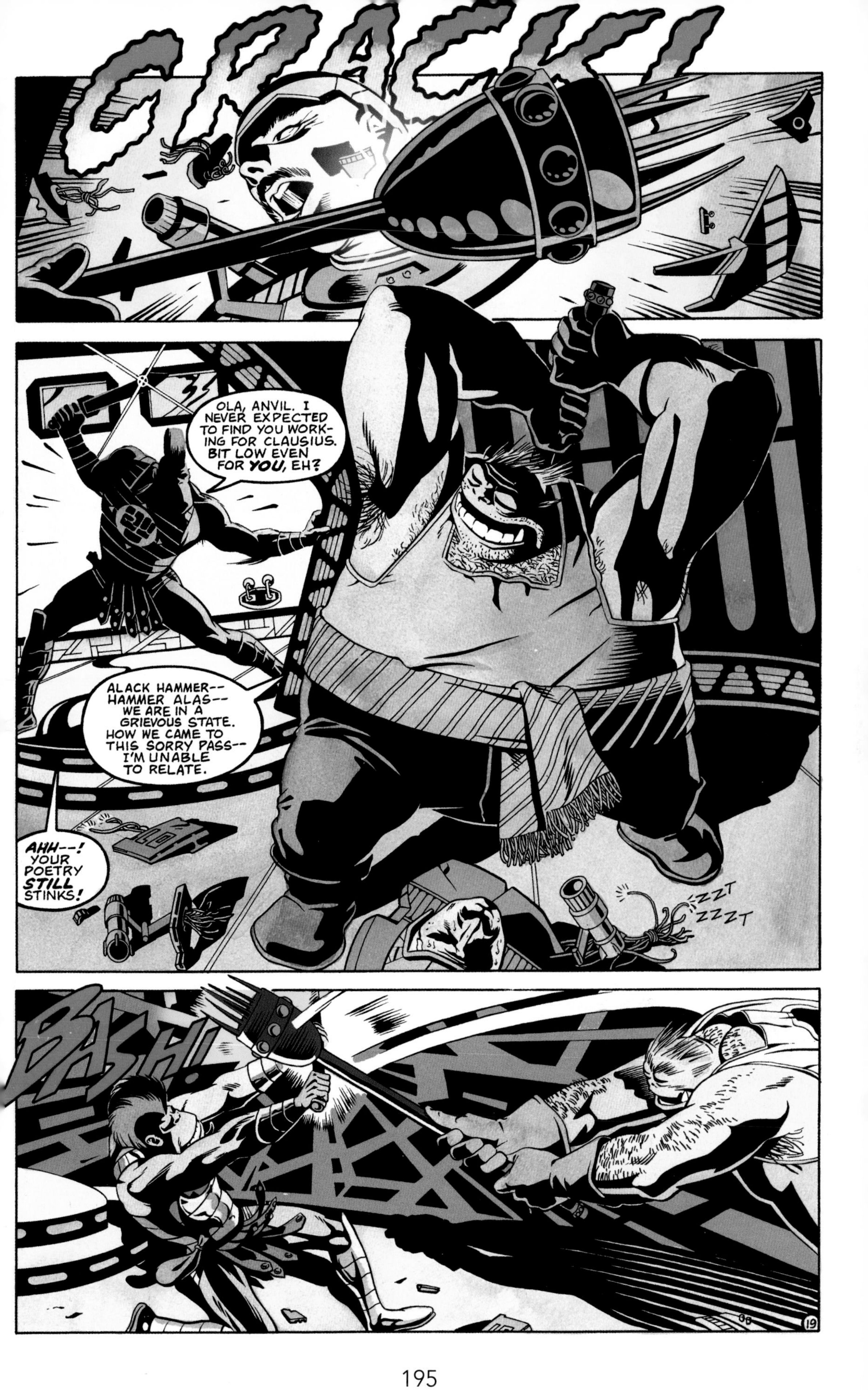
CRACK!!
OLA, ANVIL. I NEVER EXPECTED TO FIND YOU WORKING FOR CLAUSIUS. BIT LOW EVEN FOR YOU, EH?
ALACK HAMMER-- HAMMER ALAS-- WE ARE IN A GRIEVOUS STATE. HOW WE CAME TO THIS SORRY PASS-- I'M UNABLE TO RELATE.
AHH--! YOUR POETRY STILL STINKS!
ZZZT ZZZT
BASH!
19

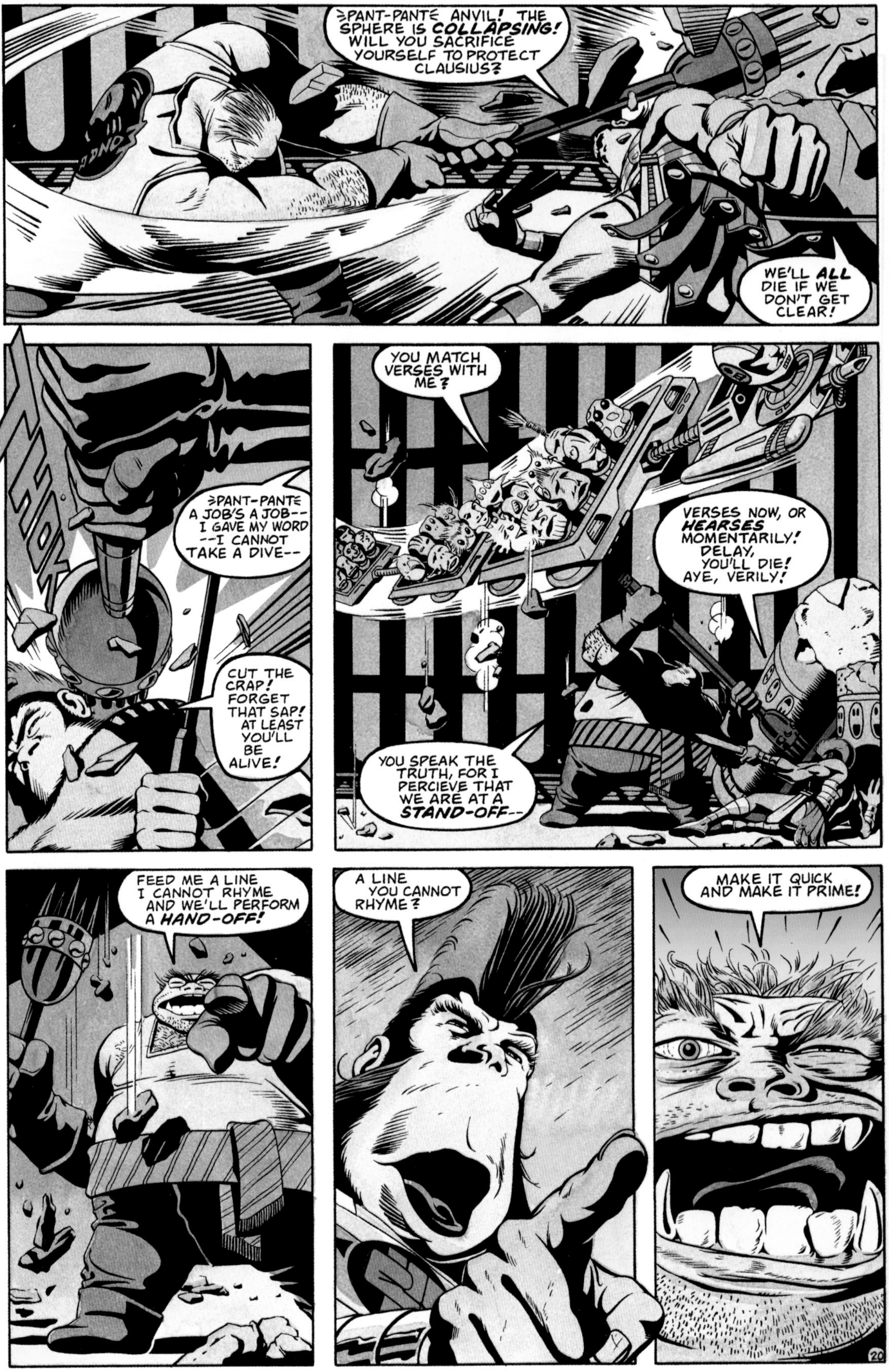

≥PANT-PANT≤ ANVIL! THE SPHERE IS COLLAPSING! WILL YOU SACRIFICE YOURSELF TO PROTECT CLAUSIUS?
WE'LL ALL DIE IF WE DON'T GET CLEAR!
THOK
≥PANT-PANT≤ A JOB'S A JOB-- I GAVE MY WORD --I CANNOT TAKE A DIVE--
CUT THE CRAP! FORGET THAT SAP! AT LEAST YOU'LL BE ALIVE!
YOU MATCH VERSES WITH ME?
VERSES NOW, OR HEARSES MOMENTARILY! DELAY, YOU'LL DIE! AYE, VERILY!
YOU SPEAK THE TRUTH, FOR I PERCIEVE THAT WE ARE AT A STAND-OFF--
FEED ME A LINE I CANNOT RHYME AND WE'LL PERFORM A HAND-OFF!
A LINE YOU CANNOT RHYME?
MAKE IT QUICK AND MAKE IT PRIME!
20

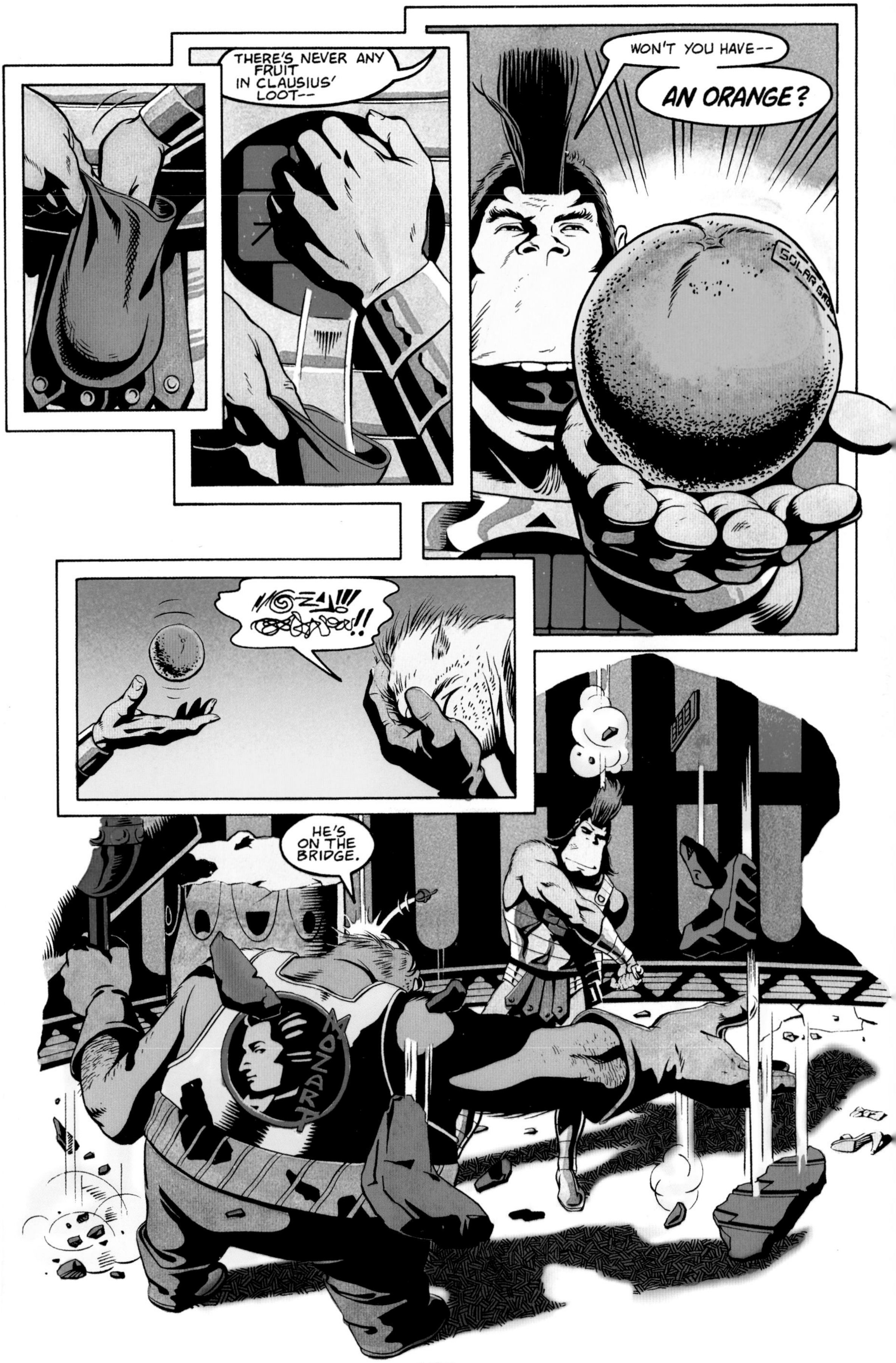
THERE'S NEVER ANY FRUIT IN CLAUSIUS' LOOT--
WON'T YOU HAVE--
AN ORANGE?
SOLAR GRO
HE'S ON THE BRIDGE.
MONDARA

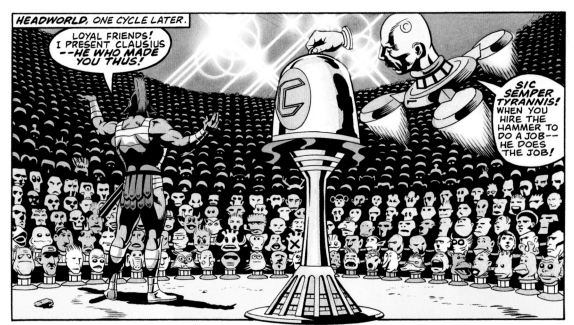

HEADWORLD, ONE CYCLE LATER.

LOYAL FRIENDS! I PRESENT CLAUSIUS --HE WHO MADE YOU THUS!

SIC SEMPER TYRANNIS! WHEN YOU HIRE THE HAMMER TO DO A JOB-- HE DOES THE JOB!

EEEEEK!

OH MY GOD!

ZUB ZUB ZUB ...

CLAUSIUS

KILL HIM!

LET'S STONE HIM!

TORTURE THE FIEND!

NO. FAR BETTER TO LEAVE HIM A DISEMBODIED HEAD, BEREFT OF TELEKINETIC POWERS!

HE SHALL BE PUT ON DISPLAY FOR ALL HIS VICTIMS TO SEE.

I WANT TO GO OUT NOW... ZIP UP MY SUIT MOMMY...

YEAH, THAT'S RIGHT CLAUSIUS. YOU CAN DISH IT OUT, BUT YOU CAN'T TAKE IT.

22

198

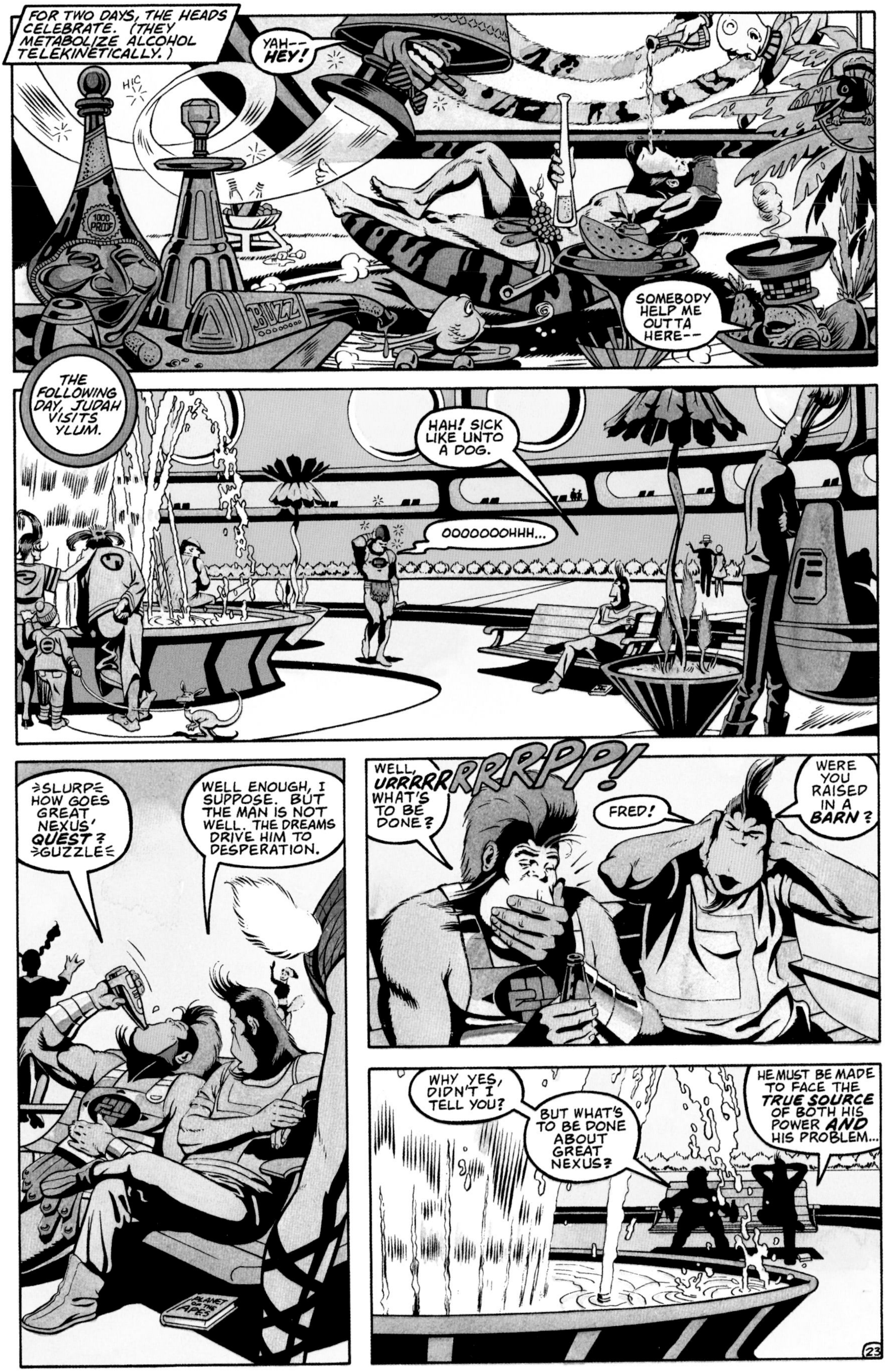

FOR TWO DAYS, THE HEADS CELEBRATE. (THEY METABOLIZE ALCOHOL TELEKINETICALLY.)
YAH-- HEY!
HIC
1000 PROOF
BUZZ
SOMEBODY HELP ME OUTTA HERE--
THE FOLLOWING DAY, JUDAH VISITS YLUM.
HAH! SICK LIKE UNTO A DOG.
OOOOOOOHHH...
≶SLURP≶ HOW GOES GREAT NEXUS' QUEST? ≶GUZZLE≶
WELL ENOUGH, I SUPPOSE. BUT THE MAN IS NOT WELL. THE DREAMS DRIVE HIM TO DESPERATION.
PLANET OF THE APES
WELL, URRRRRRRRPP! WHAT'S TO BE DONE?
FRED!
WERE YOU RAISED IN A BARN?
WHY YES, DIDN'T I TELL YOU?
BUT WHAT'S TO BE DONE ABOUT GREAT NEXUS?
HE MUST BE MADE TO FACE THE TRUE SOURCE OF BOTH HIS POWER AND HIS PROBLEM...
23

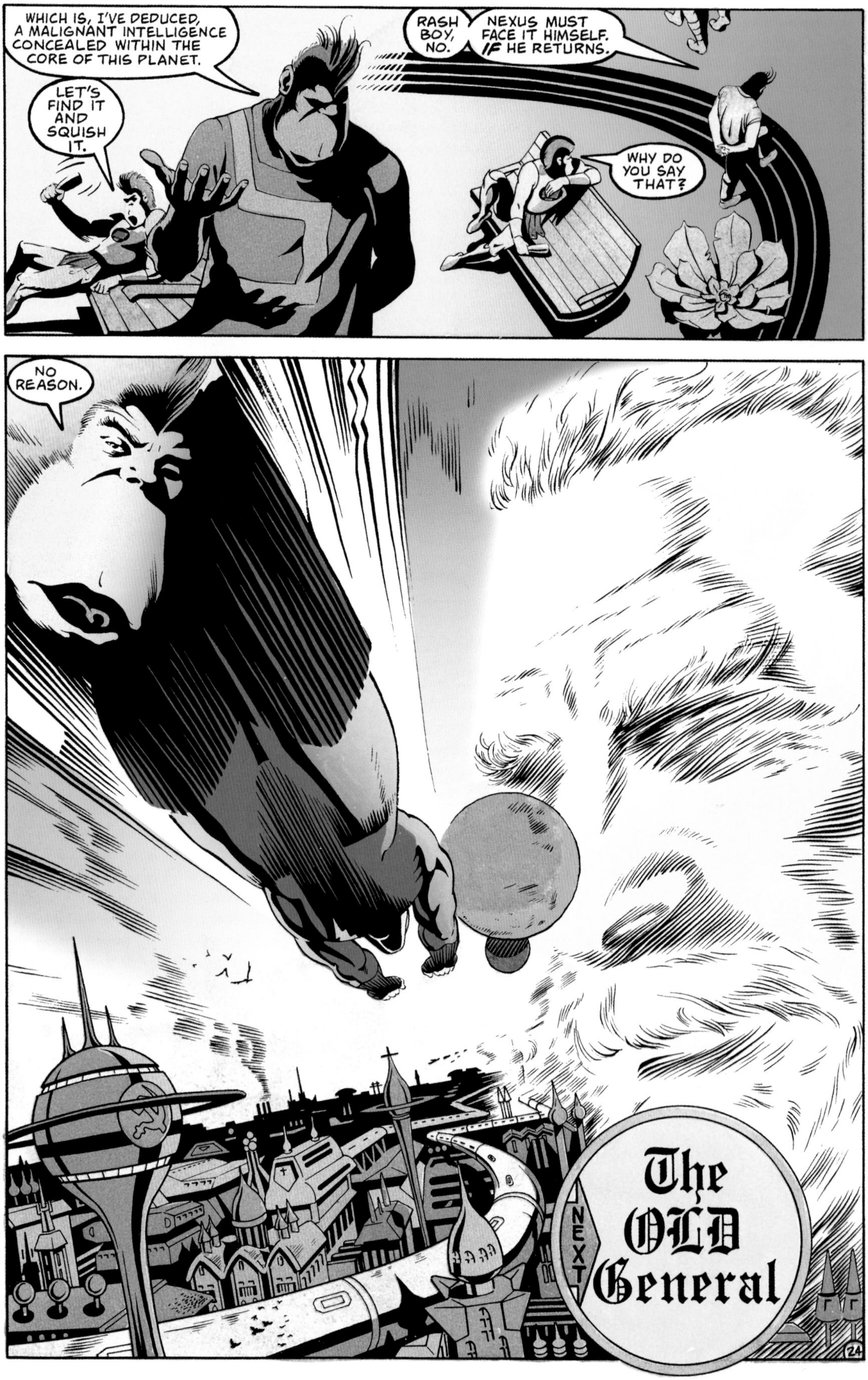
WHICH IS, I'VE DEDUCED, A MALIGNANT INTELLIGENCE CONCEALED WITHIN THE CORE OF THIS PLANET.
LET'S FIND IT AND SQUISH IT.
RASH BOY, NO.
NEXUS MUST FACE IT HIMSELF. IF HE RETURNS.
WHY DO YOU SAY THAT?
NO REASON.
NEXT
The OLD General
24

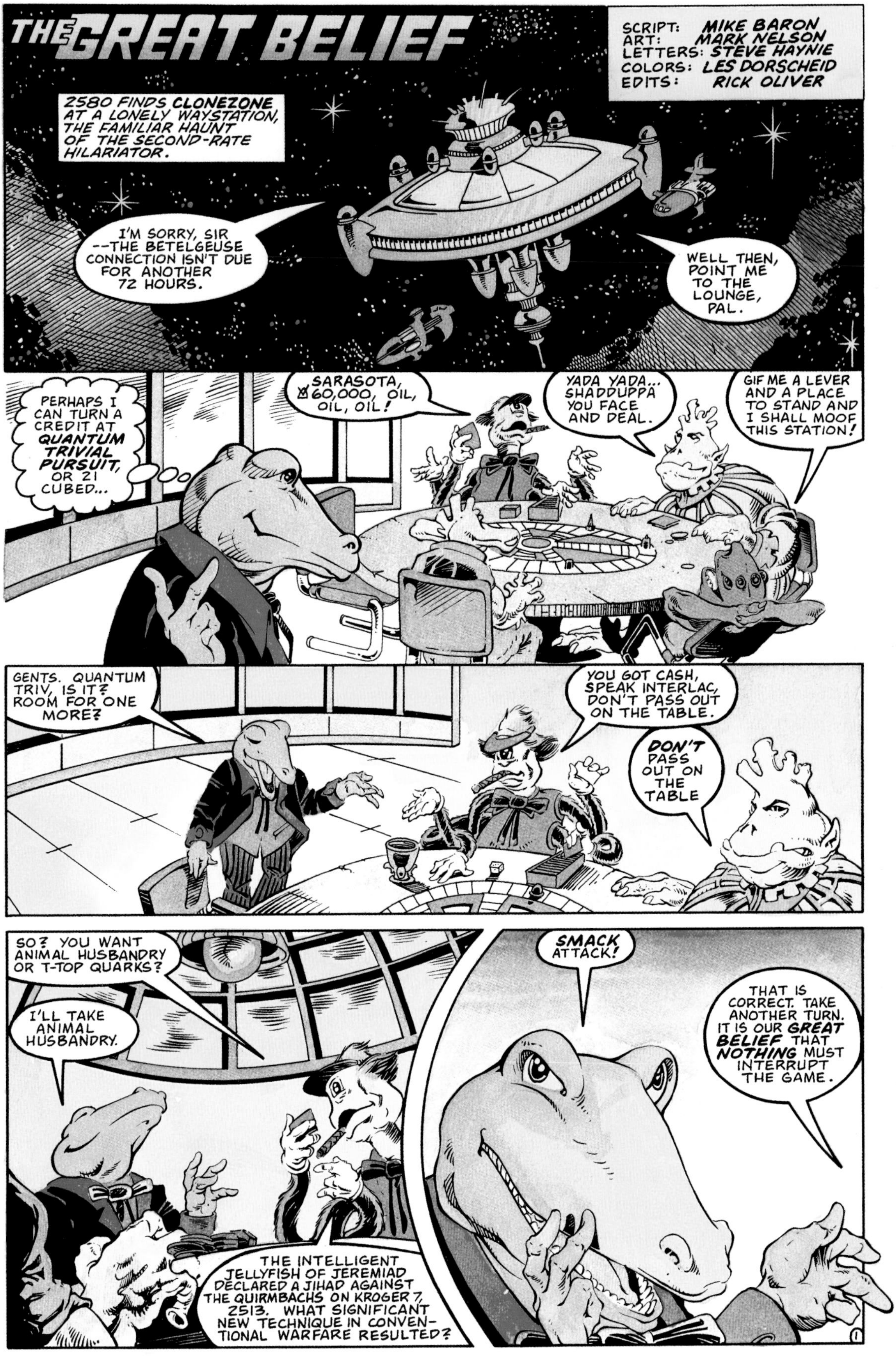
THE GREAT BELIEF
SCRIPT: MIKE BARON
ART: MARK NELSON
LETTERS: STEVE HAYNIE
COLORS: LES DORSCHEID
EDITS: RICK OLIVER
2580 FINDS CLONEZONE AT A LONELY WAYSTATION, THE FAMILIAR HAUNT OF THE SECOND-RATE HILARIATOR.
I'M SORRY, SIR --THE BETELGEUSE CONNECTION ISN'T DUE FOR ANOTHER 72 HOURS.
WELL THEN, POINT ME TO THE LOUNGE, PAL.
PERHAPS I CAN TURN A CREDIT AT QUANTUM TRIVIAL PURSUIT, OR 21 CUBED...
SARASOTA, 60,000, OIL, OIL, OIL!
YADA YADA... SHADDUPPA YOU FACE AND DEAL.
GIF ME A LEVER AND A PLACE TO STAND AND I SHALL MOOF THIS STATION!
GENTS. QUANTUM TRIV, IS IT? ROOM FOR ONE MORE?
YOU GOT CASH, SPEAK INTERLAC, DON'T PASS OUT ON THE TABLE.
DON'T PASS OUT ON THE TABLE
SO? YOU WANT ANIMAL HUSBANDRY OR T-TOP QUARKS?
I'LL TAKE ANIMAL HUSBANDRY.
THE INTELLIGENT JELLYFISH OF JEREMIAD DECLARED A JIHAD AGAINST THE QUIRMBACHS ON KROGER 7, 2513. WHAT SIGNIFICANT NEW TECHNIQUE IN CONVENTIONAL WARFARE RESULTED?
SMACK ATTACK!
THAT IS CORRECT. TAKE ANOTHER TURN. IT IS OUR GREAT BELIEF THAT NOTHING MUST INTERRUPT THE GAME.
1

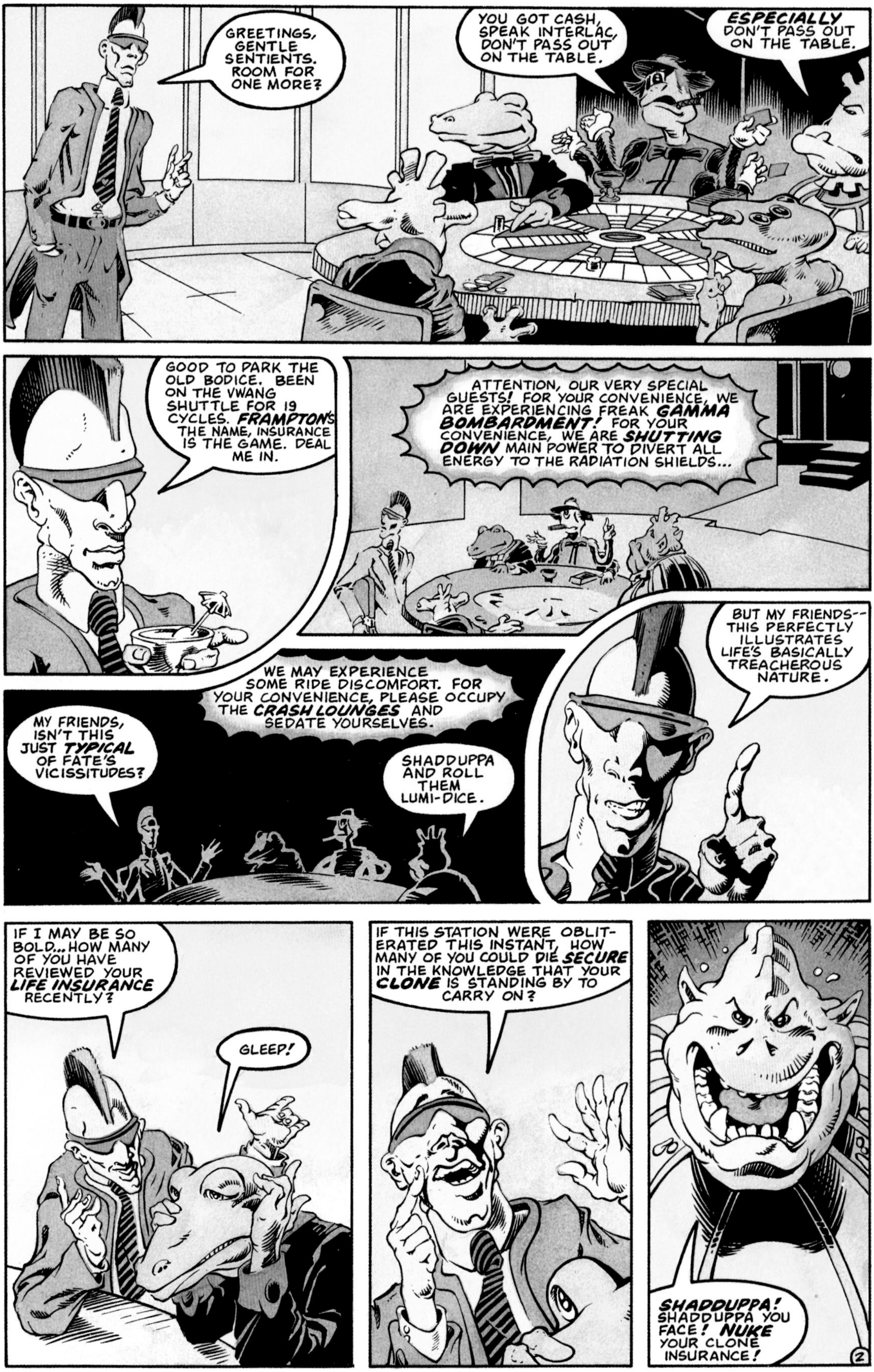
GREETINGS, GENTLE SENTIENTS. ROOM FOR ONE MORE?
YOU GOT CASH, SPEAK INTERLAC, DON'T PASS OUT ON THE TABLE.
ESPECIALLY DON'T PASS OUT ON THE TABLE.
GOOD TO PARK THE OLD BODICE. BEEN ON THE VWANG SHUTTLE FOR 19 CYCLES. FRAMPTON'S THE NAME, INSURANCE IS THE GAME. DEAL ME IN.
ATTENTION, OUR VERY SPECIAL GUESTS! FOR YOUR CONVENIENCE, WE ARE EXPERIENCING FREAK GAMMA BOMBARDMENT! FOR YOUR CONVENIENCE, WE ARE SHUTTING DOWN MAIN POWER TO DIVERT ALL ENERGY TO THE RADIATION SHIELDS...
WE MAY EXPERIENCE SOME RIDE DISCOMFORT. FOR YOUR CONVENIENCE, PLEASE OCCUPY THE CRASH LOUNGES AND SEDATE YOURSELVES.
MY FRIENDS, ISN'T THIS JUST TYPICAL OF FATE'S VICISSITUDES?
SHADDUPPA AND ROLL THEM LUMI-DICE.
BUT MY FRIENDS-- THIS PERFECTLY ILLUSTRATES LIFE'S BASICALLY TREACHEROUS NATURE.
IF I MAY BE SO BOLD... HOW MANY OF YOU HAVE REVIEWED YOUR LIFE INSURANCE RECENTLY?
GLEEP!
IF THIS STATION WERE OBLITERATED THIS INSTANT, HOW MANY OF YOU COULD DIE SECURE IN THE KNOWLEDGE THAT YOUR CLONE IS STANDING BY TO CARRY ON?
SHADDUPPA! SHADDUPPA YOU FACE! NUKE YOUR CLONE INSURANCE!
2

YOUR ODDS OF SURVIVING AN INTENSE GAMMA BOMBARDMENT ARE *SLIM*, YET AMALGAMATED MAGELLANIC IS *STILL* WILLING TO EXTEND OUR OPEN ENROLLMENT PERIOD...

EXTREMISM IN THE DEFENSE OF QUANTUM TRIVIAL PURSUIT IS NO VICE.

HUMAN, YOU ARE TREADING ON TREACHEROUS GROUND.

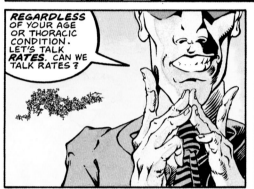

REGARDLESS OF YOUR AGE OR THORACIC CONDITION. LET'S TALK *RATES*. CAN WE TALK RATES?

BY ALL MEANS.

HILARIATOR, MAYBE YOU'D BETTER *TELL* THE HUMAN ABOUT OUR GREAT BELIEF.

"GREAT BELIEF"? WE OFFER SPECIAL RATES FOR RELIGIOUS GROUPS!

NO, NO... LET ME FILL YOU IN. THAT BUNCH THERE? *WOWZERINES*, THE LOT OF 'EM. BUY INSURANCE LIKE *CRAZY*! BUT THERE'S A CATCH... YOU FAMILIAR WITH WOWZERS?

NO... CAN'T SAY AS I AM...

I LIKE YOU. I'M GOING TO HELP YOU. THEIR "GREAT BELIEF IS THAT EVERY FRESH ENCOUNTER IS EITHER "WELL MET" OR "ILL MET," DEPENDING...

YOU WANT TO SELL A POLICY, YOU WANT TO BE WELL MET. HERE'S WHAT YOU DO: (A) BUY THEM DRINKS, AND (B) PROVE THAT YOU CAN DRINK A *DOUBLE ZONIN*, WHICH IS THE SYMBOLIC BLOOD OF WOWZER, AND PROOF OF VIRTUE. YOU FOLLOW ME?

YES... I THINK SO...

RIGHT. NOW GO OVER TO THE INTOXICATER, ORDER DRINKS FOR THE TABLE AND A DOUBLE ZONIN FOR YOURSELF, *STRAIGHT UP.*

THANKS PAL. I WON'T FORGET THIS.

3

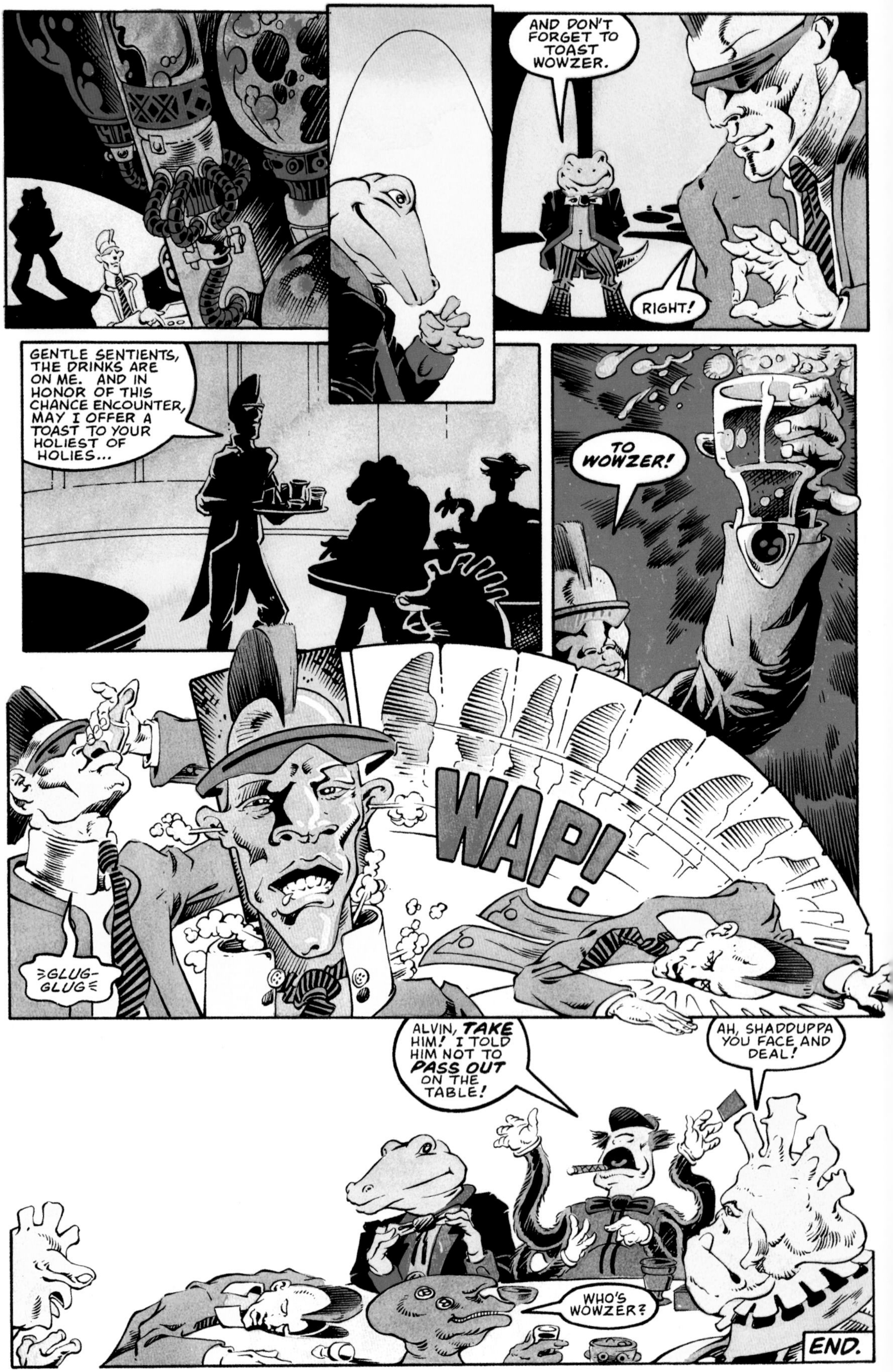
AND DON'T FORGET TO TOAST WOWZER.
RIGHT!
GENTLE SENTIENTS, THE DRINKS ARE ON ME. AND IN HONOR OF THIS CHANCE ENCOUNTER, MAY I OFFER A TOAST TO YOUR HOLIEST OF HOLIES...
TO WOWZER!
WAP!
GLUG-GLUG
ALVIN, TAKE HIM! I TOLD HIM NOT TO PASS OUT ON THE TABLE!
AH, SHADDUPPA YOU FACE AND DEAL!
WHO'S WOWZER?
END.

MIKE BARON
by Steve Rude

When I met Mike Baron on the steps of the Memorial Union at the University of Wisconsin in Madison, he was all business. A friend of his from a local newspaper that I had shown some art samples to had advised him to get ahold of me. I wanted to draw comics, Baron wanted to write them. It was in the fall of 1979 and I was in my early twenties, Baron a bit older. That meeting probably lasted no longer than fifteen minutes, but from that brief and unassuming moment, a partnership would begin that would carry us through several decades.

To think back on those early days in Madison is double-edged for me. I was perpetually poor and had to do jobs that weren't exactly my calling in life. If I wanted to meet with Baron and discuss our stories, I had to take a ten-mile bus ride to get there.

I remember one of our early meetings, before Nexus even had a name yet. We were meeting to discuss costume ideas, and Baron already had some specific thoughts, most notably the red visor and his yellow lightning bolt that overlaps his torso. It was winter at the time, and as was the norm back in those winter days, Baron would greet me with twenty layers of long johns and those thermal boot liners everyone in Wisconsin wears. He kept that apartment so cold that as I drew, I swear I could see my breath crystallize.

In spite of the cold, it was a productive evening, and everything was finalized by the end of the night. I had also missed the last bus, and that meant sleeping over in Baron's living room. Instead of turning the thermostat up a couple of degrees, he just threw a mountain of blankets at me and said, "See you in the morning, man!" At least the bus ride home was warm.

Once our exciting new series got underway, Baron would usually hand-deliver the scripts to my place. The procedure rarely varied. With Baron still sitting there, I would read these stories as a fan, laughing over the wacky stuff, and pausing at the traumatic moments that life can deliver to any of us—fictional or otherwise. Then I would go into my annoying "question mode" and begin dissecting the logic of the seemingly impossible feats Nexus was called

upon to do. No matter how seemingly implausible at the moment, Mike's answers always made a believer out of me.

I never knew how Baron came up with this crazy stuff, just that he did, story after story, and that I had to illustrate it with the same intensity.

Many people don't know this, but Baron is an excellent chef. While most guys can barely get the directions straight on the back of a frozen meatloaf, Baron excels at the tastiest of dishes. When our character Judah Maccabee—or "Fred" as I call him—started entering cook-offs in our Nexus stories, I knew from where Baron had drawn the obvious reference.

One moment I'll never forget is the day Baron dropped by with a big package in his hands. "*For me*?" I thought. He said he was always giving his girl friends gifts—why not his guy friends? Inside the package was a sleek and sporty brown leather jacket. I was so touched I could hardly choke a proper thank-you. To this day, I can't recall another moment like that with a male friend.

Interestingly, throughout our entire sixteen-year run, despite its ardent following and having received many top industry awards, *Nexus* never seemed to translate to higher sales. Another inexplicable but common example of the "art versus commerce" phenomenon.

Entering the new millennium, Mike and I saw many changes take place within our beloved profession, and sadly, some were found wanting. Many of the last decade's most prolific and top creators seemingly fell out of favor with the new editorial preferences that came into play, and hard days fell upon Mike for far too long. Throughout it all, I saw him survive it with dignity.

In my recent conversations with Baron, he's been going full tilt to succeed in his longstanding quest to break into novel writing. That he has the skills for this is the least of my worries. Mike has now reached such a confidence level, through years of toiling the exposition vineyards, that I expect you'll be seeing his name among the Clancys and the Koontzs in short order.

STEVE RUDE
by Mike Baron

Who is this tall drink of water combining the aesthetics of Andrew Loomis, Jack Kirby, and Theodor Geisel, often in the same painting? Steve Rude is a dreamer, a romantic, and a natural-born storyteller—one of those kids who filled the margins of his schoolbooks and notepads with doodles. Dude's doodles always looked more finished than everyone else's. He grew up in thrall to Marvel Comics, *Space Ghost*, and Bruce Lee, so much so that he named his first son Brandon, after Brandon Lee.

One can't look at his work without comparing it to other great artists of the twentieth century, most notably Loomis and the progenitors of the modern heroic style: N. C. Wyeth, Maxfield Parrish, and Howard Pyle. Throw in Norman Rockwell, J. C. Leyendecker, and James Montgomery Flagg, and you have a synthesis of most of the great illustrators. That effortless glow, the Rembrandt-like lighting, the natural grace of the human figure did not come easily. Steve Rude was born with extraordinary talent and has devoted his life to bringing that talent to fruition. He has studied at the feet of great masters, and although he is a master himself, he has never stopped learning. He still takes painting classes today.

I was working at an insurance company in 1981 when an editor at a newspaper called me: "There's some guy down here trying to sell us drawings and he draws just like you." Obviously, the editor was no fit judge of art. What he meant was, we were both drawing comic-book superheroes, but comparing my work to Steve's was like comparing a Yugo to a Mercedes. I met Steve on the steps of the University of Wisconsin Student Union. One look at his portfolio and I gave up trying to turn myself into an artist. Even then he had a fluidity of line and imagination that beggared most comic-book artists of the time.

When we both lived in Madison, WI, we would go over the layouts for each issue of *Nexus* like Defense Department analysts examine aerial photos of North Korea's nuclear facilities. Dude wanted to know the details of our society down to the manufacturer of the manhole covers. He never faked anything, even though he was drawing a society that existed only in our imaginations. I always told him the past was key to the future. Everything old was new again. He drew inspiration for costume design from the Third Reich, Napoleon's troops, *Star Trek*, you name it. Mostly, he studied the natural form of things. He began keeping his logs in 1976. The logs are huge sketchpads, every page filled with drawings—often in color. Page after page of nothing but the human foot, as seen from all angles. Full-color studies of Degas, Renoir, John Singer Sargent, Alex Toth (lots of Toth), Kirby, Alex Raymond, and Joseph Clement Coll. I believe he's up to log number twenty-five now. When aspiring artists approach me at a convention, I show them Dude's sketchpads. They either shrink to microbe size and vanish, or a flare goes off in their brains and they hustle away to begin drawing. If you would be an artist, carry a sketchpad at all times, and fill it as if you're being paid.

Dude often attends social functions, only to sit in the corner carefully observing and drawing people in the room. This is a cool ploy, as people will eventually wander over to try and catch a glimpse of what's going down. Dude radiates a quiet intensity that acts as a gravitational field.

Steve's a gentle soul who loves animals and has a surprisingly robust sense of humor. Many times he has reduced me to stitches with his impressions. He is also fearless. He met the beautiful Jaynelle hitchhiking. How many people meet their wives hitchhiking? He's the only guy I know (other than myself) who challenges loudmouths in movie theaters. We each have our methods. Mine involves appearing quietly behind them and whispering in their ears. Dude's involves staring them down.

Steve Rude lives in Arizona with his wife, two kids, and a couple of cats.

ALSO AVAILABLE FROM DARK HORSE BOOKS

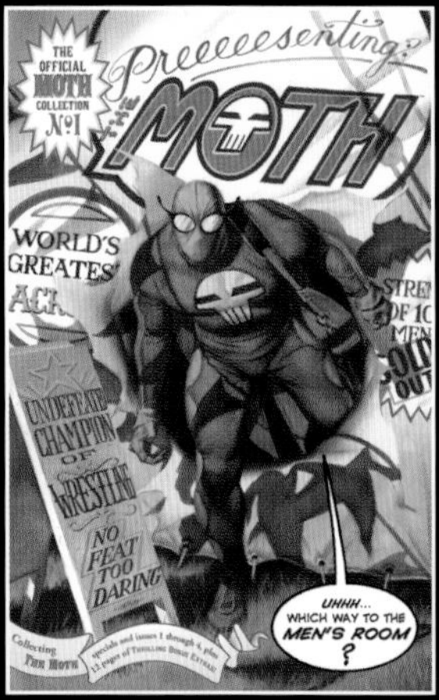
THE OFFICIAL MOTH COLLECTION No1
Preeeeesenting
MOTH
WORLD'S GREATEST
NO FEAT TOO DARING
UHHH... WHICH WAY TO THE MEN'S ROOM ?

Steve Rude's The Moth

By Gary Martin and Steve Rude

Jack Mahoney is a circus acrobat by day, masked vigilante by night! The charismatic Moth battles a savage lionman, a bounty-hunting thug, bloodthirsty mob hit men, and a trio of mischievous cat burglars!

ISBN: 1-59307-287-2 $12.95

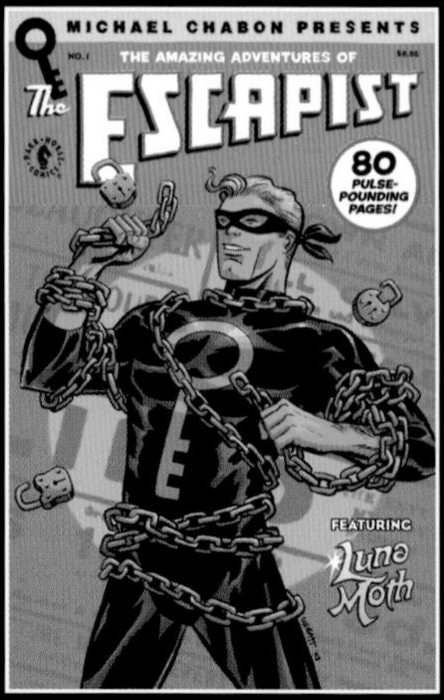
MICHAEL CHABON PRESENTS
THE AMAZING ADVENTURES OF
The ESCAPIST
80 PULSE-POUNDING PAGES!
FEATURING Luna Moth

Michael Chabon Presents: The Amazing Adventures of the Escapist Volume 1

By Michael Chabon, Mike Baron, Howard Chaykin, Bill Sienkiewicz, and others

Master of Elusion, foe of tyranny, and champion of liberation—The Escapist! Operating from a secret headquarters under the majestic Empire Theater, the Escapist and his crack team of charismatic associates roam the globe, performing amazing feats of magic to aid all those who languish in oppression's chains.

ISBN: 1-59307-171-X $17.95

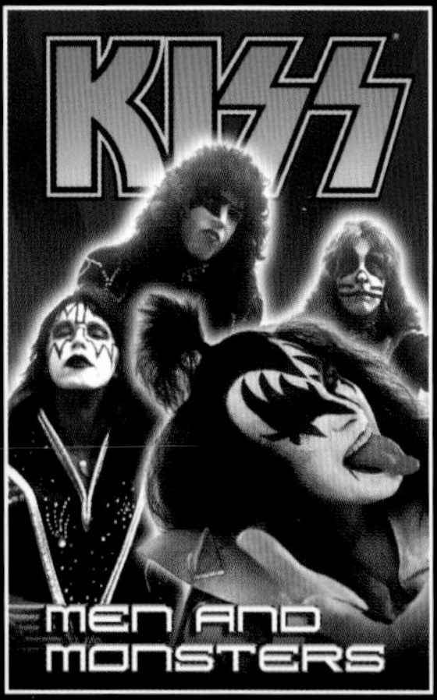
KISS
MEN AND MONSTERS

KISS Volume 3: Men and Monsters

By Mike Baron, Scott Lobdell, and Mel Rubi

Extreme dangers call for extreme heroes, and world-famous rock band-turned-superheroes KISS are here to answer the call! Immerse yourself in a world where your greatest fears and deepest fantasies come to life, where you fight alongside Mr. Speed and Christine 16, and where monsters are real—but the heroes are real kick-ass!

ISBN: 1-56971-971-3 $12.95

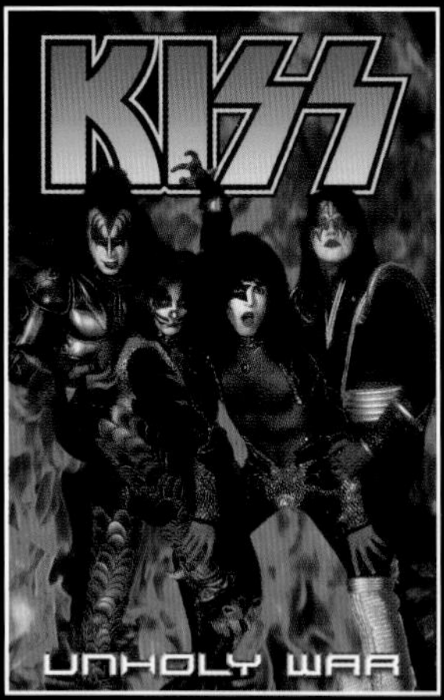
KISS
UNHOLY WAR

KISS Volume 4: Unholy War

By Mike Baron and Mel Rubi

The Demon, Starchild, Beast King, and the Celestial have been working and fighting side-by-side through the ages. Now, these superpowered beings are putting everything on the line, and their differences aside, to save the future of humanity from the darkest of threats—the malevolent and terrifying entity known as The Unholy.

ISBN: 1-59307-096-9 $9.95

DARK HORSE BOOKS

AVAILABLE AT YOUR LOCAL COMICS SHOP OR BOOKSTORE

To find a comics shop in your area, call 1-888-266-4226

For more information or to order direct visit darkhorse.com or call 1-800-862-0052

Mon.–Sat. 9 A.M. to 5 P.M. Pacific Time

*Prices and availability subject to change without notice